SPANISH

Listening Speaking Reading Writing

SECOND EDITION

SPANISH

Listening Speaking Reading Writing

SECOND EDITION

Guillermo Segreda
Manhattanville College

James W. Harris
Massachusetts Institute of Technology

With the assistance of
Robert G. Mowry
Susquehanna University

 HARCOURT BRACE JOVANOVICH, INC.
New York   Chicago   San Francisco   Atlanta

COVER DESIGN Adaptation of a bas-relief on a wall of the fortress at Chanchán, Peru, the largest city in the pre-Columbian world

Endpaper maps by J. P. Tremblay

Acknowledgment is given to Harcourt Brace Jovanovich, Inc., for use of the following materials:

"Catalina y San Antonio," from *A-LM Spanish*, Level Two, New Second Edition, copyright © 1974, 1970 by Harcourt Brace Jovanovich, Inc.

"La esquina," slightly adapted from *A-LM Spanish*, Level Two, New Second Edition, copyright © 1974, 1970 by Harcourt Brace Jovanovich, Inc.

"Se necesita sirvienta," slightly adapted from *A-LM Spanish*, Level Two, New Second Edition, copyright © 1974, 1970 by Harcourt Brace Jovanovich, Inc.

Picture credits appear on page 367.

ISBN: 0-15-583057-0

Library of Congress Catalog Card Number: 75-39394

Printed in the United States of America

Preface

This textbook has been carefully planned to include all the basic phonology, grammar, vocabulary, and cultural information necessary for comprehending, speaking, reading, and writing first-year Spanish in a volume short enough to be worked through comfortably in a single year's course—whatever the schedule of class meetings and allotted time span. Listening comprehension and speaking are stressed from the outset. In this Second Edition students are also able to choose between the continuous intensive drill of oral self-expression and the pursuit of expanded facility in reading, once they have demonstrated acceptable mastery of the phonological system. Both goals can, of course, be combined in a multitude of ways, and it is hoped that the full set of materials will be adaptable to a wide variety of teaching strategies.

The tape program for the Second Edition provides another important feature: each model sentence for the grammatical exercises is followed immediately by its English equivalent. We believe this procedure will make students aware of the meaning while they concentrate on producing the correct form.

The fifteen chapters contain cultural listening passages (described below), basic dialogs with appropriate cultural notes, related supplementary vocabulary, drills on pronunciation (Chapters 1 through 7), grammatical explanations and exercises, taped listening comprehension exercises, vocabulary lists, and a variety of reading selections suitable for development in oral or written compositions. Grammatical explanations are limited to essential generalizations: they are brief, with just enough detail to teach the point and afford the students a simple, straightforward background in the fundamentals and a firm preparation for further study.

Users of the accompanying Student Manual will find additional exercises for developing and reinforcing writing skills, as well as a complete battery of self tests and a full complement of fifteen reading selections to augment those contained in the textbook.

Spanish: Listening, Speaking, Reading, Writing includes largely the kinds of essentially audio-lingual teaching devices most teachers have become accustomed to using in recent years. A special and unique feature, however, is the cultural listening passage at the beginning of each chapter. Completely in Spanish, each passage (read aloud in class from the Instructor's Manual or played from the tape) discusses some aspects of culture related to the basic dialog, presents the dialog situation, and concludes with a list of the grammar points of the lesson. The cultural listening passage immerses students in spoken Spanish that goes beyond what they are expected to learn for active use but is sufficiently limited in structure and vocabulary to ensure its aural comprehension for the most part. A parallel English translation is provided in the textbook for students to consult while listening independently to the taped Spanish version outside class. Students should be encouraged to increase their understanding of spoken Spanish by steadily decreasing their reliance on the parallel English translation. In our own practice, students never see the Spanish version of these cultural listening passages, which are an integral part of our conception and pedagogical method. Nevertheless, the book can be used effectively by employing them as additional reading material or material for dictation or for other writing exercises.

Although many people have helped to inspire the present content and form of this book, we are especially grateful to Dr. S. N. Treviño, formerly of the Foreign Service Institute of the Department of State, for his personal encouragement during the preparation of the manuscript; and to Professors Dwight L. Bolinger, Emeritus of Harvard University; Roger M. Peel of Middlebury College; Robert Brody of the University of Texas; and W. F. Byess of the University of Tennessee for their constructive suggestions. We are also greatly indebted to Professor H. Ernest Lewald of the University of Tennessee for his valuable suggestions for cultural material and his collaboration on some of the listening passages. Finally, our thanks go to our students of the last several years at Manhattanville College, the Massachusetts Institute of Technology, Harvard University, and Susquehanna University; their suggestions and comments on previous versions of these materials helped make *Spanish: Listening, Speaking, Reading, Writing* the distinctive book we believe it to be.

GUILLERMO SEGREDA

JAMES W. HARRIS

ROBERT G. MOWRY

Contents

SPANISH

Listening   Speaking   Reading   Writing

SECOND EDITION

Venezuela:
Pan American Highway

Cultural Listening Passage
for Chapter 1

First read the English version of the passage in order to familiarize yourself with its contents. Then, as you listen to this same passage in Spanish, rely on the English as little as possible. If you need to pinpoint a specific fragment, the numbers in parentheses will help you find it. You should not expect to understand every word of the Spanish. Rather, you should concentrate on getting your ear "tuned in" to it, while grasping as much of the meaning as you can. Literal translations of some Spanish words and phrases that would sound odd in English are given in parentheses.

The passage contains two parts. One refers to the basic dialog of this chapter and explains certain cultural matters related to that conversation; the other simply mentions the grammar points of the chapter.

(The) English Classes at the Cultural Center

(1) Cultural Centers are private institutions dedicated to a better understanding between the Spanish-speaking peoples and the people of the United States of America. (2) These institutions attempt to realize this objective through a program of cultural interchange and the teaching of the two languages, English and Spanish. (3) The cultural activities they offer are numerous and varied: lectures, films, art exhibits, concerts, dances, etc. But undoubtedly the principal activity is (are) the English courses, which everybody (all the world)—men, women, old and young (children)—wants to attend.

(4) Today is the first day of classes at the Colombian–North American Cultural Center, which is situated in the city of Bogotá, capital of the Republic of Colombia. (5) In one of the classes the students are waiting for the teacher. One of them, Emilio Fonseca, is curious (has curiosity) to know who the teacher is and asks another student who is sitting beside him (at his side). (6) This other young man, whose name is Carlos María and (his) last name (is) Terán

Marín—Carlos María Terán Marín—explains to him that he doesn't know her name (last name), but that she is an American (young) woman. Emilio is glad to know that the teacher is a woman and not a man; according to him, women are better teachers than men. (7) He also wants to know what she's like (how she is). Carlos María explains to him that she's very pretty, blonde, with green eyes (eyes green). But that's not exactly what Emilio wants to know. He wants to know how she is as a teacher. Carlos María explains to him that she's a little strict but very good—so they say.

(8) (The) Colombians, and particularly (the) "bogotanos," that is (to say), the people from Bogotá, are well known (have fame) for being very formal in their personal relations and in their manner. Emilio and Carlos María give us a demonstration of this when they introduce each other (one to the other) with a great deal of ceremony, and when Carlos María then presents his sister, Luz María, who is seated next to him (at his side).

(9) Emilio greets Luz María with great formality and then, to make conversation, comments that Carlos María and his sister look (are) very much alike and asks if they are twins. But they're not; they're just brother and sister. (10) Carlos María notices that Emilio speaks with an accent that is not "bogotano" and asks him where he's from. Emilio is from Cartagena, an important seaport located on the north coast of the country.

Grammar Points

First, (the) gender in nouns, articles, and descriptive adjectives; second, plural forms of nouns and modifiers; third, personal subject pronouns; fourth, the present tense of the verb **ser** (to be); fifth, interrogative words; and sixth, (the) formation of negative sentences with the particle **no.**

San José, Costa Rica: Cultural Center

Chapter 1

Basic Dialog

Las clases de inglés en el Centro Cultural

E. *Emilio*   CM. *Carlos María*   LM. *Luz María*

I

E.   Perdón, ¿sabe usted quién es el maestro?
CM.   No sé su apellido, pero es una señorita americana.
E.   ¡Qué bueno! Las mujeres son mejores como maestras. ¿Cómo es ella?
CM.   Es muy bonita, rubia, de ojos verdes...
E.   Sí, pero como maestra, ¿qué tal es?
CM.   Según dicen, es un poco estricta, pero muy buena.

II

E.   Mi nombre es Emilio Fonseca.
CM.   Carlos María Terán Marín, mucho gusto. Mi hermana, Luz María.
E.   Encantado, señorita. ¡Qué parecidos son ustedes! ¿Son gemelos?
LM.   No, somos hermanos nada más.
CM.   ¿De dónde es usted, Emilio? Usted no es bogotano, ¿verdad?
E.   No, soy de la costa, de Cartagena.

3

(The) English Classes at the Cultural Center

E. *Emilio* CM. *Carlos María* LM. *Luz María*

I

E. Excuse me, do you know who the teacher is?
CM. I don't know her last name, but she's an American woman.
E. That's good;[1] women are better as teachers. What's she like?[2]
CM. She's very pretty, blonde, with green eyes[3]. . . .
E. Yes, but as a teacher, what's she like?[4]
CM. According to what they say, she's a little strict, but very good.

II

E. My name is Emilio Fonseca.
CM. Carlos María Terán Marín, it's a pleasure.[5] My sister, Luz María.
E. Delighted (miss). How much alike you two look! Are you twins?
LM. No, we're just brother and sister.
CM. Where are you from, Emilio? You're not a "bogotano," right?
E. No, I'm from the coast, from Cartagena.

Cultural Notes

A. *Mucho gusto* and *encantado* (or *encantada*) are expressions frequently used in introductions.
B. Both men and women commonly have María as a second given name: Carlos María, Luz María.
C. At least in official records, a person's family name is always his father's last name followed by his mother's maiden name. Some people omit the mother's maiden name in informal use; others retain it at all times. In the dialog, Emilio Fonseca prefers the short version of his last name, whereas Carlos María Terán Marín uses both names. If Carlos María should decide to use only one last name, it would be Terán, not Marín. On a visit to the United States, he would probably soon drop his mother's name to avoid being called "Mr. Marín."

[1] What good.
[2] How is she?
[3] Of eyes green.
[4] What such is?
[5] Much pleasure.

The Sounds of Spanish: I

A. **Vowels.** Spanish has five vowel sounds [a], [e], [i], [o], [u],[6] represented by the letters *a, e, i, o, u.* Each vowel is pronounced virtually the same way every time it occurs. Listen to the model voice pronounce the following exercises, and mimic what you hear as precisely as you can.

1. [a]. Spanish [a] is not produced as far back in the mouth as the vowel in English "con," nor as far front as that in English "can."

   a   a   a   a
   ma-má   Pa-na-má   ma-ña-na[7]

2. [e]. Make Spanish [e] short and clipped. It should *not* rhyme with the name of the English letter *a,* which is long and assumes the quality of "ee" at the end.

   e   e   e   e
   sé   ne-ne   e-se

3. [i]. Spanish [i] is also short and tense. Notice carefully how it differs from the name of the English letter *e.*

   i   i   i   i
   sí   Li-li   Mi-si-si-pi

4. [o]. Spanish [o] does not rhyme with the name of the English letter *o.* Round your lips at the beginning of Spanish [o] and keep them in exactly the same position. Spanish [o] does not acquire the quality of "oo" in "pool" at the end, as the most similar English sound does.

   o   o   o   o
   no   co-mo   lo-co

5. [u]. Make Spanish [u] short and tense. Round your lips at the beginning (more than for [o]) and keep them that way.

   u   u   u   u
   u-na   lu-na   A-ca-pul-co

B. **Vowels and rhythm.** Listen to the model voice and repeat each of the sentences below. These sentences are divided into syllables rather than into words to help you imitate the correct even spacing of Spanish syllables. As you repeat, try to maintain exactly the rhythm and speed of the model voice. Concentrate on the vowels. The vocabulary is not meant to be memorized.

---

[6] Brackets [ ] will sometimes be used to indicate sounds, as distinguished from spelling.
[7] The letter *ñ* (*eñe*) represents a sound roughly like that of *ny* in English "canyon."

[a]:	Va-pa-ra-Pa-na-má.[8]		(*He's headed for Panama.*)
	Va-la-ca-sa-ma-ña-na.		(*He's going to the house tomorrow.*)
[e]:	Sé-que-Pe-pe-sel-je-fe.[9]		(*I know that Pepe's the boss.*)
	Dé-me-se-que-so.		(*Give me that cheese.*)
[i]:	Di-ce-Li-li-que-sí.		(*Lily says yes.*)
	Di-fi-ci-lí-si-mo.		(*Very difficult.*)
[o]:	Co-mo-co-mo-lo-co.		(*I eat like crazy.*)
	Al-fon-so-y-yo-no-so-mos-ton-tos.		(*Alfonso and I aren't stupid.*)
[u]:	A-ca-pul-co-e-sú-ni-co.		(*Acapulco is unique.*)
	Tu-ve-mu-cho-sus-to.		(*I had a big scare.*)

Spanish Spelling: I

Spanish has one of the best spelling systems in the world, with highly regular relationships between sounds and letters—so regular, in fact, that the pronunciation of every Spanish word is unambiguously represented by the spelling. Some letters—for example, *f, m, n, s*—have the same sound values in Spanish and English; others do not. It will be extremely helpful if from the start you memorize thoroughly the following regular, completely exceptionless conventions of Spanish Spelling.

Combinations of [k] or [g] and a vowel

Sounds ⟶	[a]	[e]	[i]	[o]	[u]
↓	*Spelled:*				
[k]	ca	**que**	**qui**	co	cu
[g]	ga	**gue**	**gui**	go	gu

A. The letter *k* is used only in *kilo, kilómetro, kilogramo*, etc. The sequence *qu* is used only in *que* [ke] and *qui* [ki].

B. The sound sequence [kw] is always spelled *cu*, never *qu*, as in **cu**ota [kwóta], **cu**estión [kwestyón], *ecuación* [ekwasyón]. The sequence [gw] is spelled *gu*, as expected, before [a] and [o], but *gü* before [e] and [i]; remember that *gue* is [ge] and *gui* is [gi]. Thus: *gua* [gwa], *guo* [gwo], *güe* [gwe], *güi* [gwi]. The sequences [kwu] and [gwu] do not occur.

C. The letter sequence *ch* is always pronounced as in English "*church*" (*chico, muchacho*), never [k] as in "technical." Incidentally, *ch* is a single letter, *che*, in Spanish. It comes between *c* and *d* in the alphabet, and words are alphabetized accordingly; for example, *chico* comes after *cuánto*.

---

[8] Here the letter *v* is pronounced [b], as in "boy."
[9] The letter *j* is pronounced like the *ch* of "Bach."

D. Aside from *ch*, Spanish does not use combinations of consonant letters or double letters to represent single sounds. For example, "*physics*" is *física*, "*telephone*" is *teléfono*, "*difference*" is *diferencia*, "*illegal*" is *ilegal*, and so on. Like *ch*, *ll* is a single letter, *elle*, pronounced [y]; *rr*, also a single letter, *erre*, will be discussed in detail below.

E. The letter *h*, when not preceded by *c*, is always silent: ***hora, ahora, hermano, prohibición.*** No other letter is always silent in Spanish.

LISTENING COMPREHENSION EXERCISE A

Dialog Supplement

New vocabulary items are to be studied and memorized in context, within the framework of the related basic phrase or sentence, as shown in the example.

EXAMPLE: ¿Quién es el maestro?
                         muchacho
            ¿Quién es el muchacho?

I

¿Quién es el maestro?		**Es una señorita.**	
alumno	*student*	una señora	*a (married) lady*
muchacho	*boy*	una mujer	*a woman*
chico	*boy*	un señor	*a gentleman*
		un hombre	*a man*

Bogotá, Colombia

¿Cómo es ella? which (one)
¿Cuál

Es muy bonita.

fea	homely, ugly	joven	young
alta	tall	mala	bad, mean
baja	short, low	simpática	nice, pleasant, cute
grande	big	antipática	unpleasant
pequeña	short, small	delgada	thin, slender
nueva	new	gorda	fat
vieja	old	tonta	dumb, silly

De ojos verdes

azules	blue
pelo negro	black hair (hair black)

II

Mi hermana, Luz María		**¿De dónde es usted?**	
prima	cousin	qué país	what country
amiga	friend	qué lugar	what place
novia	sweetheart, girlfriend	qué ciudad	what city

¿Son gemelos?		**Las clases de inglés**[10]	
primos	cousins	francés	French
amigos	friends	español	Spanish

Dialog and Supplement Check

Sentence Recall

Say the dialog phrase or sentence in which each of the following words or phrases occurs.

EXAMPLE: el maestro
¿Sabe usted quién es el maestro?

apellido	Emilio Fonseca	americana
rubia	Carlos María Terán Marín	costa
las mujeres	gemelos	cultural
estricta	parecidos	bogotano
nada más	verdes	ojos

---

[10]Names of nationalities and languages are not capitalized in Spanish, except at the beginning of a sentence.

Sentence Completion

Complete the following sentences by saying many complimentary or uncomplimentary things about the person named.

EXAMPLE: La maestra es _____.
   La maestra es una señorita (mujer, señora, etc.) **muy bonita, muy buena, muy joven, de pelo rubio, etc.**

1. Luz María es _____.
2. Mi maestra es _____.
3. Mi hermana es _____.
4. Mi amiga es _____.
5. Mi prima es _____.
6. Mi mamá es _____.
7. Emilio es _____.
8. Mi novio es _____.
9. Mi hermano es _____.
10. Mi papá es _____.
11. Mi primo es _____.
12. Mi profesor es _____.

Item Substitution

Repeat each of the following sentences, substituting a related word or phrase for the parts in italics. If books are closed, your instructor will repeat the item at the end of each sentence.

EXAMPLE: No sé su *apellido*, pero es una señorita americana.
   No sé su *nombre*, pero es una señorita americana.

1. Perdón, ¿sabe usted quién es *el maestro?*
2. Pero como maestra, *¿qué tal es?*
3. Usted no es *bogotano*, ¿verdad?
4. Dicen que es *un poco* estricta.
5. ¡Qué parecidos son ustedes! ¿Son *gemelos?*
6. Es muy bonita, rubia, *de ojos verdes...*
7. No, somos *hermanos* nada más.
8. Es mi *hermana*, Luz María.

Questions

1. ¿Cuál es el apellido de Emilio?
2. Señorita, ¿cuál es su apellido? ¿Y su nombre?
3. ¿Cuál es el nombre completo de Carlos María?
4. Y usted, señor, ¿cuál es su nombre completo?
5. ¿Sabe Carlos María el apellido de la maestra de su clase?
6. ¿Sabe usted el apellido del maestro o de la maestra de su clase?
7. ¿Cómo es la maestra de Emilio, bonita o fea?
8. ¿Es ella americana?
9. ¿Qué tal es ella como maestra?
10. Y como maestro/maestra, ¿qué tal soy yo?
11. ¿Son ustedes dos gemelos?
12. Y usted, señorita, y usted, señor, ¿qué son, hermanos, o amigos nada más?
13. Según Emilio, ¿cómo son Carlos María y su hermana?
14. Usted y usted, ¿son parecidos o no?

15. ¿De dónde son Carlos María y su hermana, de Colombia o de Venezuela?
16. Y ustedes, ¿son de los Estados Unidos[11] o de Canadá?
17. ¿Es Emilio de Bogotá o de la costa?
18. ¿Es su novia bonita o fea? ¿Grande o pequeña? ¿Gorda o delgada? ¿Vieja o joven? ¿Simpática o antipática? ¿Inteligente o tonta?

Grammar

1. Gender of nouns and modifiers

Nouns

Masculine	Feminine
maestro	maestra
señor	señora
hombre	mujer
libro	ventana
nombre	clase

A. English commonly uses two entirely different nouns to distinguish male and female persons of the same category, for example, "brother" and "sister," "gentleman" and "lady," "man" and "woman." Also, other devices such as "male teacher" and "female teacher" are sometimes used. Spanish, on the other hand, typically uses the endings *-o* (masculine) and *-a* (feminine) for sex distinctions of this sort, for example, *maestro*, "male teacher," and *maestra*, "female teacher."

B. The ending *-a* is also used for the feminine counterpart of many nouns whose masculine form ends in a consonant, for example, *señor*, "gentleman," and *señora*, "lady."

C. In Spanish—as in English—there are also a number of masculine–feminine pairs made up of entirely different words, for example, *hombre*, "man," and *mujer*, "woman."

D. Unlike English, Spanish classifies as masculine or feminine *all* nouns, whether or not they refer to persons. For example, *libro*, "book," is masculine; *ventana*, "window," is feminine. In the case of nouns that do not refer to persons, "masculine" and "feminine" are only grammatical terms; Spanish speakers do not conceive of books as being somehow male and windows female.

E. As a rule, nouns ending in *-o* are masculine and those ending in *-a* are feminine, regardless of what they refer to. Among the exceptions are *día*, "day," masculine, and *mano*, "hand," feminine.

F. In general, the gender of nouns that do not end in *-o* or *-a* is unpredictable. There are, however, a few helpful rules of thumb. For example, nouns that end in *-dad*, *-ción*, and *-sión* are feminine: *la ciudad, la institución, la expresión.* In other cases it can be helpful to remember an article or some other modifier (see below).

[11]United States.

Gender Substitution

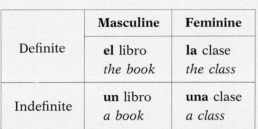

Give the feminine counterpart of the following masculine nouns.

EXAMPLE: maestro
            maestra

amigo	chico	señor	primo	hermano	español
alumno	muchacho	gemelo	novio	francés[12]	inglés

Articles

	Masculine	Feminine
Definite	**el** libro *the book*	**la** clase *the class*
Indefinite	**un** libro *a book*	**una** clase *a class*

G. The Spanish definite (*el, la*) and indefinite (*un, una*) articles have forms for each gender and agree with the nouns they modify.

Article Substitution

Read the following list of words, repeating each word and changing the definite article to the indefinite article, or vice versa.

EXAMPLES: la clase   un ojo
            una clase   **el ojo**

el inglés	la hermana	un permiso	un apellido
un perdón	la noche	una mujer	el gemelo
la clase	una tarde	la mañana	el nombre
el día	un hombre	un primo	el señor

Adjectives

Masculine	Feminine
1. un hombre **bueno** *a good man*	una mujer **buena** *a good woman*
2. un chico **italiano** *an Italian boy*	una chica **italiana** *an Italian girl*

[12]The feminine forms *francesa* and *inglesa* do not require a written accent since the stress falls on the next-to-last syllable. (See page 58.)

Adjectives (continued)

Masculine	Feminine
3. el chico **inglés** *the English boy*	la chica **inglesa** *the English girl*
4. el libro **grande** *the big book* 5. un maestro **joven** *a young (male) teacher*	la ventana **grande** *the big window* una maestra **joven** *a young (female) teacher*

H. Adjectives always agree in gender (masculine or feminine) with the nouns they modify.
I. Many adjectives end in *-o* or *-a*: *-o* when they modify a masculine noun, *-a* when they modify a feminine noun (examples 1 and 2).
J. Adjectives of nationality that end in a consonant (unlike *italiano, -a*) add *-a* when they modify a feminine noun (example 3).
K. All other adjectives are invariable (examples 4 and 5).
L. As illustrated in all the examples above, descriptive adjectives normally follow the noun they modify.

Expansion with Gender Substitutions

Give the form of the opposite gender for each of the nouns and modifiers contained in the following expanding phrases and sentences. Note that Spanish does not usually use a comma after the next-to-last word in a series (*alta, rubia y delgada*).

EXAMPLES: Una señora alta
             Un señor alto
             Una señora alta y rubia
             Un señor alto y rubio

1. Mi amigo es bogotano.
   Mi amigo es un bogotano gordo.
   Mi amigo es un bogotano gordo y tonto.
   Mi amigo es un bogotano gordo, tonto y feo.
   Mi amigo es un bogotano gordo, tonto y feo, pero simpático.

2. El maestro es americano.
   El maestro es americano o inglés.
   El maestro es americano, inglés o italiano.
   El maestro es americano, inglés, italiano o español.
   El maestro es americano, inglés, italiano, español o francés.

3. La maestra es una mujer joven.
   La maestra es una mujer joven y alta.
   La maestra es una mujer joven, alta y delgada.

La maestra es una mujer joven, alta, delgada y bonita.
La maestra es una mujer joven, alta, delgada, bonita y simpática.

4. ¿Es su novio muy gordo y muy bajo?
¿Es su novio muy gordo y muy bajo y muy feo?
¿Es su novio muy gordo y muy bajo y muy feo y muy viejo?
¿Es su novio muy gordo y muy bajo y muy feo y muy viejo, pero muy inteligente?

Replacement

For each word replacement, make all changes necessary to maintain agreement in gender between the noun and its modifiers.

EXAMPLE: El maestro es americano.

La _____.	**La maestra es americana.**
_____ simpático.	**El maestro es simpático.**
__ chica _____.	**La chica es simpática.**
_____ joven.	**La chica es joven.**
El _____.	**El chico es joven.**

1. La ciudad es muy bonita.
El país _____.
_____ pequeño.
__ clase _____.
El lugar _____.
_____ feo.

2. ¿Es una clase grande?
¿_____ centro _____?
¿_____ enorme?
¿_____ puerta _____?
¿_____ alta?
¿_____ hombre _____?

3. Mi novio es inteligente.
_____ francés.
Mi maestra _____.
_____ bogotana.
Mi amigo _____.
_____ colombiano.

Written Translation

This is your first written assignment. Do not worry too much at this time about spelling errors, but be sure that you make the proper gender agreement between nouns and modifiers, and that you place the adjectives in the proper position.

1. A large city[13] and a small country[14]
2. The tall man and the short woman

[13] *Fem.*
[14] *Masc.*

3. A Spanish lady and a French man
4. The good place and the bad place[15]
5. A fat boy and a slender girl
6. The young girl and an old woman
7. The tall, slender girl is the French teacher (teacher of French), but she's not French.
8. The short, blonde lady with (the) green eyes is the English teacher, but she's not English.
9. The city of Bogotá is a very nice place.
10. Colombia is a very large country.

Sentence Completion

Describe each of the following people, providing as many details as you can imagine. Concentrate on making the correct gender agreement with each subject.

EXAMPLE: Emilio Fonseca _____.
**Emilio Fonseca es un chico colombiano, alto,
de pelo negro,** etc.

1. La hermana de Carlos María _____.
2. La maestra de Carlos María _____.
3. Mi hermano _____.
4. Mi primo _____.
5. El amigo de mi hermana _____.
6. El maestro de francés _____.
7. Mi novia _____.
8. Mi profesor _____.

Questions

1. Señorita, ¿es su mamá alta o baja?
2. ¿Y su papá?
3. ¿Cómo es usted, señor? ¿Alto? ¿De ojos verdes? ¿Nada más?
4. ¿Verdad que su maestra es muy simpática?
5. ¿Qué es mejor en un hombre, el pelo negro o el pelo rubio?
6. Y en una mujer, ¿qué es mejor?
7. ¿Es la maestra de Emilio fea, gorda y antipática?
8. ¿Y cómo es la hermana de Carlos María?

2. Plural of nouns and modifiers

In addition to gender agreement, Spanish nouns and their modifiers show agreement in number. The formation of the plural in Spanish is the same for nouns and adjectives, and almost the same for articles.

[15]*Masc.*

	Nouns		**Adjectives**	
Singular	amigo	lugar	verde	mejor
Plural	amigos	lugares	verdes	mejores

Articles

	Definite		**Indefinite**	
	MASC.	FEM.	MASC.	FEM.
Singular	el	la	un	una
Plural	los	las	unos	unas

A. Singular nouns and adjectives ending in a vowel add -*s* to form the plural; those ending in a consonant add -*es*.

B. All of the forms of the articles follow the same pattern as nouns and adjectives, except for the masculine singular *el* and *un*. The usual English equivalent of *unos, unas* is "some."

Expansion with Number Substitutions

Give the plural form of each of the following expanding phrases and sentences. *Note:* The plural of the verb form *es* is *son.*

EXAMPLE: El lugar es grande.
            Los lugares son grandes.

1. Una maestra americana
   Una maestra americana, muy estricta
   Una maestra americana, muy estricta, pero buena
   Una maestra americana, muy estricta, pero buena y simpática

2. ¿Un hombre gordo?
   ¿Un hombre gordo y pequeño?
   ¿Un hombre gordo, pequeño y feo?
   ¿Un hombre gordo, pequeño, feo y tonto?

3. El americano es alto, ¿verdad?
   El americano es alto y gordo, ¿verdad?
   El americano es alto, gordo y rubio, ¿verdad?
   El americano es alto, gordo, rubio y joven, ¿verdad?

4. Sí, la maestra es una señorita.
   Sí sí, la maestra es una señorita muy bonita.
   Sí sí sí, la maestra es una señorita muy bonita: baja y rubia.
   Sí sí sí sí,[16] la maestra es una señorita muy bonita: baja, rubia y gorda.

---

[16]A series of *sí*'s or *no*'s spoken at a rapid pace one after the other, meaning emphatic approval or denial, is a common pattern among Spanish speakers.

Questions

Answer with complete sentences.

1. ¿Son Carlos María y Luz María primos?
2. ¿Son gemelos?
3. ¿Son Carlos María y su hermana americanos o colombianos?
4. Y Emilio, ¿es colombiano? ¿Y Luz María?
5. En general, ¿son las chicas francesas bonitas?
6. ¿Son las mujeres buenas como maestras, en general?
7. ¿Son los hombres buenos como maestros?
8. ¿Son los hombres mejores que las mujeres como maestros?
9. ¿Son ustedes dos hermanos, primos o amigos?
10. Y ustedes, señoritas, ¿son americanas o colombianas?
11. Y usted, señor, ¿es bogotano?
12. ¿Son las maestras de inglés en el Centro Cultural de Bogotá americanas, inglesas o francesas?

3. Subject pronouns

Singular		Plural	
yo	*I*	nosotros, -as	*we*
tú	*you*		
usted	*you*	ustedes	*you*
él	*he*	ellos	*they*
ella	*she*	ellas	

vosotros, -as	*you*

A. Subject pronouns are normally omitted in Spanish, as can be seen from the following dialog lines.

No sé su apellido.	(*I*) *don't know her last name.*
Es muy bonita...	(*She*) *is very pretty.* . . .
¿Son gemelos?	*Are* (*you*) *twins?*
No, somos hermanos.	*No,* (*we*) *are brother and sister.*

Use of subject pronouns indicates emphasis.

Yo no sé su apellido.	I *don't know her last name* (*but maybe somebody else does*).
Ella es muy bonita.	She *is very pretty* (*but her sister is rather plain*).
Nosotros somos hermanos.	We *are brother and sister* (*but they are cousins*).

Cartagena, Colombia

B. There are two words for "you" (singular), *tú* and *usted.* You should form the habit of using *usted,* since the use of *tú* places the speaker on an intimate basis with the listener, even more so than addressing a person by his first name in English. The acceptability of *tú* varies considerably from region to region, in accordance with differences in age, social position, degree of intimacy, and so on, among speakers. Because of this variation, you should not attempt to use *tú* freely until you have gained considerable proficiency in Spanish and have become acquainted with the relevant cultural patterns.

C. The plural form *vosotros,* although indispensable in Spain, is not used in everyday conversation or writing in Spanish America, where *ustedes* is the plural of both *tú* and *usted.*[17]

D. The feminine plural forms *nosotras, vosotras,* and *ellas* are used only to refer to a group composed exclusively of females. In all other cases the masculine form is used.

E. The English subject pronoun "it" has no commonly used Spanish counterpart: *¿Quién es?,* "Who is it?"

[17]The verb, object pronoun, and possessive adjective forms corresponding to *vosotros* will be shown in the paradigms but not included in the pattern drills. Your instructor will decide whether or not to use these forms.

4. **Present tense of** *ser,* **to be**

Usted and *ustedes,* although they mean "you," take *third* person verb forms, like "he," "she," "it," and "they."

(yo)	soy	*I am*
(tú)	eres	*you are*
(usted)	es	*you are*
(él, ella)		*he, she, it is*
(nosotros, -as)	somos	*we are*
(ustedes)	son	*you are (plural)*
(ellos, ellas)		*they are*

(vosotros, -as)	sois	*you are*

Paradigm Practice

Say the forms of the verb **ser** several times. This will enable you to do more effectively the pattern drills that follow. Say the forms alternately with and without the subject pronouns, thus:

First time	*Second time*
yo soy	soy
tú eres	eres
usted es, él es, ella es	es
nosotros somos	somos
ustedes son, ellos son, ellas son	son

Person–Number Substitution

Follow the example. Make sure that you also make the correct agreement between nouns and modifiers:

EXAMPLE: ¿Cómo es la *maestra,* simpática?
   (hombres)
   ¿Cómo son los hombres, simpáticos?

1. ¿De dónde es *usted?*
   (tú, nosotros, ustedes, su papá, ellos, yo)
2. *Yo* soy de Colombia.
   (los hermanos Terán Marín, Emilio, yo, nosotros, mi primo, usted, ustedes)

5. Interrogative words

qué	*what*	cuál, -es	*which (one)*
cómo	*how*	quién, -es	*who, whom*
dónde	*where*	por qué	*why*
cuánto, -a, -os, -as	*how much, how many*		

A. *Qué* used as an exclamatory word before an adjective corresponds to English "how."
   ¡Qué bueno!   *How nice!*
   ¡Qué parecidos!   *How similar!*

B. *Cuál* has a plural form, as does *quién.*
   ¿Cuál es?   *Which (one) is it?*
   ¿Cuáles son?   *Which (ones) are they?*
   ¿Quién es?   *Who is it (are you)?*
   ¿Quiénes son?   *Who are they (you)?*

C. *Cuánto* agrees in number and gender with the noun it modifies. Note that English uses "how much" for the singular, but "how many" for the plural.
   ¿Cuánto pelo?   *How much hair?*
   ¿Cuánta agua?   *How much water?*
   ¿Cuántos países?   *How many countries?*
   ¿Cuántas novias?   *How many girlfriends?*

D. All interrogative words have a written accent on the stressed syllable.

E. In Spanish, prepositions (if present) always precede interrogative words and cannot be left dangling, as in the English "Where are you from?"

   ¿De dónde es usted?   *Where are you from?*
   ¿Con qué se escribe   *How (With what) do you spell*
      "centro," con *s* o con *c*?   centro, *with (an)*
                                                      s *or with (a)* c?

You Ask the Questions

Use interrogative words in questions that could elicit each of the following replies.

EXAMPLE: La maestra es de los Estados Unidos.
                    ¿De dónde es la maestra?

   1. Yo soy de México.
   2. Mi nombre es José.[18]
   3. Mi apellido paterno es Jiménez.
   4. Mi apellido materno es Jijón.

---

[18]Use the Spanish for "which," not "what."

5. Mi nombre completo es José Jiménez Jijón.
6. Soy bueno, simpático, pequeño, de pelo verde y ojos feos.
7. Yo soy alumno del Centro Cultural de Baja California.
8. Hay seis alumnos en mi clase; mi papá, mi mamá, mi hermano, mi amigo Pedro, mi prima Luisa y yo.
9. Mi maestra de inglés es una señorita inglesa.
10. Ella es una chica gorda y muy baja, pero muy bonita.
11. Ella y yo somos novios.

Substitution

Notice the use of *qué* as "how." Make sure that the adjectives agree with the nouns they modify.

1. ¿Mi novia? ¡Qué bonita es!
   ¿El Centro Cultural? ¡_____!
   ¿Las clases de español? ¡_____!

2. ¿El profesor Campos? ¡Qué simpático es!
   ¿Los hermanos Terán Marín? ¡_____!
   ¿Nosotros? ¡_____!

3. ¿Los profesores americanos? ¡Qué estrictos son!
   ¿El profesor de francés? ¡_____!
   ¿Tú? ¡_____!
   ¿El papá de la chica? ¡_____!

6. Negative sentences with *no*

¿Es o no es el maestro?	*Are you or aren't you the teacher?*
No, no soy.	*No, I'm not.*

A. Affirmative sentences, whether declarative or interrogative, are made negative by placing the particle *no* before the verb.

B. *No* is also used alone, like *sí*. Therefore, when a question is answered with *no* first, followed by a negative verb construction, two *no*'s may occur in a sequence.

Affirmative ⟶ Negative

EXAMPLE: Usted es francés
          Usted no es francés.

1. Yo soy de la capital.
2. Bogotá es la capital de Chile.
3. Es una ciudad muy grande.
4. Los colombianos somos muy simpáticos.
5. ¿Es usted americano?
6. ¿Habla usted español?
7. Ustedes son unos alumnos muy buenos.

Emphatic Denial

Answer the following questions with a rapid sequence of three *no*'s followed by a complete negative statement.

EXAMPLE: Perdón, ¿es usted el profesor de español?
No no no, no soy el profesor de español.

1. ¿Es la ciudad de Nueva York la capital del estado?
2. ¿Son ustedes buenos alumnos en español?
3. ¿Es Rusia un país pequeño?
4. ¿Son las mujeres mejores que los hombres?
5. ¿Somos usted y yo parecidos?

Useful Expressions

Buenos días. (Buenas tardes.) (Buenas noches.)	Good morning. (Good afternoon.) (Good night.)
¿Cómo está usted? (¿Cómo sigue usted?) (¿Qué tal?)	How are you? (How are you coming along?) (How are things?)
Bastante bien, gracias. (Muy bien, gracias.)	Pretty good, thanks. (Very well, thanks.)
Yo estoy muy bien.	I'm fine.
¡Qué bueno! Me alegro.	That's good! I'm glad.
Yo estoy muy mal.	I'm doing badly (feeling bad).
¡Qué lástima! Lo siento mucho.	What a shame! I'm very sorry.
¿Habla usted inglés?	Do you speak English?
Sí, yo hablo un poco. ¿Por qué?	Yes, I speak a little. Why?
¿Cómo se dice "tomorrow" en español?	How do you say "tomorrow" in Spanish?
Se dice "mañana."	You say "mañana."
Gracias.	Thanks.
De nada.	You're welcome.
Con permiso.	Excuse me.
Cómo no.	Of course.

Rejoinders

Respond in any appropriate way to the following questions or statements.

EXAMPLES: El profesor Campos está mal.
Lo siento mucho.
¿Habla usted inglés?
Sí, hablo un poco.
No, yo hablo español.

1. Buenos días.
2. Gracias.
3. ¿Cómo está usted?
4. ¿Habla usted español?

5. Y usted, ¿habla inglés?
6. ¿Cómo se dice "professor" en español?
7. Yo estoy muy mal.
8. ¿Cómo se dice "good afternoon" en español?
9. Con permiso.

Conversation Stimulus

The whole class answers with a complete, meaningful phrase, which need not be a grammatically complete sentence. You may agree or disagree by starting your reply with *Sí, señor (señorita),...* or *No, señor,...* Your instructor will signal the yes and no answers. Don't be shy; let yourself go along with the others in the class, even if the first time you can give only a partial answer.

EXAMPLES: Buenos días, señores (señoritas), buenos días.
            Buenos días, profesor(a), buenos días.
            Yo no soy un profesor estricto, ¿verdad?
            No, señor, usted no es un profesor muy estricto.

1. ¿Son ustedes buenos alumnos?
2. Bogotá es la capital de Venezuela, ¿verdad?
3. ¿Son ustedes de Bogotá?
4. Carlos María y Luz María son bogotanos, ¿verdad?
5. ¿Son importantes los Centros Culturales?
6. ¿Hay ciudades viejas en los Estados Unidos? ¿Hay ciudades nuevas?
7. ¿Cuál es la ciudad capital de los Estados Unidos? ¿Es bonita?
8. Cartagena es uno de los puertos de Panamá, ¿verdad?
9. ¿Cuál ciudad de los Estados Unidos es un puerto principal?
10. ¿De qué país son ustedes?
11. Ustedes y yo somos amigos, ¿no es verdad?
12. Las mujeres son mejores como maestras, ¿verdad?
13. Estados Unidos es un país muy grande, ¿no?
14. ¿Es muy bonito Estados Unidos?
15. Nueva York es otro país, ¿verdad? ¿Qué es Nueva York?
16. ¿Hay un estado con el nombre de Nueva York también?
17. Los americanos son muy antipáticos, ¿verdad?
18. Perdón, ¿quién es el maestro de español aquí? ¿Es bueno o malo?

LISTENING COMPREHENSION EXERCISE B

Reading and Performing

Read the following dialogs several times each until you familiarize yourself with the lines and can put some feeling into them. Then close your books and try to act out each situation, without necessarily repeating all the lines verbatim. (NOTE: New words occurring only in the reading selections are not listed in the chapter vocabularies. If they are not footnoted, and you cannot guess their meanings from context, you will find them in the vocabulary at the end of the book.)

Un alumno nuevo

PIRI. *Pirimpimpín*[19]   PROF. *Profesor*

PIRI.   Con permiso, buenas tardes.

PROF.   Buenas[20], ¿qué tal?

PIRI.   Muy bien, señor, gracias. Perdón, ¿es usted el profesor de filosofía?

PROF.   A sus órdenes.

PIRI.   Yo soy uno de los nuevos alumnos, Mi nombre es Pirimpimpín Soto.

PROF.   Ah, mucho gusto. ¿De dónde es usted, Pirimpimpín? Usted no es colombiano, ¿verdad?

PIRI.   No, señor, soy peruano. Perdón, señor, ¿es verdad que usted es un profesor muy estricto?

PROF.   ¡No no no no no, no es verdad, no es verdad!

PIRI.   ¡Qué bueno, cuánto me alegro! Su clase es por la mañana, ¿no?

PROF.   No, por la tarde.

PIRI.   Ah... Bien, con permiso, profesor. Muchas gracias.

PROF.   De nada Pirimpimpín, cómo no.

Con Luis y Ana, sus nuevos amigos

PIRI.   Pst, Luis, ¿quién es la chica de pelo rubio y ojos verdes? ¡Qué fantástica, qué fenomenal, qué...!

LUIS.   Es mi hermana.

PIRI.   Oh, perdón.

LUIS.   ¿Por qué? ¡ANA! ¡ANA!

PIRI.   No, por favor, yo soy muy tímido.

ANA.   ¿Sí, Luis?

LUIS.   Pirimpimpín, mi hermana Ana.

PIRI.   Encantado, señorita. Pirimpimpín Soto.

ANA.   Mucho gusto.[21]

[19] Pirimpimpín is a nickname. It is used here so that you will practice pronouncing a series of unstressed *i*'s, every one of which must sound as distinct and clear as the stressed *i* in the last syllable.

[20] *Buenas* (or *buenos*) alone is a common and less formal way of responding to any of the "good . . ." greetings (*buenos días; buenas tardes, noches*).

[21] *Mucho gusto* can be used not only as "How do you do?" but also as "Very happy to have met you."

Quito, Ecuador: Street scene

Por la tarde, con Ana

PIRI. Usted y su hermano son muy parecidos. Pero usted es mucho más bonita.

ANA. Gracias, ¡qué simpático es usted!

PIRI. Y su nombre es muy bonito, Ana.

ANA. Mi nombre completo es Ana de los Angeles.[22]

PIRI. ¿Ana de los Angeles qué? ¿Cuál es su apellido?

ANA. Montenegro. Ana de los Angeles Montenegro.

PIRI. ¿Montenegro qué?

ANA. Montenegro de Gaulle.

PIRI. ¿De Gaulle? ¿Su mamá es francesa?

ANA. No, ella es colombiana, pero de origen francés. Dicen que es descendiente de un hombre muy famoso en la historia de Francia.

Por la noche, con Ana

ANA. Pirimpimpín, ¿cómo son las chicas peruanas?

PIRI. Unas son altas, otras[23] son bajas, otras son gordas, otras son simpáticas, otras antipáticas...

ANA. ¿Qué más?

PIRI. ¿Qué más qué? Nada más. Ah, sí, son muy bonitas.

ANA. ¿Muy *muy* bonitas?

PIRI. Sí, pero ustedes las colombianas son más bonitas.

[22] *Angeles* is stressed on the first syllable. [23] Others.

For Oral or Written Composition

Using the following key words and phrases, summarize the main ideas of the preceding passages in a series of complete sentences.

Nombre y nacionalidad del alumno nuevo.
Con quién habla Pirimpimpín.
Cómo es el profesor.
Cuándo son las clases del profesor.
Quiénes son Luis y Ana.
Información sobre Ana.

LISTENING COMPREHENSION EXERCISE C

Vocabulary

a to; at
el **agua** *f* water
ah ah, oh
alto, -a tall
el **alumno,** la **alumna** student
americano, -a American
la **amiga** friend, girlfriend
el **amigo,** friend, boyfriend
antipático, -a unpleasant, disagreeable
el **apellido** surname
azul blue
Baja California Lower California
bajo, -a low, short
bastante enough; quite; fairly
bien well; okay
bogotano, -a from Bogotá, Colombia
bonito, -a pretty
bueno, -a good; nice
la **capital** capital city
el **centro** center
la **ciudad** city
la **clase** class
colombiano, -a Colombian
como like; as
¿cómo? how

cómo no of course
completo, -a complete
con permiso excuse me
la **costa** coast
cuál which; what
cuándo when
cuánto, -a how much
cultural cultural
la **chica** girl
el **chico** boy
de from; of; about
de nada you're welcome
del from the; of the; about the
delgado, -a thin, slender
el **día** day
dicen they say; you *pl* say
¿dónde? where
el the
él he
ella she
ellas *f* they
ellos *m* they
en in; on; at
encantado, -a charmed, delighted; delighted to meet you
español, -a Spanish

está   he, she, it is; you *sing* are

el **estado**   state

Estados Unidos *sing* or *pl*   United States

estricto, -a   strict

la **expresión**   expression

feo, -a   ugly

francés, -esa   French

gemelo, -a   twin

general   general

gordo, -a   fat

las **gracias**   thanks

grande   big, large; great

el **gusto**   pleasure

habla   he speaks, talks; she speaks, talks; you *sing* speak, talk

hablo   I speak, talk

hay   there is, there are

la **hermana**   sister

el **hermano**   brother

el **hombre**   man

importante   important

inglés, -esa   English

la **institución**   institution

inteligente   intelligent

italiano, -a   Italian

joven   young

el **joven**   young man

la **joven**   young woman

la(s)   the

la **lástima**   pity

el **libro**   book

lo siento   I'm sorry

los   the

el **lugar**   place

mal   sick, ill

malo, -a   bad; sick, ill

la **mamá**   mother, mom

mañana   tomorrow

la **mañana**   morning

mañana por la mañana   tomorrow morning

más   more

materno, -a   maternal

me alegro   I'm glad

mejor   better

mi   my

la **muchacha**   girl

el **muchacho**   boy

mucho, -a   plenty, much, a lot; *pl* many

la **mujer**   woman

muy   very

nada   nothing

nada más   only, nothing more

negro, -a   black

no   no

la **noche**   night

el **nombre**   name

nosotros, nosotras   we

la **novia**   sweetheart, girlfriend; fiancée

el **novio**   sweetheart, boyfriend; fiancé

nuevo, -a   new

el **ojo**   eye

el **país**   country

el **papá**   father, dad

parecido, -a   alike, similar

paterno, -a   paternal

el **pelo**   hair

pequeño, -a   small; short

perdón   pardon me, excuse me

el **perdón**   pardon

el **permiso**   permission

pero   but

poco, -a   little, scanty; *pl* few

¿por qué?   why

el **puerto**   port

que   that, which; who

¿qué tal?   how are you?

quien   who, whom

quién   who, whom

rubio, -a   blonde

Rusia   Russia

sabe   he knows; she knows; you *sing* know

sé   I know

se dice   you say, they say, one says

según   according to

seis   six

la **señora**   Mrs.; lady

la **señorita**   Miss; girl

ser   to be

sí yes

sigue he continues (to be); she continues (to be); you continue (to be)

simpático, -a nice, pleasant, charming

sobre about

su your; his; her; their

también too, also

la **tarde** afternoon

tonto, -a dumb; silly

tú you

un, una a, an; *pl* **unos, unas** some

uno one

usted(es) you

la **ventana** window

la **verdad** truth

¿verdad? isn't that so?; right?

viejo, -a old

vosotros, vosotras you

y and

yo I

Cultural Listening Passage
for Chapter 2

Sunday: An Outing in the Country

(1) During their summer or Easter vacations, groups of North American students usually (are accustomed to) visit some of the Latin American countries. These are short visits of two or three days in each country, but with lots of activity and fun, not only for the visitors but also for the students of the country they are visiting. (2) Right now (in these moments) there is a group (that is) visiting one of the small Central American countries, Costa Rica. Costa Rica, situated between Panama and Nicaragua, is a tiny republic of the tropics, with a population of almost two million inhabitants. Its territorial extension is approximately half that of the state of New York. It is one of the most democratic and advanced countries in Latin America, although, like the other Central American republics, it is still an essentially agricultural country, coffee being its main product for export.

(3) The most beautiful and picturesque part of Costa Rica is the countryside, with its coffee, banana, and sugar plantations; with the poor (humble) but clean and cheerful homes of the peasants; with the impressive tropical vegetation; with the cows and the oxen and the horses and the chickens and the birds and the flowers that abound everywhere. Yes, the Costa Rican countryside is an ideal place for outings. (4) It is precisely at an outing in the country, in a place called Tres Ríos (Three Rivers), about ten or fifteen kilometers from San José, the capital, where this group of students, all girls from a high school in Florida, is right now. Accompanying them there is, naturally, a very large group of "ticos," as they call the Costa Ricans.

(5) Over there in the shade of a magnificent (splendorous) mango tree is Vickie talking to Manuel and Jorge. Vickie says that she likes Costa Rica very much, that the outing is beautiful, and that everybody seems to be having such a good time (so merry). (6) Manuel then

explains—jokingly, of course—that they are in a happy mood not only because they are on the outing but because the "ticos" are like that by nature; they are always cheerful people. (7) Jorge intervenes to say that that's a lie, that the "ticos" are very dull, and that if now they look very happy it's because they, the American girls, are visiting Costa Rica.

(8) And way over there, walking by the bank of the river, we see beautiful Linda accompanied by Enrique and Hernán. It is almost one o'clock in the afternoon and Linda probably is tired from walking—although she says she isn't and she's not hungry (hasn't hunger). She says she's only thirsty (has thirst) and doesn't want to eat anything; she just wants to drink (take) something cold. (9) Enrique says that he'll be glad to go and get (with much pleasure he will bring) some Cokes that are in the car. Linda says that she's not tired and suggests that the three of them go look for the Cokes.

(10) Today is Sunday; this group of American students is going to be in Costa Rica until Tuesday. Then they're going to go to Nicaragua, where they're going to spend two days.

Grammar Points

First, the present tense of the verb **estar** (to be); second, the difference between the verbs **ser** and **estar;** third, cardinal numbers and the time of day; fourth, the present tense of the verb **ir** (to go); fifth, the infinitive form of verbs; and sixth, the construction **ir a** + *infinitive* (to be going to).

Costa Rica: Folk
dancing

Chapter 2

Basic Dialog

Domingo: un paseo al campo

I

VI. *Vickie*   MA. *Manuel*   JO. *Jorge*

VI. ¡Qué lindo está el paseo! ¡Todos están tan alegres!
MA. Los ticos somos así por naturaleza; somos gente alegre.
JO. Mentira, Vickie, somos muy apagados. Hoy estamos alegres porque ustedes están en Costa Rica.
VI. Gracias, muy amable. Costa Rica me gusta mucho.
MA. ¿Le gusta, de veras? ¿Cuánto tiempo van a estar aquí?
VI. Hasta el martes. Luego vamos a Nicaragua. Allí vamos a pasar dos días.

II

LI. *Linda*   EN. *Enrique*   HE. *Hernán*

LI.   ¿Alguien sabe qué hora es? No tengo mi reloj.
EN.   Es casi la una. ¿Ya tiene hambre? ¿Quiere comer?
LI.   No, gracias, tengo sed solamente. Quiero tomar algo frío.
HE.   Enrique, por favor, las Coca-Colas están en el carro. Linda está un poco cansada. Ella y yo esperamos aquí.
LI.   No no. Yo no estoy cansada. ¿Por qué no vamos los tres?

Sunday: An outing in the country[1]

I

VI. *Vickie*   MA. *Manual*   JO. *Jorge*

VI.   What a nice outing![2] Everybody looks so happy![3]
MA.   We "ticos" are naturally[4] like that; we are cheerful people.
JO.   That's not true,[5] Vickie, we're very dull. Today we are happy because you are in Costa Rica.
VI.   Thank you, that's nice of you. I like Costa Rica very much.[6]
MA.   Do you like it, really? How long are you going to be here?
VI.   Until Tuesday. Then we're going to Nicaragua. We're going to spend two days there.

II

LI. *Linda*   EN. *Enrique*   HE. *Hernán*

LI.   Does anybody know what time it is? I don't have my watch.
EN.   It's almost one. Are you hungry already? Do you want to eat?
LI.   No, thank you, I'm only thirsty. I want to drink something cold.
HE.   Enrique, would you please?[7] The Cokes are in the car. Linda's a little tired. She and I will wait here.
LI.   No, no. I'm not tired. Why don't the three of us go?

Cultural Notes

A.   In Spanish-speaking areas Sunday is listed as the last day of the week, not the first. Rather than a day of rest, *el domingo* (morning and afternoon) is a day for festivities and all kinds of outdoor and indoor activities. People go to church, but they also go on picnics, to the stadium (the most important sports events and other spectacles

[1]Countryside.
[2]How beautiful is the outing.
[3]In a festive mood.
[4]By nature.
[5]Lie.
[6]Costa Rica pleases me much.
[7]For (a) favor.

take place on Sunday), dancing, to the movies, and to birthday parties. Presidential elections usually occur on Sunday, and in some countries the winners are drawn in the national lottery on that day.
B. Bottled water and soft drinks are more common as accompaniments to meals in Hispanic countries than in the United States.

The Sounds of Spanish: II

A. **The consonant *t*.** Spanish *t* differs from English *t* in two principal respects. First, for Spanish *t*, the front part of the tongue is pressed against the back of the upper teeth, *not* against the gum ridge above and behind the upper teeth as in English. Second, Spanish *t* is *never* followed by a puff of air (technically, *aspiration*) as English *t* frequently is. Mispronunciation of *t* is one of the most unattractive characteristics of a foreign accent in Spanish. To appreciate the effect of mispronounced *t*'s and to familiarize yourself with the sound of Spanish *t*, listen to a Spanish speaker mispronounce English by using Spanish *t*'s.

> You take too much time, Tom.
> Take two tokens, Tina.
> It takes two to tango.

Listen again to these sentences and, if you are not shy, imitate the Spanish speaker's foreign accent. This is an excellent way to learn to pronounce Spanish correctly.

Now listen and repeat the following sentences. Concentrate on the *t*'s but do not neglect the pronunciation of previously learned vowels and the maintenance of an even rhythm.

> Los-ti-cos-no-to-ma-mos-té.   (*We Costa Ricans don't drink tea.*)
> Yo-no-ten-go-tan-tos-tan-gos.   (*I don't have so many tangos.*)
> Tan-tos-ton-tos-to-man-te-qui-la. (*So many fools drink tequila.*)

B. **The consonant *d*.** In Spanish, the letter *d* stands for two distinct sounds. At the beginning of an utterance or after a pause, and after *l* or *n*, Spanish *d* is pronounced [d], much like the English *d* of "dog," "day," and "adopt." In all other positions Spanish *d* is pronounced [đ], much like the *th* of "mother," "lather," and "then." Listen to the similarity between English *th* and Spanish *d* in the following words; repeat only the Spanish words.

mother	moda	(*fashion*)
either	ida	(*departure*)
soothing	suden	(*perspire*)
lather	lado	(*side*)
than	Adán	(*Adam*)

A word obviously does not appear in the same context every time it is used. For example, the word *dónde,* "where," might be used in the sentence *¿Dónde estás?,* "Where are you?" In this case the first *d* occurs after silence (let's suppose), and is accordingly pronounced [d]. But *dónde* might also be used in *No sé dónde,* "I don't know where." Here the first *d* of *dónde* does *not* occur after silence (or after *n* or *l*), and is accordingly pronounced [đ]. Listen and repeat the following examples, in which *d*'s in the same word are pronounced differently according to context. As a reminder, all *d*'s pronounced [đ] are underlined.

de Juan	(*John's*)	casa <u>d</u>e Juan	(*John's house*)
dónde	(*where*)	de <u>d</u>ónde	(*from where*)
delga<u>d</u>a	(*slender*)	la <u>d</u>elga<u>d</u>a	(*the slender one*)
domingo	(*Sunday*)	qué <u>d</u>omingo	(*what a Sunday*)

We will give you additional practice pronouncing Spanish [đ]. In the following words, the *d*'s pronounced [đ] are underlined as a reminder. Listen and repeat.

na<u>d</u>a	(*nothing*)	ocupa<u>d</u>o	(*occupied, busy*)
pareci<u>d</u>os	(*similar*)	preocupa<u>d</u>o	(*worried*)
ciu<u>d</u>ad	(*city*)	mie<u>d</u>o	(*fear*)
uste<u>d</u>	(*you,* singular)	vi<u>d</u>a <u>d</u>iaria	(*daily life*)
uste<u>d</u>es	(*you,* plural)	i<u>d</u>ea	(*idea*)
cansa<u>d</u>a	(*tired*)	desocupa<u>d</u>a	(*unoccupied, free*)
to<u>d</u>avía	(*still*)	estu<u>d</u>ia	(*he studies*)
limpia<u>d</u>ita	(*cleaning*)	Faculta<u>d</u> <u>d</u>e Derecho	(*Law School*)
to<u>d</u>os	(*all*)	pe<u>d</u>acito	(*piece*)
enamora<u>d</u>o	(*in love*)	cui<u>d</u>a<u>d</u>o	(*care*)

C. **r between vowels.** Spanish *r*, [r], is totally unlike any kind of *r* heard in normal American English. There is, however, a very common sound in English which works very well for Spanish [r], although it is not spelled *r* in English. This is the sound of the *t* (or *tt*) and the *d* (or *dd*) in words like "Betty," "Eddie," "ladder," "caddie," "got it," and so on, in casual pronunciation. Listen to the similarity of the English *t*'s and *d*'s to the Spanish *r*'s in the following words.

better	Vera (*a proper name*)	cotter	cara (*face*)
Eddies	eres (*you are*)	pot o' tea	para ti (*for you*)

Listen and repeat the following words and phrases. Pay particular attention to [r].

hora	(*hour*)	pero	(*but*)	cara	(*face*)
ahora	(*now*)	para	(*for*)	señora	(*lady*)
mujeres	(*women*)	estar aquí	(*to be here*)	americana	(*American*)
mejores	(*better*)	mira	(*look*)	lotería	(*lottery*)

No-sé-qué-(h)o-ra-e-sa-(h)o-ra.	(*I don't know what time it is now.*)
Las-mu-je-re-son-me-jo-res.	(*Women are better.*)
¿Pe-ro-pa-ra-qués-ta-ra-quí?	(*But what's the purpose of being here?*)
Mi-ra-la-ca-ra-de-la-se-ño-ra-me-ri-ca-na.	(*Look at the American lady's face.*)

The following exercise will give you practice in discriminating between Spanish *d*'s and *r*'s between vowels.

	[d]		[r]	
cada	(*each*)	cara	(*face*)
codo	(*elbow*)	coro	(*chorus*)
mido	(*I measure*)	miro	(*I look*)
mudo	(*mute*)	muro	(*wall*)
pudo	(*he was able*)	puro	(*pure*)
todos	(*everybody*)	toros	(*bulls*)

Spanish Spelling: II

Although pronunciation is unambiguously predictable from spelling in Spanish, the converse is not true. That is, some sounds have more than one spelling, as shown in the following chart:

Sound	Spellings	Examples
[b]	*b* or *v*	*b*ueno, *b*aja, tam*b*ién; *v*iejo, *v*erde
[h]	*g* or *j*	*g*emelos, *g*ente; mu*j*eres, me*j*ores
[s]	*c*, *s*, or *z*	on*c*e; *s*í, ca*s*a*s*; *z*apato, die*z*
[y]	*ll* or *y*	*ll*amo, e*ll*a, a*ll*í, *y*o, *y*a, o*y*e

In general, you cannot predict the spelling of Spanish words that have any of the sounds [b, h, s, y] or those spelled with a silent *h*; the spelling must simply be memorized. However, in an extremely large number of cases Spanish spelling may be deduced from English spelling. A tiny sample follows.

ENGLISH	SPANISH	ENGLISH	SPANISH
alpha*b*et	alfa*b*eto (*not* alfa*v*eto)	*J*esus	*J*esús (*not* Gezúz)
*v*alid	*v*álido (*not* *b*álido)	difference	diferencia (*not* diferensia)
*h*abit	*h*ábito (*not* _ávito)	expression	expresión (*not* expreción)
*h*onor	*h*onor (*not* _onor)	*z*one	*z*ona (*not* *s*ona)
general	general (*not* *j*eneral)	cas*t*le	cas*t*illo (*not* ca*z*tiyo)

LISTENING COMPREHENSION EXERCISE A

Dialog Supplement

Study and memorize the new vocabulary items in context, within the framework of related basic phrases or sentences, as in the preceding chapter.

Branch of a coffee tree

I

Un paseo al campo

al mar	*to the sea*
al lago	*to the lake*
al río	*to the river*
a la playa	*to the beach*
a la montaña	*to the mountain*

Allí vamos a pasar dos días.

una semana	*a week*
un mes	*a month*
un año	*a year*
un ratito	*a little while*

¿Cuánto tiempo van a estar aquí?

estudiar	*to study*
trabajar	*to work*
hablar	*to talk*
esperar	*to wait, hope*

¡Qué lindo está el paseo!

	el cielo	*the sky*
¡Qué linda está la fiesta!	la casa	*the party*
	la casa	*the house*

¡Todos están tan alegres!

contentos	*happy, satisfied*
tristes	*sad*
ocupados	*busy*
preocupados	*worried*
aburridos	*bored*

Luego vamos a Nicaragua.

Después	*afterwards*
Antes	*before*
También	*also*
Siempre	*always*

II

¿Alguien sabe qué hora es?		Quiero tomar algo.	
Nadie	*nobody*	hacer	*to do, to make*
Todo el mundo	*everybody*[8]	decir	*to say*
		ver	*to see*

¿Ya tiene hambre?		Quiero tomar algo frío.	
Todavía	*still*	caliente	*hot*

No, tengo sed.		Las Coca-Colas están en el carro.	
calor	*hot*	La cerveza está en el carro.	*the beer*
frío	*cold*	la leche	*the milk*
sueño	*sleepy*	el agua[9]	*the water*
miedo	*afraid*	el café	*the coffee*
prisa	*in a hurry*	el té	*the tea*

Dialog and Supplement Check

Sentence Recall

Say the dialog phrase or sentence in which each of the following words or phrases occurs.

Costa Rica	Coca-Colas	de veras
alegres	reloj	hambre
Nicaragua	hora	sed
apagados	martes	esperamos
cansada	por naturaleza	

Next-Sentence Rejoinders

Say the dialog sentence that follows the one you hear.

EXAMPLE: ¡Qué lindo está el paseo!
          ¡Todos están tan alegres!

1. Costa Rica me gusta mucho.
2. Las Coca-Colas están en el carro.
3. ¿Alguien sabe qué hora es?
4. Mentira, Vickie, somos muy apagados.
5. ¿Quiere comer?
6. Quiero tomar algo frío.
7. ¿Cuánto tiempo van a estar aquí?
8. Es casi la una.
9. Yo no estoy cansada.
10. Luego vamos a Nicaragua.

[8]All the world.
[9]Although *agua* is a feminine noun, it takes the article *el*. All other modifiers are feminine (*agua fría, las aguas*, etc.).

Item Substitution

Repeat each of the following phrases or sentences, substituting one or more related words or phrases for the one in italics. If books are closed, your instructor will repeat the item to be substituted.

EXAMPLE: Allí vamos a pasar *un mes.*
Allí vamos a pasar dos días.
Allí vamos a pasar una semana.
Etc.

1. Un paseo *a la montaña.*
2. *¿Nadie* sabe qué hora es?
3. Allí vamos a pasar *un ratito.*
4. ¿Cuánto tiempo van a *esperar* allí?
5. ¡Todos están tan *cansados!*
6. ¡Qué lindo está *el cielo!*
7. ¿Cuánto tiempo van a *trabajar* allí?
8. *¿Alguien* sabe qué hora es?
9. *Después* vamos a Nicaragua.
10. Un paseo *al río.*

Questions

1. ¿En qué país están Vickie y Linda?
2. ¿Está Costa Rica al norte o al sur de Nicaragua?

Mexico City:
Chapultepec
Park

3. ¿Cuál es la capital de Costa Rica? ¿De Nicaragua?
4. ¿Está Vickie con uno o con dos muchachos?
5. ¿En qué parte de Costa Rica están, en una ciudad?
6. ¿Cómo está el paseo, alegre o triste?
7. ¿Cómo está el día hoy, bonito o feo?
8. ¿Sabe Linda qué hora es? ¿Por qué no sabe?
9. ¿Cuánto tiempo más van a estar las chicas en Costa Rica?
10. Y ¿adónde van a ir después?
11. ¿Quiere usted ir a un paseo mañana o ahora?
12. ¿Adónde quiere ir, a un lago, a la playa?
13. ¿Tiene hambre Linda? ¿Tiene sueño? ¿Tiene frío? ¿Qué tiene?
14. Y usted, ¿tiene calor o tiene frío?
15. ¿Tiene usted sed? ¿Qué quiere tomar, cerveza o té?
16. ¿Cuánto tiempo van a pasar las chicas en Nicaragua?
17. ¿Le gusta a usted la clase de español? ¿De veras?
18. ¿Quiere estudiar más ahora?

Grammar

7. **Present tense of** *estar,* **to be**

(yo)	estoy
(tú)	estás
(usted) } (él, ella)	está
(nosotros, -as)	estamos
(ustedes) } (ellos, ellas)	están

(vosotros, -as)	estáis

Paradigm Practice

Say the forms of the verb **estar** several times. Alternate saying them with and without the subject pronouns. This will enable you to do more effectively the pattern drills that follow. The *vosotros* form should be included in this practice if your instructor wishes to include it in the pattern drills.

Alternate Substitution

Concentrate not only on *estar* but on making the correct number–gender agreement between subject and modifiers. Follow the example.

1. Yo no estoy cansada.
   Jorge _____.
   Jorge no está cansado.
   _____ estoy _____.
   Nosotros _____.
   _____ ocupadas.
   Ellos _____.
   _____ está _____.
   _____ aburrido.
   Vickie y Linda _____.

2. El cielo está lindo.
   __ casa _____.
   _____ fantástica.
   __ paseo _____.
   _____ aburrido.[10]
   Ella y yo[11] _____.
   _____ está _____.
   _____ preocupado.
   Todo el mundo _____.

3. ¡Qué bonito está el paseo!
   ¡_____ montañas!
   ¡_____ está _____!
   ¡____ verde _____!
   ¡_____ mar!
   ¡____ fantástico _____!
   ¡_____ playa!

8. ser *vs.* estar

A. Both **ser** and **estar** mean "to be." For Spanish speakers, however, these two verbs are just as different as "do" and "make" (both *hacer* in Spanish) or "say" and "tell" (both *decir* in Spanish) are for English speakers.

   As shown in the chart below, *estar* is used in just two cases (a third will be added in Chapter 3): to refer to the *location* of a person or thing, and to refer to the *condition* of a person or thing at a particular time. *Ser* covers all other meanings of "to be," which are many and varied (examples 4 through 9 provide a small sample). Thus your learning task is relatively simple. When confronted with making a choice between *ser* and *estar*, ask two questions: "Location of something?" If so, use *estar*. "Condition of something at a particular time?" If so, use *estar*. If the answer to both questions is "no," then use *ser*, regardless of meaning. In time you will learn to make the choice automatically, without having to ask these questions consciously.

---

[10] In this case *aburrido* means "boring."

[11] If *yo* is a male, then use the masculine plural form to agree with subject.

estar

A. *Location*

  1. ¿Dónde **está** Bogotá? **Está** en Colombia. *Where is Bogotá? It's in Colombia.*
  2. ¿Dónde **está** María? **Está** aquí. *Where is María? She's here.*

B. *Condition*

  3. ¿Cómo **está** María? **Está** muy cansada. *How is María? She's very tired.*

ser

  4. ¿Quién **es** María? **Es** una chica. *Who is María? She's a girl.*
  5. ¿Qué **es** María? **Es** colombiana. *What is María? She's Colombian.*
  6. ¿De dónde **es** María? **Es** de Colombia. *Where's María from? She's from Colombia.*
  7. ¿Cómo **es** María? **Es** muy alegre. *What's María like? She's very cheerful (a very cheerful person).*
  8. ¿Qué día **es** hoy? Hoy **es** domingo. *What's today? Today is Sunday.*
  9. ¿Qué hora **es?** **Es** casi la una. *What time is it? It's almost one.*

B. The only sentences in which either *ser* or *estar* may be used are those with predicate adjectives (examples 3 and 7). *Ser* expresses the normal, characteristic, usual classification of the subject as to appearance, personality, intelligence, size, etc. (*María es bonita, es simpática, es inteligente, es alta*, etc.). *Estar*, on the other hand, expresses the state of appearance, health, etc., that the subject happens to be in at a particular time. Obviously, the state or condition of a subject at a particular time (*estar*) may or may not coincide with the normal, characteristic classification (*ser*). This is illustrated in the basic dialog of this chapter: Manuel says that Costa Ricans are characteristically cheerful (**somos** *así por naturaleza*); Jorge denies this, saying that they are normally dull (**somos** *muy apagados*); whatever the correct facts are about the usual nature of Costa Ricans, they happen to be happy on this particular occasion because of the American girls (*Hoy* **estamos** *alegres porque ustedes están en Costa Rica*).

Similar distinctions are often made in English with some word other than "be"; for example, *María es muy bonita, pero* **está** *fea en la foto*, "María is very pretty, but she *looks* ugly in the photo"; *El café* **está** *bueno porque es café bueno*, "The coffee *tastes* good because it's good coffee."

Some predicate adjectives are normally used only with *estar*. These are adjectives that describe a situation usually thought of as out-of-the-ordinary or as a departure from a norm: *ocupado* (busy), *enfermo* (sick), *preocupado* (worried), etc.

Ser or Estar?

After having carefully read the preceding discussion, listen to each of the following English sentences and decide whether the same sentence in Spanish would require the *ser* verb form or the *estar* verb form given alongside it. *Note:* Do not translate the sentences.

1. How is your mother this morning? (*Es* or *está?*)
2. Where are you from, my friend? (*Eres* or *estás?*)
3. What's that? (*Es* or *está?*)
4. Do I look okay with this hat? (*Soy* or *estoy?*)
5. What nationality is your uncle? (*Es* or *está?*)
6. What does he look like? (*Es* or *está?*)
7. You must be tired. (*Ser* or *estar?*)
8. Who is that man over there? (*Es* or *está?*)
9. Well, here we are. (*Somos* or *estamos?*)
10. You sound very intelligent today. (*Eres* or *estás?*)
11. But I am intelligent! (*Soy* or *estoy?*)
12. Sorry. Are we friends? (*Somos* or *estamos?*)
13. Don't bother me, I'm busy! (*Soy* or *estoy?*)
14. What day is today? (*Es* or *está?*)
15. What beautiful eyes she has. One is green, the other one black. (*Es* or *está?*)

Paired Questions

Use the appropriate form of *ser* or *estar*. The first question must be answered affirmatively.

EXAMPLES: ¿Está usted triste?
Sí, estoy triste.
¿Por qué está triste?
Porque yo soy así por naturaleza.

1. ¡Qué estricta está la maestra hoy! ¿No? ¿Por qué está tan estricta?
2. ¿Está Pedro muy gordo en la foto? ¿Pero por qué está tan gordo?
3. ¿Están aburridos los alumnos? ¿Por qué? ¿Es una clase aburrida?
4. ¡Qué bonita está Teresita con su vestido nuevo! ¿No? Pero ella no está bonita por el vestido nada más, ¿no?
5. ¡Qué inteligentes estamos todos hoy! ¿No es verdad? ¿Y por qué estamos todos tan inteligentes?

Questions

EXAMPLES: ¿Emilio Fonseca? ¿De la costa?
Sí, Emilio Fonseca es de la costa.
¿Vickie y Linda? ¿En Costa Rica?
Sí, Vickie y Linda están en Costa Rica.

1. ¿Qué? ¿Casi la una?
2. ¿Usted? ¿Muy bien?
3. ¿Ustedes? ¿De los Estados Unidos?
4. ¿Carlos María? ¿Hermano de Luz María?
5. ¿Ellos? ¿Gemelos?
6. ¿Yo? ¿Americano?
7. ¿Los rusos? ¿Aquí?
8. ¿Usted y yo? ¿Amigos?
9. ¿Mañana? ¿Domingo?
10. ¿Su papá? ¿Muy bien?

Performing

Read the following dialog several times until you are able to put some feeling into the lines. Then act out a similar situation, expanding the conversation with other subjects, such as asking the other person if he is hungry, etc., but leaving the names out until the very end.

Error

A. ¡Ah! ¡Francisco! Mi amigo, ¿cómo está usted?
B. ¡Ah! ¡Buenos días, mi amigo! ¡Mucho gusto! ¿Qué tal está?
A. Estoy bien, muchas gracias. Está muy bonito el día, ¿no es verdad?
B. Sí, ¡está fantástico! ¡Pero usted está muy bien! Está un poco más gordo, nada más, pero ¡está muy bien!
A. Gracias, muchas gracias. Y... ¿cómo están todos en su familia, Francisco?
B. Todos están bien, gracias. ¿Y qué tal su familia, Alfredo, cómo están todos?
A. Pero mi nombre no es Alfredo.
B. Y mi nombre no es Francisco.
A. Oh, perdón
B. Cómo no. Con permiso.

LISTENING COMPREHENSION EXERCISE B

9. Cardinal numbers; the time of day

Numbers

1 uno	11 once	21 veintiuno
2 dos	12 doce	22 veintidós
3 tres	13 trece	23 veintitrés
4 cuatro	14 catorce	30 treinta
5 cinco	15 quince	31 treinta y uno
6 seis	16 dieciséis	32 treinta y dos
7 siete	17 diecisiete	40 cuarenta
8 ocho	18 dieciocho	50 cincuenta
9 nueve	19 diecinueve	
10 diez	20 veinte	

A. *Dieciséis* (16), *diecisiete* (17), *dieciocho* (18), and *diecinueve* (19) are actually *diez y seis,* "ten and six," *diez y siete,* "ten and seven," and so on, but they are customarily written as one word, as shown.
B. *Veintiuno* (21), *veintidós* (22), *veintitrés* (23), and so on through *veintinueve* (29) are actually *veinte y uno,* "twenty and one," *veinte y dos,* "twenty and two," and so on.

These may be written either way, but the one-word spelling is more common. The final *e* of *veinte* is dropped in the one-word forms, in both spelling and pronunciation.

C. No other compound number is written as one word: *treinta y uno* (31), *treinta y dos* (32), *cuarenta y tres* (43), *cincuenta y nueve* (59), and so on.

Counting Aloud

1. Count the people in your class.
2. Count the chairs.
3. One student counts from 1 to 10, the next one from 11 to 20, etc.
4. One student counts in even numbers to 10, the next one from 12 to 20, etc.
5. Repeat exercise 4 with odd numbers.
6. One student counts in fives from 5 to 25, the next one from 30 to 50.
7. Count in tens to 50.

The time of day

¿Qué hora es?	*What time is it?*
Es la una y cuarto.	*It's a quarter past one.*
Es la una y media.	*It's one thirty.*
Es la una en punto.	*It's one on the dot.*
Son las dos de la mañana.	*It's two in the morning.*
Son las tres y cinco.	*It's five past three.*
Son las cuatro menos cinco.	*It's five to four.*

D. Normally, when asking the time of day, singular *es* is used. In responding to the question, singular *es* is used for the hour of one, plural *son* for all the other hours.
E. There is no Spanish counterpart for the phrase "o'clock."
F. The feminine article is always used before the number indicating the hour.
G. The period of the day is expressed by the phrases *de la mañana, de la tarde,* and *de la noche.*
H. Fractions of the hour are expressed with the words *y* (and) and *menos* (less).

Telling Time: The Hours

Practice saying the hours of the day in order several times. Use *es* for the hour of one and *son* for the rest. Add the period of the day (*de la mañana, de la tarde, de la noche*).

EXAMPLE: **Es la una de la mañana. Son las dos de la mañana.** Etc.

Telling Time: Hours with Fractions

Practice saying the hours of the day plus (*y*) and minus (*menos*) all the fractions represented by five-minute intervals.

EXAMPLE: **Es la una en punto. Es la una y cinco. Es la una y diez. Es la una y cuarto (quince).** Etc.

Oral Exercise
Read the following times of the day in Spanish.

Shaded clocks indicate P.M.

10. Present tense of *ir,* to go

(yo)	voy
(tú)	vas
(usted) (él, ella)	va
(nosotros, -as)	vamos
(ustedes) (ellos, ellas)	van

| (vosotros, -as) | vais |

A. The verb endings for *ir* are the same as those for *estar*.
B. *Ir* requires the preposition *a* (to) before any noun or verb complement: *Voy a casa; allí vamos a pasar dos días.*
C. *Vamos*, used alone, also means "let's go."

Paradigm Practice

Say the forms of the verb *ir* several times until you are ready to do the pattern drills that follow. Repeat the forms one time with the subject pronouns, the next time without them.

Person–Number Substitution

1. Usted siempre va a la playa, ¿verdad?
   (Jorge, Manuel y yo, los hermanos de Luz María, ustedes, alguien, yo)
2. ¿Adónde van ustedes?
   (yo, Vickie y Linda, su primo, nosotros, usted, ellos)

11. The infinitive form of verbs

-ar	-er	-ir
estar	ser	ir
pasar	hacer	decir
tomar	comer	
estudiar	ver	
trabajar		
hablar		
esperar		

A. The infinitive is the form of a verb from which the verb takes its name. It corresponds to the English verb form that is usually preceded by the particle "to": ***ser o no ser,*** "to be or not to be."
B. In Spanish all infinitives end in *r* preceded by *a, e,* or *i*. There are then three groups of verbs, as shown in the chart above. Of the three, the largest is the *-ar* group. In fact, any new verb that comes into the language is almost invariably assigned to this group.
C. The infinitive often serves as the complement, or object, of another verb.[12] Infinitive complements are sometimes preceded by the preposition *a* (*Allí **vamos a pasar** dos días*), but usually not (***Quiero tomar** algo frío*). The presence or absence of *a* is determined by the preceding verb (*vamos a, quiero*), not by the infinitive (*pasar, tomar*).

---

[12]This will be taken up in more detail in Chapter 12.

Oral Translation

In all translation drills use *usted* for "you" unless otherwise specified.

1. I want to be somebody.
2. Why do you want to study Spanish?
3. Because I want to go to Costa Rica.
4. Don't you want to work here?
5. What do you want to do now?
6. I want to say something.
7. What do you want to say?
8. I'm hungry; I want to eat something hot.
9. Do you want to see something?
10. No, I want to wait in the car.

12. *Ir a* + infinitive, to be going to

¿Cuánto tiempo **van a estar** aquí?	*How long are you going to be here?*
Allí **vamos a pasar** dos días.	*There we're going to spend two days.*
¿Vas a ir tú, Enrique?	*Are you going to go, Enrique?*

As in English, this construction is very frequently used to refer to the future.

Person–Number Substitution

If the cue is given in English, do not include the subject or subject pronoun in your response.

1. ¿Cuánto tiempo van a estar aquí?
   (we, you, Carlos María and his sister, Emilio, I, they, you and I)
2. Allí vamos a pasar dos días.
   (they, I, my sister, Vickie and Linda, we, he, you *pl*)
3. ¿Vas a ir tú?
   (nosotros, ustedes, yo, Enrique, Enrique y Hernán, todos ellos)

Alternate Substitution

1. ¿Cuánto tiempo van a estar aquí?
   ¿——————— trabajar ———?
   ¿——————— vamos ————?
   ¿Por qué ———————————?
   ¿——————— voy ————?
   ¿——————— comer ———?
   ¿Qué ——————————?
   ¿——————— hacer ———?

2. Yo no voy a ir allí.
   Nosotros ————————————.
   ————— comer ——————.
   Vickie ——————————.
   ————— estudiar ————.
   Usted ——————————.
   ————— ir ——————.
   Yo ——————————.

Substitution and English Meaning

Change each of the following sentences to the "going to" form. Then give the English equivalent of the new sentence.

EXAMPLE: ¿Quién es el maestro?
           ¿Quién va a ser el maestro?
           Who's the teacher going to be?

1. Es muy gorda.
2. Somos amigos.
3. ¡Qué lindo está el paseo!
4. Yo voy.
5. Yo no estoy cansada.

6. Linda y yo esperamos aquí, entonces.
7. ¿Quién habla español aquí?
8. Es casi la una.
9. ¡Todos están tan alegres!

Conversation Stimulus

The whole class responds to each of the following statements and questions. Your instructor will signal the yes and no answers. In answering yes or no, give three very quick *sí*'s or *no*'s in sequence, and then the rest of your answer.

EXAMPLES: Hoy vamos a trabajar mucho, ¿no?
            ¡No no no! ¡Hoy no vamos a trabajar mucho!
            ¿Son ustedes muy buenos alumnos?
            ¡Sí sí sí! ¡Somos muy buenos alumnos!

1. ¿En qué país están Linda y Vickie ahora?
2. ¿Hasta qué día van a estar allí?
3. Y luego, ¿adónde van a ir?
4. No es verdad. Ellas van a ir a México después.
5. Ustedes son muy simpáticos.
6. Yo soy muy simpático también.
7. Ustedes están en Nicaragua ahora.
8. ¿Cuántos días van a pasar las muchachas americanas en Nicaragua?
9. ¿Están Linda y Vickie contentas o tristes en el paseo?
10. ¿Son ustedes inteligentes y simpáticos por naturaleza?
11. ¿Están ustedes muy ocupados?
12. Yo estoy muy triste y muy preocupado.
13. ¿Están ustedes contentos o tristes en la clase?
14. ¿En qué país estamos ahora?

LISTENING COMPREHENSION EXERCISE C

Reading

América Latina

La mayor[13] parte del inmenso territorio situado al sur de los Estados Unidos tiene el nombre de América Latina o Latinoamérica. América Latina incluye a dieciocho naciones independientes descendientes de España, más Puerto Rico, un estado también libre y también antigua colonia española, pero hoy día políticamente asociado a los Estados Unidos.

Este[14] grupo de estados americanos lleva[15] el nombre de Hispanoamérica, y son los siguientes[16]: México, directamente al sur de los Estados Unidos, y al sur de México las seis repúblicas de América Central, que son: Guatemala, Honduras, El Salvador, Nicaragua, Costa Rica y Panamá. Siguen luego los países de Sudamérica: Colombia, Venezuela, Ecuador, Perú, Bolivia, Chile, Argentina, Paraguay y Uruguay. Y finalmente, en las Antillas, tenemos a Cuba, Puerto Rico y la República Dominicana. Dos países más completan el bloque latinoamericano: la inmensa nación de Brasil, donde el idioma oficial es el portugués, ya que[17] es una antigua colonia de Portugal, y Haití, ex-colonia francesa, nación que tiene el honor de ser el primer país independiente de todo el continente de América.

[13] Major.
[14] This.
[15] Has (lit., carries).

[16] Following.
[17] Since.

Washington, D.C.: General Assembly, Organization of American States

For Oral or Written Composition

inmenso territorio
naciones independientes
Puerto Rico
Hispanoamérica
directamente al sur

países de América Central
países hispanoamericanos de Suramérica
Antillas
bloque latinoamericano
Brasil
Haití

Vocabulary

aburrido, -a   bored; boring
adónde   (to) where
ahora   now
al   to the; at the
alegre   happy, cheerful
algo   something
alguien   someone; anyone, anybody
allí   there
amable   kind
antes   before
el **año**   year
apagado, -a   dull
aquí   here
así   thus, so, like that, this way
el **café**   coffee; café
caliente   hot
el **calor**   heat
el **campo**   country; countryside
cansado, -a   tired
el **carro**   car
la **casa**   house; home
casi   almost, nearly
catorce   fourteen
la **cerveza**   beer
el **cielo**   sky
cinco   five
cincuenta   fifty
la **Coca-Cola**   Coke
comer   to eat
con   with
contento, -a   content, happy, satisfied
cuarenta   forty

el **cuarto**   quarter (of an hour)
cuatro   four
de veras   really
decir   to say, tell
después   afterward
diecinueve   nineteen
dieciocho   eighteen
dieciséis   sixteen
diecisiete   seventeen
diez   ten
doce   twelve
el **domingo**   Sunday
dos   two
en punto   on the dot
entonces   then
esperamos   we wait, are waiting
esperar   to wait
estar   to be
estudiar   to study
la **familia**   family
fantástico, -a   fantastic, wonderful
el **favor**   favor
la **fiesta**   party
la **foto**   photo
frío, -a   cold
la **gente**   people
gusta   is pleasing to
hablar   to speak, talk
hacer   to do; make
el **hambre** *f*   hunger
hasta   until, up to
la **hora**   hour

hoy today
ir to go
el **lago** lake
le him, to him; her, to her; you, to you
le(s) gusta(n) you like; he likes; she likes
la **leche** milk
lindo, -a pretty, nice
luego later; then
el **mar** sea
el **martes** Tuesday
más more; plus
me me, to me
me gusta(n) I like
medio, -a half, half a
menos less; minus
la **mentira** lie
el **mes** month
el **miedo** fear
la **montaña** mountain
el **mundo** world
nadie no one, nobody; anyone, anybody (after negative)
la **naturaleza** nature
el **norte** north
nueve nine
ocupado, -a busy, occupied
ocho eight
once eleven
la **parte** part
pasar to spend (time)
el **paseo** outing
la **playa** beach
por by; because of
por favor please
porque because
preocupado, -a worried
la **prisa** speed, haste
la **puerta** door
el **punto** point
quiere he wants; she wants; you *sing* want

quiero I want
quince fifteen
el **ratito** little while
el **reloj** clock; watch
el **río** river
ruso, -a Russian
sabe he knows; she knows; you *sing* know
la **sed** thirst
seis six
la **semana** week
siempre always
siete seven
solamente only
el **sueño** sleep(iness)
el **sur** south
tan so; as
el **té** tea
tengo I have
tengo sed I'm thirsty
el **tico, -a** nickname for Costa Rican
el **tiempo** time; weather
tiene he has; she has; you *sing* have
tiene hambre he's hungry; she's hungry; you're hungry
todavía still; yet
todo, -a all; every; *pl* everybody; all
todo el mundo everybody
tomar to take; to drink; to eat
trabajar to work
trece thirteen
treinta thirty
tres three
triste sad
uno one
veinte twenty
ver to see
el **vestido** dress
la **voz** voice
ya already; now

Cultural Listening Passage
for Chapter 3

Aspects of (the) Daily Life: In a Café

(1) Everywhere in almost all the cities in Spain and Spanish America there are outdoor cafés. They are not only places where people go to eat or drink something. (2) With the pretext of having a cup of coffee, a soft drink or a beer, or eating a sandwich or a dish (plate) of something (whatever thing), people —especially men—go there to chat, to discuss politics, to read the paper, and to look at the women passing by on the street.* (3) The café is like a free club, a social center, where the customers may spend several hours, if they desire, without anybody protesting (and nobody protests). It is a custom, an aspect of daily life.

(4) Not always, however, is the café the place where one can read the paper or chat with his friends peacefully (with all tranquility). The café

*See Cultural Note E.

is a place where beggars, shoeshine boys, and lottery vendors also hang around (arrive). They (these) go from table to table begging (asking for alms), offering their services, interrupting conversations, and, at times, even intervening in them. (5) Poor people! They have to live, too. The trouble is that this occurs so frequently that one cannot even chat with a friend. (6) Such is the case with (of) Juan José and his friend, who enter a café and in a matter of a few minutes are interrupted several times—first by a woman selling lottery tickets, then by a shoeshine boy, and finally by a beggar.

(7) Juan José and his friend Gabriel are talking about one of the girls in the café, thinking that she is a waitress (employee). Gabriel calls to her to order two coffees, but it turns out that she's not a waitress; she's the owner's daughter. The girl, according to Juan José, is studying at the Law School of the National University, and since she is very attractive and

probably is the only woman, everybody is in love with her.

(8) The shoeshine boy interrupts to say that a guy who is looking toward Juan José's table is her boyfriend, and that he's very jealous. At the same time, the beggar appears, asking for a little something "for the love of God." Juan José and his friend become impatient (lose patience) and leave without drinking their coffee.

Grammar Points

First, the demonstratives **este** (this), **ese** (that), **esto** (this), and **eso** (that); second, the present tense of regular verbs ending in **-ar;** third, the days of the week; fourth, the present progressive construction; and fifth, the definite article with titles.

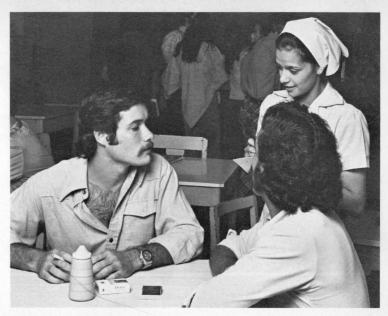

San José, Costa Rica: In
a café

Chapter 3

Basic Dialog

Aspectos de la vida diaria: en un café

JJ. *Juan José* G. *Gabriel* VE. *Vendedora* L. *Limpiabotas* ME. *Mendigo*

I

JJ. ¿Por qué no entramos y tomamos un café?
G. Buena idea. Mira, esta mesa está desocupada.
VE. ¿Compra lotería para el domingo, señor?
G. No, gracias. ¡Señorita! Dos cafés.
JJ. Esa no es una empleada, hombre. Es la hija del dueño, el Sr.[1] Pérez.

II

L. ¿Le limpio los zapatos, señor?
JJ. No, mis zapatos están limpios.
G. ¡Hombre! ¿No es ésa la chica que estudia en la Facultad de Derecho?
JJ. La misma. Y todo el mundo está enamorado de ella.

[1]Abbreviation of *señor*.

III

L. Ese tipo que está mirando hacia acá es el novio. Dicen que es muy celoso.

JJ. ¡Ah caramba! ¿Qué estás haciendo tú aquí? ¡Vete o llamo a la policía!

ME. Una limosnita, por amor de Dios...

JJ. ¡Esto es imposible! No podemos ni hablar. ¡Vámonos!

Aspects of daily life: in a café

JJ. *Juan José* G. *Gabriel* W. *Woman lottery vendor* S. *Shoeshine boy* B. *Beggar*

I

JJ. Why don't we go in and have a cup of coffee?

G. Good idea. Look, this table is empty.

W. Will you buy a lottery ticket for Sunday, sir?

G. No, thanks. Miss! Two coffees.

JJ. That's not a waitress, man. She's the daughter of the owner, Mr. Pérez.

II

S. Shall I shine your shoes, sir?

JJ. No, my shoes are clean.

G. Hey, isn't that the girl who's studying at the Law School?

JJ. The same. And everybody's in love with her.

III

S. That guy looking this way is her boyfriend. They say he's very jealous.

JJ. For Pete's sake! What are you doing here? Go away or I'll call the police!

B. Can you spare a little something, please. . . .

JJ. This is impossible! We can't even talk. Let's get out of here![2]

Cultural Notes

A. People who wait on tables are seldom addressed as "waiter" or "waitress" (*mesero, -a*), for this form of address belittles them. A common, more dignified, and more generally acceptable term is *señor* or *señorita*.

B. Government-run lotteries are well-established institutions in the Hispanic countries and supplement the revenues from taxation. The sale of lottery tickets provides steady employment to a considerable number of poor people, both men and women. In Madrid, for example, the lottery vendors who stand on the strategic street corners equipped with dark glasses and canes are licensed by the welfare agency serving the blind.

[2]Let's go away.

C. Keeping a glossy shine on one's shoes is a matter of considerable concern to the well-dressed Latin urbanite. To serve this ever growing clientele—as well as the steady stream of foreign tourists—an army of itinerant shoeshine specialists has sprung up in every large city. The "do-it-yourself-in-the-home" mentality hardly exists in Latin America.

D. Sidewalk begging, while officially illegal in most Hispanic countries, is often a flourishing activity. By and large, those who beg do so out of necessity, for a subsistence living.

E. On the streets of some Spanish-speaking areas, especially urban centers, women are commonly ogled and bombarded with *piropos*. A *piropo* is a complimentary, flattering, or flirtatious remark.

The Sounds of Spanish: III

"Double r." In addition to the single *r*, Spanish has another *r*-type sound, traditionally called "double *r*." This traditional name is a handy label, but it is slightly misleading on two counts: (1) the sound in question is spelled *rr* between vowels (*carro, perro*), but with a single *r* at the beginning of a word (*rubia, reloj*) and after *n, l,* or *s* (*Enrique, alrededor, Israel*); (2) the "double *r*" usually consists of a rapid series of three, four, or five—not just two—taps of the tongue against the top of the mouth. In extremely emphatic pronunciation there may be as many as ten or more taps.

Normal American English has no sound even approximately like Spanish "double *r*." This sound is produced by placing the tongue in roughly the position for English *t* or *d*, and then expelling air forcefully over the top of the tongue, which makes the tip flutter.

Try now to produce a series of "double *r*'s," first in long spurts and then in shorter ones. The sound should be something like an imitation of a small motor.

Now listen and repeat the following nonsense jingle, some version of which nearly every Spanish speaker knows.

> Erre con erre cigarro
> Erre con erre barril
> Rápidos corren los carros
> Del ferrocarril

It is absolutely essential not to confuse "single *r*"—exactly one tap—with "double *r*"—more than one tap. For Spanish speakers, these two sounds are just as different as *t* and *d* or *m* and *n*. Many pairs of words are distinguished *solely* by the contrast between the two kinds of *r*. Listen and repeat the following examples.

caro	(*expensive*)	carro	(*car*)
cero	(*zero*)	cerro	(*hill*)
ahora	(*now*)	ahorra	(*he economizes*)

coro	(*choir*)	corro	(*I run*)
pero	(*but*)	perro	(*dog*)

Listen and repeat the following words, all included within the basic material of the first five chapters.

rubia	reloj	Enrique
Costa Rica	carro	ropa
aburrido	ratito	arroz

COGNATES

horrible	Rusia	cigarro	roca
terrible	Puerto Rico	errático	resto
rápido	ruinas	irritación	ocurre

Spanish Spelling: III

The written accent mark and stressed syllables. We will use the word "stress" to refer to the relative prominence of syllables in *pronunciation,* and the expression "written accent" to refer to the mark ´ which occurs over some vowels in Spanish *spelling.* We use two different words to avoid confusion, since the stress of a Spanish word is not always indicated by a written accent. In Spanish, unlike English, the location of the stressed syllable of a word is always predictable from the spelling, according to the following rules.

A. If a word has a written accent, the syllable with the written accent is stressed. Read aloud the following examples.

simpática	todavía	después	órdenes	azúcar	inglés
antipática	lotería	adiós	lógico	fácil	café
miércoles	Jiménez	también	sábado	difícil	según

B. If a word has no written accent and ends in any consonant except *n* or *s*, the *last* syllable is stressed. Read aloud the following examples.

usted	animal	profesor	mujer	español
ciudad	escribir	reloj	estoy	lugar

C. If a word has no written accent and ends in *n*, *s*, or a vowel (that is, every word not covered by rules A and B), the *next-to-last* syllable is stressed. Read aloud the following examples.

buenos	americano	ocupados
escribe	delgada	bastante
dicen	apellido	personajes

LISTENING COMPREHENSION EXERCISE A

Dialog Supplement

I

Esta mesa está desocupada.

silla	*chair*

Es la hija del dueño. *owner*

esposa	*wife*
madre	*mother*
abuela	*grandmother*
tía	*aunt*
sobrina	*niece*

II

Mis zapatos están limpios.

sucios	*dirty*

Mi camisa está limpia. *shirt*

blusa	*blouse*
corbata	*tie*
ropa	*clothes*
falda	*skirt*

Mis zapatos están limpios.

calcetines	*socks*
pantalones	*pants*

Mi vestido[3] está limpio. *dress*

traje	*suit*
sombrero	*hat*

Mis cosas están limpias. *things*

gafas	*(eye)glasses*
medias	*stockings*

[3] In some countries men's suits are also referred to as *vestidos*.

Guatemala City, Guatemala: Vendor of lottery tickets

III

Ese tipo que está mirando hacia acá.

hacia allá[4]   *that way, over there*

¿Qué estás haciendo tú?   **Es el novio.**

comiendo   *eating*   padre   *father*

pariente   *relative*

No podemos ni hablar.   **Voy a llamar a la policía.**

conversar   *chat*   buscar   *look for*

cantar   *sing*

fumar   *smoke*

pensar   *think*

Dialog and Supplement Check

Sentence Recall

Say the dialog phrase or sentence in which each of the following words or phrases occurs.

mira	¡caramba!	amor	enamorado
limosnita	un café	celoso	zapatos
señor	dueño	empleada	policía
entramos	tipo	mirando	hablar

Word Recall

Give a Spanish equivalent for the following words.

love	stockings	world	dirty
clothes	boyfriend	Law School	to think
we drink	daily	life	waitress
in love with	God	a relative	jealous
niece	looking	shoes	owner

Item Substitution

Repeat each of the following sentences, substituting one or more related words or phrases for the one in italics. If books are closed, your instructor will say the item at the end of each sentence.

[4]*Acá* differs from *aquí* in that *acá* is less precise; it means "here," "in this general area." *Allí* and *allá*, both meaning "there," differ in the same way, *allá* being less precise.

1. Esa es *la hija* del dueño.
2. Mis *zapatos* están limpios.
3. ¿Compra lotería para *el domingo?*
4. No podemos ni *hablar.*
5. Mi *camisa* está limpia.

6. Mira, esta *mesa* está desocupada.
7. ¿Le limpio *las gafas?*
8. Voy a *buscar* a la policía.
9. Aquí no podemos ni *fumar.*
10. Es el *novio.*

Questions

1. ¿Dónde están Juan José y su amigo?
2. ¿Van a tomar o van a comer algo?
3. ¿Van a tomar una cerveza?
4. ¿Quién es la señorita que está en el café, una empleada?
5. ¿Hay mesas desocupadas en el café?
6. ¿Compra Gabriel lotería?
7. ¿Están limpios o sucios los zapatos de Juan José?
8. ¿Y los zapatos de usted?
9. ¿Es la hija del dueño estudiante de la escuela secundaria o de la universidad?
10. ¿Estudia ella en la Facultad de Filosofía y Letras?
11. ¿En qué facultad de la universidad está ella?
12. ¿Va usted a estudiar medicina o derecho en la universidad?
13. ¿Qué va a estudiar usted?
14. ¿Cómo está su camisa, limpia o sucia? ¿Y su sombrero?
15. ¿Quién está mirando hacia la mesa de Juan José?
16. ¿Qué dicen del novio de la hija del dueño?
17. ¿Hay otras interrupciones en la conversación de Juan José y su amigo?
18. ¿Qué quiere el mendigo?
19. ¿Hay muchos mendigos en los Estados Unidos?

Grammar

13. Demonstratives

Descriptive adjectives (see Chapter 1) refer to some property of the noun they modify—for example, its size, shape, color, or condition. *Limiting* adjectives, on the other hand, relate the noun they modify to its environment. They may specify its position relative to the speaker, state the possessor, indicate the quantity, etc., and are classified accordingly as demonstratives, possessives, quantifiers ("many," "few," numbers), and so on.

Spanish descriptive adjectives pose two problems for the English-speaking student: gender and number agreement, and position *after* the noun they modify. Limiting adjectives pose only the problem of agreement, since they *precede* the noun they modify, in Spanish just as in English.

A. The usual Spanish equivalents of the English demonstratives "this" (*pl* "these") and "that" (*pl* "those") are shown below. Note that the masculine singular forms *este* and *ese* end in *e*, instead of the expected *o*.

Demonstrative Adjectives

	this	these	that	those
masculine	este	estos	ese	esos
feminine	esta	estas	esa	esas

B. There is also a third set of demonstrative adjectives: *aquel* (*m sing*), *aquella* (*f sing*), *aquellos* (*m pl*), *aquellas* (*f pl*). Like *ese, aquel* is equivalent to English "that"/"those," but suggests greater remoteness from both speaker and hearer than does *ese. Aquel*, which is less commonly used than *ese*, will not be used in the following exercises.

Noun Substitution

EXAMPLES: Este sombrero
  (zapatos)
  Estos zapatos
  (traje)
  Este traje

1. Ese señor
  (señora, sobrino, hijos, padre, esposo, maestras, profesora, empleado, dueños, abuela)
2. Esos días
  (domingos, mes, semana, horas, reloj, ratitos, año)
3. Esta montaña
  (cielo, lagos, mar, playas, lugares, país, ciudad, campo, mundo, vida)

Double Item Substitution

Point with your finger as you do this exercise.

EXAMPLE: Este sombrero que está aquí
  _____ allí
  Ese sombrero que está allí

Esas cosas que están allí
  _____ aquí
  ____ señores _____
  _____ allí
  ____ mesa _____
  _____ aquí
  ____ sillas _____
  _____ allí
  ____ zapatos _____
  _____ aquí
  ____ camisa _____

Demonstrative Pronouns

este vestido y **ése**	*this dress and that one*
esas cosas y **éstas** también	*those things and these too*
¿Cuál traje quiere, **éste** o **ése?**	*Which suit do you want, this one or that one?*

C. Spanish demonstratives are sometimes used without a following noun; they then function as *demonstrative pronouns*. In English we say "these" and "those" in the plural, but "this one" and "that one" in the singular. As the above examples indicate, the Spanish singular demonstratives are just like the plurals; they are never followed by *uno.*

D. Note that there is a written accent on the stressed syllable of demonstratives not followed by a noun. This accent is purely a writing convention to distinguish the pronoun from the adjective; it reflects no change in pronunciation.[5]

¿Cuál es?

Give one-word answers to the following *¿cuál?* questions, pointing with your finger as you answer.

EXAMPLE: ¿Cuál es su corbata?
 Esta[6] (pointing).
 ¿Cuáles son mis zapatos?
 Esos.

¿su amigo?	¿ustedes?	¿mi traje?	¿su camisa?
¿la clase?	¿yo?	¿mi camisa?	¿mis alumnos?
¿sus ojos?	¿la puerta?	¿mi blusa?	¿su maestro?
¿el profesor?	¿sus zapatos?	¿mis ojos?	¿la ventana?
¿su ropa?	¿mis pantalones?	¿mi ropa?	¿su libro?

Neuter Demonstratives

¡Esto es imposible!	*This is impossible!*
¿Qué es **eso?**	*What is that?*

E. *Esto* and *eso* never modify a noun. Consequently, they never change for number or gender and are called *neuter demonstratives. Esto* and *eso* are used to refer to situations, ideas, actions, etc., for which no particular noun exists (first example), and to things (not people[7]) that are identified by a particular noun only later in the sentence or discourse, if ever (second example).[8]

---

[5]*Aquél, aquélla,* etc., also function as pronouns, entirely analogous to *éste* and *ése.*

[6]*Esta* does not have a written accent here because, to avoid printing problems, accents are usually not used on capital letters.

[7]If a woman were to introduce her husband by saying

Esto es mi esposo, she would be saying something quite outrageous. The implication would be something like "This (unidentified thing) is my husband." She should say *Este es mi esposo.*

[8]*Aquello* is the neuter demonstrative that corresponds to masculine *aquel* and feminine *aquella.*

Tegucigalpa, Honduras: Shoeshine boys

Translation

1. What's this?
2. That? I don't know.
3. Is that (stuff) French or English?
4. This is Spanish!

5. Do you want this?
6. What's that? That's Coca-Cola.
7. What's this, coffee or tea?
8. This is coffee; that's tea.

14. Present tense of regular -ar verbs

cantar

(yo)	cant	-o
(tú)	cant	-as
(usted) (él, ella)	cant	-a
(nosotros, -as)	cant	-amos
(ustedes) (ellos, ellas)	cant	-an

(vosotros, -as)	cant	-áis

A. The part of a verb to which *-ar, -er,* or *-ir* is added to form the infinitive is called the *stem.* Regular verbs, such as *cantar,* have the same stem throughout their entire conjugation.
B. The present tense endings are the same for all *-ar* verbs except the first person singular of *estar* (*estoy*), and of *dar,* "to give" (*doy*).
C. The simple present tense forms of a verb in Spanish (those illustrated in the chart above) correspond to both the simple present and the present progressive in English.

Juan canta bien.   *John sings well.*
Juan canta en este momento.   *John is singing right now.*

D. Spanish may also use a simple present tense verb form to express the near future.

Linda y yo esperamos aquí.   *Linda and I will wait here.*

Paradigm Practice

Practice saying the forms of the verbs listed below until you can do them without hesitation. Say the forms one time with the subject pronouns, the next time without them. This will enable you to do more effectively the pattern drills that follow. If your instructor wishes to add the *vosotros* form in the pattern drills, include this form in your paradigm practice.

tomar	esperar	cantar	ocupar
hablar	mirar	fumar	limpiar
estudiar	comprar	buscar	
trabajar	conversar	llamar	

Person–Number Substitution

If the cue is given in English, do not say the subject or subject pronoun.

1. ¿Por qué no esperan?
   (you, you and I, my niece, I, they)
2. La chica estudia en la Facultad de Derecho.
   (nosotros, ese tipo, yo, todo el mundo, ellos, la chica)
3. ¿Con quién hablan Juan José y su amigo?
   (tú, usted, el limpiabotas, la mujer y yo, Juan José y su amigo)
4. Juan José no busca a la policía.
   (yo, nosotros, el mendigo, ustedes, Juan José)
5. ¿Por qué no entramos y tomamos un café?
   (they, John, John and you, I, you and I, the girls, we)
6. Juan José y su amigo no toman el café, ¿verdad?
   (el novio de la chica, mis tíos, el mendigo, nosotros)

Sí o No

The whole class answers. Listen carefully to each of the following statements. Then give as long an answer as possible, indicating whether the statement is true or false. Begin your answer with sí or *no*.

EXAMPLE: Juan José y su amigo entran a⁹ una casa. ¿Sí o no?
            No, ellos no entran a una casa, entran a un café.

1. Hay seis mesas desocupadas en el café. ¿Sí o no?
2. Hay muchas mesas desocupadas en esta clase. ¿Sí o no?
3. Ustedes hablan español muy muy muy bien. ¿Sí o no?
4. Todo el mundo en la Facultad de Derecho está enamorado de la hija del dueño del café. ¿Sí o no?
5. Todos ustedes están enamorados. ¿Sí o no?
6. El tipo que está mirando hacia la mesa de Juan José es el hermano de la chica. ¿Sí o no?
7. Usted, señorita, está mirando hacia acá. ¿Sí o no?
8. Y usted, señor, está mirando hacia allá. ¿Sí o no?
9. Gabriel compra lotería para el domingo. ¿Sí o no?
10. La hija del dueño conversa durante una hora con Juan José. ¿Sí o no?
11. Juan José va a llamar a la policía porque el limpiabotas todavía está allí. ¿Sí o no?
12. Todo el mundo conversa con el mendigo. ¿Sí o no?
13. Alguien llama a la policía. ¿Sí o no?
14. En esta clase no podemos tomar cerveza, porque esto no es un café. ¿Sí o no?

15. Days of the week

Días de la semana

lunes	*Monday*
martes	*Tuesday*
miércoles	*Wednesday*
jueves	*Thursday*
viernes	*Friday*
sábado	*Saturday*
domingo	*Sunday*

A. The days of the week are masculine and are normally preceded by the definite article.

Hasta **el** martes.   *Till Tuesday.*
¿Compra lotería para **el** domingo?   *Will you buy a lottery ticket for Sunday?*
La fiesta es **el** sábado.   *The party is Saturday.*
Yo no trabajo **los** lunes.   *I don't work (on) Mondays.*

⁹The preposition *a* usually follows the verb *entrar*.

B. When they are listed, as in a calendar, and when they are equated with an adverb or noun of time (*hoy, ya, ahora, mañana*, etc.), the days of the week are not preceded by an article.

    Hoy es domingo.   *Today is Sunday.*
    Mañana va a ser lunes.   *Tomorrow is (going to be) Monday.*

C. The days of the week are always written with a lower-case letter.

D. Only *sábado* and *domingo* add an *s* to form the plural; the others remain the same.

    No tengo clases los sábados.   *I don't have classes (on) Saturdays.*
    Tengo tres clases los miércoles.   *I have three classes (on) Wednesdays.*

Questions

1. ¿Cuántos días hay en la semana?
2. ¿Cuáles son?
3. ¿Qué día es hoy?
4. ¿Va usted a la universidad los sábados o los domingos?
5. ¿Qué días de la semana van ustedes a la escuela?
6. ¿Qué día de la semana le gusta más, el sábado o el domingo?
7. Y el lunes, ¿no le gusta?
8. ¿Cuál le gusta a usted más, el lunes o el viernes?

16. The present progressive

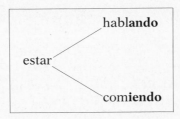

A. The present progressive construction in English consists of a form of the verb "to be" plus the present participle, the "*-ing*" form of a verb.

    I *am studying* now.
    Are you *sleeping?*

The present progressive in Spanish is very similar. It consists of a form of *estar* (never *ser*) plus the Spanish equivalent of the "*-ing*" form. This form consists of the verb stem plus *-ando* for *-ar* verbs and *-iendo* for *-er* and *-ir* verbs. Only *estar* agrees with the subject; the *-ando/-iendo* form is invariable.

    (Yo) **estoy estudiando** ahora.   *I am studying now.*
    Las chicas **están comiendo.**   *The girls are eating.*

B. The use of the present progressive in Spanish is similar to the use of the present progressive in English. There is one important difference, however. In Spanish the present progressive is used only to refer to an action *in progress at the moment of speaking.* Thus, unlike English, Spanish *never* uses the present progressive to refer to an event which will take place in the future. For example, "I'*m eating* with some friends this evening" *cannot* be translated *Estoy comiendo...* in Spanish; it can be only *Como con unos amigos esta noche* or *Voy a comer con unos amigos esta noche.*

Present Participle Substitution

Substitute the present participle of each of the following verbs as shown in the example.

EXAMPLE: Estoy hablando.
            mirar
            Estoy mirando.

trabajar	hacer	cantar	llamar
tomar	comprar	ver	buscar
entrar	conversar	fumar	comer

Construction Substitution

The whole class responds.

EXAMPLE: Juan José y su amigo entran a un café.
            Juan José y su amigo están entrando a un café.

1. Llaman a la empleada.
2. En este momento entra una mujer.
3. Ahora Juan José compra lotería.
4. Ellos no comen todavía.
5. También entra un limpiabotas.
6. La abuela del dueño estudia en la universidad.
7. Los dos amigos conversan con el limpiabotas.
8. Hablan de la tía del dueño.
9. Un tipo mira hacia la mesa de Juan José.
10. Juan José llama a la policía.
11. ¿Qué haces tú?

Group Questions

The whole class answers. Give full answers, not just the present participle.

1. ¿Qué están estudiando ustedes, español o francés?
2. ¿Están trabajando mucho o poco?
3. ¿Está el profesor hablando por teléfono o hablando con los alumnos?
4. ¿Estoy yo fumando?
5. ¿Estoy comiendo?

6. ¿Están ustedes fumando?
7. ¿Están comiendo?
8. ¿Qué estamos haciendo, cantando?

Individual Questions

Individual students answer the following questions with a progressive construction.

EXAMPLE: ¿Dónde estudia inglés Emilio Fonseca?
            Está estudiando en el Centro Cultural.

1. ¿Con quién conversa usted en este momento?
2. ¡Señor! ¿Por qué fuma usted ahora, en la clase? ¿No sabe usted que aquí no podemos fumar, ah?
3. ¡Y usted, señorita! ¿Por qué canta?
4. Ah no, ¡esto es imposible! ¿Por qué come usted, señor?
5. ¡Y usted! ¿Por qué mira hacia allá? ¿Por qué no mira hacia acá?

17. **The definite article with titles**

> 1. ¿Quién soy yo, **la** Srta.[10] Fonseca?
> 2. No, usted es **la** Srta. González.
> 3. Francisco quiere conocer a **la** señora Fonseca.
> 4. Mucho gusto, señora Fonseca.

When a person is *referred to* by his name and an accompanying title, the definite article *always* precedes the title (examples 1, 2, and 3). On the other hand, when a person is *addressed directly* by his name and title, the definite article is *not* used (example 4).

Oral Translation

I

A. Good morning, Mrs. Solano. Is Professor Gil here today?
B. No, Professor Gil is here on Tuesdays and Thursdays only.

II

A. Sr. Gamboa, aren't you going to the outing?
B. The outing is not today, it's Friday. Today is Wednesday.
A. But Mrs. Lobo says (that) it is today.
B. Mrs. Lobo doesn't know anything.[11]

LISTENING COMPREHENSION EXERCISE B

[10] Abbreviation of *señorita*.
[11] In Spanish the double negative is correct: "Mrs. Lobo doesn't know nothing."

Reading

En el café del papá de Carmencita

CA. *Carmencita*   AN. *Antonio*   MAR. *Mario*   PA. *Papá*   MA. *Mamá*

CA. ¡Hola Mario! ¿Qué tal, Antonio? ¡Ah! Allá también están Fernando y el profesor Lobo, en esa mesa. ¡Qué sorpresa!

AN. Y en esa otra mesa están Chucho, Jacinto y José. Toda la universidad está aquí. ¡Qué tragedia!

MAR. ¿No va a ir a clase, Carmencita?

CA. No, hoy no puedo[12] ir; dos de los empleados que trabajan en las mesas están quién sabe dónde. ¡Son unos irresponsables! Bien ¿y?... ¿Van a tomar algo? Hay una cerveza mexicana de-li-cio-sa, Carta Negra.

AN. ¿Por qué no conversa con nosotros un ratito primero? Siéntese,[13] después trabaja.

CA. Ay, lo siento mucho, Antonio, pero ahora no puedo, estoy muy ocupada. Más tarde tal vez,[14] ¿eh?

MAR. Carmencita, ¿quién es ese señor que está mirando hacia acá tan serio?

CA. ¡Ay, Dios! Es mi papá. Está furioso. Rápido, ¿van a tomar algo?

AN. ¡No, no, y NOOO! ¡Vete inmediatamente o llamo a la policía!... ¡Perdón, Carmencita! ¡No es a usted! ¡Es al limpiabotas! ¡Carmencita! ¡Por favor! Carmencita...

PA. ¡CARMEN! ¿Con quién está usted conversando? ¿Quiénes son esos dos tipos?

MA. Ay, por Dios, Francisco, ¿por qué eres así? Carmencita no está haciendo nada malo. Está conversando con dos jóvenes muy simpáticos. ¿Qué hay de malo en eso?

CA. Son dos amigos de la universidad, dos muchachos muy decentes y de muy buena familia.

PA. ¡¡Yo no permito que mi hija...!!

MA. Shh, silencio un momento. ¿Ah, sí? ¿Qué apellido son?

CA. Gómez Castro uno y Gómez Pinto el otro. Son primos.

PA. ¡Primos o no primos, usted es mi hija y usted...!

MA. Shh, Francisco, por favor. ¿Ah, sí? ¿De los Gómez millonarios? ¿Por qué no invitas a los dos muchachos a la fiesta del domingo?

CA. ¡No, mamá!

MA. Entonces al paseo del sábado.

[12]Can't.
[13]Sit down.
[14]Maybe.

CA.   ¡Mamá, yo tengo novio! ¡No puedo!

MA.   ¡Ay, ese tipo no me gusta! ¡No no no no no, imposible! Un hombre que no trabaja, no estudia, no sabe hacer nada; cantar y comer, comer y cantar, nada más. ¡Qué perezoso[15] es!

PA.   Pero canta muy bien, ¿no crees[16] tú, mi vida?

MA.   ¡CANTA HORRIBLEMENTE! Francamente, no sé cómo mi hija, una señorita de la mejor sociedad, tan atractiva, tan inteligente, tan, tan, tan... ¿Adónde vas, Francisco? ¿Adónde vas, Carmencita? ¡Francisco! ¡Carmen! ¡Qué tragedia! ¡Qué vida!

[15] Lazy.
[16] Think.

For Oral or Written Composition

¡Qué sorpresa!   esos dos tipos
están quién sabe dónde   ¿Qué apellidos son?
un ratito primero   yo tengo novio
estoy muy ocupada   no sabe hacer nada
está mirando hacia acá   pero canta muy bien
¡Es al limpiabotas!   una señorita de la mejor sociedad

Vocabulary

la **abuela**   grandmother
el **abuelo**   grandfather
acá   here; over here
allá   there; over there
el **amor**   love
aquel, aquella *adj*   that; *pl* **aquellos,**
  -as   those
aquél, aquélla   that one; *pl*
  aquéllos, -as   those
aquello   that
la **blusa**   blouse
buscar   to look for
el **calcetín**   sock
la **camisa**   shirt
cantar   to sing
¡caramba!   for Pete's sake!
celoso, -a   jealous
la **cerveza**   beer
comprar   to purchase, buy
conocer   to know, be acquainted
  with; to meet
la **conversación**   conversation
conversar   to converse, chat
la **corbata**   necktie
la **cosa**   thing
el **derecho**   jurisprudence
desocupado, -a   unoccupied, free
diario, -a   daily
dicen   they say; you *pl* say
Dios   God
el **doctor,** la **doctora**   doctor
doy   I give, am giving
el **dueño,** la **dueña**   owner
durante   during, for
el **empleado,** la **empleada**   employee
enamorado, -a   in love
entrar   to enter, go in, come in
la **escuela**   school
ese, -a *adj*   that; *pl* **esos, -as**   those
ése, -a   that one; *pl* **ésos, -as**
  those
eso   that
la **esposa**   wife

el **esposo**   husband
este, -a *adj*   this; *pl* **estos, -as**   these
éste, -a   this one; *pl* **éstos, -as**
  these
esto   this
la **facultad**   school (of a university)
la **falda**   skirt
la **filosofía**   philosophy; **filosofía y letras**
  humanities
fumar   to smoke
las **gafas**   (eye)glasses
hacia   toward
la **hija**   daughter
el **hijo**   son
los **hijos**   children
la **idea**   idea
imposible   impossible
la **interrupción**   interruption
el **jardín**   garden
el **jueves**   Thursday
la **limosnita**   a little alms
el **limpiabotas**   shoeshine boy
limpiar   to clean
limpio, -a   clean
la **lotería**   lottery; lottery ticket
el **lunes**   Monday
llamar   to call
la **madre**   mother
la **madre superiora**   mother superior
la **media**   stocking
la **medicina**   medicine
el **mendigo**   beggar
la **mesa**   table
el **miércoles**   Wednesday
mira   look
mismo, -a   same
el **momento**   moment
ni   neither, nor; (not) even
ocupar   to occupy
la **oficina**   office
el **padre**   father
los **pantalones**   trousers, pants
para   for; to, in order to

el **pariente** relative
el **parque** park
   pensar to think
   perfectamente perfectly
la **piscina** swimming pool
   pobre poor
   podemos we can
el **policía** policeman
la **policía** police (force)
   por for
   por teléfono on the telephone
la **ropa** clothes, clothing
el **sábado** Saturday
   secundario, -a secondary
la **silla** chair
la **sobrina** niece

el **sobrino** nephew
el **sombrero** hat
   sucio, -a dirty
el **taxi** taxi
la **tía** aunt
el **tío** uncle
el **tipo** guy
el **traje** suit
la **universidad** university
   vámonos let's go (away)
el **vendedor,** la **vendedora** vendor
el **vestido** dress
   vete go away
la **vida** life
el **viernes** Friday
el **zapato** shoe

Cultural Listening Passage
for Chapter 4

Appearances Are Deceiving

(1) In Latin America there are rich people, there are poor people, and there are rich people who are poor or who, if they are not really poor, at least pretend to have more than (what) they really have. (2) This third group is very numerous, more numerous than (what) one would imagine. I am in this group. We are people who go through (pass) life accumulating debts and eluding bill collectors (collectors of bills) or keeping them busy with promises of payment and all kinds of excuses. This comes about because our laws, or the judges who apply them, are not sufficiently strict in this respect. We are very sentimental, perhaps, and except in rare or extreme cases, we almost never see a man end up in (go to stop in) jail or lose prestige because of his debts. (3) Those of us who owe money here, there, and every-

where are so many that we don't really worry too much about it, because, as the saying goes, misery loves company (suffering of many, consolation of fools).

(4) Many times, in order to collect a bill, the creditor has to depend more on the skill of his bill collector than on the protection that the law itself affords him. This individual must be an expert in the art of collecting bills, a person who has tact, infinite patience, perseverance, and optimism. When the bill collector goes to a house for the first time, he knows beforehand that the person who opens the door already has a reply ready: "Come back tomorrow," or "The master has visitors," or "They just went out," or "Come back tomorrow; the master is in the bathroom," or "He's not in; I don't know what time he'll get back (arrive)." And so it happens each time the poor fellow goes back to collect. But he goes back again and again (one and

another time) without losing his patience or his good humor, or the hope of trapping his victim at last, some day.

(5) The basic dialog of this lesson presents a typical case. Here I am, the husband, in the dining room with my wife and children, making my usual comment about the fact that we owe money everywhere; but that's not really important to me. What makes (puts) me furious is this stinking lottery. I never win. This time, same as ever, NOTHING! Some day perhaps; that's everybody's hope. That's why everybody here, from the richest to the poorest, buys lottery tickets (lottery).

(6) However, notice how I, in spite of my debts, am planning (thinking) to sell my house in order to buy another one, better, much more expensive, with an enormous garden, with a swimming pool, with one bath on the first floor and two on the second, with many bedrooms, cement walls, many windows, and a beautiful red roof. (7) Notice how I also permit (give) myself the luxury of having a gardener, besides the cook and Lucrecia, the new maid. Poor Lucrecia! My wife shouts at her all the time because she doesn't know how to set the table yet. Sometimes I can't cut the meat because there aren't any knives on the table. Other times there aren't any spoons (tablespoons), or teaspoons, or napkins, or glasses. . . . Poor Lucrecia! She has to learn.

(8) Incidentally, my wife says she is going to fire the cook because she is very insolent. But that's not true. The cook only wants to know when we are going to pay her the three months' overdue salary we owe her. That's why she is very insolent, and that's why my wife wants to fire her.

Grammar Points

First, the present tense of regular verbs ending in **-er** and in **-ir;** second, some verbs of this type that are irregular in the first person—**poner** (to put), **traer** (to bring), **salir** (to go out), **hacer** (to do, to make), **saber** (to know), **conocer** (to know), and **ver** (to see); third, the construction **acabar de** + *infinitive;* fourth, the personal **a;** fifth, the contraction **al;** sixth, prepositions; seventh, the use of the infinitive after a preposition; and eighth, review of verb constructions.

Chapter 4

Basic Dialog

Las apariencias engañan

MA. *Marido* MU. *Mujer* H. *Uno de los hijos* L. *Lucrecia, la nueva criada*[1]

I

MA. Debemos dinero en todas partes, mujer. Y la lotería, como siempre... NADA. ¿Con qué corto la carne?

MU. ¡Lucrecia! ¡Los cuchillos! ¡Siempre debe poner todos los cubiertos!

MA. Calma,[2] mujer, la pobre es nueva; tiene que aprender.

MU. A propósito, voy a despedir a la cocinera; es muy insolente. Esta mañana...

MA. No quiero saber, gracias. Y ustedes, hijitos, ninguno está comiendo. ¿Qué pasa?

[1] When *nuevo, -a* precedes the noun it modifies, it means "recently acquired or arrived"; when it follows, it means "recently formed or made." Similarly, *pobre* means "unfortunate," "pitiful" before a noun, but "impoverished" after a noun.

[2] *Calma* is a noun here; the idea is, "Proceed with calm."

II

H.   ¿De veras vamos a vender esta casa, papá?

MA.   Sí, pero es para comprar una más linda.

H.   ¿Cuándo vamos a verla? ¿Después de comer?

MU.   Tal vez. Tiene un jardín enorme y... ¡Lucrecia! ¡La puerta!

L.   Creo que es el mismo cobrador del otro día.

MU.   Dígale que acabamos de salir.

L.   Sí, señora.—Dice la señora que acaban de salir.

Appearances are deceiving

H. *Husband*   w. *Wife*   c. *One of the children*   L. *Lucrecia, the new maid*

I

H.   We owe money everywhere, dear. And the lottery—like always, NOTHING. What do I cut the meat with?

w.   Lucrecia! The knives! You must always put all the silverware (on the table).

H.   Easy, dear, the poor (girl) is new; she has to learn.

w.   Incidentally, I'm going to fire the cook; she's very insolent. This morning . . . .

H.   I don't want to know, thank you. And you, children, none of you is eating. What's the matter?

II

c.   Are we really going to sell this house, Dad?

H.   Yes, but it's for the purpose of buying a nicer[3] one.

c.   When are we going to see it? After we eat?

w.   Maybe. It has an enormous garden and . . . Lucrecia! The door!

L.   I think it's the same bill collector as the other day.

w.   Tell him we've just gone out.

L.   Yes, ma'am.—The lady says they just went out.

Cultural Notes

A.   There are three acceptable ways of referring to someone's wife: *la mujer de Pedro, la esposa de Pedro,* and *la señora de Pedro. La mujer* is rather informal; *la esposa,* a little more formal; and *la señora,* the most formal. In direct address from husband to wife, only *mujer* can be used; it is equivalent to "dear" in this case.

B.   Middle-income families usually have a maid and a cook. They can afford this luxury because Latin American servants are among the most underpaid people in the world. A good cook, for instance, earns not more than thirty dollars a month in most countries.

C.   Here, the lady of the house addresses Lucrecia, the maid, with the *usted* form of the verb rather than with the familiar form *tú.* This usage varies from country to country. The maid, however, would always answer in the *usted* form.

[3]More beautiful.

The Sounds of Spanish: IV

A. **The consonants *b* and *v*.** The letters *b* and *v* are not distinguished in pronunciation. Spanish *v* is never pronounced with the sound of English *v*.

At the beginning of an utterance and after *n* or *m*, both *b* and *v* are pronounced [b], like English *b*. The letter combination *nb* is pronounced [mb]. Repeat the following examples.

b (be larga)	verdes	en vez de	vamos	invierno
v (be corta)	vieja	blusa	vender	en verano
buenos	bonita	bogotano	nombre	un vaso

After a vowel, both *b* and *v* have the sound [ƀ], which is not found in English. The lips are brought close together so that they are almost touching, but not quite; the flow of air is not stopped even momentarily, as it is for English *b* and Spanish [b]. In the following examples, *b* and *v* in the left-hand column are pronounced [b]. In the right-hand column they have the Spanish sound [ƀ]. As a reminder, the *b*'s and *v*'s with the unfamiliar sound are underlined. Remember that Spanish *v* is never pronounced like English *v*.

voy	me voy
vemos	debemos
bonita	qué bonita
vestido	ese vestido
bueno	qué bueno
voy	no voy
van	acaban

Practice saying the following sentences. Do not stop between words. Each sentence must be said as if it were one long word. *Note:* The English meaning alongside each sentence is given for your information and need not be learned.

Eva bebe vino blanco.	(*Eva drinks white wine.*)
¡Que viva Cubita bella!	(*Long live beautiful little Cuba!*)
¡Qué bueno sabe este vaso de vino!	(*This glass of wine sure tastes good!*)

In all other positions, *b* and *v* can be pronounced as either [b] or [ƀ]. Thus, you may hear native speakers say either *cor*[b]*ata* or *cor*[ƀ]*ata*, *el* [b]*aile* or *el* [ƀ]*aile*.

B. **The consonant [h].** Compare Spanish [h] with the sound of English *h* (or *wh*) as you listen to the following pairs of words.

high	Jaime (*James*)
hen	gente
who goes	jugos (*juices*)
holly	jale (*pull*)

The Spanish sound is produced by the friction of the air passing through a narrow opening between the tongue and the roof of the mouth. Hold your tongue high when you imitate this sound, in order to create enough friction. Listen again to the same pairs of words, and then repeat each pair.

Imitate the way a Spanish speaker would mispronounce the following English utterances with a very strong Spanish [h] sound.

He is *h*ere.   *H*ilda *h*ates *h*im.
*Wh*o's *Wh*o in America.   *H*ippies *h*ave *h*epatitis.
*H*i! *H*ow are you?   *H*ello, *h*oney! I'm *h*ome!

Now repeat the following Spanish words.

japonés	jefe	gente	ojos	enojar
jamón	Jorge	joven	Jesús	mujer
jardín	José	jota	Jiménez	vieja
jardinero	hijos	ge	Jijón	trabaja

LISTENING COMPREHENSION EXERCISE A

Dialog Supplement

I

¡Lucrecia! ¡Los cuchillos!

el tenedor	*the fork*
la cuchara	*the spoon (tablespoon)*
la cucharita	*the teaspoon*
el plato	*the plate, dish*
la taza	*the cup*
el vaso	*the glass*
la servilleta	*the napkin*
el mantel	*the tablecloth*
la comida	*the dinner, food*

¿Con qué corto la carne?

el pan	*the bread*
la mantequilla	*the butter*
el queso	*the cheese*

¿Con qué tomo la sopa? *the soup*
¿Con qué como los huevos? *the eggs*

el arroz	*the rice*
el postre	*the dessert*
la ensalada	*the salad*

A propósito

Sin embargo	*however*
De todos modos	*anyway*
Por consiguiente	*therefore, consequently*
Por eso	*that's why, therefore*

No quiero saber.

beber	*drink*
vivir	*live*
escribir	*write*
prometer	*promise*
leer	*read*

Voy a despedir a la cocinera.

al jardinero	*the gardener*
conocer	*to meet, get acquainted with*
traer	*to bring*

II

Mi casa tiene un jardín enorme.

una sala	*a living room*
un comedor	*a dining room*
un patio	*a patio*
una cocina	*a kitchen*
un piso	*a floor*
un baño	*a bathroom*
una pared	*a wall*
un techo	*a roof*
un cuarto	*a room, bedroom*
una piscina	*a swimming pool*

Dialog and Supplement Check

Sentence Recall

Say the dialog line in which each of the following words or phrases occurs.

dinero	vender	hijitos	calma
carne	dígale	insolente	de veras
despedir	para comprar	jardín	cobrador

Next-Sentence Rejoinders

Listen to each of the following dialog lines; then say the line that follows.

1. ¿Con qué corto la carne?
2. ¡Lucrecia! ¡La puerta!
3. ¡Caramba!
4. Dígale que acabamos de salir.
5. Es muy insolente. Esta mañana...

Questions

1. ¿Quién es Lucrecia? ¿Qué no sabe hacer?
2. ¿Va a despedir la señora a Lucrecia?
3. ¿Por qué va a despedir a la cocinera?
4. ¿Qué quiere tener el señor para cortar la carne?
5. ¿Es verdad que el marido y la mujer van a vender la casa?
6. ¿Para qué, según él?
7. Cuando la familia está comiendo, ¿quién llama a la puerta?
8. ¿Qué le dice Lucrecia al cobrador?
9. ¿Con qué toma usted la sopa?
10. ¿Toma usted café en una taza o en un vaso?
11. ¿Cómo se escribe "vaso," con *b* o *v*?
12. ¿Hay teléfono en su casa? ¿Qué número es?

Bogotá, Colombia: Patio of
an upper-class residence

13. ¿Tiene usted una casa o un apartamento?
14. ¿Cómo es su casa, o su apartamento?
15. Y su casa, señorita, ¿tiene puertas y ventanas? ¿Cuántas?
16. ¿Es su casa de estilo español o inglés? ¿Tiene patio? ¿Piscina?

Grammar

18. Present tense of regular -*er* and -*ir* verbs

beber		vivir
beb		**viv**
	-o	
	-es	
	-e	
-emos		-imos
	-en	

vosotros	beb	-éis
	viv	-ís

Regular *-er* and *-ir* verbs have the same endings in all tenses, except for the *nosotros* forms of the present (*-emos/-imos*) and the *vosotros* present tense and command forms. (See Chapter 14 for *vosotros* command forms.)

Paradigm Practice

1. Practice saying the present tense forms of the verbs listed, first with and then without the subject pronouns.

comer	prometer	insistir	deber
creer	vender	decidir	recibir
leer	escribir	describir	aprender

2. Practice saying the first person plural forms (*nosotros*) of the following pairs of verbs.

1. leer y escribir
2. beber y vivir
3. recibir y vender
4. insistir y salir
5. creer y aprender
6. ver y creer

Person–Number Substitution

If the cue is in English, do not repeat the subject.

1. Nosotros debemos dinero en todas partes.
   (yo, el marido, el marido y la mujer, usted y yo)
2. Tal vez venden la casa.
   (I, we, these gentlemen, she, they all)
3. La cocinera come y bebe mucho.
   (el señor y la señora, todo el mundo, ustedes, yo, tú)
4. ¿Por qué no escribimos tú y yo una novela?
   (él y ella, usted, todos, nosotros, el jardinero)
5. ¿Dónde viven ellos ahora?
   (los hijos, ese pariente, el marido, la criada y yo, tú, el cobrador y la cocinera)

Questions

1. ¿Quiénes son los personajes principales del diálogo de esta lección?
2. ¿Son el marido y la mujer gente rica o gente pobre?
3. ¿Deben dinero? ¿Dónde, en una parte nada más?
4. ¿Creen ustedes que el marido es un hombre responsable o irresponsable? ¿Por qué?
5. ¿Cuántos sirvientes hay en esa casa?
6. ¿A quién quiere despedir la señora, al jardinero? ¿Por qué?
7. Si ellos venden su casa, ¿dónde van a vivir?
8. ¿Quién quiere describir la casa que ellos van a comprar?
9. ¿Quiere usted describir su casa, por favor?
10. ¿Cuál es para usted el tipo ideal de casa?

19. Irregular first person singular forms

Infinitive	First person singular	
poner	**pongo**	*I put*
traer	**traigo**	*I bring*
salir	**salgo**	*I leave, go out*
hacer	**hago**	*I do, make*
saber	**sé**	*I know*
conocer	**conozco**	*I know**
ver	**veo**	*I see*

*The meanings of *saber* and *conocer* are explained on page 149.

A. The rest of the present tense forms of the above verbs are regular.
B. The irregular forms have to be learned individually, since it cannot be predicted from the infinitive whether or not a verb has an irregular first person form. Before going on with the drills that follow, study each of the above forms in "paradigm practice" (*pongo, pones, pone,* etc.; *hago, haces, hace,* etc.).

Questions

Answer with a full sentence each time. Select the *yo* answer whenever there is a choice.

EXAMPLE: ¿Quién sabe más español, usted o su hermano? **Yo sé más español.**

1. ¿Quién pone más attención en la clase, usted o ella?
2. ¿A qué hora sale usted de su casa, a las ocho o a las nueve?
3. ¿Conoce usted mi casa?
4. ¿Quién hace la comida en su casa, usted o su mamá?
5. ¿Cuántas ventanas y cuántas puertas ve usted en esta clase?
6. ¿Siempre trae usted su libro de español a la clase?

Person–Number Substitution

1. Si no pones los cubiertos, no comes.
   (I, they, he, my sister and I, you *pl*)
2. Si usted no sabe la lección, no sale el domingo.
   (nosotros, los alumnos, yo, mi hija, tú, ustedes)
3. ¿Estudiamos, salimos o hacemos otra cosa?
   (you, Emilio and Luz María, I, my children)
4. ¡Ustedes! ¿Por qué no hablan o hacen algo?
   (usted, maestro, usted y yo, yo, hijitos, señorita)

20. Acabar de + *infinitive*

> La señora dice que **acaban de salir.**
> *The lady says (that) they have just gone out.*

A. This construction corresponds to the English expression "to have just (done)" or "just (did)."
B. *Acabar* also means "to finish," "to end."
   ¿Qué día acaban las clases?   *What day do classes end?*

¿Qué acabo de decir?

Listen to the following statements. After each statement the instructor will ask *¿Qué acabo de decir?* Begin your answer with *Usted acaba de decir que.* (What was said?)

EXAMPLE: Ustedes son muy buenos y muy simpáticos. ¿Qué acabo de decir?
      Usted acaba de decir que nosotros somos muy buenos y simpáticos.

1. Aquí no podemos ni hablar.
2. Ustedes comen mucho. Por eso están tan gordos.
3. Usted, señorita, hace todo perfectamente.
4. Usted no sabe dónde está Costa Rica.
5. Usted sale todas las noches. Por eso no estudia.
6. Mañana no hay clase de español.
7. Es la verdad.
8. No, es mentira.
9. Los mendigos son pobres.
10. Todo el mundo está enamorado de la hija del dueño.
11. Voy a llamar a la policía.

21. The personal *a*

Voy a llamar a la policía.	*I'm going to call the police.*
Voy a llamar un taxi.	*I'm going to call a taxi.*
Busco a mis primos.	*I'm looking for my cousins.*
Busco una silla.	*I'm looking for a chair.*
Estoy mirando a la maestra.	*I'm looking at the teacher.*
Estoy mirando la pared.	*I'm looking at the wall.*

The particle *a* normally precedes all verb objects that refer to people.

Object Substitution

EXAMPLE: No veo a la maestra.
            (puerta)
            No veo la puerta.

1. No quiero conocer a nadie.
    (la cocina, su cuarto, su familia, los hijos, nadie, nada)
2. ¿Ven ustedes el techo de la casa?
    (el jardín y la piscina, la dueña, los cuartos, la cocinera, el comedor, la señora)
3. ¿A quién[4] busca usted?
    (qué, cuál maestro, cuál piso, cuántas sillas, cuántos chicos)
4. ¿Qué quiere usted?
    (quién, cuánto dinero, cuánta gente, cuál silla, cuál señorita)
5. ¿Traigo a María aquí?
    (dos mesas, dos chicas, la señora, la ropa)

22. The contraction *al*

$$a + el \longrightarrow \textbf{al}$$

The other forms of the definite article do not contract.

Object Substitution

Remember to use the personal *a* when the substitution is a personal noun.

EXAMPLE: No conozco a la Srta. Malo.[5]
            (Sr. Bueno)
            No conozco al Sr. Bueno.

1. Buscan a la Sra. Jiménez.
    (profesor Gil, Srta. Cuevas, Dr. Caro,
    Padre Jesús, Madre Superiora)
2. Vamos a la playa.
    (parque, Centro Cultural, oficina,
    clase, campo)
3. La mujer llama a la criada.
    (policías, hija, hijo)
4. No conocemos al marido.
    (tía, maestro, piscina, primo)

---

[4] *Quién* is the object of *busca;* since it refers to a person, it is preceded by *a*.

[5] *Malo* and *Bueno* are fairly common family names in Spanish.

23. Prepositions

Simple Prepositions

a	*to, at*	hasta	*up to, until*
con	*with*	para	*for, in order to, to*
contra	*against*	por	*for, by, through*
de	*from, of, about*	según	*according to*
en	*in, on, at*	sin	*without*
entre	*between, among*	sobre	*on, on top of, about*
hacia	*toward(s)*		

A. The prepositions given above are among the commonest in Spanish and the easiest to learn. Further details will be taken up in later lessons. The most important thing to remember about prepositions at this point is that they are never used in Spanish at the end of a sentence. They must always precede their objects, even when these are question words. For example, in English we may say either "Who(m) are you talking *about?*" or "*About* whom are you talking?" but in Spanish there is just one possibility: *¿De quién está usted hablando?*

Quito, Ecuador: Plaza de la Independencia

Written Translation

Don't forget the article before titles.
According to Professor Campos and Miss Bueno, in order to go from Peru (*Perú*) to New York by sea one must pass through the Panama Canal (*canal de Panamá*).

B. Like English, Spanish also has compound prepositions, most of which consist of an adverb followed by the preposition *de*.

ADVERB	COMPOUND PREPOSITION
Está **encima**.	Está **encima de** la mesa.
It's on top.	*It's on top of the table.*

Compound Prepositions

además de	*besides, in addition to*	delante de	*in front of*	en vez de	*instead of*
al lado de	*beside, at the side of*	dentro de	*inside (of),*	encima de	*on top of*
antes de	*before*		*within*	enfrente de	*facing, opposite*
cerca de	*near*	después de	*after*	fuera de	*outside (of)*
debajo de	*under, underneath*	detrás de	*behind*	lejos de	*far from*

The commonest compound prepositions in Spanish are those listed above.

Written Translation

1. What is that for?
2. You! Who are you talking about?
3. What are you talking about?
4. I know! You are talking about me (*mí*)!
5. And without my permission!
6. You and you and you, against the wall!
7. But we are among friends!
8. Only until tomorrow, according to the boss.
9. Poor Lucrecia, she doesn't know how to set the table: she places the glasses on top of the plates, and the napkins under the cups.
10. We can't see because the person (who is) in front of us is very tall.

Sí o No

The whole class confirms or corrects the following statements, according to your instructor's cue. If a correction is to be made, first deny the statement and then correct it.

EXAMPLE: El profesor está al lado de la ventana.
Confirmation: **Sí, el profesor está al lado de la ventana.**
   Correction: **No, el profesor no está al lado de la ventana; está detrás de la puerta.**

1. Ustedes siempre estudian español antes de la clase y después de la clase.
2. Este libro está debajo de la mesa.
3. Ustedes están detrás del profesor.
4. Yo estoy al lado de la puerta.
5. Los alumnos están fuera de la clase.
6. Argentina está cerca de México.
7. Yo estoy delante de ustedes.
8. Yo estoy enfrente de ustedes.

24. The infinitive after a preposition

después de **comer**	*after eating*
su manera de **ser**	*their way of being*
sin poner atención	*without paying attention*
además de **estudiar**	*besides studying*

After a preposition, *only* the infinitive form of the verb is used, *never* the present participle (*-ando/-iendo*), as is usually the case in English.

Written Translation

1. Talking about owning money, the bill collector is here.
2. Is this water good for (*para*) drinking, Lucrecia?
3. Before selling his house, he's going to buy another.
4. What do you do, besides work?
5. This is for (*para*) María, for (*por*) being so good.[6]
6. Instead of doing that, why don't you pay attention?

Questions

The whole class answers using complete sentences.

1. ¿Estudia usted para saber más, o solamente para pasar el tiempo?
2. ¿Está usted contento con aprender un poco nada más?
3. ¿De qué está hablando él, de ir a la playa?
4. ¿Es posible vivir sin deber dinero?
5. ¿Es bueno comprar una casa sin tener suficiente dinero?
6. ¿Qué acaba de decir él?

[6]The difference between *para* and *por* will be taken up in Chapter 7.

25. Review of verb constructions

1. Simple present	El marido **vende** la casa.	*The husband sells (is selling) the house.*
2. Present progressive	El marido **está vendiendo** la casa.	*The husband is selling the house (right now).*
3. "Wants to"	El marido **quiere vender** la casa.	*The husband wants to sell the house.*
4. "Going to"	El marido **va a vender** la casa.	*The husband is going to sell the house.*
5. "Just did"	El marido **acaba de vender** la casa.	*The husband just sold the house.*

Verb constructions in Spanish may contain a single verb form (example 1); a form of *estar* followed by a present participle (example 2); a verb form followed directly by an infinitive (example 3); or a verb form followed by an infinitive, with an intervening preposition, usually *a* or *de* (examples 4 and 5). Verb constructions will be taken up in greater detail in Chapter 12.

Construction Substitution

EXAMPLES: **¿Qué hago ahora?**   *What am I doing now?*
       (voy)
      ¿Qué voy a hacer ahora?
       (debe)
      ¿Qué debe hacer ahora?
       (estoy)
      ¿Qué estoy haciendo ahora?

1. Compramos otra casa.
   (vamos, está, no quiere, acaban)
2. Voy a llamar a la policía.
   (debo, estamos, vamos, quiero, debes, acabo)
3. Lucrecia no sabe poner la mesa.
   (no quiere, no está, no va)
4. No, gracias, acabo de tomar una taza de té.
   (voy, acabamos, debemos, quiere)
5. ¿Qué pasa?
   (acaba, va, está)
6. ¿Dice usted una cosa finalmente?
   (quiere, debe, está, va, acaba)
7. Participo más en la clase.
   (debo, estoy, voy, quiero)

8. Aprendemos el diálogo de memoria.
   (vamos, queremos, debemos, acabamos, estamos)
9. ¿Pongo más atención en la clase?
   (estoy, voy, debo)

LISTENING COMPREHENSION EXERCISE B

Reading

Quito

Capital de mi país, Ecuador. Ciudad típica latinoamericana, como muchas otras construidas[7] por los españoles durante la época colonial. En el sector viejo de la ciudad, intacto y de gran valor histórico, pueden admirarse[8] el Palacio Presidencial, la Plaza de la Independencia, la Catedral, la Iglesia de la Compañía de Jesús y otros templos famosos por su estilo arquitectónico y decorativo. Hay otros sectores de construcción más reciente, pero no siempre de mejor construcción: uno, en el extremo norte de la ciudad, con casas residenciales modernas y de gran lujo,[9] donde viven los ecuatorianos ricos y las familias del cuerpo diplomático; otro, en el extremo sur, donde viven, más o menos, en casas que casi no son casas, los ecuatorianos pobres y los indios, que son muchos y muy pobres. Hay también sectores residenciales en otras partes de Quito, pero especialmente en el centro de la ciudad, donde vivimos en casas de construcción modesta y relativamente viejas, los ecuatorianos que no somos ni ricos ni pobres, los ecuatorianos de la clase media, que somos muy pocos.

Quito, ciudad pintoresca del trópico, no es realmente[10] tropical. Sus características no son típicas de una ciudad tropical. Situada allá en la alta sierra[11] de los Andes, Quito es una ciudad de clima agradable y fresco[12] durante el día y casi frío en las noches. No tiene el clima caliente de La Habana, Santo Domingo o Veracruz. Y su gente, los quiteños, son de carácter reservado, conservador y serio en su manera de hablar, en su manera de vestir[13] y en su manera de ser. Allí la gente prefiere el "usted" al "tú," la ropa de estilo conservador a la ropa de brillantes colores, la moderación al exceso. Hay muchas otras ciudades grandes y bonitas en la América española. Más grandes que Quito, sí, pero más bonitas, ¡no! Quito es la mejor de todas.

[7] Built.	[10] Really.	[13] Dress.
[8] Can be admired.	[11] Mountains.	
[9] Luxury.	[12] Cool.	

Quito, Ecuador

For Oral or Written Composition

ciudad típica	en el extremo sur
la época colonial	la clase media
de gran valor histórico	ciudad pintoresca
otros sectores	el clima caliente
de gran lujo	los quiteños

LISTENING COMPREHENSION EXERCISE C

Vocabulary

a propósito by the way; incidentally
acabar to finish, end
acabar de to have just (done something)

además besides
además de besides, in addition to
al lado de beside, at the side of
antes de before

el **apartamento**
aprender   to learn
el **arroz**   rice
la **atención**   attention
el **baño**   bath; bathroom
básico, -a   basic
beber   to drink
la **calma**   calm
la **carne**   meat
cerca   near, nearby
cerca de   near
el **cobrador**   bill collector
la **cocina**   kitchen
la **cocinera**   cook
el **comedor**   dining room
la **comida**   meal; food; dinner
contra   against
cortar   to cut
creer   to believe
la **criada**   maid
cuando   when
el **cuarto**   room
los **cubiertos**   silverware
la **cuchara**   (table)spoon
la **cucharita**   teaspoon
el **cuchillo**   knife
de memoria   by heart
de todos modos   anyway, at any rate
debajo de   under, underneath
deber   to owe
decidir   to decide
delante de   in front of
dentro de   inside (of), within
describir   to describe
despedir   to fire
después de   after
detrás   behind
detrás de   behind
el **diálogo**   dialog
dígale   tell him; tell her
el **dinero**   money
en todas partes   everywhere
en vez de   instead of
encima de   on top of, above
enfrente de   facing, opposite
la **ensalada**   salad

entre   between, among
escribir   to write
el **estilo**   style
Europa   Europe
finalmente   finally
francamente   frankly
fuera de   outside (of)
el **hijito**   small child, sonny (diminutive)
el **huevo**   egg
ideal   ideal
el **idioma**   language
insistir   to insist
insolente   insolent
irresponsable   irresponsible
el **jardinero**   gardener
la **lección**   lesson
leer   to read
lejos   far
lejos de   far from
el **mantel**   tablecloth
la **mantequilla**   butter
el **marido**   husband
ninguno, -a   no; none; no one; not any; any, anyone (after *neg*)
la **novela**   novel
el **pan**   bread
la **pared**   wall
participar   to participate
el **patio**   patio
el **personaje**   character
el **piso**   floor
el **plato**   plate; dish
poner   to put
poner atención   to pay attention
poner la mesa   to set the table
por   for, by, through
por consiguiente   therefore
por eso   that's why; therefore
posible   possible
el **postre**   dessert
principal   principal
prometer   to promise
el **propósito**   purpose
el **queso**   cheese
recibir   to receive
responsable   responsible

rico, -a   rich
saber   to know
la **sala**   living room
salir   to go out, leave
se escribe   you write, one writes
la **servilleta**   napkin
si   if
sin   without
sin embargo   however
el **sirviente**, la **sirvienta**   servant
sobre   on, on top of
la **sopa**   soup
suficiente   sufficient
tal vez   perhaps, maybe

la **taza**   cup
el **techo**   roof
el **teléfono**   telephone
el **tenedor**   fork
tener   to have
tener que   to have to
el **tipo**   type; guy
traer   to bring
las **vacaciones**   vacation
el **vaso**   glass
vender   to sell
la **vez**   time (instance)
vivir   to live

Cultural Listening Passage
for Chapter 5

Notes from a History Class

(1) It wasn't Columbus but the Scandinavians, five hundred years before him, who were the first Europeans who arrived at the lands of the New World. (2) It is Christopher Columbus, nevertheless, whom the world recognizes as the true discoverer of America. Columbus, unlike (differently from) his predecessors, had the good fortune to represent such an enterprising nation as was Spain at that time. (3) After Columbus' first discoveries, other explorers followed in his footsteps and discovered new lands. Then came (arrived) the conquistadors, and later on the missionaries, the settlers, and the farmers. (4) The small flat world of those days was then converted into a marvelous world, round and enormously larger. A new era was initiated for humanity, and Christopher Columbus' great feat passed into history as one of the most important events of all times.

(5) Columbus was born in Genoa, Italy, in the year 1451, of humble family. In his youth he worked as a weaver of woolen fabrics (fabrics of wool) and then he became interested in trading and navigation. He worked as a seaman on ships that sailed the Mediterranean. He was shipwrecked off (in front of) the coast of Portugal and, when he arrived in that country, he decided to settle (establish himself) in Lisbon, the capital. (6) He got married in Portugal and there too was born his only son, Diego. It was also in Portugal that he conceived the idea that it was possible to reach India and Japan by a shorter route, (and) traveling west (toward the occident) rather than traveling east (toward the orient). (7) After many (long) investigations and studies, he finally developed a plan that he presented to the king of Portugal. The project was turned down (rejected) and then Columbus went (directed himself) to the king and queen of Spain, Ferdinand and Isabella. After much

doubt and hesitation the Spanish monarchs—particularly the queen—finally gave him their support.

(8) On the third day of August of 1492, Christopher Columbus sailed (departed) from the port of Palos, in command of three small caravels with a crew of 120 men. Seven weeks later, when most of the crew were beginning to show (give) signs of despair and rebellion, one of the sailors, named Triana, sighted for the first time the lands of our continent. The date was the 12th of October, 1492.

(9) Columbus returned to Spain on the 15th of March of the following year. Then he made three more voyages. On the 25th of September, 1493, he left Spain in command of 17 ships and 1500 men. During that second voyage he discovered several islands in the Caribbean, including the Virgin Islands and Puerto Rico. (10) On his third trip he discovered the island of Trinidad and the coast of Venezuela. His last trip was in 1502. He returned to Spain in 1504 and two years later, on the 20th of May, 1506, he died in the city of Valladolid at the age of 55. Years later, his remains were taken to the Dominican Republic; they are now buried in the Cathedral in Santo Domingo, the capital city.

Classmates

(11) These are the notes that Cecilia, one of the characters of the dialog that follows, took during a history class. Cecilia is an excellent student, at the top (the first) of her class. She knows by heart (from memory) any date or historical fact, the length of any river, the height of any mountain, any chemical or mathematical formula, the statistics on the population or the products of any country.

(12) She is in her third year of high school (secondary) and in every subject she's taking—literature, English, French, math, history, geography, physics, chemistry, biology, psychology, and civic education—she's always the first in her class. (13) When the teacher dictates his lesson, Cecilia is always the only one who never remains behind and the one who takes the clearest notes. For this reason her classmates admire her so much and they all want to study with her for the exams.

(14) Yesterday (during the) afternoon at about two o'clock her friend Anita called her to find out if she could go and study with her, but nobody answered the phone. There was nobody home. Cecilia was out shopping.

(15) A while ago (it makes a while) Anita called again and Cecilia invited her to come to her house. Anita is going over right away.

Grammar Points

First, past tense forms; second, uses of the preterit and the imperfect; third, more cardinal numbers; and fourth, ordinal numbers.

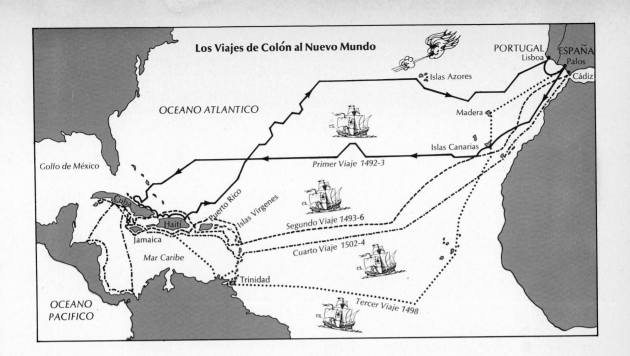

Los Viajes de Colón al Nuevo Mundo

Chapter 5

Basic Dialog

Compañeras de clase

A. *Anita*   C. *Cecilia*

I

A.   ¿Aló? ¿Cecilia? Te habla Anita, ¿qué tal? Te llamé ayer pero no estabas.

C.   ¡Ay qué lástima! Andaba de compras. ¿A qué hora llamaste?

A.   Eran como las dos. Nadie contestó.

C.   Sí, no había nadie en casa. Todos salimos ayer.

A.   Ah, con razón. Yo también iba a ir al centro pero hacía mucho calor.

II

c. Y... ¿qué hay de nuevo? ¿Estudiaste para el examen de historia?

A. Un poco. A propósito, Ceci, ¿cuándo descubrió Colón la isla de Trinidad, en el segundo o en el tercer viaje?

c. En el tercero. El 31 de octubre de 1498 (mil cuatrocientos noventa y ocho).

A. ¡Qué genio! Por eso quería ir a tu casa ayer. Mis apuntes son un desastre.

c. ¿Por qué no vienes hoy? ¿A qué hora te conviene?

A. A cualquier hora. Ahora mismo si te parece.

c. Perfecto. Te espero, entonces.

Classmates

A. *Anita*   c. *Cecilia*

I

A. Hello, Cecilia? This is Anita, hi! I called you yesterday but you weren't in.

c. Oh, too bad! I was out shopping.[1] What time did you call?

A. It was about two. Nobody answered.

c. Yes, there was nobody home. We all went out yesterday.

A. Oh, no wonder, I was going to go downtown too, but it was very hot.

II

c. And . . . what's new? Did you study for the history exam?

A. A little. By the way, Ceci, when did Columbus discover the island of Trinidad, on his second or on his third trip?

c. On his third. October 31, 1498.

A. What a genius! That's why I wanted to come over to your house yesterday. My notes are a mess.

c. Why don't you come over today? What time suits you?

A. Any time. Right now if it's okay with you.[2]

c. Fine. I'll be waiting for you, then.

Cultural Notes

A. *¿Aló?* is one of the more common greetings given when answering the telephone. In Mexico the accepted form is *¿Bueno?* and in Spain it is *¿Diga?*

B. The curriculum of the secondary school system in Latin America is much broader than the U.S. high school curriculum, and a *bachiller*, or graduate of a Latin American secondary school, usually has come into contact with more fields of the

---

[1]*Andar,* literally "to walk," is also used with the meaning of "to be out (somewhere or doing something)."

[2]If it seems to you.

humanities and sciences than most U.S. high school graduates. One of the main reasons for the wide scope of the Latin American system is that only a small percentage of secondary students are able to go on to the universities.

C. It is still a matter of pride among the upper classes to send children abroad for secondary school or university study, either to Europe or preferably to the United States. But since, due to seasonal differences, the school years in North and South America do not coincide, it is difficult to arrange successful exchanges of large groups.

The Sounds of Spanish: V

A. *s* **and** *z* **between vowels.** In Spanish there is never a [z] sound between vowels, even when the spelling is *z*.[3] Listen to the following English and Spanish words and compare the sound of *s* or *z* between vowels.

Venezuela	Venezuela
president	presidente
visit	visitar

Now listen and repeat.

visitar	música	taza
presidente	azul	brazos
Venezuela	rosas	resultado
razón	Brasil	Jesús
presente	museo	pedazo

B. **The consonant** *g.* At the beginning of an utterance and after *n*, Spanish *g* is pronounced [g], like English *g*. After a vowel, it is pronounced [ǥ], with the back of the tongue almost, but not quite touching the roof of the mouth. In all other positions either sound is acceptable. Listen and repeat the following pairs of words and phrases. Notice that the same word can have a [g] or a [ǥ], depending on what sound precedes it. The *g*'s that are pronounced [ǥ] are underlined.

gusto	mucho gusto	góndola	una góndola
grande	qué grande	gusta	me gusta
gato	ese gato	gano	nunca gano

[3] In Castilian pronunciation the letter *z* is pronounced like the *th* in "think."

Now listen and repeat the following series of words containing the sounds [b̶], [d̶], and [g̶].

[b̶]		[d̶]	[g̶]
esta<u>b</u>as	cu<u>b</u>iertos	na<u>d</u>a	se<u>g</u>undo
ha<u>b</u>ía	i<u>b</u>a	to<u>d</u>os	fu<u>g</u>a
nue<u>v</u>o	de<u>b</u>emos	despe<u>d</u>ir	ha<u>g</u>o
no<u>v</u>enta	E<u>v</u>a	pu<u>d</u>o	si<u>g</u>o
	u<u>v</u>a	na<u>d</u>ie	dí<u>g</u>ale
	ha<u>b</u>a	su<u>d</u>a	so<u>g</u>a
		ni<u>d</u>o	hi<u>g</u>o
		estu<u>d</u>iaste	trai<u>g</u>o

Finally, practice the following sentences. All occurrences of [b̶], [d̶], and [g̶] are underlined. Each sentence should be said as if it were one long word. Imitate the model voice as closely as possible.

Hugo es el a<u>b</u>oga<u>d</u>o <u>d</u>e Gonzalo.   (*Hugo is Gonzalo's lawyer.*)
Dice que <u>v</u>i<u>v</u>e en la Ha<u>b</u>ana, Cu<u>b</u>a.   (*He says he lives in Havana, Cuba.*)
Yo no <u>d</u>igo ni ha<u>g</u>o na<u>d</u>a.   (*I don't say or do anything.*)

LISTENING COMPREHENSION EXERCISE A

Dialog Supplement

I

Un examen de historia
química *chemistry*
matemáticas *mathematics*

Una lección de historia
alemán *German*
biología *biology*

Te llamé ayer.
anoche *last night*
anteayer (*the*) *day before yesterday*
anteanoche (*the*) *night before last*
hace unos días *a few days ago*

Pero hacía mucho calor.
viento *windy*
tanto *so much*
demasiado *too much*

II

Nadie contestó.

ganó	*won*	
nació	*was born*	
murió	*died*	

Ahora mismo voy.

Hoy mismo	*today for sure*
Mañana mismo	*tomorrow for sure*

Dialog and Supplement Check

Sentence Recall

Say the dialog phrase or sentence in which each of the following words or phrases occurs.

octubre	mismo	apuntes
lástima	de compras	nuevo
Colón	calor	estudiaste
contestó	centro	había
viaje	ayer	conviene

Questions

1. ¿En qué año descubrió Colón América? ¿En qué fecha?
2. ¿Descubrió la isla de Trinidad en su tercero o en su cuarto viaje?
3. ¿Había alguien en la casa de Cecilia ayer por la tarde?
4. Según Anita, ¿hacía calor ayer o hacía frío?
5. ¿Iba a ir ella al centro ayer o al mercado?
6. ¿Con quién quería ella estudiar ayer?
7. ¿Qué quería estudiar, historia o geografía?
8. ¿Quería ella estudiar con Cecilia anoche, anteanoche o ayer por la tarde?
9. ¿Va ella a estudiar con su amiga ahora mismo o después?

Grammar

26. Past tense forms

Spanish verbs have two sets of past tense forms, the **preterit** and the **imperfect**, which refer to past time in different ways. You will learn first the two sets of forms, and then when to use the preterit and when the imperfect. It is essential for you to learn the forms thoroughly, so that they will not be a problem later, when you are concentrating on their use.

A. Note that in the preterit forms, stress never falls on the stem. Moreover, the position of the stress is the only difference between certain forms, for example preterit *llamó*, "he called," and present *llamo*, "I'm calling." (See chart on p. 102.)

(handwritten: to call)
(handwritten: when or what you did)
(handwritten: to eat   to go out)

Preterit

	llamar	comer	salir
stem	llam	com	sal

(handwritten: yo) · *(handwritten: tú)* · *(handwritten: usted, el, ella)* · *(handwritten: nosotros)* · *(handwritten: ustedes, ellos, ellas)*

-é	-í	
-aste	-iste	
-ó	-ió	
-amos	-imos	
-aron	-ieron	

llamasteis	comisteis	salisteis

B. For *-ar* verbs, the first person plural is the same in the preterit and the present: *trabajamos ayer,* "we worked yesterday"; *trabajamos ahora,* "we're working now."

C. Regular *-er* and *-ir* verbs have the same endings in the preterit.

D. For *-ir* verbs, the first person plural is the same in the preterit and the present: *salimos ayer,* "we went out yesterday"; *salimos ahora,* "we're going out now." This is *not* true of *-er* verbs: *comimos ayer,* "we ate yesterday," but *comemos ahora,* "we're eating now."

E. The verb **dar,** "to give," takes the endings of *-er* and *-ir* verbs in the preterit: *di, diste, dio dimos, dieron, (disteis).*

Paradigm Practice

Before proceeding with the pattern drills, do as much paradigm practice in the preterit as possible with the verbs listed below, all of which you have learned in the present and preceding chapters.

-ar VERBS

hablar	entrar	esperar	contestar	ganar
tomar	cantar	trabajar	fumar	cortar
estudiar	pasar	comprar	buscar	conversar

-er AND *-ir* VERBS

comer	ver	leer	creer	vivir
vender	aprender	conocer	salir	escribir
prometer	nacer	deber	descubrir	(dar)

F. All the verbs listed above are regular in the preterit except for *dar.* There are, however, some spelling rules to be observed.

1. No written accent mark is required on monosyllabic forms.

di, dio
vi, vio

Monterrey, Mexico: Classroom in the Technological Institute

2. In the first-person singular preterit forms of *-ar* verbs, the following spelling changes occur with respect to the final consonant of the stem.

    a. *z* ⟶ *c*. It is an arbitrary rule that *z* cannot be written before *e*.

       empe*z*ar (*to begin*): empecé

    b. *c* ⟶ *qu*. This change is required to represent the pronunciation correctly.

       bus*c*ar: busqué
       to*c*ar (*to touch*): toqué

    The incorrect spellings *buscé* and *tocé* would represent [bussé] and [tosé].

    c. *g* ⟶ *gu*. This change, too, is needed for correct representation of pronunciation.

       llegar (*to arrive*): llegué

    The incorrect spelling *llegé* would represent [yehé].

3. The third person singular and plural endings of *-er* and *-ir* verbs, usually spelled *-ió* and *-ieron*, are spelled *-yó* and *-yeron* in the verbs whose stem ends in a vowel. It is an arbitrary rule that *y* must replace unstressed *i* between vowels.

       creer: creyó, creyeron
       leer: leyó, leyeron

Person–Number Substitution

1. Nosotros vendimos la casa y compramos una nueva.
   (papá, mis tíos, Napoleón, tú, los dueños, nosotros)

leyeron

leyó

2. Yo leí la carta pero no contesté.
    (mis padres, nosotros, mi novia, tú, él, todos)
3. ¿Ayer estudiaste o saliste?
    (we, I, Anita and Cecilia, the girl, they)
4. Cuando la mujer recibió el dinero, salió de compras.
    (él y yo, mis parientes, la cocinera, el jardinero y la criada, tú, el marido)
5. La chica acabó el examen y después leyó sus apuntes.
    (ellos, tú, el maestro, ustedes, la empleada)
6. Yo lo encontré y llamé a la policía.
    (mis hijos, alguien, nosotros, usted y ella, los alumnos)

Questions

1. ¿A qué hora llamó Anita a Cecilia ayer?
2. ¿Cecilia salió a la calle ayer?
3. ¿Estudiaron Anita y Cecilia ayer o van a estudiar hoy?
4. Cuando Anita llamó a su amiga ayer, ¿quién contestó el teléfono?
5. ¿A qué hora salió usted de su casa esta mañana?
6. ¿Estudiaron ustedes español ayer?
7. ¿En qué año descubrió Cristóbal Colón América?
8. ¿Escribió usted una composición ayer?
9. ¿Usted llamó a la policía anoche?
10. ¿Dónde aprendió usted a leer y a escribir?
11. ¿En qué mes y en qué lugar nació usted?
12. ¿Qué comieron ustedes anoche a la hora de la comida?
13. ¿Entendieron ustedes todas estas preguntas?
14. ¿Aprendieron algo?

Imperfect   *describing*

llamar	comer	salir
llam	com	sal
-aba	-ía	
-abas	-ías	
-aba	-ía	
-ábamos	-íamos	
-aban	-ían	

llamabais	comíais	salíais

llovía—used stem to do
usted

G. Only the following verbs are irregular in the imperfect.

to be ser: era, eras, era, éramos, eran, (erais)
to go ir: iba, ibas, iba, íbamos, iban, (ibais)
to see ver: veía, veías, veía, veíamos, veían, (veíais)

same in preterit 3 fui, fuiste, fue, fuimos, fueron

Paradigm Practice

Do paradigm practice in the imperfect with the following verbs.

-*ar* VERBS		-*er* AND -*ir* VERBS		
estar	hablar	saber	querer	descubrir
acabar	pensar	tener	traer	escribir
dar	continuar	ser	aprender	salir
ganar	llegar	deber	hacer	permitir
		ver	leer	

Person–Number Substitution

Read the following paragraph aloud. Then reread it four times, each time substituting one of the following subjects for *Rodolfo*: *yo, tú, nosotros, Rodolfo y Juanita.*

Cuando Rodolfo era pequeño, cuando tenía diez años de edad, más o menos, vivía en el campo. Era un chico muy feliz. Iba a la escuela por la mañana y trabajaba con su padre por la tarde. El sabía hacer muchas cosas. Durante las vacaciones, cuando no iba a la escuela, montaba a caballo todos los días. Iba a caballo al río, iba al lago, iba a todas partes. No tenía horas para comer. Cuando tenía hambre, comía un sandwich, una tortilla o una fruta. Cuando tenía sed, tomaba agua del río. Francamente, Rodolfo pasaba una vida muy feliz cuando era pequeño.

27. Uses of the preterit and the imperfect

A. Both the imperfect and the preterit refer to past activities, events, states, and conditions, but they do so in quite different ways. Essentially, the preterit views past events, etc., as noncontinuous and the imperfect views them as continuous. That is, the preterit is used to report events, situations, etc., which begin or end—or both—at some time in the past which the speaker has in mind. The imperfect, on the other hand, is used to report events, situations, etc., which neither begin nor end at the time the speaker is thinking of, but rather which have already begun and are in progress or in existence at this time.

B. The following trivial story illustrates the most important distinctions between the preterit and the imperfect. Read the entire story in English first. Then read it again, this time considering carefully the Spanish verb forms given at the right. These are the most likely equivalents of the corresponding English verb forms, in the context of the story. Comments on these equivalents follow.

Yesterday I *called* (1) a man who *had* (2) a house for sale. He *came by* (3) for me and *took* (4) me to see the house. It *was* (5) pretty old, but on careful inspection it *seemed* (6) to me to be in good condition. I *met* (7) the owner's

(1) *llamé*, pret.
(2) *tenía*, imperf.   (3) *pasó*, pret.
(4) *llevó*, pret.
(5) *era*, imperf.
(6) *pareció*, pret.
(7) *conocí*, pret.

wife. To my surprise, she *knew* (8) my wife. They *used to work* (9) in the same office. We *chatted* (10) for a while. When I *got* (11) home, my wife *was fixing* (12) supper. I *told* (13) her about the house—that it *looked* (14) like a bargain.

(8) *conocía*, imperf.
(9) *trabajaban*, imperf.
(10) *conversamos*, pret.
(11) *llegué*, pret.
(12) *preparaba*, imperf. (13) *conté*, pret.
(14) *parecía*, imperf.

(1) Preterit: the calling was begun and completed at the time the speaker is thinking about. (2) Imperfect: the owner neither began to have nor stopped having the house at that time. (3) and (4) Preterit: both activities were begun and completed, one after the other. (5) Imperfect: the house was already old, and continued to be so. (6) Preterit: the speaker's impression of the house came into existence as a result of the inspection, not before. (7) Preterit: the speaker's acquaintance with the owner's wife began at that moment. (8) Imperfect: the acquaintance of the owner's wife with the speaker's wife continued, having begun earlier. Compare (7) and (8) carefully. (9) Imperfect: the speaker reports a situation which existed at a previous time, not the beginning or end of this situation. (10) Preterit: the conversation is reported as an activity which began and ended, regardless of its duration, in the period the speaker has in mind. (11) Preterit: the speaker's arrival was completed. (12) Imperfect: the wife's activity was in progress when the speaker arrived, having begun earlier. (13) Preterit: the story of the house began and ended, no matter how long it took, during the time the speaker is now telling about. (14) Imperfect: the speaker's impression of the house was formed earlier, and continues to exist at this moment. Compare (6) and (14) carefully.

C. Spanish *consistently* distinguishes between events in progress and events that begin and/or terminate, by choosing the imperfect for the former and the preterit for the latter. English *may or may not* explicitly make the same distinction by choosing particular verb forms. For example, in (9) and (12), the expressions "used to" and "was ____ -ing" clearly indicate habitual or ongoing events. However, in all other cases where Spanish has an imperfect, English has a simple past tense form ("had," "was," "knew," etc.) just as in all the cases where Spanish has the preterit. Thus, in deciding whether to use the imperfect or the preterit in Spanish, you cannot depend on English verb *forms* for a consistently reliable clue. You must think instead about the *meaning*, as illustrated and explained above.

Another striking difference between English and Spanish is that English sometimes uses completely different verbs to express distinctions that are made in Spanish by choosing the imperfect or the preterit. For example, in (7) above, the preterit of *conocer* is equivalent to "meet," that is, "begin an acquaintance," while in (8) the imperfect of *conocer* is "know," "be acquainted with." Another common verb that has different English equivalents in the preterit and the imperfect is *saber*. In the imperfect, *saber* is "know," "have factual information," while in the preterit, it is "learn," "hear," "acquire information." (The preterit of *saber* is irregular, and will be taken up later.) You will learn other examples of this sort.

D. As a preliminary exercise on the imperfect and the preterit, go back over the basic dialog of this chapter, find all the imperfect and preterit forms, and make sure you understand the reason for using each. For example, Anita says to Cecilia, *Te llamé ayer pero no estabas.* Here, *no estabas* (imperfect) reports a state of affairs already in existence, while *te llamé* reports an act that was begun and completed during the time the speaker has in mind.

Tense Substitution

Read the following paragraphs, making sure that you understand each one thoroughly. Then read each again in the past tense, substituting the appropriate forms of either the preterit or the imperfect for those in the present tense.

I

Es la una de la tarde. Estoy cansado y tengo hambre. No tengo comida en la casa. Busco en la refrigeradora pero solamente veo un poco de pan francés. Salgo a la calle. Hace un frío fenomenal. Después de andar casi un kilómetro descubro finalmente un pequeño restaurant. Todas las mesas están ocupadas. Pregunto cuánto tiempo tengo que esperar. El dueño contesta que tengo que esperar dos horas. Salgo furioso del restaurant y entro de nuevo a mi casa. En ese momento llega[4] mi madre del mercado. Pocos minutos después estoy yo comiendo un enorme y delicioso sandwich de jamón con queso.

II

Emilio es un alumno nuevo. El primer día él entra a la clase y toma asiento al lado de Carlos María. Quiere saber quién es la maestra y entonces pregunta a Carlos María. Carlos María no sabe el apellido de la maestra pero sabe que ella es una señorita americana.

III

Vickie está en un paseo fantástico y todos están muy alegres. Los ticos, gente alegre por naturaleza, ese día están más contentos todavía. Vickie conversa con Manuel, quien quiere saber si a ella le gusta Costa Rica y cuánto tiempo va a estar allí. Vickie contesta que sí, que Costa Rica le gusta mucho, pero que no va a estar mucho tiempo más porque tiene que ir a Nicaragua. En ese instante llega Jorge e[5] interrumpe la conversación. Pregunta a Vickie si ella tiene hambre. Manuel está furioso con su amigo.

IV

Son como las dos de la tarde. Anita llama a su amiga Cecilia. Nadie contesta el teléfono. Llama otra vez, la misma cosa. Llama cinco veces en total pero nadie contesta. Claro, nadie contesta porque no hay nadie en la casa. Cecilia y sus padres andan de compras en el centro. Anita también va a ir al centro pero no está segura porque hace mucho calor.

[4]Either imperfect ("was arriving") or preterit ("arrived") is possible.
[5]*E* is used in place of *y* when the next word begins with the sound [i].

Discussion

Without rereading them, retell in the past tense the situations in each of the preceding paragraphs.

Questions

1. ¿Dónde completó usted sus estudios secundarios?
2. ¿Quién era su maestro favorito?
3. ¿Cómo era él (o ella)?
4. ¿Estudió usted historia en la escuela secundaria?
5. ¿A qué hora entraban ustedes a clase?
6. ¿A qué hora salía usted de la escuela?
7. ¿Conocía usted a este señor el año pasado?
8. ¿Cuándo conoció usted a esta señorita?
9. ¿Dónde estaban ustedes ayer a esta misma hora?

28. More cardinal numbers

A. The conjunction *y* is always used in combinations with the multiples of ten: *sesenta y uno, ochenta y nueve.*
B. Units and tens are added directly to hundreds without *y*: *ciento treinta y ocho, ochocientos setenta y dos.*

San Juan, Puerto Rico:
View of El Morro from Isla
de Cabra

Números cardinales

1 uno	11 once	21 veintiuno	80 ochenta
2 dos	12 doce	22 veintidós	90 noventa
3 tres	13 trece	23 veintitrés	100 cien
4 cuatro	14 catorce	30 treinta	101 ciento uno
5 cinco	15 quince	31 treinta y uno	200 doscientos
6 seis	16 dieciséis	32 treinta y dos	300 trescientos
7 siete	17 diecisiete	40 cuarenta	400 cuatrocientos
8 ocho	18 dieciocho	50 cincuenta	500 quinientos
9 nueve	19 diecinueve	60 sesenta	600 seiscientos
10 diez	20 veinte	70 setenta	700 setecientos

800 ochocientos

900 novecientos

1000 mil

1,000,000 un millón (de)

C. From 200 on, the suffix -cientos changes to -cientas to agree with feminine nouns: doscientos hombres, cuatrocientas mujeres.
D. The numbers 500, 700, and 900 have the irregular forms quinientos, setecientos, and novecientos.
E. The word mil is not attached to dos, tres, etc., and, unlike the suffix -cientos, it remains singular: cinco mil niños, siete mil niñas.
F. Spanish does not use constructions like English "seventeen hundred" or "nineteen forty-five." The year 1984, for instance, can be expressed only as mil novecientos ochenta y cuatro.
G. Millón is a noun. Its multiples use the plural millones. De is added before another noun: un millón de libros, cinco millones de habitantes.

Counting Aloud

1. One student counts from 1 to 10, the next one from 11 to 20, etc.
2. One student counts in even numbers to 10, the next one from 12 to 20, etc.
3. Repeat exercise 2 with odd numbers.
4. One student counts in fives from 5 to 25, the next one from 30 to 50, the next from 50 to 100.
5. Count in tens to 100; in hundreds to 1000; in thousands to 1,000,000.

Oral Translation

1. Columbus discovered America in 1492.
2. He was born in 1451.

3. I was born in 1960.
4. There are 210 million inhabitants[6] in this country. There are fifty states.
5. My grandfather is (has) almost one hundred years old (*de edad*).

Questions

1. ¿En qué año nació usted?
2. ¿Cuántos estudiantes hay en esta universidad?
3. ¿En qué año murió el presidente Kennedy?   *morir – die*
4. ¿En qué año descubrió Colón América?
5. ¿En qué año estamos ahora? ¿Cuál es la fecha exacta?
6. ¿En qué año ganaron los Estados Unidos su independencia?
7. ¿Cuántos habitantes hay en este país?

29. Ordinal numbers

Números ordinales

primero	*first*	sexto	*sixth*
segundo	*second*	séptimo	*seventh*
tercero	*third*	octavo	*eighth*
cuarto	*fourth*	noveno	*ninth*
quinto	*fifth*	décimo	*tenth*

A. Ordinal numbers above ten are seldom used in Spanish. Cardinal numbers are generally preferred. Thus a construction like *Te he llamado quince veces* (I've called you fifteen times) is more commonly used than *Esta es la décimoquinta vez que te llamo* (This is the fifteenth time I've called you).
B. Ordinal numbers show agreement in number and gender with the noun they modify: *los **primeros** días, la **quinta** semana*.
C. *Primero* and *tercero* drop the final *o* before a masculine singular noun: *mi **primer** libro, el **tercer** viaje*.
D. Only the first day of the month is designated by the ordinal number, *primero*. Cardinal numbers are used for all the other days: ***primero** de enero, **cuatro** de julio, **treinta y uno** de diciembre*.

Questions

1. ¿Cuál es la fecha de la independencia de los Estados Unidos?
2. ¿Cuál es el primer día del año?
3. ¿En qué fecha exacta nació usted?
4. ¿En qué fecha nació Jorge Washington?

[6]*Habitantes.*

5. ¿Cuál es el primer día de la semana?   7. ¿Qué fecha es hoy?
   ¿El segundo? ¿Cuáles son los otros?   8. ¿Cuántos días hay en un año?
6. ¿Cuál es el sexto mes del año?

LISTENING COMPREHENSION EXERCISE B

Reading

Quiénes son los latinoamericanos

Hay varias hipótesis sobre el origen de los primeros habitantes de América. Una de ellas es la de que los primeros americanos fueron[7] el producto de varios movimientos migratorios originados en el Asia y que entraron a nuestro continente procedentes de Siberia por el estrecho de Bering, hace[8] unos quince o veinte mil años. De allí poco a poco continuaron hacia el sur, pasando de Alaska al Canadá, por los Estados Unidos y México y luego a través[9] de Centroamérica a la América del Sur, llegando finalmente hasta la parte sur de Chile y Argentina.

Algunos de estos grupos continuaron su vida nómada de cazadores y pescadores.[10] Pero otros empezaron a establecer colonias en tierras fértiles y a interesarse en la agricultura. Se dedicaron al cultivo de varios productos vegetales, especialmente el maíz,[11] que es todavía uno de los ingredientes básicos en la comida del campesino latinoamericano.

La necesidad de descubrir las épocas del año más apropiadas para el cultivo de los diversos productos dio origen a la investigación de los fenómenos naturales, al establecimiento de observatorios astronómicos, y al desarrollo[12] de las ciencias y de las artes. Nacieron entonces grandes civilizaciones indias en América. Las tres más avanzadas son la tolteca–azteca del valle central de México; la civilización maya en Honduras, Guatemala y la parte sur de México; y el imperio de los incas, situado en la alta cordillera[13] de los Andes.

Cuando los primeros españoles llegaron a América, la civilización maya estaba ya casi extinta, pero la de los aztecas y la de los incas estaban en su apogeo.[14] Los españoles, sin embargo, conquistaron a estos dos grandes imperios de una manera relativamente fácil. Pero, al contrario de los ingleses que llegaron a América con sus mujeres y sus familias, los españoles llegaron solos y se mezclaron[15] con los indios. Apareció entonces, además del europeo (español y portugués) y del indio, un tercer elemento racial: el mestizo.

[7] Were.
[8] Ago.
[9] Through.
[10] Hunters and fishermen.
[11] Corn.

[12] Development.
[13] High mountain range.
[14] Peak.
[15] Mixed.

New York: Spanish
American students

Luego llegó el cuarto componente de la población latinoamericana, el negro, importado de Africa para trabajar como esclavo en las minas, en las plantaciones de azúcar y en otras regiones donde el indio era escaso[16] o estaba desapareciendo rápidamente.

Hoy día los descendientes de otros europeos—italianos en particular, y también ingleses, alemanes, y franceses—constituyen también una buena parte de la población latinoamericana.

El total de esta población es ahora de casi doscientos setenta y cinco millones. Sin embargo, al contrario de los Estados Unidos donde el elemento europeo predomina en la mayor parte del país, la distribución racial de nuestros pueblos es menos uniforme. Hay cuatro países, por ejemplo, donde predomina el elemento indio: Guatemala, Ecuador, Perú y Bolivia. En otros, como Colombia, Honduras, El Salvador, Nicaragua, Venezuela, Paraguay, Chile y México, el porcentaje de población mestiza es el más alto. En Panamá, la República Dominicana, Cuba, Haití, y en ciertas regiones de la costa de Colombia, Venezuela, Honduras, Ecuador y Nicaragua, viven gran número de negros y mulatos. En el Brasil un cincuenta por ciento de la población es también negra, mulata y zamba[17], y el otro cincuenta por ciento es blanca. Y finalmente, sólo en tres países, Argentina, Uruguay y Costa Rica, predomina casi en su totalidad el elemento racial de origen europeo.

[16] Scarce.
[17] Racial cross of Indian and black.

For Oral or Written Composition

hipótesis
movimientos migratorios
a través de
vida nómada
los fenómenos naturales
civilizaciones indias
en su apogeo
el mestizo
la población latinoamericana
el elemento europeo
la distribución racial
el porcentaje

LISTENING COMPREHENSION EXERCISE C

Vocabulary

ahora mismo right now, right away
alemán, -a German
¿aló? hello
andar to walk; to go
anoche last night
anteanoche the night before last
anteayer the day before yesterday
el **apunte** note
el **árbol** tree
el **asiento** seat
¡ay! oh!; ah!
ayer yesterday
la **biología** biology
el **caballo** horse
la **calle** street
el **centro** downtown
Colón Columbus
el **compañero,** la **compañera** companion, classmate
completar to complete
la **composición** composition
la **compra** purchase
con razón no wonder
contestar to answer

conviene it is suitable, it suits
cualquier(a) any; whatever
cuarto, -a fourth
de compras shopping
de nuevo again, once more
décimo, -a tenth
delicioso, -a delicious; delightful
demasiado, -a too much; too many
el **desastre** disaster
descubrir to discover
diez ten
la **edad** age
enorme enormous
especialmente especially
exacto, -a exact
el **examen** exam, examination
explicar to explain
fantástico, -a fantastic, great
favorito, -a favorite
la **fecha** date
feliz happy
fenomenal great, terrific
furioso, -a furious
ganar to win; to earn

generalmente   generally
el **genio**   genius
la **geografía**   geography
  haber   to be (in existence)
el **habitante**   inhabitant
  hace   ago
  hacer calor   to be hot (weather)
  hacer frío   to be cold (weather)
  hacer viento   to be windy
la **historia**   history
  hoy mismo   today for sure
la **independencia**   independence
  informar   to inform
el **instante**   moment
  interrumpir   to interrupt
la **isla**   island
el **jamón**   ham
el **kilómetro**   kilometer
  llegar   to arrive
  mañana mismo   tomorrow for sure
las **matemáticas**   mathematics
el **mercado**   market
  mil   thousand
el **millón**   million
  montar a caballo   to ride horseback
  nacer   to be born
  nadar   to swim
  normalmente   normally

noveno, -a   ninth
noventa   ninety
octavo, -a   eighth
octubre   October
ocho   eight
parecer   to seem
perfecto, -a   perfect
la **pregunta**   question
preparar   to prepare
primero, -a   first
¿qué tal?   hi; how's it going?
querer   to want
la **química**   chemistry
quinto, -a   fifth
la **razón**   reason
la **refrigeradora**   refrigerator
el **restaurant**   restaurant
el **sandwich**   sandwich
segundo, -a   second
séptimo, -a   seventh
sexto, -a   sixth
tanto, -a   so much, as much
te   you; to you; for you
temprano   early
tercero, -a   third
tocar   to play (music)
el **viaje**   trip
el **viento**   wind

Cultural Listening Passage
for Chapter 6

Latin American Students Abroad

(1) Eighteen of the twenty Latin American nations—all except Brazil and Haiti—constitute the block called Spanish America. These are the former colonies of Spain, born as independent republics approximately a hundred fifty years ago (it makes approximately one hundred fifty years), except Cuba and Panama, the babies of the family, (with) about seventy years old (of age) each. (2) Many people in the United States and (in) Europe are under the impression that these sister republics are very closely bound (united) nations, and they do not understand why they don't live all together in the same house, under the same roof, under a single government, like the fifty states that constitute the great colossus of the North.

(3) "Sisters yes! United no!" answer the Guatemalans in the face of (before) such a possibility. "Sisters yes! United no!" exclaim the Mexicans. "Sisters yes! United no!" shout the Bolivians and the Paraguayans and the Chileans and the Argentineans and the Venezuelans. "What a pity!" the Great Liberator Simón Bolívar is probably (will be) saying from the great beyond; and his golden dream—a united America, one great nation—is still (continues being) only a dream.

(4) "Yes, we are terribly nationalistic," they all confess; "our fatherland and nothing else!" "Join (unite ourselves) with Venezuela? Never!", say the Colombians. "Join with Argentina? Death first!", say the Chileans. "Central America a single country? No, thanks!", they answer in each one of these tiny nations.

(5) Historical reasons and the formidable geographical barriers that separate these nations from one another are the principal causes of this extreme nationalistic feeling that makes impossible the realization of Bolívar's dream. (6) The curious thing, however, is that, in spite

116

of their nationalism and (of) their wars and (of) the great (long) distances that separate them, there exists among all the Spanish American nations a true feeling of fraternity, a feeling constantly expressed in many situations and under all kinds of circumstances. An example in miniature is the case of (the) Latin American students abroad.

(7) In many of the universities in the United States, for example, there is a group—sometimes small, sometimes large—of foreign students, the majority of whom are young Spanish Americans, or Latins, as they are more commonly called. And each new Latin who arrives joins "the group," the impenetrable group of Latins who always go around together, eat together, live together. (8) Here political differences cease; here there are no cultural differences; here the Mexican and the Argentinean, separated by a distance of ten thousand kilometers, discover that they are alike, that they think alike. Here there is only one nationality: Spanish American.

(9) In the basic conversation that follows we present a typical picture: a group of Latins in an American university chatting in their dormitory. There we see Miguel, a Honduran, who has just come in (returned) from the street, conversing with a Chilean. It is extremely cold

(it makes an extreme cold) in the street and (the) poor Miguel's ears are (Miguel has the ears) so cold that he can't (doesn't) even feel them. Today is the first of December, and they are almost in the middle of winter (in full winter). The Chilean, poor guy, looks like he's homesick (misses his fatherland). How he would love to be in Chile now!

(10) Over there are a Salvadoran named Sánchez and his friend Rodolfo, a Paraguayan, getting ready to go to the movies. They are in a hurry (have haste) because the movie is going to start very soon. They are worried because they are going to arrive late, but fortunately their good friend Pepe, the Panamanian, lends them his car.

(11) And in another corner of the dormitory we see a Cuban and a "chapín" (native of Guatemala) chatting. The "chapín" has a headache (pain of head) and is also worried because they still haven't sent him his (the) check from home (the house).

Grammar Points

First, the present tense of some slightly irregular verbs; second, pronouns after a preposition; third, the months of the year and dates; and fourth, direct and indirect object pronouns.

Caracas, Venezuela: Bolívar
Memorial

Chapter **6**

Basic Dialog

Estudiantes latinos[1] en el extranjero

I

MI. *Miguel (hondureño)*   CHI. *Chileno*

MI.   ¡Qué frío hace en la calle! Parece que va a nevar. ¡Ay, mis orejas! Ni las siento.

CHI.   Ah, cómo quisiera estar en Chile. Allá estamos en pleno verano.

MI.   ¿No piensas ir a tu tierra para Navidad?

CHI.   ¿Estás loco? ¿Sabes cuánto cuesta el viaje?

[1] Short for *latinoamericanos.*

II

RO. *Rodolfo (paraguayo)*   SA. *Sánchez (salvadoreño)*   PE. *Pepe (panameño)*

RO.   ¿Vas a preguntarle al panameño o no? Vamos a llegar tarde. La película empieza a las ocho.

SA.   Si lo veo le pregunto. Ah, aquí viene. Hola, Pepe. ¿Quieres ir al cine con nosotros?

PE.   No, prefiero quedarme. Mañana tengo un examen difícil.

SA.   ¿Nos prestas el coche, entonces? Te prometo cuidarlo mucho.

III

CU. *Cubano*   CHA. *Chapín*

CU.   ¿Qué te pasa, chapín?

CHA.   Tengo un pequeño dolor de cabeza. ¿Qué fecha es hoy?

CU.   Primero de diciembre.

CHA.   Si no me mandan un cheque pronto, no sé qué voy a hacer.

Latin American students abroad

I

MI. *Miguel (Honduran)*   CHI. *Chilean*

MI.   It sure is cold outside! It looks like it's going to snow. Ow! My ears! I don't even feel them.

CHI.   Oh, how I'd love to be in Chile. We're right in the middle of summer down there.

MI.   Aren't you planning to go home for Christmas?

CHI.   Are you crazy? Do you know how much the trip costs?

II

RO. *Rodolfo (Paraguayan)*   SA. *Sánchez (Salvadoran)*   PE. *Pepe (Panamanian)*

RO.   Are you going to ask the Panamanian or not? We're going to be late. The picture starts at eight.

SA.   If I see him, I'll ask him. Oh, here he comes. Hi, Pepe. Do you want to go to the movies with us?

PE.   No, I'd rather stay here. I have a difficult test tomorrow.

SA.   Will you lend us your car, then? I promise you I'll take good care of it.[2]

[2]To care for it much.

III

cu. *Cuban*   cha. *Chapín*

cu.   What's the matter,[3] Chapín?
cha.   I have a slight headache. What's today's date?[4]
cu.   December first.
cha.   If they don't send me a check soon, I don't know what I'm going to do.

[3]What's happening to you?   [4]What date is today?

The Sounds of Spanish: VI

A. **The clusters [sya], [sye], and [syo].** In English, *c*, *t*, and *s* are usually pronounced like *sh* in words like "gracious," "nation," and "expansion." In similar words in Spanish, however, *c* and *s* are always pronounced [s], as in "say," never like *sh*.
Pronounce the following words, paying close attention to the [s] clusters.

FAMILIAR WORDS	COGNATES		
gracias	introducción	paciencia	Alicia
diecisiete	pronunciación	social	posición
dieciocho	eficiente	conversación	construcción
asiento	inicial	combinación	vacaciones
Lucrecia	concentración	sección	estación
atención	apariencia	ejercicio	internacional

B. **The clusters [tyo], and [tu].** Because of the influence of English words like "question," where *tion* is pronounced almost like "chin," and "natural," where *tu* is pronounced almost like "chew," students tend to mispronounce the sequences *tio* and *tu* in many Spanish words. In these Spanish combinations there is no fusing of sounds: the *t* is pronounced [t], never like *ch*. Listen carefully to the following pairs of words.

question	cuestión
natural	natural
intellectual	intelectual

Now listen and repeat.

naturalmente	puntual	fortuna
cuestión	Portugal	impetuoso
cultural	mutuamente	fractura
intelectual	indigestión	bastión

LISTENING COMPREHENSION EXERCISE A

Dialog Supplement

I

¡Qué frío hace!

buen tiempo	*good weather*
mal tiempo	*bad weather*
sol	*sunny*
viento	*windy*

Allá estamos en pleno verano.

	invierno	*winter*
	otoño	*fall*
Allá estamos en plena primavera.	primavera	*spring*
	estación	*season*

¡Qué frío hace en la calle!

en el centro	*downtown*
en las afueras	*on the outskirts*
afuera	*outside*
adentro	*inside*

¡Ay, mis orejas!

mis oídos	*my ears (inner)*
mis manos	*my hands*
mis dedos	*my fingers; my toes*
mis brazos	*my arms*
mis piernas	*my legs*
mis pies	*my feet*
mis dientes	*my teeth*
mi cara	*my face*
mi nariz	*my nose*
mi boca	*my mouth*

Parece que va a nevar.

llover	*to rain*

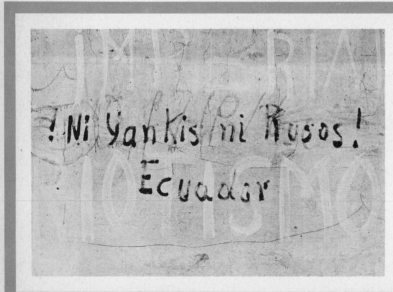

Quito, Ecuador: Graffito

II

¿Vas a preguntarle al panameño?
    contestarle   *answer*

Mañana tengo un examen difícil.
                        fácil   *easy*

Vamos a llegar tarde.
        temprano   *early*
        a tiempo   *on time*

¿Nos prestas el coche?
    das   *give*

III

Tengo dolor de cabeza.
    dolor de oídos   *earache*
    dolor de muelas[5]   *toothache*
    dolor de estómago   *stomach ache*
    dolor de garganta   *sore throat*

Dialog and Supplement Check

Sentence Recall

Say the dialog phrase or sentence in which each of the following words or phrases occurs.

calle	con nosotros	película	nevar
verano	quisiera	el coche	cheque
Navidad	fecha	cuidarlo	examen
viaje	en el extranjero	al cine	quedarme
diciembre	dolor	panameño	tierra

Item Substitution

Repeat each of the following sentences, substituting a related word or phrase for the part in italics. If books are closed, your instructor will say the item at the end of each sentence.

1. ¡Qué frío hace en *la sala*!
2. ¡Ay, *mis piernas*!
3. Parece que va a *llover*.
4. ¡Qué *buen tiempo* hace!
5. Vamos a llegar *a tiempo*.
6. Tengo dolor de *muelas*.
7. ¿Vas a *preguntarle* al panameño?
8. Allá estamos en plena *primavera*.
9. Mañana tengo un examen *fácil*.
10. ¡Ay, mi *estómago*!

Questions

1. ¿Con quién está hablando el chileno?
2. ¿Dónde quisiera estar el chileno ahora?
3. ¿Dónde quisiera estar usted ahora?
4. ¿En qué estación están los estudiantes en Chile ahora? ¿Y nosotros?

[5]*Muela* means "molar," but the expression *dolor de muelas* includes the front teeth as well.

5. ¿Cómo está el tiempo hoy, bonito, feo o regular? ¿Hace frío afuera o hace calor?

6. ¿Va a ir el chileno a su tierra para Navidad?

7. ¿Y adónde van a ir Rodolfo y su amigo Sánchez?

8. ¿Es Sánchez un nombre o un apellido?

9. ¿Va a ir el panameño al cine? ¿Por qué no?

10. ¿Sabe usted qué película van a ver Rodolfo y su amigo?

11. ¿Van a ir ellos a pie o en coche?

12. ¿Cómo puede ir uno a Chile—en taxi, en tren, en avión o en autobús?

13. ¿Cuál de los amigos tiene dolor de cabeza?

14. ¿Cuál de ustedes tiene dolor de estómago? ¿De muelas?

15. ¿Cuáles son las cuatro estaciones del año? ¿Cuál le gusta más a usted?

16. ¿Parece que va a llover, o ya está lloviendo?

17. Señor, ¿usted siempre llega tarde o temprano a clase?

18. ¿A qué hora sale de su casa, generalmente?

19. ¿Vive usted en el centro o en las afueras de la ciudad?

20. ¿Cuál es el nombre de la calle y el número de la casa donde usted vive?

Grammar

30. **Stem-changing verbs:** *e → ie*

pen*sar*	qu*erer*	sen*tir*[6]
*pien*so	*quie*ro	*sien*to
*pien*sas	*quie*res	*sien*tes
*pien*sa	*quie*re	*sien*te
pen*sa*mos	qu*ere*mos	sen*ti*mos
*pien*san	*quie*ren	*sien*ten

pen*sáis*	qu*eréis*	sen*tís*

A. The chart illustrates a large class of verbs whose stem vowel changes from *e* to *ie* in certain forms. This stem change cannot be predicted from the infinitive form; it has to be learned through practice. Notice that the change occurs only when the stress is on the stem. (In the chart, the stressed syllable is indicated by italics.) Thus this stem change does not occur in the infinitive or in the *nosotros* or *vosotros* forms of the present tense.

B. The verbs **tener** (to have, to hold) and **venir** (to come) are like **querer** and **sentir,** except for the first person singular forms *tengo* and *vengo*.

C. The "it" form of **nevar** (to snow) is *nieva*.

[6]The -*ir* verbs of this class undergo an additional change. In the present participle and in certain other forms, which will be discussed later, the stem vowel changes from *e* to *i: sentir, sintiendo; venir, viniendo.*

(The stem vowel of a verb is the last vowel in the stem of the infinitive form. For example, the stem vowel of the verb *comenzar,* to begin, is *e*.)

Paradigm Practice

Before proceeding with the pattern drills, do paradigm practice with the following verbs, alternating each verb form with the *nosotros* form, as suggested by the example.

EXAMPLE: empezar
yo empiezo, nosotros empezamos, tú empiezas, nosotros empezamos, usted empieza, nosotros empezamos, él empieza, nosotros empezamos, ustedes empiezan, nosotros empezamos, ellos empiezan, nosotros empezamos

pensar   sentir   cerrar   preferir
querer   venir   tener

Person–Number Substitution

If the cue is given in English, do not include the subject in your responses.

1. Hola, Pepe. ¿Quieres ir al cine con nosotros?
   (Pepe y Juan, amigos, Srta. García)
2. No, prefiero ir otro día.
   (we, my sister, they, you and I, everybody, you, I)
3. Lo siento mucho.
   (they, we, Mary, your friends, all of us, you *pl*)
4. ¿En qué piensan ustedes?   ~thinking about?~
   (el panameño, los cubanos, nosotros, el estudiante, yo, usted)
5. Ah, aquí viene Pepe.
   (yo, nosotros, los latinos, el coche, mi novia)
6. El chapín tiene dolor de estómago.
   (el profesor, yo, nosotros, su abuela, mis hijos, todo el mundo)

Alternate Substitution

Besides saying the correct verb form, you must also make the proper number-gender agreement between nouns and modifiers.

1. Mañana yo tengo un examen difícil.
   _____ ~unos examenes~ difíciles.
   _____ nosotros ~tenemos~ _____.
   _____ ~los examenes~ fácil~es~
   _____ los _____.
   _____ prefiero _____.
   _____ clases _____.
   _____ venimos a _____.

2. La película empieza a las ocho.
   Las~películas~ ~empiezan~ _____.
   _____ temprano.
   Nosotros ~empiezemos~ _____.
   _____ empiezo _____.
   _____ a la una.
   _____ cerramos _____.
   Yo _____.

J *You Ask the Questions*

Ask questions that would elicit the following answers.

1. Nosotros queremos ir a Chile.
2. No vamos porque no tenemos dinero.
3. Yo pienso ir a mi tierra para Navidad.
4. Usted tiene dolor de pies.
5. Ellos quieren ir a Florida porque allá hace calor.
6. Nosotros preferimos ir al cine.
7. Rodolfo y su amigo quieren ir al cine.
8. La película empieza a las nueve menos diez.
9. Ustedes tienen frío porque estamos en invierno.
10. Sí sí sí, yo lo siento mucho.

31. Pronouns after a preposition

para mí	*for me*	después de nosotros	*after us*
sin ti	*without you*		
por usted	*for you*	con ustedes	*with you*
de él	*of him*	según ellos	*according to them*
a ella	*to her*	hacia ellas	*toward them*

para vosotros	*for you*

A. With the exception of *mí* and *ti,* the prepositional pronouns are identical to subject pronouns.
B. *Con* has the special forms *conmigo* (with me) and *contigo* (with you, *fam*).

Oral Translation

1. near them
2. without me
3. according to us
4. from them
5. under you *pl* debajo ustedes
6. with me con mego
7. toward her
8. after you (*formal*) despues de ustede
9. on top of him ensemade el
10. behind them detras de ellos
11. for us para nosotros
12. with her con ella

Questions

The whole class answers, giving *negative* responses. Replace the nouns after prepositions with the appropriate pronouns.

EXAMPLE: ¿Quiere Pepe ir al cine con Sánchez y con Rodolfo?
No, no quiere ir al cine con ellos.

Bolivia: The Andes

1. ¿Quiere Pepe ir con el chileno? ✓
2. ¿Quiere él ir con ustedes?
3. ¿Quieren ustedes ir conmigo?
4. ¿Quieren ustedes ir al cine con la chica mexicana?

No, usted no esta detras nosotros

5. ¿Estoy yo detrás de ustedes?
6. ¿Puedo yo vivir sin ustedes?
7. ¿Pueden ustedes vivir sin mí?
8. ¿Están ustedes hablando de mi abuela?

Questions

Individual students answer.

1. ¿Vive usted con sus padres? ✓
2. ¿Con quién está hablando usted en este momento?
3. ¿Y yo estoy hablando con este alumno?
4. ¿Está usted pensando en su novia?
5. ¿Quién está delante de usted?
6. ¿Vive usted lejos de su suegra?

7. ¿Quiere ir al cine conmigo?
8. ¿Es fácil el español, según el profesor?
9. ¿Hay otros alumnos inteligentes en esta clase, además de usted?
10. ¿Tiene usted problemas con sus hermanos?

32. Months and dates

Meses y fechas

1°[7] de enero	7 de julio
2 de febrero	8 de agosto
3 de marzo	9 de septiembre
4 de abril	10 de octubre
5 de mayo	11 de noviembre
6 de junio	31 de diciembre

[7]Abbreviation for *primero*.

A. Except for the first day of the month, Spanish uses cardinal numbers for dates. The names of the months are written with lower-case letters.

B. The word order *primero de diciembre* or *diez de abril*—rather than *diciembre primero* or *abril diez*—is practically the only one used in the spoken language.

Questions

The whole class answers briefly.

1. ¿Qué fecha es hoy?
2. ¿En cuál estación estamos?
3. ¿Cuándo empieza la primavera?
4. ¿Cuándo acaba?
5. ¿Y cuándo empieza el verano?
6. ¿Cuáles son los meses del verano?
7. ¿Cuáles son los meses del otoño?
8. ¿Cuáles son los meses del invierno?
9. ¿Cuál es la fecha de la independencia de los EE. UU.?
10. ¿En qué fecha empieza el año?
11. ¿Cuál es el último día del año?
12. ¿Cuántos días hay en el mes de mayo?
13. ¿Cuántos meses hay en el año?
14. ¿Cuántas semanas hay en el año?
15. ¿Cuántas horas hay en un día?

La fecha es el cuarto de julio de mil setecientos setenta y seis.

33. Direct object pronouns

me	*me*	nos	*us*
te	*you*		
lo	*you / him / it*	los	*you / them*
la	*you / her / it*	las	*you / them*

os	*you*

A. Direct object pronouns immediately precede single verb forms that are conjugated for person and number.

Nos buscan.   *They're looking for us.*
No **los** veo.   *I don't see them.*

In verb constructions with an infinitive or a present participle, the object pronoun may precede or follow the whole construction, with no change in meaning. In writing, an object pronoun that follows the verb is attached to it.

Nos están buscando.⎫
Están buscándo**nos**.[8]⎭   *They're looking for us.*
No **los** voy a ver.⎫
No voy a ver**los**.⎭   *I'm not going to see them.*

B. Direct object pronouns make no distinction between persons and things.

Veo a la chica.⎫
Veo la mesa.⎭ **La** veo.   Veo al chico.⎫
Veo el libro.⎭ **Lo** veo.[9]

Item Substitution

EXAMPLES: ¡Ay qué frío! *Las orejas,* ni las siento.
   (*los pies*)
   ¡Ay qué frío! Los pies, ni los siento.
   ¡El teléfono! *Es para usted.*
   ¿Quién me llama?

1. ¡Ay qué frio! *La boca,* ni la siento.
   (el brazo, los dedos, la cara, el pie, las manos, la nariz)
2. ¡El teléfono! *Es para Rodolfo.*
   (es para mí, es para Juanita, es para nosotros, es para ustedes, es para el cubano, es para los chilenos, es para las chicas, es para ti)

√ *Questions*

Answer each question twice, putting the object pronoun first before and then after the present participle or infinitive.

EXAMPLES: ¿Estás buscando al chileno?
   Sí, lo estoy buscando. Sí, estoy buscándolo.
   ¿Tú vas a ver la casa?
   Sí, yo la voy a ver. Sí, yo voy a verla.

---

[8]There is no shift of stress when a pronoun is added to a present participle. Thus a written accent is necessary.

[9]In some areas singular *le* and plural *les* replace masculine *lo* and *los*—but not feminine *la* and *las*—when they refer to people. The text reflects standard usage in Spanish America.

1. ¿Estás buscando a la profesora?
   (el número de teléfono, la casa de Juan, a los cubanos, tus apuntes)
2. ¿Tú vas a ver al doctor?
   (a mis amigas, el libro, la fecha, a los latinos, a Pepe)

34. Indirect object pronouns

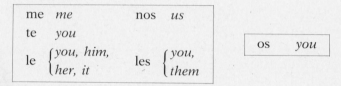

me	*me*	nos	*us*
te	*you*		
le	*you, him, her, it*	les	*you, them*

os	*you*

A. The position of indirect object pronouns is the same as that of direct object pronouns.

Les escribo una carta. *I'm writing them a letter.*

Les estoy escribiendo una carta.}
Estoy escribiéndo**les** una carta. } *I'm writing them a letter.*

Les quiero escribir una carta. }
Quiero escribir**les** una carta. } *I want to write them a letter.*

B. Indirect object pronouns make no distinction between persons and things or between masculine and feminine.

Le compré algo. *I bought something for him/her/it.*

C. There is a fundamental difference in grammar between direct and indirect object pronouns in Spanish. With *direct* objects, nouns and pronouns do not occur together. With *indirect* objects, however, an indirect object noun (always preceded by *a*) is normally accompanied by a redundant indirect object pronoun.

Le escribo una carta *a María.*
(*To her* = Mary) *I'm writing a letter to Mary.*

¿Vas a preguntar- -*le* al panameño o no?
Are you going to ask (him =) the Panamanian or not?

Item Substitution: Indirect Object Pronouns

EXAMPLES: Aquí está *Pepe.* ¿Por qué no le preguntas?
    (yo)
  Aquí estoy yo. ¿Por qué no me preguntas?
  ¿Les escribiste *a tus padres?*
    (a tu padre)
  ¿Le escribiste a tu padre?

1. Aquí están ellos. ¿Por qué no les preguntas?
   (el chileno, nosotros, Cecilia, Cecilia y Anita, el profesor, la profesora)
2. ¿Le escribiste al chileno?
   (a Susana y a Berta, a tus amigos, a Roberto, a mí, a Linda)

✓ *Written Translation*

1. I'm going to write my girlfriend a long letter.
2. They're going to send us a check soon.
3. We're going to ask Pepe if he can lend us the car.
4. Anita asked Cecilia if she was a genius.
5. I must bring my teacher something nice (pretty).
6. What are you going to buy your mother for Mother's Day?

35. Direct vs. indirect objects

Many verbs take both direct and indirect objects. Typical are verbs that refer to an exchange of objects or information. The thing exchanged is the direct object; the participant in the exchange (besides the subject) is the indirect object.

DIRECT OBJECT	INDIRECT OBJECT
Vendo **la casa.** → **La** vendo. *I'm selling **the house.** → I'm selling **it.***	**Le** vendo la casa. *I'm selling **him** the house.*
Escribo **la carta.** → **La** escribo. *I'm writing **the letter.** → I'm writing **it.***	**Le** escribo (una carta). *I'm writing **him** (a letter).*
Hablo bien **español.** → **Lo** hablo bien. *I speak **Spanish** well. → I speak **it** well.*	**Les** hablo. *I'm talking/speaking **to them.***
Debo **dinero.** → **Lo** debo. *I owe **money.** → I owe **it.***	**Les** debo dinero. *I owe **them** money.*
Quiero contestar **la carta.** → Quiero contestar**la.** *I want to answer **the letter.** → I want to answer **it.***	Quiero contestar**le** (su pregunta). *I want to answer **him** (his question).*
Pide **el cheque.** → **Lo** pide. *He's asking for **the check.** → He's asking for **it.***	**Les** pide (el cheque). *He's asking **them** (for the check).*

Estoy diciendo **la verdad.** → Estoy diciéndo**la.**

*I'm telling **the truth.*** → *I'm telling **it.***

No quieren mandar **dinero.** → No quieren mandar**lo.**

*They don't want to send **money.*** → *They don't want to send **it.***

Estoy diciéndo**le** (algo).

*I'm telling **her** (something).*

No quieren mandar**le** dinero.

*They don't want to send **her** money (send money **to her**).[10]*

Writing Exercise

Complete the following sentences according to the example.

EXAMPLE: ¿Al *panameño?* Si lo veo le pregunto.
¿A mis hermanas? _____
¿A mis hermanas? Si las veo les pregunto.

1. ¿A *él?* Si lo veo le pregunto.
   ¿A esos señores? *Si los veo les pregunto.*
   ¿A mis parientes? *Si me veo les pregunto.*
   ¿A mi abuela? *Si me veo le pregunto.*
   ¿Al mendigo? *Si lo veo le pregunto.*
   ¿A ellas? *Si las veo les pregunto.*

2. ¿A *Luz María?* ¿Va a escribirle para invitarla?
   ¿A los chicos? *¿Va a escribirles para invitarlos?*
   ¿A su novio? *¿Va a escribirle para invitarlo?*
   ¿A nosotros? *¿Va a escribirnos para " ?*
   ¿A Carmencita? *¿Va a escribirle para " ?*
   ¿A él? *¿Va a escribirle para invitarla ?*

3. ¿A *tu padre?* ¿Lo estás llamando para decirle algo?
   ¿A los chilenos? *¿Los están llamando para decirles algo?*
   ¿A la boliviana? *¿La está llamando para decirle algo?*
   ¿Al cubano? *¿Lo está llamando para decirle " ?*
   ¿A las mexicanas? *¿Las están llamando para decirles algo?*
   ¿Al nicaragüense? *¿Lo está llamando para decirle algo?*

4. ¿A *los chicos?* ¿Les pediste dinero o los llevaste al cine?
   ¿A tus hijas? *¿Les pediste dinero o las llevaste al cine?*
   ¿A tus hermanos? *" " " los " " ?*
   ¿A tu primo? *¿Le pediste dinero o lo llevaste al cine?*
   ¿A tu compañera? *" " la " " ?*
   ¿A tu compañero? *lo*

[10]***Mandar*** can take a direct object referring to a person: *No quieren mandar* a María *a esa escuela.* → *No quieren mandar*la *a esa escuela.* They don't want to send *Mary* to that school. → They don't want to send *her* to that school.

Santiago, Chile: Street scene

Reading

El béisbol en Hispanoamérica

En general, dice la gente hispanoamericana que el deporte[11] más popular de nuestros países es el fútbol, es decir el fútbol estilo europeo, que se juega[12] como Dios manda[13]—con los pies, la cabeza y una pelota redonda[14]. Igual que[15] el fútbol norteamericano, el fútbol latino es el gran espectáculo de las masas. Todos los domingos grandes multitudes llenan[16] hasta el último asiento de los estadios—estadios pequeños, estadios grandes, ¡estadios enormes! como el estadio de Maracaná en Río de Janeiro, que tiene capacidad para acomodar a más de 200.000 espectadores.

Pero existe otro deporte en muchas partes de Hispanoamérica, el cual es tan popular o más popular que el fútbol: es el béisbol, producto puro de América del Norte. Los mexicanos, los puertorriqueños, los venezolanos, los nicaragüenses, los cubanos, los panameños y los dominicanos se sienten verdaderamente orgullosos[17] de haber producido para las grandes ligas un gran número de "estrellas"[18]. ¿Quién no reconoce el nombre de Roberto Clemente, Juan Marichal, Félix Millán, "Mannie" Sanguillén, los hermanos Alou y muchísimos otros entre los famosos jugadores en la historia del béisbol?

En los barrios[19] más pobres de Caracas, de la Ciudad de México, de Bogotá

[11] Sport.
[12] *Se juega:* is played.
[13] *como* . . . as it should be played.
[14] *Pelota redonda:* round ball.
[15] *Igual que:* like.

[16] Fill.
[17] *Verdaderamente orgullosos:* truly proud.
[18] Stars.
[19] Sections, neighborhoods.

Guatemala City,
Guatemala:
North–Central
American and
Caribbean
Amateur
Baseball
Championship

y en muchas capitales de provincia colombianas y centroamericanas vemos a chicos de todas las edades jugando al béisbol con implementos primitivos, mientras[20] sus padres escuchan[21] entusiasmadamente en la radio de una cantina[22] el resultado de los partidos[23] profesionales. Muchos padres aspiran a ver a sus hijos jugando algún día como profesionales en los equipos[24] de los Mets, de los Yankees, de los Padres de San Diego, de los Piratas de Pittsburgh.

El béisbol es un juego muy rápido y lento al mismo tiempo. El jugador tiene que[25] emplear toda su astucia[26] y debe ser muy ágil con los pies, con las manos y con los ojos. Además, debe contar con una buena porción de suerte[27], como ocurre en toda actividad humana.

Hay nueve jugadores en cada[28] equipo. El más importante es el pícher (o "lanzador") quien, junto[29] con el cácher (o "receptor") forman la "batería" del equipo. Luego hay otros cuatro jugadores—la primera base (barrera), la segunda base, la tercera base y el shortstop—estacionados en el infield. Y finalmente, los tres outfielders. Si el bateador del otro equipo llega a primera base, tiene luego que pasar a segunda, a tercera y finalmente a home; esto cuenta como una carrera[30]. Pero hay bateadores que golpean[31] la pelota tan fuerte que la hacen salir del estadio y ellos meten[32] entonces lo que[33] se conoce por el nombre de jonrón. Es algo muy emocionante ver a un jugador batear un jonrón.

El partido normalmente dura nueve inings (turnos) y cada equipo tiene el mismo número de oportunidades al bate. Pero no hay un término fijo[34] para la duración de un ining o de un partido. En esto difiere mucho el béisbol del fútbol. Un aspecto de este deporte en el cual el público se entretiene[35] mucho, son las continuas y acaloradas disputas entre los jugadores y el referí (el árbitro); claro que[36] los jugadores siempre pierden y el referí siempre gana. El es la autoridad máxima. Es tal vez este fuerte carácter individualista y la falta[37] de restricciones respecto al límite de tiempo lo que hace tan atractivo para los hispanoamericanos el deporte del béisbol.

Cultural Note

Since *fútbol* (called "soccer" in North America) and *béisbol* are of English and American origin, much of the terminology used in these sports is not translated into Spanish. Thus it is quite common to hear Spanish speakers say, for instance, that so-and-so "es un *pícher* (o un *cácher*) muy bueno." The language purists, however, are always struggling to counter this trend by trying to find true corresponding Spanish words, some of which are given in parentheses in the reading. But the purists are not always successful. For instance, Spanish has both the English word *fútbol* and the Spanish *balompié*, but *fútbol* is gradually displacing *balompié*. This struggle is evident in the sports sections of newspapers. Some papers prefer to use as much Spanish terminology as possible, while others, trying to be more realistic, use words like *cácher*, *pícher*, and *jonrón*.

For Oral or Written Composition

el deporte más popular
los estadios
el estadio de Maracaná
otro deporte
se sienten verdaderamente orgullosos
chicos de todas las edades

en la radio de una cantina
rápido y lento
la "batería" del equipo
el nombre de jonrón
las disputas acaloradas
este fuerte carácter individualista

LISTENING COMPREHENSION EXERCISE C

[30] Run.
[31] Hit.
[32] Make.
[33] *Lo que:* what.

[34] Fixed.
[35] *Se entretiene:* is amused.
[36] *Claro que:* of course.
[37] Lack.

Vocabulary

a tiempo on time
abril April
adentro within, inside
afuera outside
las **afueras** outskirts
agosto August
el **autobús** bus
el **avión** plane
¡ay! ow!
la **boca** mouth
el **brazo** arm
la **cabeza** head
la **cara** face
el **centro** center of town, downtown
cerrar (ie) to close
el **cine** movies, movie theater
el **coche** car
conmigo with me
contigo with you *fam*
cubano, -a Cuban
cuidar to take care of
el **chapín** nickname for native of
   Guatemala
el **cheque** check
chileno, -a Chilean
dar to give
el **dedo** finger
diciembre December
el **diente** tooth
difícil difficult
el **dolor** pain, ache
EE.UU. U.S.A.
empezar (ie) to begin
en el extranjero abroad
en pleno verano in the middle of
   summer
enero January
la **estación** season
el **estómago** stomach
fácil easy
febrero February
la **garganta** throat
¡hola! hi!

el **invierno** winter
invitar to invite
julio July
junio June
lo(s) he, it; *pl* them
loco, -a crazy
llover to rain
mandar to send
la **mano** hand
marzo March
mayo May
mexicano, -a Mexican
la **muela** tooth (molar)
la **nariz** nose
la **Navidad** Christmas
nevar (ie) to snow
nos us, to us
noviembre November
el **número** number
el **oído** (inner) ear
la **oreja** (outer) ear
os you *pl;* to you *pl*
el **otoño** autumn
los **padres** parents
panameño, -a Panamanian
la **película** film
pensar (ie) to think, intend
pensar en to think about
el **pie** foot
la **pierna** leg
preferir (ie) to prefer
preguntar to ask (a question)
prestar to lend
la **primavera** spring
pronto quickly
quedarse to stay, remain
quisiera I would like; he would like;
   she would like; you *sing* would like
regular so-so, fair
salvadoreño, -a Salvadoran
se dice you say, one says
sentir (ie) to feel
septiembre September

el **sol** sun
la **suegra** mother-in-law
el **tiempo** weather
la **tierra** homeland

el **tren** train
último, -a last
venir (ie) to come
el **verano** summer

Cultural Listening Passage
for Chapter 7

At Last They're Leaving!

(1) My name is (I call myself) Jim Davis; I'm a North American citizen living in Mexico for many years. I'm married to a Mexican woman; her name is (she calls herself) Margarita. We have five children and we're very happy. I can't complain about anything. Mexico is a marvelous country and I hope to stay here with my family for the rest of my life.

(2) Tonight we're having guests for dinner (to eat)—we had, rather (better said), because dinner ended three hours ago. Now we're in the living room chatting with them, our dear friends Napoleón Gamboa and his wife Pepita. They are Bolivian. They are old friends of ours and we are very fond of them (love them much). (3) The only thing wrong with them (bad thing that they have) is that, like typical Latins, they always arrive one or two hours late to engagements (invitations) of this type; and then that, since Pepita likes to chat so much and my wife does too, they stay for hours and hours and never leave even if you push them out (pushing them). It's true that in the course of the evening they say good-bye three or (and) four times— but they don't leave. The slightest little word added to a "good-bye" or to a "thank you" is sufficient motive to start a new theme of conversation. (4) That's why (for that) I've warned my wife that when we go to pay (make) a visit, when it's time to leave (at the hour of saying farewell) she must say only "good-bye and thank you very much, see you tomorrow," and nothing else. Of course, my wife never pays attention (to me) to these warnings; it's like talking to the wall, because she's always full of extra little words and "by the way's" and things.

(5) As for me, this business of saying good-bye in stages kills me, more so when one is as sleepy as I am (has a sleepiness like the one I have) now. Here we are in the living room,

138

but we're not sitting; we're standing (on foot) because we're already on the second good-bye. Pepita is telling us that they have to leave because tomorrow they have to get up early. They're invited to a wedding at eight in the morning. Right away comes the "by the way" from Margarita. She says—speaking of weddings—that some friends of ours are going to get divorced because the woman is very jealous and follows her husband everywhere, and so on and so forth. And more and more details follow and nobody moves for a long while, despite my many hints and efforts to end the conversation. Finally it ends. But then comes (the) number three.

(6) We start to walk toward the door when Napoleón suddenly remembers that he has forgotten his overcoat. I run back like crazy and bring it for him. In the meantime Pepita is saying good-bye to my wife and takes advantage of the opportunity to add a small comment about the dinner, especially about the main dish, the *paella*. "Delicious," according to her, and she asks Margarita for the recipe. I give my wife the eye (twist my eyes on my wife); she smiles at me and starts telling Pepita that in a very big (wide) frying pan you put a little onion and garlic and you fry it in (with) oil. Then you put in a little bit of tomato and then you put in some pieces of chicken and the rice, then

you throw other things in, you cover the pan and—I don't remember the rest. There, nailed down to that spot in the living room, we spend the next twenty minutes.

(7) At last we reach the door. There Napoleón asks me how to get to (how one arrives at) the center of town. I explain to him that you go (follow) straight ahead on the street that passes in front of our house, but that it is necessary to turn right at the corner by the hospital. The word reminds Pepita of something she must tell us: "They say that . . . uh . . . what's his name is seriously ill and that . . . ." Jesus, Mary, and Joseph! Another story—no! But fortunately Napoleón is as tired as I am and doesn't let her go on. Thank God! Bravo, Napoleón!

Grammar Points

First, another group of verbs that are slightly irregular in the present tense; second, reflexive pronouns; third, the construction **tener que** + *infinitive;* fourth, the difference between the verbs **saber** and **conocer;** fifth, the difference between the verbs **pedir** and **preguntar;** sixth, the prepositions **para** and **por;** seventh, the particle **se** as an unspecified subject; and eighth, emphatic object pronouns.

Spanish paella

Chapter 7

Basic Dialog

¡Por fin se van!

NA. *Napoleón Gamboa*   PE. *Pepita, su esposa*
JIM. *Jim Davis*   MA. *Margarita, su esposa*

I

NA.   Esta vez sí[1], Pepita, debemos irnos.
MA.   Ay, ¿por qué? Mañana es domingo; no tienen que levantarse.
PE.   Nosotros sí. Estamos invitados a una boda, ¡a las ocho! Se casa la hija de un peón.
MA.   ¿Ah sí? Y hablando de bodas, ¿conoce a Amadeo Gil?
PE.   Sí, sé que él y su mujer se divorcian. Dicen que ella es muy celosa.

---

[1]*Sí* is used for emphasis; it is often equivalent to
"do" in English: "We *do* have to go."

II

Media hora después.

NA. Bueno, ahora sí nos vamos. Muchas gracias por todo. ¡Ah! El[2] abrigo.

JIM. Ah, sí, perdón. Ya[3] lo traigo.

PE. ¡Qué paella tan deliciosa, Margarita! Si le pido la receta, ¿me la da?

MA. Con mucho gusto. Mire: en una sartén grande se pone un poco de ajo y cebolla. Luego,...

III

Veinte minutos después.

NA. Para llegar al centro sigo derecho por aquí, ¿no, Jim?

JIM. No, hay que doblar a la derecha en la esquina del hospital.

PE. Ah, ahora, que dice "hospital," este[4], cómo se llama... está muy enfermo.

NA. ¡No, Pepita, por favor! ¡Chao! ¡Buenas noches!

At last they're leaving!

NA. *Napoleón Gamboa*   PE. *Pepita, his wife*
JIM. *Jim Davis*   MA. *Margarita, his wife*

I

NA. This time, Pepita, we really must go.

MA. Oh, why? Tomorrow is Sunday; you don't have to get up.

PE. Yes, we do. We're invited to a wedding, at eight! The daughter of one of our workers is getting married.

MA. Oh, really? And talking about weddings, do you know Amadeo Gil?

PE. Yes, I know that he and his wife are getting divorced. They say that she's very jealous.

II

A half hour later.

NA. Well, this time we *are* leaving. Thanks for everything. Oh, my coat.

JIM. Oh, yes, excuse me. I'll get it for you right away.

PE. What a delicious *paella*, Margarita! If I ask you for the recipe, will you give it to me?[5]

MA. I'll be glad to. Look, in a large frying pan you put a little bit of garlic and onion. Then . . .

III

Twenty minutes later.

NA. To go downtown I go straight ahead this way, right, Jim?

JIM. No, you have to turn right at the corner by the hospital.

PE. Oh, now that you say "hospital," uh, what's his name . . . is very ill.

NA. No, Pepita, please! So long! Good night!

---

[2]The definite article is often used in Spanish where English uses a possessive, if it is obvious who the possessor is.

[3]*Ya* (already) is used to imply promptness of action.

[4]*Este...* (often with an extended final [e] sound) is a "fumble word," used to fill the silence while one is thinking (like "uh" in English).

[5]To me it you give.

The Sounds of Spanish: VII

Syllabication and rhythm. The attainment of an even syllabic rhythm in Spanish is a great aid to acquiring an even, clear, precise pronunciation of the vowels. And this even, clear, precise pronunciation of the five vowels—whether stressed or unstressed—is in turn the basis for the acquisition of a generally good pronunciation of Spanish.

Reading aloud is an excellent rhythm exercise; but it will not help you much unless you know—and apply to your reading—the rules for syllable division in Spanish. By applying these rules to your spoken Spanish, you can attain the even, staccato rhythm that native speakers of Spanish have.

The rules are quite simple, although they differ from the English rules. In the spoken language they apply not only to single words but also to sequences of words uttered as a single breath group (*mi nombre es Emilio, adiós, buenas noches, yo no estoy cansada,* etc.). In writing of course, the rules apply to single words only. They are listed below.

A. A single consonant between vowels always begins a syllable.

a *sus* órde*n*es	a-*s*u-*s*ór-de-*n*es
qué *t*al es	qué-*t*a-*l*es
to*d*os están a*q*uí	to-*d*o-*s*es-tá-*n*a-*q*uí

B. Clusters of two consonants whose second member is *r* or *l* (*br, cr, fr,* etc.; *bl, cl, fl,* etc.) are treated as single consonants, the entire cluster going with the following vowel.

ha*blo* mucho	(h)a-*blo*-mu-cho[6]
tan ale*gres*	ta-na-le-*gres*

C. Other consonant clusters are separated, the first consonant ending the preceding syllable, the second (plus *r* or *l*) beginning the next.

el alu*mn*o	e-la-lu*m*-*n*o
a sus ór*d*enes	a-su-sór-*d*e-nes
e*l m*aestro	e*l*-*m*a-es-tro

D. The sequence consisting of *any vowel* preceded or followed by unstressed *i* or unstressed *u* comprises a single syllable and is therefore pronounced in the same length of time as a single vowel.

t*ie*ne	t*ie*-ne	b*ue*no	b*ue*-no
ag*ua*	a-g*ua*	v*ei*nte	v*ei*n-te
qu*ie*n es	qu*ie*-nes	ca*u*sa	ca*u*-sa
ci*u*dad	ci*u*-dad	ad*ió*s	a-d*ió*s
c*ui*dado	c*ui*-da-do	d*ue*ño	d*ue*-ño

E. If the same vowel or consonant sound occurs at the end of one word and the beginning of the next, the two sounds are normally pronounced as one single vowel or consonant, and the words are linked together.

[6]Remember that the letter *h* alone represents no sound, and that *ch, ll,* and *rr* are single letters.

mi nombr*e es C*ielito	mi-nom-bre-*c*ie-li-to
la*s* silla*s s*on feas	la-*s*i-lla-*s*on-fe-as
Ev*a* h*abl*a *a*lemán	e-v*a*-bla-le-mán

F. If the final vowel of one word and the beginning vowel of the next are not the same, they are both pronounced but are linked together.

n*o* h*abl*a *e*spañol	no (h)a-bla es-pa-ñol
cóm*o está e*lla	có-mo es-tá e-lla
María *o E*milio	ma-rí-a o e-mi-lio
José *o A*licia	jo-sé o a-li-cia

You should review the six rules above before you do the following exercise and whenever you do any practice reading, particularly on your own.

Syllabication

Written word boundaries do not necessarily coincide with spoken syllable boundaries—in fact, very commonly do not—as is illustrated in the following sentences. Read them aloud several times in a natural manner, using the spoken syllabic divisions provided as a guide.

1. ¿Quié-ne-sel-ma-es-tro?
2. E-su-na-se-ño-ri-ta-me-ri-ca-na.
3. Di-cen-que-sun-po-co-es-tric-ta.
4. Mi-nom-bre-sE-mi-lio.
5. So-mo-s(h)er-ma-nos.
6. Los-ti-co-so-mo-sa-sí.
7. Quie-ro-to-ma-ral-go-frí-o.
8. Lue-go-va-mo-sa-Ni-ca-ra-gua.
9. U-na-vi-si-ta-la-go.
10. ¿Qués-ta-s(h)a-cien-do?
11. Voy-a-lla-ma-ra-la-po-li-cí-a.

LISTENING COMPREHENSION EXERCISE A

Dialog Supplement

I

Debemos irnos.

acostarnos	*go to bed*
sentarnos	*sit down*

No tienen que levantarse.

vestirse	*get dressed*	quedarse	*stay*
bañarse	*take a bath, bathe*	quejarse	*complain*
lavarse	*wash (oneself)*	preocuparse	*worry*
peinarse	*comb (one's hair)*	enojarse	*get angry*
afeitarse	*shave*	desmayarse	*faint*

II

¡Ah! El abrigo.

Los guantes	*the gloves*
El impermeable	*the raincoat*
La cartera	*the purse, wallet, briefcase*
El paraguas	*the umbrella*

¡Qué paella tan deliciosa!

cena	*supper*
comida	*meal*
¡Qué almuerzo tan delicioso!	*lunch*
desayuno	*breakfast*

En una sartén se pone un poco de ajo.   **Si le pido la receta...**

cocina	*cook*	consigo	*get*
calienta	*heat*	digo	*tell*

III

Hay que doblar a la derecha.   **Está enfermo.**

izquierda	*left*	peor	*worse*
		mejor	*better*

En la esquina del hospital.

cementerio	*cemetery*

Dialog and Supplement Check

Sentence Recall

Say the dialog line in which each of the following words or phrases occurs.

invitados	levantarse	peón
Amadeo	receta	doblar
debemos	derecho	gusto
paella	a la derecha	enfermo
sartén	muy celosa	

Supplement Recall

Make one or more substitutions within each of the following utterances.

¡Ah! El paraguas.
Mañana no hay que preocuparse.
Está muy enfermo.
¡Qué comida tan deliciosa!
Hay que doblar a la derecha.
Debemos irnos.

Questions

1. ¿Quiénes son los invitados a la comida?
2. ¿Tienen que levantarse ellos temprano mañana?
3. ¿Adónde están invitados Napoleón y su señora?
4. ¿A qué hora es la boda, a las cinco de la tarde?
5. ¿Quién se casa?
6. ¿Y quiénes se divorcian?
7. ¿Por qué se divorcian Amadeo y la mujer?
8. ¿Es usted celoso?
9. Pepita y Napoleón, ¿están divorciados o están casados?
10. ¿Sabe usted cocinar?
11. ¿Quién sabe cocinar arroz? Si le pido la receta, ¿me la da?
12. ¿Le gusta a usted el ajo? ¿Y la cebolla?
13. Según Pepita, ¿quién está muy enfermo?
14. Y ustedes, ¿cómo están, están enfermos?

Grammar

36. Stem-changing verbs: *e* ⟶ *i*

pe*dir*

> *pi*do
> *pi*des
> *pi*de
> pe*di*mos
> *pi*den

> pe*dís*

A. In a few very common *-ir* verbs like **pedir,** the stem vowel *e* becomes *i* in forms in which the stress is on the stem, and in the present participle (*pidiendo*). (In the chart, the stressed syllable is indicated by italics.) Thus only the infinitive and the *nosotros* and *vosotros* forms have *e* in the stem of the verb. There is no way to predict which *-ir* verbs are like *pedir;* this must simply be memorized.

B. *Repetir, seguir, conseguir, despedir, servir,* and *vestir* are conjugated like *pedir.*

C. *Decir* is like *pedir* except that the first person singular form has an irregularity: *digo, dices, dice, decimos, dicen,* (*decís*).

Paradigm Practice

Alternate the *nosotros* form with each of the other forms of the following verbs.

EXAMPLE: pedir
> **yo pido, nosotros pedimos, tú pides, nosotros pedimos, usted pide, nosotros pedimos, él pide, nosotros pedimos, ustedes piden, nosotros pedimos, ellos piden, nosotros pedimos.**

seguir[7]	repetir	servir
conseguir[7]	decir	despedir

Person–Number Substitution

If the cue is given in English, do not include the subject in your response.

1. Si le pido la receta...
    (we, they, she and I, I)

---

[7]Remember that the *u* is not pronounced in the combinations *gue* and *gui*; its function here is to indicate that *g* is *not* pronounced [h], as in *gente.*

2. Y Pepita sigue hablando.
   (Pepita y Margarita, usted también, tú y yo, los Gamboa[8], todo el mundo)
3. ¿Dónde consigue Jim tanto dinero?
   (tú, nosotros, mis amigos, el peón, "cómo se llama", yo)
4. Si mi mujer despide a la cocinera, no consigue otra.
   (tú, nosotros, yo, "cómo se llama", ustedes, mi tía)
5. Lo digo una vez nada más; no repito.
   (a man, we, women, you *pl*, I, Jim, they)
6. ¿Lucrecia sirve la comida?
   (sus padres, la hija del peón, nosotros, yo, usted)
7. ¿Por qué no vistes a Juanito?
   (we, she, they, I, he)

37. Some uses of reflexive pronouns

Reflexive Pronouns

Yo	**me**	veo.	*I see myself.*
Tú	**te**	vas.	*You are leaving.*
Usted			
El	**se**	viste.	*You (he, she) get(s) dressed.*
Ella			
Nosotros	**nos**	quedamos.	*We are staying.*
Ustedes			
Ellos	**se**	levantan.	*You (they) get up.*
Ellas			

Vosotros **os** bañáis.	*You are taking a bath.*

A. Reflexive pronouns in English are those which end in "-self" or "-selves": "myself," "himself," "ourselves," and so on. The Spanish reflexive pronouns are almost the same as the direct and indirect object pronouns. Only the third-person pronoun is different: **se** is the third person reflexive pronoun for singular and plural, masculine and feminine.
B. The position of the reflexive pronouns is the same as that of the direct and indirect object pronouns, *i.e.*, attached to the present participle and infinitive forms, or preceding the other verb forms you know.
C. Reflexive pronouns appear much more often in Spanish than in English. In general, Spanish uses reflexive pronouns wherever English does, but also in a number of situations where English does not.

1. Spanish and English are parallel.
   Me veo en la foto.   *I see myself in the photo.*
   ¿Por qué no **te** compras un para-   *Why don't you buy yourself an umbrella?*
   guas?

[8]The plural form of family names is rarely used in Spanish.

2. Spanish has a reflexive direct object, English has an expression with "get."

¿Por qué no **te** vistes? | *Why don't you get dressed?* Literally, *Why don't you dress yourself?*

No tienen que levantar**se**. | *You don't have to get up.* Literally, *You don't have to raise yourselves.*

María y Juan **se** divorcian. | *María and Juan are getting divorced (a divorce).* Literally, *María and Juan are divorcing themselves (each other).*

3. Spanish has a reflexive indirect object, English has a possessive adjective.

Se pone el abrigo. | *He's putting on his coat.* Literally, *He's putting the coat on himself.*

Se está lavando la cara. | *She's washing her face.* Literally, *She's washing herself the face.*

4. Spanish has a few verbs which *must* be used reflexively, although the English equivalents are not reflexive.

¿Por qué **te** quejas? | *Why are you complaining?*

¡**Se** está desmayando! | *She's fainting!*

5. Some verbs may be used nonreflexively with one meaning, and reflexively with another meaning; English uses entirely different verbs.

Vamos. | *We're going (somewhere).*

Nos vamos. | *We're leaving, getting out of here.*

Atlanta queda en Georgia. | *Atlanta is (located) in Georgia.*

Me quedo aquí. | *I'm staying (remaining) here.*

Despiden a la cocinera. | *They are firing the cook.*

Se despiden de sus amigos. | *They are saying good-bye to their friends.*

Person–Number Substitution

If the cue is in English, do not include the subject in your response.

1. Ahora sí nos vamos.
(I, they, we, you *fam*, he)
2. ¿Por qué? Ustedes no deben levantarse.
(las visitas, yo, usted y su mujer, nosotros, nadie)
3. Ustedes se quejan mucho.
(ella, tú, usted, las visitas, yo, alguien)
4. Se desmayó alguien.
(yo, tú y yo, mi novia, ellos)
5. Iba a bañarme.
(we, they, Pepita and Napoleón, he, you *fam*)
6. ¡Amadeo y su mujer se divorciaron!
(yo, Jim y Margarita, nosotros, el profesor)
7. Napoleón está poniéndose el abrigo[9].
(yo, tú, todo el mundo, nosotros, ellos)
8. Yo no sé si me voy o me quedo.
(nosotros, Napoleón y Pepita, tú, Pepita, tú y yo, usted, mi mujer, mis hijos)

[9]Like other single articles of clothing, *abrigo* is singular with both singular and plural subjects: each person puts on one coat.

Questions

1. ¿Dónde están Pepita y Napoleón?
2. ¿Quiere irse a su casa[10] Napoleón o quiere quedarse?
3. ¿Quiere usted irse a su casa o quiere quedarse aquí?
4. Y mañana, ¿no tiene usted que levantarse?
5. ¿Por qué dice Margarita que Napoleón y Pepita no tienen que levantarse mañana?
6. ¿Por qué tienen ellos que levantarse, entonces?
7. ¿A qué hora se casa la hija del peón?
8. Y hablando de bodas, ¿quiénes van a divorciarse?
9. ¿Cuándo van a casarse ustedes?
10. ¿Es usted muy celoso? ¿Se enoja mucho?
11. Y usted, señorita, ¿se levanta temprano todos los días?
12. ¿Y se baña con agua fría o con agua caliente?
13. Cuando usted se viste, ¿se pone primero el zapato derecho o el zapato izquierdo?
14. Señor, ¿usted se afeita primero y luego se peina o viceversa?
15. ¿Cómo se llama usted?

38. tener que + *infinitive*

Tenemos que vender la casa.   *We have to sell the house.*

This construction corresponds to English "must" or "have to" before an infinitive.

Written Translation

This is a combination exercise; use either *tener que* + infinitive or *acabar de* + infinitive as the individual sentence requires.

1. Lucrecia has to go to bed early.
2. They just got married.
3. I have to get dressed.
4. We just turned to the left.
5. Margarita just said that she has to leave.
6. They say that Amadeo and his wife just got divorced.
7. You don't have to stay.
8. His son just asked her for the raincoat.
9. Do I have to put on my hat?
10. Someone just fainted in the garden.

[10]*Irse a (su) casa:* to leave for (one's) home.

39. saber *vs.* conocer

---

1. **Conozco** un lugar muy bonito.   *I know a very pretty place.*
2. Quiero **conocer** a su prima.   *I want to meet your cousin.*
3. **¿Conoces** a Amadeo Gil?   *Do you know Amadeo Gil?*

4. Sí, **sé** que él y su mujer se divorcian.   *Yes, I know that he and his wife*
                                              are getting a divorce.
5. Emilio **sabe** quién es la maestra.   *Emilio knows who the teacher is.*
6. Luz María **sabe** hablar inglés.   *Luz María knows how to speak English.*

A. **Conocer** means "to know" in the sense of being or getting acquainted with something or someone. *Conocer* is used in Spanish where "meet" (a person for the first time) is used in English (example 2).
B. **Saber** means "to know" in the sense of having factual information or data that could be communicated to someone else (examples 4 and 5), or in the sense of possessing a skill—knowing how to do something (example 6). *Saber* is not normally followed by *cómo* before an infinitive.

Reading and Completion

Read the following paragraph, filling in the blanks with the correct form of either *saber* or *conocer*. Do not write the answers; force yourself to try to say the correct form as you read. Don't forget the definite article before titles or the personal *a*.

   Mañana vamos a ver la casa que vamos a comprar. Yo no _____ cuántos cuartos tiene, pero dice mi hermana que es muy grande. El dueño es un señor de apellido Caremango. Yo no _____ quién es él. Mi hermana _____. Ella _____ Sr. Caremango muy bien. Mi hermana _____ todo el mundo y _____ muchas cosas. Yo _____ que ella _____ mucho y que _____ mucha gente. Ella _____ Europa y los países de Africa y _____ los nombres de las capitales de todos esos países. Francamente, mi hermana es muy inteligente.

40. pedir *vs.* preguntar

Yo no le **pido** a usted favores.   *I'm not asking you for favors.*
Yo le **pregunto** su nombre, nada más.   *I'm asking you your name only.*

A. **Pedir** means "to ask (for)" in the sense of requesting or soliciting, and also ordering something in a restaurant. **Preguntar** means "to ask" in the sense of inquiring or seeking information.

B. "To ask for" is simply *pedir;* no preposition is used.

Reading and Completion

Read the following sentences, filling in the blanks with either *pides* or *preguntas,* whichever is appropriate. Do not write in the answers, but rather force yourself to try to say the correct form as you read.

1. ¿Por qué me ___ favores?
2. ¿Por qué me ___ mi nombre?
3. ¿Por qué me ___ qué día es hoy?
4. ¿Por qué me ___ el carro?
5. ¿Por qué me ___ cómo es el carro?
6. ¿Por qué me ___ la hora?
7. ¿Por qué me ___ el reloj?
8. ¿Por qué me ___ dinero?
9. ¿Por qué me ___ cómo estoy?
10. ¿Por qué me ___ ser tu amigo?

41. para *and* por

para		
for (destination)	Voy **para** Panamá.	*I'm headed for Panama.*
	El dinero es **para** Juan.	*The money is for Juan.*
for (deadline)	¿Qué tenemos que hacer **para** mañana?	*What do we have to do for tomorrow?*
by (deadline)	Tiene que estar aquí **para** el lunes.	*He has to be here by Monday.*
in order to	Venden su casa **para** comprar otra.	*They're selling their house (in order) to buy another one.*
	¿Para qué?	*What for? (In order to do what?)*
por		
for (duration)	Voy a estar en Panamá **por** tres semanas.	*I'm going to be in Panama for three weeks.*
for (exchange)	Le doy un dólar **por** el libro.	*I'll give you a dollar (in exchange) for the book.*
for (the sake of)	Lo hago **por** mi familia.	*I do it for (the sake of) my family.*
by (place)	Siempre paso **por** su casa.	*I always pass by your house.*
through	Vamos **por** la otra puerta.	*Let's go through the other door.*
along	¿Caminamos **por** el río?	*Shall we walk along the river?*
because	**Por** usted, voy a llegar tarde.	*Because of you, I'm going to be late.*
	Por comer tanto, tiene dolor de estómago.	*Because he ate (of eating) so much, he has a stomachache.*
	¿Por qué?	*Why? (Because of what?)*

A. The most common meanings of **para** and **por** are illustrated above. You will learn other meanings later. *Para* and *por* are tricky because both sometimes correspond to English "for." Although *por* looks and sounds a lot like "for," *para* is much more frequently the correct Spanish equivalent.

B. The meanings of **para** all have something in common, namely, the idea of *aim, goal, destination,* or *terminal point.* This provides a useful device for deciding whether to use *para* or *por* in many sentences. Consider, for example, "He gave me a radio for the car." If "for the car" means "to put in the car," then the car is the destination of the radio, and the Spanish would be *para el carro.* But if it means "in exchange for the car" (*i.e.,* "I gave him the car, and he gave me the radio in exchange"), then the Spanish would be *por el carro.*

C. In addition to the meanings given above, **por** occurs in a number of fixed expressions that must be learned one by one. The title of the dialog of this chapter provides an example: *por fin,* "finally," "at last."

Written Translation

1. Who is that for, for him or for me?
2. I work in order to have money.
3. How much do you want for your car?
4. Why do you want to work for nothing?
5. When do you leave for Caracas?
6. I am here on account of you.
7. And I'm going to tell you why and what for.
8. Who just passed by our room?

Reading and Completion

As you read, fill in the blanks with *por* or *para.* Do not write in the words, so that you can do the exercise more than once.

_____ ir de Nueva York a Lima en barco hay que pasar _____ el canal de Panamá. Nosotros salimos _____ Lima el domingo. ¡Qué fantástico! ¡Pensar que vamos a estar allá _____ las fiestas de Año Nuevo! Pobre Jorge, _____ no tener visa de residencia en los Estados Unidos no puede venir con nosotros. El siempre está diciendo que va a ir al Departamento de Inmigración y Naturalización _____ ver si puede cambiar su visa de turista _____ una de residencia. Pero nunca lo hace.

42. Unspecified subjects

The construction *se + third person verb form* is often used in sentences in which the speaker considers it unnecessary or irrelevant to state exactly the subject of the verb. The verb usually agrees in number with the object. The most common English equivalents are passive sentences with no actor or agent indicated (examples 1 and 4), or expressions with "one," "you," "they," "people," or "we" meaning "someone," "anybody," or "everyone" (examples 2, 3, 5, and 6). Notice examples 2 and 6, where the English object pronouns "it" and "them" have no Spanish equivalent.

Singular verb	
1. ¿Cómo **se escribe** "ventana"?	*How is "ventana" spelled?*
2. ¿Cómo **se hace?**	*How does one do it?*
3. **Se pone** un poco de cebolla...	*You put in a little bit of onion . . .*
Plural verb	
4. Aquí **se venden** sartenes grandes.	*We sell large frying pans here.*
5. **Se necesitan** dos tazas de agua.	*You need two cups of water.*
6. **Se comen** calientes.	*People eat them hot.*

Rejoinders

EXAMPLES: Usted tiene que decir "buenos días" en inglés.
¿Cómo se dice "buenos días"?
Esta noche voy a hacer paella.
¿Cómo se hace paella?

1. Quiero escribir un libro.
2. ¿Quiere usted ir al centro, por favor?
3. Ustedes no pronuncian bien en español la palabra "immediately."
4. ¡Mirando la televisión y hablando por teléfono! ¡Santa María! ¡Esa no es manera de estudiar para un examen, hijito!
5. Voy a poner la mesa.
6. Queremos llamar a México larga distancia.

Oral Translation

Use expressions with *se*.

1. How do they eat (the) paella, hot or cold?
2. And how do you make it?
3. You need many things.
4. First you put in a little onion and garlic.
5. Then you . . . you . . . how do you say "you add"?
6. *Se agrega.* Then you add pieces of chicken,[11] right?
7. Yes, but other things are added, too.
8. How long do you cook the whole thing?[12]
9. Five hours. Then you put the paella on the table.
10. I know. Then you eat it, you wash the dishes, and that's all.

[11] *Pedazos de pollo.*
[12] *Todo.*

43. Emphatic object pronouns

me . . . a mí		nos . . . a nosotros/-as	
te . . . a ti			
lo/le . . .	a usted	los/les . . .	a ustedes
	a él		a ellos
la/le . . .	a usted	las/les . . .	a ustedes
	a ella		a ellas

os . . . a vosotros/-as

Spanish direct and indirect object pronouns cannot be stressed. In order to emphasize or to clarify the reference of an object pronoun, the appropriate prepositional phrase (see chart) is added, either before or after the verb phrase. The unstressed object pronouns are not dropped when the prepositional phrases are added; but in phrases containing no verb, the prepositional phrase alone is used.

A mí no **me** mandan dinero, sólo **a ti te** mandan.
*They don't send **me** money; they only send it to **you**.*
El **nos** va a comprar la casa **a nosotros,** no **a ella.**
*He's going to buy the house for **us**, not for **her**.*

Questions

Use a complete sentence in your reply and stress the object by adding the appropriate prepositional phrase at the end.

EXAMPLES: ¿A quién llama usted, al hombre o a la mujer?
La llamo a ella.
¿A quién le presta Pepe el coche, a ella o a ellos?
Le presta el coche a ella.

1. Rodolfo no nos pregunta a nosotros si queremos ir al cine, ¿verdad?
2. ¿Usted me ve a mí o lo ve a él?
3. Usted me debe dinero a mí, ¿no es verdad?
4. ¿A quién le ponen ustedes más atención, a él o a mí?

Written Translation

EXAMPLES: I'm not calling *you*. I'm calling *her*.
No te estoy llamando a ti. La estoy llamando a ella.
or
No estoy llamándote a ti. Estoy llamándola a ella.
Will you lend me the car? To *you*? No, thanks.
¿Me prestas el carro? ¿A ti? No, gracias.

1. If they don't wait for *me,* why are they going to wait for *them?*
2. Who do you want, *him* or *her?*
3. You see *us* and you don't see *them?*
4. She's looking at *me,* not *you.*
5. I know *you,* but you don't know *me.*
6. Are they going to buy the house from *us* or from *them?*

LISTENING COMPREHENSION EXERCISE B

Reading

La madre de mi mujer

Soy uno de esos maridos quienes admiten que la suegra es o puede ser una señora agradable y útil—a veces—especialmente si sabe cocinar. Mi suegra no vive con nosotros pero tiene la simpática costumbre[13] de venir a pasar todos los fines de semana, desde[14] las cinco de la tarde del viernes hasta las once de la noche del domingo, con sus "hijitos"[15], como llama ella a Lupe, mi mujer, y a Roberto, que soy yo. Mi suegra se llama Pepita. Doña Pepita es una mujer muy buena. Vive sola porque su esposo, mi suegro don Napoleón, murió el año pasado. Por eso a ella le gusta mucho venir a pasar los fines de semana con nosotros, y a nosotros también nos gusta tenerla aquí. Claro, su presencia causa problemitas[15] aquí y problemitas allá, pero no son importantes. Por ejemplo, cuando abro[16] la puerta el viernes, entra hablando y cuando se va para su casa el domingo por la noche, todavía está hablando. Los viernes se acuesta muy tarde y nosotros tenemos que acompañarla. Los sábados se levanta a la hora exacta en que yo me levanto, y cuando yo voy a entrar al baño, encuentro siempre la puerta cerrada; doña Pepita "acaba de entrar un momentito." ¿Un momentito? Allí se queda ella dos o tres horas bañándose, lavándose los dientes, peinándose, arreglándose[17] la cara con todo cuidado[18] y mirándose en el espejo[19] por media hora más. Mi pobre Lupe no puede bañarse hasta el mediodía y yo nunca tengo la oportunidad ni[20] de afeitarme durante todo el fin de semana.

Pero no importa. Es precisamente durante estas visitas—sin embargo—cuando se revela que una madre política tan obstinada en pasar todos, pero absolutamente todos, los fines de semana con sus hijos, puede ser también alegría[21] y de gran utilidad para ellos. Porque el caso es que mi suegra sabe preparar platos deliciosos de cualquier tipo y estilo imaginable de comida.

---

[13] Custom.
[14] From.
[15] The suffix *-ito, -ita* adds the connotation of "little" to the noun to which it is attached.
[16] I open.

[17] Making up.
[18] Care.
[19] Mirror.
[20] *Here,* even.
[21] Joy.

Un plato que en mi opinión es especialmente suculento es el famoso arroz con pollo. ¡Arroz con pollo! ¿No es eso lo mismo que la muy popular "paella valenciana" y sus muchas variantes que encontramos en todos los libros de cocina del mundo y que cualquiera de nosotros debe saber preparar sin dificultad? Ah, pero no, no es lo mismo. Claro que los ingredientes principales son el arroz y el pollo, pero luego empieza lo verdaderamente artístico[22], lo genial. Todo el efecto depende de cuánto caldo[23], cuánta salsa de tomate, cuánto ajo y cebolla, cuánta sal[24], cuánta pimienta[25], etc., etc., se agrega al pollo. Además, el arroz con pollo se sirve con otros platos: ensalada, sopa, vino, postre y todo el resto del menú que varía mucho de país a país o de región a región. Finalmente, si se quiere—y mi suegra siempre quiere—se pueden incluir unos ingredientes misteriosos que nunca figuran en las recetas de los libros. Son ingredientes que sólo doña Pepita conoce. Y es eso lo que realmente me gusta, me encanta, de mi suegra. Además, cada vez que nos prepara el arroz con pollo, ella nos sorprende[26] con algo completamente inesperado, algo extra. Para este sábado dice ella que nos tiene una sorpresa muy grande. ¿Qué puede ser? Tengo una pequeña sospecha[27] de que es algo que se llama "seviche ecuatoriano"

[22] The truly artistic part.
[23] Broth.
[24] Salt.

[25] Pepper.
[26] Surprises.
[27] Suspicion.

porque Lupe dice que la oyó[28] hablando con una amiga sobre un plato del Ecuador. Quién sabe. Yo soy puertorriqueño y no conozco ese plato. Pero estoy muy ansioso de probarlo[29].

Algún[30] día me va a matar[31] doña Pepita con sus extravagantes recetas. Si así[32] ocurre, que en paz descanse yo[33]. Pero si no ocurre, estoy resignado a aguantar[34] a mi suegra por el resto de mi vida (fines de semana solamente), si nos promete seguir cocinando de manera tan creativa.

For Oral or Written Composition

si sabe cocinar
los fines de semana
hijitos
don Napoleón
problemitas
cuando se levanta
el caso es
suculento

los libros de cocina
lo verdaderamente artístico
me encanta
algo completamente inesperado
puertorriqueño
estoy muy ansioso
que en paz descanse yo

Recetas de cocina

Seviche ecuatoriano

Ingredientes:

medio kilo[35] de camarones[36]
un poquito de cebolla picada[37]
una taza de jugo de naranja[38]
media taza de jugo de limón[39]

un poquito de salsa de ají picante[40]
salsa de tomate (un cuarto de taza)
sal y pimienta

Cómo se prepara:

En agua hirviendo[41] se ponen los camarones por aproximadamente un minuto. Luego se sacan[42] y se ponen en otro recipiente[43] para servirse. Se agregan los otros ingredientes y eso es todo. El seviche se sirve frío con un poco de maní[44] tostado encima. Es un plato parecido al coctel de camarones americano, pero mejor.

---

[28] Heard.
[29] Try it.
[30] Some.
[31] Kill.
[32] This way.
[33] *Que ... yo:* May I rest in peace.
[34] Endure.
[35] Kilogram, equal to about 2.2 lbs.

[36] Shrimp.
[37] Chopped, diced.
[38] *Jugo de naranja:* orange juice.
[39] Lemon, lime.
[40] *Salsa ... picante:* hot pepper sauce.
[41] Boiling.
[42] *Sacar:* to take out.
[43] Dish.
[44] Peanuts.

SOPAS SOUPS	**ENTREMES** APPETIZERS
SOPA DE GARBANZOS Mexican Chick Pea Soup	*GUACAMOLE* Avocado Dip
SOPA DE FRIJOLES Mexican Black Bean Soup	*NACHOS* Tortillas with Melted Cheese, Hot Pepper

PLATILLOS COMBINACION
MEXICAN COMBINATION PLATTERS

CUERNAVACA - Enchilada, Taco, Tostada, Arroz y Frijoles
ACAPULCO - Enchilada, Taco, Tamal, Arroz y Frijoles
CHIHUAHUA - Stuffed Pepper, Taco, Enchilada, Carne Azada, Rice, Beans

POSTRES DESSERTS	**BEBIDAS** BEVERAGES	
FLAN Brandied Caramel Custard	*CAFE* Coffee	*TE* Tea
HELADO Ice Cream	*LECHE* Milk	*ESPRESSO* Espresso

Arroz con pollo centroamericano

Ingredientes:

medio kilo de arroz
un pollo
dos cucharadas[45] de salsa de
tomate

dos cucharadas de mantequilla
cebolla y ajo[46] picados
sal y pimienta

Cómo se prepara:

Primero se cocina el pollo con un poco de agua, sal, pimienta, ajo y cebolla. Luego se fríe todo en mantequilla. Después se agrega el caldo del pollo, el arroz y el resto de los ingredientes. Cuando el arroz ya está cocinado, se puede agregar, si se quiere, un poco más caldo. Se sirve con ensalada de lechuga[47] y tomate.

Huevos rancheros mexicanos

Ingredientes:

huevos
tortillas[48]
aceite[49]

sal
salsa picante (de chilitos[50] y cebollitas
picados y tomates molidos[51])

Cómo se prepara:

Se calienta una sartén con aceite. Se pone a freír[52] una tortilla. En otra sartén caliente con aceite se fríen los huevos. Se ponen los huevos sobre la tortilla y se agregan sal y salsa picante al gusto.

LISTENING COMPREHENSION EXERCISE C

[45]Tablespoonfuls.
[46]*Ajo* may also mean a single clove of garlic.
[47]Lettuce.
[48]*Tortillas* are thin pancakes made of cornmeal, very common in Mexico.

[49]Oil.
[50]Hot peppers.
[51]Ground.
[52]Fry.

Vocabulary

el **abrigo**   overcoat
  acostarse   to go to bed
  afeitarse   to shave
  agregar   to add
el **ajo**   garlic
el **almuerzo**   lunch
el **Año Nuevo**   New Year
  bañarse   to take a bath, bathe
el **barco**   boat
la **boda**   wedding
  calentar (ie)   to heat
  cambiar   to change
la **cartera**   wallet; purse; briefcase
  casarse   to get married
la **cebolla**   onion
el **cementerio**   cemetery
la **cena**   supper
  cocinar   to cook
  con mucho gusto   gladly
  conseguir (i)   to get, obtain
  ¡chao!   so long!
  debemos   we should
  delicioso, -a   delicious, delightful
la **derecha**   right
  derecho   straight ahead
el **desayuno**   breakfast
  desmayarse   to faint
  despedirse (i)   to say good-bye
la **distancia**   distance
  divorciarse   to get a divorce
  doblar   to turn
  enfermo, -a   sick
  enojarse   to get angry
la **esquina**   corner
  este...   uh . . .
el **guante**   glove
  hay que   it is necessary to, you have
    to
el **hospital**   hospital
el **impermeable**   raincoat
  inesperado   unexpected

la **inmigración**   immigration
  invitado, -a   invited
  irse   to leave, go away
la **izquierda**   left
  largo, -a   long
  lavarse   to get washed, wash
    oneself
  levantarse   to get up
la **manera**   way
la **naturalización**   naturalization
  necesitar   to need
  nunca   never
la **paella**   paella: a Spanish dish made
    with rice
el **paraguas**   umbrella
  pedir (i)   to ask for
  peinarse   to comb one's hair
el **peón**   day laborer
  peor   worse
  ponerse   to put on
  por aquí   this way, over here
  por fin   at last
  preocuparse   to worry
  pronunciar   to pronounce
  quejarse   to complain
la **receta**   recipe
  repetir (i)   to repeat
  rico, -a   delicious
  ¡Santa María!   Holy Mary!
la **sartén**   frying pan
  se   himself, herself, yourself, oneself,
    itself, yourselves, themselves
  seguir (i)   to continue, go on
  sentarse (ie)   to sit down
  servir (i)   to serve
  suculento   juicy, scrumptious
la **televisión**   television
el/la **turista**   tourist
  vestirse (i)   to get dressed
  viceversa   vice versa
la **visa de residencia**   resident visa

Cultural Listening Passage
for Chapter 8

How Lucky Are Those
Who Study Spanish!

(1) Among people who study or teach foreign languages, controversies sometimes arise over whether one language is more difficult (presents greater difficulty) to study (it) and learn (it) than another. This is something very relative, since it depends largely (in great part) on (what is) the native language of the student. For example, it is no doubt easier for an Argentinean to learn to speak Portuguese or Italian than it is for an American, since these are both Romance languages, like Spanish. On the other hand (for the other part), Germans can learn to speak English more easily than Frenchmen can, because English and German are languages that belong to the same Germanic family and have, therefore (by consequence), many linguistic features in common.

(2) As for English and Spanish, only in the aspect of (the) written language is there not the least doubt as to which of these two languages is easier: Spanish, naturally. But it's this and nothing else, really, that makes many people believe (have the opinion) that English is harder to learn than Spanish—which is an inaccurate (inexact) judgment, because we must not confuse the spoken language with the written language.

(3) In the basic conversation that follows, we can observe this erroneous concept in (through) the comments of Emilio and Luz María, who, as we remember, are students at the Cultural Center in Bogotá. Both complain that English is too difficult and envy the lucky ones who study Spanish. Emilio asks Luz María if she knows how to pronounce the word r-o-u-g-h. She's not sure. She thinks that it's "rof." But the dictionary doesn't say.

(4) So they decide to go to the bookstore to see if they can find a good grammar. There they see the book they're looking for and they point it out to the clerk. But this young man seems to be a little dumb and he touches all the books—the gray book, the yellow book, the blue one, the purple one, this one, that one, the one that's up high, the one that's down below—all except the red one, the one on (of) grammar.

(5) At last he finds it and shows it to Luz María and (to) Emilio. But he doesn't know how much it costs. He says that he's going to (go to) ask the price and that he'll be right back.

Grammar Points

First, the last group of verbs that are slightly irregular in the present tense; second, the sequence of direct and indirect object pronouns; third, the possessive adjectives; and fourth, nominalization.

Chapter 8

Basic Dialog

¡Qué suerte tienen los que estudian español!

E. *Emilio*   LM. *Luz María*   EM. *Empleado*

I

E.   ¿De quién es ese diccionario, tuyo? ¿Me lo prestas?

LM.   No es mío, pero te lo presto si me lo devuelves.

E.   Cómo no. ¡El inglés[1] es tan difícil.

LM.   Tienes razón. El español es mucho más fácil.

E.   ¿Tú recuerdas, Luz María, cómo se pronuncia esta palabra: erre-o-u-ge-hache?

LM.   "Rof", creo. No estoy segura. ¿No dice el diccionario?

E.   No. Vamos a la librería a ver si encontramos una buena gramática.

[1]The definite article usually precedes the name of a language, particularly when the language functions as the subject of a sentence. The names of all languages are masculine. Remember also that the names of languages and nationalities are not capitalized.

II

LM. Señor, ¿cuánto cuesta ese libro? No, el otro, más arriba.

EM. ¿Este?

E. El rojo, el que acaba de tocar. ¡Ese! ¿Es muy caro?

EM. Ah, el de gramática. No sé el precio. Voy a preguntar. Ya vuelvo.

How lucky are those who study Spanish!

E. *Emilio* LM. *Luz María* c. *Clerk*

I

E. Whose[2] dictionary is that—yours? Will you lend it to me?

LM. It's not mine, but I'll lend it to you if you return it to me.

E. Sure. English is so difficult.

LM. You're right. Spanish is much easier.

E. Do you remember, Luz María, how this word is pronounced: *r-o-u-g-h*?

LM. "Rof," I think. I'm not sure. Doesn't the dictionary say?

E. No. Let's go to the bookstore and see if we can find a good grammar.

II

LM. Sir, how much does that book cost? No, the other one, a little higher.

c. This one?

E. The red one, the one you just touched. That one! Is it very expensive?

c. Oh, the grammar.[3] I don't know the price. I'm going to ask. I'll be right back.

Spanish Spelling: IV

El alfabeto

a	a	f	efe	l	ele	p	pe	u	u
b	be	g	ge	ll	elle	q	cu	v	ve
c	ce	h	hache	m	eme	r	ere	w°	doble ve
ch	che	i	i	n	ene	rr	erre	x	equis
d	de	j	jota	ñ	eñe	s	ese	y	i griega
e	e	k°	ka	o	o	t	te	z	zeta

°These letters occur only in a few words that Spanish has borrowed from other languages.

[2]Of whom; Spanish has no one-word equivalent of
the interrogative "whose."
[3]The (book) of grammar.

The alphabet. By now you have heard or read the names of most of the letters. The complete alphabet is shown above.

Names of letters are used primarily in initials and abbreviations, and occasionally to clarify the spelling of a word—in which case only the letters in doubt are included (*b, v, c, s, z, s, h.*)

LISTENING COMPREHENSION EXERCISE A

Dialog Supplement

I

¿De quién es ese diccionario?

cuaderno	*notebook*
lápiz	*pencil*
papel	*(piece of) paper*
periódico	*newspaper*

¿De quién es esa revista?   *magazine*

pluma	*pen*
carta	*letter*

¿Me lo prestas?

regalas	*give (as a present)*
muestras*[4]*	*show*

Vamos a la librería.

biblioteca	*library*
tienda	*store*
oficina	*office*

¡Qué suerte tienen los que estudian español!

enseñan	*teach*
entienden*[5]*	*understand*

II

No, el otro, más arriba.

más abajo	*lower*

¿Es muy caro?

barato	*inexpensive, cheap*

El rojo

amarillo	*yellow*	café*[6]*	*brown*
blanco	*white*	anaranjado	*orange*
gris	*gray*	morado	*purple*
azul	*blue*		

---

[4] The infinitive is *mostrar.*
[5] The infinitive is *entender.*
[6] Some speakers say *de color café;* others use *marrón, pardo, castaño,* or *habano.* There is no one universally accepted term in Spanish for "brown."

Dialog and Supplement Check

Sentence Recall

Say the dialog phrase or sentence in which each of the following words or phrases occurs.

razón	precio	te lo presto
se pronuncia	libro	librería
difícil	arriba	
diccionario	tocar	

Item Substitution

Repeat each of the following sentences, substituting a related word or phrase for the part in italics. If books are closed, your instructor will repeat the item at the end of each sentence.

1. Vamos a *la tienda.*
2. El *azul,* señorita.
3. ¿Me lo *regalas?*
4. El *verde,* señorita.
5. No, el otro, *más abajo.*
6. ¡*Ese!*
7. ¿De quién es *esta pluma?*
8. Vamos a *la librería.*
9. ¡Qué suerte tienen los que *aprenden* español!
10. ¿Me lo *das?*
11. El *anaranjado,* señor.

Grammar

44. Stem-changing verbs: *o* ⟶ *ue*

mostr**ar**	volv**er**	mor**ir**
*mue*stro	*vuel*vo	*mue*ro
*mue*stras	*vuel*ves	*mue*res
*mue*stra	*vuel*ve	*mue*re
mos*tra*mos	vol*ve*mos	mo*ri*mos
*mue*stran	*vuel*ven	*mue*ren
mos*tráis*	vol*véis*	mo*rís*

A. There is a large group of verbs in which the vowel of the stem changes from *o* to *ue.* The diphthong *ue* occurs when the stress falls on the last vowel of the stem; otherwise the stem vowel is *o.* (In the chart, the stressed syllable is indicated by italics.) This group includes *-ar,* *-er,* and *-ir* verbs. This stem change cannot be predicted from the infinitive.
B. Some of the most common verbs with the *o* → *ue* alternation are listed below.

-ar		*-er*		*-ir*	
mostrar	*to show*	devolver	*to return, give back*	morir(se)	*to die*
costar	*to cost*	volver	*to return, go back*		
encontrar	*to find*	poder	*to be able*		
recordar	*to remember*				

Paradigm Practice

Do paradigm practice with each of the verbs listed above, alternating the *nosotros* form with the other forms.

EXAMPLE: **yo muestro, nosotros mostramos, tú muestras, nosotros mostramos, usted muestra, nosotros mostramos, él muestra,** etc.

Person–Number Substitution

If the cue is given in English, do not include the subject pronoun in your response.

1. Un momento, ya vuelvo.
    (we, they, I, she, she and he, you *fam*, he and I)
2. Emilio le devuelve el diccionario a Luz María.
    (nosotros, tú, él y Pedro, "cómo se llama", todos)
3. El empleado le muestra la gramática a Emilio.
    (yo, nosotros, los empleados, todo el mundo)
4. ¿A qué hora vuelven ustedes?
    (nosotros, la empleada, tú, Emilio y Luz María, usted y yo, los empleados)
5. Si no encuentro la revista, no puedo ir.
    (we, they, you *fam*, you *pl*, she)
6. No recuerdo cómo se pronuncia.
    (we, they, I, nobody, he and I)

Alternate Substitution

¿Cuánto cuesta ese libro rojo?

¿_____ libros _____?

¿_____ amarillo?

¿_____ cuestan _____?

¿_____ pluma _____?

¿_____ azul?

¿_____ lápiz _____?

¿_____ estos _____?

Havana, Cuba: Bookstore

Infinitive Drill

Give the infinitive for each of the verb forms listed below, attaching object pronouns whenever they are given.

EXAMPLE: nos vamos   lo sabes
          irnos   **saberlo**

voy	estamos	vuelvo	comiendo	me alegro
me voy	te despides	me da	haciendo	lo sé
es	se casa	sigo	somos	quiere
lo traigo	le pido	dicen	se divorcian	viene
muero	los devuelves	nos muestra	lo presto	te prometo
nevando	tengo	lo entiende	le gusta	se acuesta

45. Sequence of object pronouns

A. The most frequent combinations of object pronouns are those illustrated below. In these combinations the pronouns beginning with *l* are always second; that is, they directly precede the verb form.

B. *Le* and *les* are always replaced by *se* before another pronoun beginning with *l*.

Me lo da	(a mí).		*He gives it to me.*
Te lo da	(a ti).		*He gives it to you.*
Se lo da	(a usted, a ustedes).		*He gives it to* { *you.*
	(a él, a ella).		*him, her.*
	(a ellos, a ellas).		*them.*
Nos lo da	(a nosotros).		*He gives it to us.*

Os lo da	(a vosotros).	*He gives it to you.*

Le traigo el abrigo.	*I'll bring him his coat.*
Se lo traigo. (*Not* Le lo traigo.)	*I'll bring it to him.*
Les doy la receta.	*I'll give you the recipe.*
Se la doy. (*Not* Les la doy.)	*I'll give it to you.*

C. The prepositional phrases *a mí, a ti, a él*, etc., may be used for emphasis or clarity, the same as they are with single pronouns.

> Este libro, ¿se lo doy **a usted, a él** o **a ella?**   *Shall I give this book to you, to him, or to her?*

D. The position of a sequence of two object pronouns with respect to the verb is the same as that of a single pronoun. That is, sequences of pronouns precede conjugated verb forms (as in the examples in the chart and in paragraph B) or they may optionally be attached to infinitives and present participles (as in the following examples).

> ¿La casa? Quiero comprár**sela,** pero él no **me la** quiere vender.   *The house? I want to buy it from him, but he doesn't want to sell it to me.*

A sequence may *not* be split, with one pronoun going before the conjugated verb and the other after the infinitive or participle. In the present progressive construction, the object pronouns may either be attached to the present participle or come before the form of *estar.*

> ¿La casa? Están terminándo**mela.** ¿La casa? **Me la** están terminando.   *The house? They're finishing it for me.*

E. The position of stress does not shift in infinitives and participles when pronouns are attached. Thus written accents are required, as shown in the examples above, since each pronoun adds to the total number of syllables and relocates the position of stress relative to the end of the word.

Writing Exercise

Rewrite the following conversation between two sisters, filling in the blank spaces with the appropriate object pronouns.

EXAMPLE: ¿Y ese reloj? ¿Quién ____ ____ regaló?
              ¿Y ese reloj? ¿Quién te lo regaló?

ANA: ¿Cuándo ____ vas a devolver a don Pedro los libros que ____ prestó a ti hace ya casi un mes?

LUZ: Mañana. Yo ____ prometo a ti, y ____ ____ repito: mañana ____ devuelvo los libros a don Pedro. Mañana mismo ____ ____ devuelvo. ¿Estás contenta?

ANA: Mañana, mañana, mañana. ¡Siempre mañana! ¿Por qué no ____ ____ das a mí ahora mismo y yo ____ ____ doy a don Pedro? Esta noche voy a su casa.

LUZ: Está bien. Pero tienes que pedir____ perdón a don Pedro en mi nombre y explicar____ que yo ____ siento mucho pero que estaba enferma.

ANA: Eso es mentira. Y otra cosa: nunca más voy a prestar____ a ti mi ropa. Todas las cosas que ____ presto, o ____ ____ devuelves sucias o no ____ ____ devuelves o crees que son tuyas.

LUZ: Eso no es verdad. A propósito, ¿dónde está mi blusa blanca? ¿A quién ____ ____ diste?

ANA: Esa blusa estaba muy vieja. ____ ____ regalé a la criada.

LUZ: ¿Y quién, puedo preguntar____, mi linda hermana, ____ dio a ti permiso para hacer eso? ¡Mi blusa favorita! La blusa que ____ dio abuelita. Recuerdo que ____ ____ regaló para mi graduación. ¡Tú eres muy desconsiderada[7]! ¡Tienes que decir____ a Lucrecia que debe devolver____ inmediatamente!

Noun–Pronoun Substitution

EXAMPLE: El diccionario, ¿me lo prestas?
(la pluma)
La pluma, ¿me la prestas?

1. ¿El abrigo? Ya se lo traigo.
   (su ropa, los calcetines rojos, su sombrero gris, los pantalones anaranjados, la camisa morada, los zapatos blancos, la corbata amarilla, un doctor y un policía)
2. ¿El diccionario? Sí, te lo presto si me lo devuelves.
   (los zapatos, este sombrero, mis servilletas, el mantel blanco, estos cuchillos, las tazas, el carro, mis gafas)
3. Ese libro, señor, ¿puede mostrárnoslo?
   (esas cosas, la casa, el jardín, la piscina, los cuartos, el comedor, la cocina y la sala, los baños)

Reading and Retention

Read the following paragraph enough times for you to retain the details of the situation it describes. Then answer the questions that follow.

Juanito siempre les presta sus cosas a sus amigos y muchas veces ellos no se las devuelven. Y cuando él les pide algo a ellos, ellos no le dan nada. Ahora acaba de prestarle su pluma a Pedro, su diccionario a María, y en este momento Pirimpimpín le está pidiendo[8] el reloj. Estoy seguro de que Juanito también va a prestárselo y Pirimpimpín no va a devolvérselo. ¡Pobre Juanito!

Questions. Answer with complete sentences each time.

[7] Thoughtless, inconsiderate.
[8] In *-ir* verbs like *pedir* (see page 145), *i* occurs in the stem of the present participle. This is discussed further in Chapter 12.

EXAMPLES: ¿Qué les presta Juanito a sus amigos?
Les presta todas sus cosas.
¿Y sus amigos le devuelven las cosas siempre?
No, muchas veces no se las devuelven.

1. ¿Qué le dan ellos a Juanito cuando él les pide algo?
2. ¿Qué acaba de prestarle Juanito a Pedro?
3. ¿A quién acaba de prestarle Juanito su pluma?
4. ¿Qué acaba de prestarle a María?
5. ¿A quién acaba de prestarle el diccionario?
6. ¿Qué le está pidiendo Pirimpimpín a Juanito en este momento?
7. ¿A quién le está pidiendo Pirimpimpín el reloj?
8. ¿Cree usted que Juanito va a prestarle el reloj a Pirimpimpín?
9. ¿Y cree usted que Pirimpimpín va a devolverle el reloj?
10. ¿Qué le presta Juanito a usted?[9]
11. ¿Qué les presta Juanito a ustedes?
12. ¿A quién va a prestarle Juanito su reloj?
13. ¿Pirimpimpín acaba de pedirle, va a pedirle o está pidiéndole el reloj a Juanito en este momento?
14. Si Juanito le presta algo a usted, ¿usted se lo devuelve?
15. Y si yo le presto a usted dinero, ¿me lo devuelve usted después?
16. Y si yo le pido a usted cinco dólares, ¿me los presta usted?
17. Y si le pido a usted un favor, ¿me lo hace?
18. En el diálogo de esta lección, ¿qué le pide Emilio a Luz María?
19. ¿Y Luz María le presta el diccionario?
20. ¿Va a devolverle el diccionario Emilio a Luz María?

Written Translation: Capsule Review

Many previously discussed grammar points are reviewed in the following exercise. If you are in doubt about how to translate a phrase, do not guess, but consult the appropriate grammar section.

A. What's that (that)[10] you have in your hands?
B. It's a picture (*una foto*) of the house that I'm going to give (as a gift) Luisita.
A. When is your daughter getting married?
B. In November, I believe, but I don't remember the exact date. The seventeenth, perhaps.
A. It's a very nice house. Whose is it?
B. Do you know Dr. Campos? He's the owner. If he sells it to me cheap, I'll buy it from him tomorrow.
A. The house looks very nice. Before buying it, however, why don't you go see others?

[9] In Spanish the double negative is the correct form. Thus you must say in Spanish, "Juanito doesn't lend me nothing."
[10] *Que* is never omitted in Spanish.

B. What for? After seeing two or three already, I'm sure that we're not going to find a better one (one better).

A. What are you doing now? Do you want to go with me to see the house that my uncle just bought?

B. No, thanks, I don't have time now. I have to do my work for tomorrow.

46. Possessive Adjectives

Before a noun		*After a noun*
mi tío	*my uncle*	el tío **mío**
tu tío	*your uncle*	el tío **tuyo**
su tío	*his, her, your, their uncle*	el tío **suyo**
nuestro tío	*our uncle*	el tío **nuestro**

vuestro tío	*your uncle*	el tío **vuestro**

A. There are essentially two ways of expressing possession in Spanish: with a possessive adjective, as shown in the chart, and with *de*.

> Es la hija **del** dueño.   *She's the owner's daughter.*
> El libro es **de** Marta.   *The book is Marta's.*

B. *Mi, tu,* and *su* show inflection for number only.

SINGULAR   PLURAL

$$\text{mi} \begin{cases} \text{tío} \\ \text{tía} \end{cases} \qquad \text{mis} \begin{cases} \text{tíos} \\ \text{tías} \end{cases}$$

C. *Nuestro, vuestro, mío, tuyo,* and *suyo* show inflection for both number and gender.

SINGULAR	PLURAL
nuest**ro** tí**o**	nuest**ros** tí**os**
nuest**ra** tí**a**	nuest**ras** tí**as**
el tí**o** tuy**o**	los tí**os** tuy**os**
la tí**a** tuy**a**	las tí**as** tuy**as**

D. The biggest problem the possessive adjectives present to English-speaking students is that they agree in number and gender with the *thing possessed*, not with the possessor. Study the following examples carefully.

ONE THING POSSESSED
Esa es **su** casa.
That's his (her, your, their) house.

MORE THAN ONE THING POSSESSED
Esas son **sus** casas.
Those are his (her, your, their) houses.

E. The phrases *su casa* and *la casa suya* may mean *la casa de él, de ellos, de ella, de ellas, de usted,* or *de ustedes.* When the intended meaning of *su* or *suyo* is not clear from the context, or when the speaker wishes to emphasize one possessor rather than another, the appropriate phrase with *de* is used. *Suyo* is more common when the possessor is *usted;* and *de él, de ella,* etc., more common in the other cases.

Item Substitution

Remember that the possessive adjective agrees with the noun possessed, not with the possessor.

EXAMPLE: ¿De quién es este diccionario, tuyo o de ella?
        (cosas)
     ¿De quién son estas cosas, tuyas o de ella?

1. Ese tenedor no es suyo, es mío.
    (plato, cuchara, servilletas, manteles, gafas, taza, huevos, ensalada, pan)
2. Esta casa no es de nosotros, es de mi tío.
    (cuarto, piscina, jardines, árboles, hotel, cosas)
3. No sé si la librería es de él, de ella o de los dos.
    (hoteles, dinero, coche, hijos, casa)

Questions

Answer with a possessive adjective or phrase and point with your finger as you respond.

EXAMPLE: ¿De quién son esos zapatos?
     Míos (or **suyos, de él, de María,** etc.).

1. ¿De quién son estas cosas?
2. ¿De quién es este reloj?
3. ¿De quién es esa revista?
4. ¿De quién son esas gafas?
5. ¿De quién son estos zapatos?
6. ¿Y esta cabeza?
7. ¿Y esos ojos?
8. ¿Y estas manos?
9. ¿Y esta clase?
10. ¿Y estas orejas?

47. Nominalization

1. El libro azul y **el** (libro) **rojo**	*The blue book and the red one*
2. Las camisas mías y **las** (camisas) **suyas**	*My shirts and yours*
3. El libro de recetas y **el** (libro) **de gramática**	*The recipe book and the one on (of) grammar*
4. El libro que está allí y **el** (libro) **que acaba de tocar**	*The book that's over there and the one you just touched*
5. Un lápiz anaranjado y **uno** (lápiz) **negro**	*An orange pencil and a black one*
6. Esta (chica) y **ésa** (chica)	*This one and that one*
7. Este (muchacho) y **otro** (muchacho)	*This one and another one*

A. English frequently uses the word "one" or expressions such as "that which" and "those of" in order to avoid repetition of a noun. Spanish, on the other hand, simply omits the repeated noun under certain conditions. The noun modifiers minus the omitted noun function just like the original noun phrase, and are thus said to be "nominalized."

B. Repeated nouns preceded by a definite article may be omitted *only* if followed by a simple adjective (examples 1 and 2), an adjective phrase beginning with *de* (example 3), or an adjective clause beginning with *que* (example 4).

C. Repeated nouns may also be omitted—regardless of what modifiers may follow—if they are preceded by an indefinite article (example 5), a demonstrative adjective (examples 6 and 7), or *otro* (example 7).

D. Only two changes occur in nominalized noun phrases: *un* becomes *uno* (example 5), and nominalized demonstratives have a written accent on the stressed syllable (example 6). "Another (one)" is simply *otro*, not *un otro* or *uno otro* (example 7).

Reading Exercise

Read the following conversations, using nominalizations where appropriate to make the language more natural. In answering the questions, use nominalizations to avoid unnecessary repetitions.

I

A. ¿Cuál casa prefiere usted, la casa del Dr. Colón, la casa de la familia Vega o la casa del jardín grande?

B. No recuerdo cuál es la casa del Dr. Colón y cuál es la casa de la familia Vega.

A. La casa de los Vega es la casa que tiene el techo rojo.

B. Ah, claro. Esa casa es la casa que me gusta más. Es la casa que cuesta más, pero es la casa más bonita.

1. ¿Cuáles son las tres casas que el Sr. A menciona?
2. ¿Recuerda el Sr. B cuál es la del Dr. Colón y cuál es la de la familia Vega?
3. ¿De quién es la que tiene un techo rojo?
4. ¿Cuál le gusta más al Sr. B?
5. ¿Es la de los Vega más cara o más barata que la que tiene un jardín grande?

II

C. ¡Qué confusión de libros! ¿Cuáles libros son los libros míos y cuáles libros son los libros tuyos?

CH. Los libros míos son un libro verde, un libro gris y otro libro, no recuerdo el color.

C. ¿Y adónde vas con esa corbata, hombre? ¡Esa corbata es la corbata que acabo de comprar!

CH. ¡Esta corbata no es tuya! La corbata tuya es morada; esta corbata es azul.

1. ¿Cuáles son los libros del Sr. Ch?
2. ¿Y es la corbata que tiene el Sr. Ch la que el Sr. C acaba de comprar?

  3. ¿De qué color es esa corbata?
  4. Y la del Sr. C, ¿de qué color es?
  5. ¿Y de qué color es la corbata de usted? ¿Y la mía?

Questions

  1. ¿De quién es el diccionario, de Luz María?
  2. ¿Le presta ella el diccionario a Emilio?
  3. ¿El va a devolvérselo o no?
  4. ¿Qué dice Emilio respecto al idioma inglés?
  5. Y según Luz María, ¿tiene Emilio razón o no?
  6. ¿Por qué dice ella que tienen suerte los que estudian español?
  7. ¿Cuál es uno de los muchos problemas que tienen los que estudian inglés, según Luz María?
  8. ¿Cómo se pronuncia la palabra inglesa "hache-o-te", "jot" o "jat"?
  9. ¿Cómo son los verbos en español, fáciles o difíciles de aprender? ¿Por qué?
  10. ¿Cómo se escribe la palabra *gente*, con *ge* o con *jota*? ¿Y la palabra *ahora*?
  11. ¿Adónde van Luz María y Emilio después?
  12. ¿Qué buscan ellos allí?
  13. ¿Cuál libro quieren ellos, el amarillo?
  14. ¿Quieren el que está más arriba o el que está más abajo?
  15. ¿El de filosofía?
  16. ¿El que el empleado acaba de tocar?
  17. ¿Sabe el empleado cuánto cuesta el libro?
  18. ¿Qué va a hacer él?

LISTENING COMPREHENSION EXERCISE B

Reading

Nociones lingüísticas[11]

Nadie sabe cuántos exactamente son los idiomas que existen en el mundo, pero se calcula que el total varía entre tres mil y cinco mil. La mayor parte de ellos, sin embargo, son los lenguajes de pequeñas sociedades que se encuentran todavía en un estado primitivo de desarrollo[12], y hay como consecuencia muchas lenguas sobre las cuales sabemos muy poco. Estas lenguas "desconocidas" representan el habla de muchas tribus americanas, de muchos negros africanos,

[11] In the sequences *güe* and *güi*, the dieresis (two dots) indicates that the *u* is pronounced. Thus, *lingüístico* is *lin*[gwí]*stico*, and *vergüenza*, "shame," is *ver*[gwe]*nza*.
[12] Development.

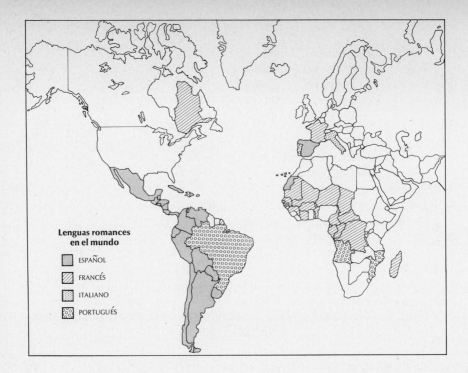

Lenguas romances en el mundo

- ESPAÑOL
- FRANCÉS
- ITALIANO
- PORTUGUÉS

de muchos nativos de Australia. Nueva Zelanda, Indonesia y China y de otros pueblos asiáticos, cuya[13] población total puede alcanzar[14] a las dos terceras partes de los casi cuatro mil millones de personas que habitan nuestro planeta.

Las lenguas de Europa, del Mediterráneo y del Cercano Oriente, geográficamente más accesibles al análisis lingüístico, han sido clasificadas y agrupadas en "familias" de acuerdo con ciertas características similares que revelan un antepasado común.

La más grande y la más importante de estas familias es la indoeuropea, así llamada porque cubre casi toda Europa y se extiende hasta el norte de la India. Dentro de este grupo hay otras subdivisiones lingüísticas llamadas también familias. Estas ramificaciones del antepasado indoeuropeo tienen su origen en los movimientos migratorios de esta gente hacia diferentes rumbos[15], iniciados aproximadamente tres mil años antes de Jesucristo. Así, algunos grupos se dirigen hacia la India, y surge[16] allí a través del tiempo el idioma sánscrito. Otros van hacia Persia, donde la lengua original de esa región se convierte en el persa antiguo. Otros llegan a la península de Grecia, y nacen con el tiempo los primeros dialectos del griego antiguo. Otros a la península italiana, y surgen las lenguas itálicas, siendo el latín una de ellas. Y otros van a las regiones escandinavas y a la Europa Occidental, originándose entonces las lenguas de la familia germánica, de la cual desciende el inglés.

[13]Whose.
[14]Reach.

[15]Directions.
[16]*Surgir:* to arise.

Con la expansión del imperio romano a través de Europa, el latín sufre poco a poco cambios en las diferentes regiones, y se origina de esta manera otro subgrupo de idiomas llamados lenguas romances, las principales de las cuales son el español, el francés, el italiano, el portugués y el rumano.

Es obvio entonces que aunque[17] el inglés y el español tienen el mismo antepasado, existe entre ellos una relación menor que entre dos lenguas romances. Sin embargo, a causa de la invasión de Inglaterra por los normandos en el año 1066, la lengua inglesa contiene gran cantidad de vocabulario y de formas gramaticales franceses y latinos, siendo por consiguiente, de la familia germánica, la más cercana al español o a cualquier otra lengua romance.

[17]Although.

For Oral or Written Composition

número de idiomas que existen en el mundo
población total
antepasado común
familia indoeuropea
origen de la familia germánica
lenguas romances
por qué es más cercano al español, entre las lenguas germánicas, el inglés

LISTENING COMPREHENSION EXERCISE C

Vocabulary

abajo below
amarillo, -a yellow
anaranjado, -a orange
arriba above
azul blue
barato, -a cheap, inexpensive
la **biblioteca** library
blanco, -a white
café brown
caro, -a expensive
la **carta** letter
claro of course

el **color** color
la **condición** condition
la **confusión** confusion
costar (ue) to cost
el **cuaderno** notebook
devolver (ue) to return (something)
el **diccionario** dictionary
el **dólar** dollar
encontrar (ue) to find
enseñar to teach
entender (ie) to understand
la **gramática** grammar; grammar book

gris gray
el **hotel** hotel
el **lápiz** pencil
la **librería** bookstore
más abajo farther down
más arriba farther up
mencionar to mention
morado, -a purple
morir (ue) to die
mostrar (ue) to show
la **oficina** office
el **papel** paper
el **periódico** newspaper
la **pluma** pen

poder (ue) to be able
el **precio** price
recordar (ue) to remember
regalar to give as a gift
respecto a with respect to
la **revista** magazine
la **suerte** luck
seguro, -a sure
tener razón to be right
la **tienda** store
tocar to touch
el **verbo** verb
volver (ue) to return

Cultural Listening Passage
for Chapter 9

Militarism in Latin America

(1) There exists a curious parallel between the epoch that followed the wars of independence in Latin America and the decades that came after the Second World War. In both instances we note the tendency toward military dictatorship, which consequently brought about (produced) suppression of political parties and individual freedom of expression.

(2) At the present time a large part of the inhabitants of the Southern Hemisphere have lost the right to live as free citizens. There exists today, as it has always existed, the case of the legally elected government that has been overthrown by a military junta—a term sadly famous throughout the entire world because of its frequent occurrence (appearance) in Latin America.

(3) What are the causes of this repeated intervention on the part of the military forces in the political field? No doubt there are a number of factors that have contributed to the phenomenon of the *caudillo* [military strong-man] and the military coup d'état. (4) For example, in countries like Paraguay, Ecuador, or Haiti there still exists a great gap between the rich and the poor classes, and there is no middle class capable of offering social and political stability. (5) In other nations, like Argentina with its strong (developed) middle class, and Peru with its large Indian population, there emerged suddenly—and dangerously for the rich classes—the vote of the masses. This brought about fear and distrust on the part of the oligarchy and consequently the use of armed forces again and again.

(6) Lack of civic responsibility on the part of the ruling class, lack of educational and economic opportunities for the people (mass), and the consequent difficulty in bringing about social mobility, continuously create demands that

alarm those in charge of the established order. Hence constant military intervention and the enormous expense for weapons and maintenance.

Coup d'état in Andivia

(7) In the republic of Andivia—a ficticious name—there has just been a coup d'état, and the country is (finds itself) now under the command of a military junta.

(8) Sitting on a bench in Central Park in Miraflores, a small town in a province of Andivia, we find three respectable men of that community. They are don* Alfredo, don Luis, and *Licenciado** Vargas. They have just heard the news on the radio and are commenting on the matter without showing (giving signs of) much alarm, an indication that this is not the first time a military junta has seized power in Andivia. (9) As we can see by the conversation among the three gentlemen, all kinds of rumors are circulating. Some say that the president was killed; others say that the president took refuge in a foreign embassy; others, that they put him on a plane and sent him into exile. In short, nobody knows for sure.

(10) A while ago General Méndez, head of the junta, spoke on the radio. The general addressed (directed himself to) the nation to explain the reasons that obligated the armed forces to take charge—temporarily, according to him—of the government (power). Repeating the well-known and already worn-out words of other military men in Latin America, he said that the coup d'état was necessary "in order to save the fatherland from communism."

(11) This reasoning sounded (seemed) amusing to don Luis and his friends, because the reasons that really provoked the fall of the government legally elected by the people of Andivia were others: The president, with the support of his cabinet, attempted (wanted) to impose (establish) a small additional tax on the rich class. At the same time he proposed to Congress a reduction in the enormous budget of the armed forces. The reaction of the military was immediate.

Grammar Points

First, a group of verbs which are irregular in the preterit; second, certain negative and affirmative words; third, shortening of some adjectives; and fourth, position of the subject in statements and questions.

*See Cultural Notes.

Chapter **9**

Basic Dialog

Golpe de estado en Andivia

DON A. *Don Alfredo*   LIC. V. *Licenciado Vargas*   DON L. *Don Luis*

I

DON A.   ¿Supieron la noticia? ¡Cayó el gobierno!
LIC. V.   Sí, la oímos por radio. ¡Qué barbaridad!
DON L.   Se dice que mataron al presidente. ¿Es cierto?
DON A.   Nadie sabe. Algunos dicen que se refugió en una embajada.
LIC. V.   A mí me contó alguien que lo pusieron en un avión y lo mandaron al exilio.
DON L.   ¡Qué gran tragedia! ¡Otra junta militar!

II

DON A.   Hace un rato habló el general Méndez, jefe de la junta.
LIC. V.   ¿De veras? ¿Qué dijo?
DON A.   Dijo que el golpe de estado fue necesario para salvar a la patria del comunismo.
DON L.   ¡Qué divertido! Ustedes saben cuál fue el verdadero motivo.
LIC. V.   Claro, el nuevo impuesto a los ricos.
DON L.   Y la rebaja en el presupuesto de defensa. El gobierno no cayó; simplemente se suicidó.

Coup d'état in Andivia

DON A. *Don Alfredo*   LIC. V. *Licenciado Vargas*   DON L. *Don Luis*

I

DON A.   Did you hear[1] the news? The government fell!
LIC. V.   Yes, we heard it on the radio. Terrible!
DON L.   They say the president was killed. Is it true?
DON A.   Nobody knows. Some people say he took refuge in an embassy.
LIC. V.   Somebody told me that they put him on a plane and sent him into exile.
DON L.   That's a great tragedy! Another military junta!

II

DON A.   General Méndez, the head of the junta, spoke a while ago.
LIC. V.   Really? What did he say?
DON A.   He said that the coup d'état was necessary in order to save the country from communism.
DON L.   What a joke! You know what the real reason was.
LIC. V.   Sure, the new tax on the wealthy.
DON L.   And the reduction in the defense budget. The government didn't fall; it simply committed suicide.

Cultural Notes

A. The diverse conditions in the twenty countries constituting Latin America make it difficult to present a general and yet accurate political picture of the whole region. The concentration and nature of political power are apt to change in these dynamic societies, which are developing at different speeds, and any overall appraisal of Latin American politics must vary from year to year. In recent times, military intervention in Latin American governments has been very frequent; yet there is a real need to differentiate among these military regimes. In some countries the governments have been taken over by traditional rightist and pro-upper-class generals or juntas.

[1] Find out.

Such was the case in Chile in 1973. In Peru, however, the military leaders who overthrew the president in 1968 decreed the expropriation of foreign corporations and large landholdings in an attempt to bring about social justice and land reform that would benefit millions of underprivileged citizens.

B. *Don* is a title used with male first names; it is equivalent to *señor* used with last names. Thus, José Mata may be addressed as either *don José* or *Sr. Mata*. The feminine counterpart of *don* is *doña*.

C. *Licenciado* (abbreviated *Lic.*) is the title conferred on graduates of a law school in several countries. Titles such as *licenciado* and *ingeniero* (abbreviated *Ing.*) carry considerable prestige and are commonly used with last names, just like "doctor" and "professor."

The Sounds of Spanish: VIII

Regional differences in pronunciation. You are of course aware that English is not pronounced exactly the same throughout the English-speaking world. The same is true of Spanish. In neither case, however, are regional differences in pronunciation any great barrier to communication. The Spanish described in this book is typical of the great majority of Spanish speakers, and would be accepted and understood anywhere. It would be very time-consuming—and not very useful—to list here a large number of minute and inconsequential regional variations in Spanish pronunciation. Instead, we shall give only the three most striking differences.

A. In southern Spain and all of Spanish America, the letter *z* in any position and the letter *c* before *e* or *i* are pronounced [s], as in English "say." In northern and central Spain only, *z* in any position and *c* before *e* or *i* are pronounced like *th* in English "think." Thus, most speakers pronounce *casa* and *caza* alike: [kasa]; but in northern and central Spain *casa* is [kasa] while *caza* is [katha]. This pronunciation is a characteristic of what is known as Castilian Spanish.

B. In parts of Spain and most of Spanish America, the letter *ll* is pronounced [y], as in English "yes." In other parts of Spain and isolated pockets of Spanish America, *ll* is pronounced similar to *lli* in English "million." Thus, most speakers pronounce *cayo* and *callo* alike: [kayo]; but for a minority of speakers *cayo* is [kayo] while *callo* is roughly [kalʸo].

C. In several areas, notably around the Caribbean, *s* before a consonant or at the end of a word is reduced to an aspiration—like English *h*—in normal unguarded speech. Thus, in these areas *gasta* may be heard as [gaʰta] and *las casas* as [laʰ kasaʰ].

LISTENING COMPREHENSION EXERCISE A

Dialog Supplement

I

¡Cayó el gobierno!		**Se refugió en una embajada.**	
Perdió[2]	*lost*	Se metió[3]	*got inside*
La oímos por radio.		**Se refugió en una embajada.**	
escuchamos	*listened*	una iglesia	*a church*
		un edificio	*a building*
Mataron al presidente.		**Lo pusieron en un avión.**	
Derrocaron	*overthrew*	barco	*ship*
¡Otra junta militar!			
dictadura	*dictatorship*		

II

El general Méndez		**¿De veras? ¿Qué dijo**		
almirante	*admiral*	trajo[4]	*brought*	
coronel	*colonel*	hizo[5]	*did*	
mayor	*major*	propuso[6]	*proposed*	
capitán	*captain*			
teniente	*lieutenant*	**Y la rebaja en el presupuesto**		
sargento	*sergeant*	el aumento	*the increase*	

Jefe de la junta			
de la Marina	*of the Navy*	**se suicidó**	
del Ejército	*of the Army*	se volvió loco	*went crazy*
de las Fuerzas Aéreas	*of the Air Force*		
de la Infantería de la Marina	*of the Marines*		

Dialog and Supplement Check

Sentence Recall

Say the dialog phrase or sentence in which each of the following words or phrases occurs.

barbaridad	rebaja	se suicidó
gobierno	embajada	cierto
presidente	avión	mataron
general Méndez	impuesto	noticia
patria	supieron	exilio

[2]The infinitive is *perder*.
[3]The infinitive is *meterse*.
[4]The infinitive is *traer*.
[5]The infinitive is *hacer*.
[6]The infinitive is *proponer*.

Santiago, Chile:
September 11, 1973

Item Substitution

Listen to and repeat each of the following sentences, substituting a related word or phrase for the part in italics. If books are closed, your instructor will repeat the item at the end of each sentence.

1. Hace un rato habló el *sargento* Méndez.
2. *Cayó* el gobierno.
3. ¿De veras? ¿Qué *propuso?*
4. Y la *rebaja* en el presupuesto.
5. ¡Qué *terrible!*
6. Se refugió en una *iglesia.*
7. El general Méndez, Jefe del *Ejército.*
8. ¡Otra *junta* militar!

Questions

1. ¿Es Andivia una nación verdadera o imaginaria?
2. ¿Qué pasó allí recientemente?
3. ¿Cómo cayó el gobierno?
4. ¿Son los golpes de estado raros o frecuentes en América Latina?
5. ¿Quién derrocó al gobierno de Andivia?
6. ¿Qué le pasó al presidente, lo mataron?

7. ¿Dónde se refugió él, según unas personas?
8. Y según otros rumores, ¿adónde mandaron los militares al presidente?
9. ¿Cómo lo mandaron al exilio, lo pusieron en un barco?
10. ¿Quiénes son los tres señores que estaban comentando este golpe de estado en Andivia?
11. ¿Piensan ellos que esto es una cosa buena para su patria?
12. ¿Quién es el jefe de la junta militar?
13. ¿Cuándo habló por radio?
14. ¿Para qué habló por radio?
15. ¿Cuál fue el motivo del golpe de estado, según el general Méndez?
16. ¿Cuál fue la verdadera razón, según el Lic. Vargas?
17. ¿Y cuál otra, según don Luis?
18. ¿Cómo es el gobierno de los Estados Unidos, una dictadura o una democracia?
19. ¿Cuáles son otros países democráticos del mundo?
20. ¿En cuáles países de América Latina hay gobiernos militares o dictaduras en estos momentos?

Grammar

48. Irregular preterit forms

The preterit forms shown below have irregularities in both stem and endings. The stems must simply be memorized, but the observations that follow the charts may be helpful.

andar	an**duv-**	
estar	es**tuv-**	
poner	**pus-**	
saber	**sup-**	
poder	**pud-**	-e, -iste, -o, -imos, -ieron, (-isteis)
tener	**tuv-**	
querer	**quis-**	
hacer	**hic-**	
venir	**vin-**	

A. The endings of this first group are those of regular *-er* and *-ir* verbs, except that the first person singular ending is unstressed *-e* (*anduve, tuve*) rather than stressed *-í* (*comí, viví*); and the third person singular ending is unstressed *-o* (*anduvo, tuvo*) rather than stressed *-ió* (*comió, vivió*).

B. The preterit forms of **hacer** are *hice, hiciste, hizo, hicimos, hicieron, (hicisteis). Hizo* is spelled with a *z* because a *c* would incorrectly indicate [íko].

traer	tra**j**-	⎫
decir	di**j**-	⎭

traer traj- ⎫
decir dij- ⎭ -e, -iste, -o, -imos, -eron, (-isteis)

C. The preterit stems of the second group end in *j*. The endings have one peculiarity in addition to those of the first group: the third person plural ending is *-eron* (*trajeron, dijeron*) rather than *-ieron* (*comieron, tuvieron*).

ser ⎫
ir ⎬ fui, fuiste, fue, fuimos, fueron, (fuisteis)

D. **Ser** and **ir,** the third group, have identical preterit forms with the stem *fu-;* their endings are slightly different from those of the other groups.

E. Many of the verbs listed in the charts have derivatives formed by the addition of a prefix. Derivatives almost always have the same irregularities as the corresponding simple verbs. For example, *componer* (to compose; to fix) has the same endings as *poner: compuse, compusiste,* etc. Listed below are some common derivatives of the irregular verbs shown in the charts.

poner (*puse*)
componer *to compose; to fix*
descomponer *to decompose; to break down*
proponer *to propose*
reponer *to replace*
posponer *to postpone*
oponerse *to oppose*
imponer *to impose*

traer (*traje*)
atraer *to attract*
contraer *to contract; to shrink*

decir (*dije*)
bendecir *to bless*
maldecir *to curse*
contradecir *to contradict*

tener (*tuve*)
contener *to contain*
retener *to retain*
entretener *to entertain*
obtener *to obtain*
mantener *to maintain*
detener *to detain, stop;* refl., *to come to a stop*

venir (*vine*)
convenir *to be suitable*
provenir de *to originate from*
prevenir *to prevent; to warn*
intervenir *to intervene*

hacer (*hice*)
deshacer *to tear down; to break up*

Paradigm Practice

You need not memorize all the compound verbs given above. You should, however, include some of them in your paradigm practice.

Person–Number Substitution

1. ¿Supieron la noticia?
   (we, they, you *fam*, I, your friend)
2. Los militares lo pusieron en un avión.
   (el general, los sargentos, usted, nosotros, el jefe, tú)
3. ¿Qué dijo el jefe de la junta?
   (tú, yo, los generales, tú y yo, ustedes, el Lic. Vargas, usted)
4. Después vino una dictadura.
   (unos coroneles, yo, nosotros, otro golpe de estado, tú)
5. El presidente no pudo hacer nada.
   (nosotros, la gente, usted, ustedes, tú, yo)
6. Yo no fui a la iglesia porque no quise.
   (mi hermano, ellos, María y Pedro, Pedro y yo, tú, ustedes)

Tense Substitution

Say aloud the following sentences, first in the imperfect, then in the preterit.

EXAMPLE: ¿Sabe usted quién es el maestro?
   ¿Sabía usted quién era el maestro?
   ¿Supo usted quién fue el maestro?

1. ¡Qué lindo está el paseo!
2. ¡Todos están tan alegres!
3. Luego vamos a Nicaragua.
4. La señora tiene un hijo.
5. Quiero tomar algo frío.
6. Voy a llamar a la policía.
7. ¡Qué frío hace en la calle!
8. Ah, por fin viene.
9. Estamos invitados a una boda.
10. ¡Por fin se van!
11. Tienes razón.
12. No estoy segura.
13. Voy a preguntar.
14. Es muy caro.
15. Ando de compras.
16. ¡Por qué no vienes?

Written Composition

Write a composition using both past tenses (preterit and imperfect) of approximately one hundred words on a subject of your choice. Include as many preterit forms of the derivative verbs in paragraph E above as you can.

¿Qué dije yo?

Listen to the following statements. After each statement the instructor will ask, *¿Qué dije yo?* The whole class answers. Start your answers simply with *Que*, as in the example.

EXAMPLE: Yo fui presidente de la república de Andivia. ¿Qué dije yo?
Que usted fue presidente de la república de Andivia.

1. Cuando era presidente ganaba mucho dinero.
2. Estaba muy contento. No podía quejarme.
3. Sin embargo, tuve mala suerte.
4. Un día mis ministros y yo propusimos una rebaja en el presupuesto de defensa.
5. Inmediatamente vinieron tres generales a hablar conmigo.
6. Me dijeron que yo estaba loco y yo les dije muchas malas palabras.
7. Me puse furioso e hice un gran escándalo.
8. Esa misma noche me dieron un golpe de estado.
9. Mis ministros y yo tuvimos que refugiarnos en una embajada.
10. Estuvimos en esa embajada un año.
11. El embajador, pobre hombre, se volvió loco.
12. Lo pusieron en un avión y lo mandaron a su país.
13. Por fin yo pude salir de Andivia.
14. Vine a los Estados Unidos y traje a mi familia.
15. Los primeros días tuve dificultad en encontrar trabajo.
16. Yo no sabía hacer nada; sabía ser presidente nada más.
17. Gracias a Dios sé hablar español también.
18. Un día supe que aquí necesitaban un profesor de español.
19. Vine y hablé con el presidente—de presidente a presidente.
20. Aquí estoy ahora: su profesor, a sus órdenes.

Chain Narration

One student relates the beginning of the story the instructor has just told. Another student continues, and then another, until the story is completed.

49. Negative and affirmative words

A. Negative words can be used either before or after the verb. If they follow the verb, the verb must be preceded by *no* or another negative word.

Nada me gusta. *or* **No** me gusta **nada.**	*I don't like anything.*
Nadie viene. *or* **No** viene **nadie.**	*No one's coming.*
Tampoco bailo. *or* **No** bailo **tampoco.**	*I don't dance either.*
Nadie come **nada.** *or* **No** come **nada nadie.**	*No one eats anything.*

"Double negation" is not only not incorrect in Spanish, it is *required* when *no* precedes the verb in sentences like the examples above.

B. When *no* precedes the verb, no other negative word may. Several negative words other than *no*, however, may precede the verb. The following example is possible, though rather extreme.

Aquí **ninguno tampoco ni** le pide **ni** le da **nada** a **nadie nunca.**
Nor does anyone here ever ask anyone for anything or give anything to anyone.
(Literally, *Here no one neither neither asks nor gives nothing to no one never.*)

Negative		Affirmative	
nada	*nothing, not anything*	algo	*something*
		todo	*everything*
nadie	*no one, not anyone*	alguien	*someone, anyone*
		todo el mundo	*everyone*
		todos	*all*
ni	*neither, nor; not even*	o	*either, or*
		hasta	*even*
ninguno, -a	*no, none, not any, no one, not anyone, neither one*	alguno(s), -a(s)	*some, someone, any*
nunca	*never, not ever*	una vez	*once*
		a veces, algunas veces	*sometimes*
		siempre	*always*
tampoco	*neither, not either*	también	*also*

Transformation

Repeat each sentence as you hear it. Then say it once more, placing the negative word after the verb.

EXAMPLE: ¡En esta clase ninguno estudia!
        ¡En esta clase no estudia ninguno!

1. ¡Nada están aprendiendo!
2. ¡Nunca hacen silencio!
3. ¡Tampoco llegan temprano a clase!
4. ¡Nadie pone atención!
5. ¡Esto es imposible; aquí ni se puede enseñar!

Bolivia: Crowd listening to a speech by the late
President Barrientos

Affirmative ⟶ Negative

The whole class answers.

EXAMPLE: Nosotros supimos absolutamente todo.
          Nosotros no supimos absolutamente nada.

1. Yo también hice un examen muy
   bueno.
2. Todo el mundo estaba preocupado.
3. Alguien se suicidó después del examen.
4. Algunos de los alumnos se des-
   mayaron.
5. Yo voy a pasar este curso—¡algún[7] día!
6. Bueno, o nos vamos o nos quedamos.
7. A mí todo me pasa.

No es cierto

The whole class answers. Deny the following statements about your class, beginning each
denial with *No es cierto.*

EXAMPLE: El profesor dice que ustedes saben muchísimo.
          No es cierto, no sabemos nada.

1. Que en esta clase todo el mundo estudia.

[7]*Alguno* drops the *o* before masculine nouns. See
grammar section 50.

2. Que ustedes siempre hacen silencio.
3. Que todos ponen atención.
4. Que siempre llegan temprano también.
5. Que ustedes o son muy inteligentes o estudian mucho.

Written Translation

JUAN.   You don't know anybody or know anything.
LUIS.   And you don't know much either.
JUAN.   You don't even know who Socrates (Sócrates) was.
LUIS.   Wasn't he the one who said, "I know only that I know nothing"?
JUAN.   No, he never said that.

50. Shortened modifiers

una mujer	**un** hombre
buena mujer	**buen** hombre
mala mujer	**mal** hombre
alguna mujer	**algún** hombre
ninguna mujer	**ningún** hombre
primera mujer	**primer** hombre
tercera mujer	**tercer** hombre
gran mujer	**gran** hombre
cualquier mujer	**cualquier** hombre

A. The first section of the chart above lists some adjectives which, like *uno* and the ordinal numbers *primero* and *tercero*, drop the final *o* before the singular form of masculine nouns.

B. These modifiers are shortened even when two occur together, and when they are separated from the noun.

> **ningún mal** hombre   *no bad man*
> **ningún** otro hombre   *no other man*

C. *Grande* loses its final syllable before any singular noun, either masculine or feminine; *gran* usually means "great" rather than "big." Its plural form remains unshortened: *grandes*.

D. *Cualquiera* means "any" in the sense of "whichever," "just any (old)." The shortened form *cualquier* occurs before masculine and feminine singular nouns. The plural *cualesquiera* is seldom used.

> ¿Qué vas a darle a Mauricio?   *What are you going to give Maurice?*
> **Cualquier** cosa.   *Any old thing.*

Noun Substitution

1. ¡Qué gran tragedia!
     (tragedias, hombres, almirante, capitán, jefes)
2. Esa fue una buena idea.
     (presidente, coroneles, defensa, periódico, mujer, hombre)
3. No vino ninguna mala noticia.
     (momento, persona, doctor, criada, jefe)
4. ¿Hay aquí algún problema?
     (tragedia, sargentos, alumno inteligente, maestras simpáticas, profesor de español)

Oral Translation

1. The third week, the third man
2. A great president, but a great tragedy
3. No woman is better than I.
4. I'm not going to read just any old book.
5. Some day I'm going to write a good book.

51. Word order

Information Questions

> ¿Por qué se refugió el presidente en la embajada?
> *or*
> ¿Por qué se refugió en la embajada el presidente?
> *Why did the president take refuge in the embassy?*

A. The basic word order of "information questions"—those that begin with interrogative expressions like *qué, cómo, cuánto tiempo,* etc.—is either

   interrogative expression + verb + subject + remainder

or

   interrogative expression + verb + remainder + subject

as shown in the chart.

Oral Translation

1. What does your friend want?
2. What are the other boys doing?
3. Where is your father going to work?
4. How long is the president going to be in the embassy?
5. When did General Méndez speak on (through) the radio?
6. What did the general say?

Yes-No Questions

¿Usted supo la noticia?	
¿Supo usted la noticia?	*Did you hear the news?*
¿Supo la noticia usted?	

Statements

Anita te habla.	*This is Anita.*
Te habla Anita.	
El gobierno cayó.	*The government fell.*
Cayó el gobierno.	
Alguien me dijo eso.	
Me dijo alguien eso.	*Someone told me that.*
Me dijo eso alguien.	

B. As the charts show, word order is quite free in yes-no questions and statements. Subtle shifts of meaning accompany the various arrangements of the same set of words. It takes time to master all these subtleties, but the following are the crucial points:

1. Change in word order does not necessarily imply change in grammatical function (unlike "Dog bites man" *vs.* "Man bites dog" in English).
2. Whether a given string of words is a statement or a yes-no question is determined solely by intonation—rising for questions, falling for statements—and, in written sentences, by punctuation. Listen to the differences in the intonation of the following pairs of sentences.

STATEMENTS	YES-NO QUESTIONS
Anita te habla.	¿Anita te habla?
Te habla Anita.	¿Te habla Anita?

3. In general, the *end* of a statement or question is the focus of attention; it gives or asks for information that is new, important, or surprising. The beginning supplies information that is known, in the background, or taken for granted. For example, in a previous dialog one of the speakers says on the phone, *Te habla Anita.* It is obvious that somebody is speaking; therefore *Te habla* comes first. What is informative is that the person speaking is Anita, so this word comes last.

Questions

Answer with a full utterance, placing the subject last.

EXAMPLE: ¿Quién sabe más, el maestro o el alumno?
   Sabe más el maestro.

1. ¿Quién cayó, el gobierno constitucional o la junta?
2. ¿Cuántos alumnos pasaron el examen, tres o cuatro?

3. ¿Va a hablar usted o voy a hablar yo?
4. ¿Quién llamó, Anita o Teresa?
5. ¿Es la capital de Colombia Caracas o Bogotá?
6. ¿Quién estuvo más contenta en el paseo, Vickie o Linda?
7. ¿Quién tiene razón, él o yo?

LISTENING COMPREHENSION EXERCISE B

Reading

Aniversario de la independencia

El día 22 de noviembre, tres meses después de que una junta militar derrocó al gobierno constitucional del país, la república de Andivia celebró con una imponente parada militar la fecha del aniversario de su independencia. Su excelencia general Antonio Méndez, Presidente Provisional, acompañado de los otros dos miembros de la junta, mariscal Napoleón Bonavena, Jefe de las Fuerzas Aéreas, y el almirante Nelson Quesada, Jefe de la Marina, pasó revista[8] a las tropas que con impecable precisión marchaban frente al Palacio Presidencial. El desfile[9] continuó luego hacia la Avenida de los Héroes donde casi un millón de andivianos esperaban ansiosamente desde tempranas horas de la mañana. Durante más de tres horas, estos miles de espectadores, que en su gran mayoría eran la gente del pueblo, gente pobre, desnutrida y mal vestida, vieron pasar ante sus ojos el poderío de las fuerzas armadas de su patria: tanques de guerra, cañones y otros armamentos modernos, todo tipo de vehículos de transporte, cadetes de la Academia Militar con sus relucientes[10] uniformes y montando grandes y hermosos caballos, cadetes de la Academia Naval con sus uniformes blancos, soldados de infantería con botas negras de la mejor calidad, aviones militares volando en precisas formaciones, varias bandas militares y muchas cosas más. Fue en realidad un grandioso espectáculo que recibió la admiración y los aplausos de muchos espectadores; pero no de todos.

De regreso[11] a su casa el hijo de uno de ellos le preguntó a su padre:

—Papá, ¿cuánto cuestan los tanques y los aviones?

—Mucho dinero, hijo.

—¿Para qué necesitamos un ejército tan grande, papá?

—Para defender a la patria.

—¿Contra quién?

—Quién sabe.

—Papá, si algún día puedes comprarme un par de zapatos, yo quiero botas, como las de los soldados.

—Está bien, hijo, algún día... tal vez...

---

[8] *Pasar revista:* to review.
[9] Parade.
[10] Glittering.
[11] *De regreso:* back.

Questions for Oral or Written Compositions

1. ¿Es Andivia un país verdadero o imaginario?
2. ¿En qué aspecto representa Andivia la realidad de algunos países americanos?
3. ¿Está la república de Andivia gobernada en estos momentos por un gobierno constitucional?
4. ¿Cómo llegó al poder la junta militar?
5. ¿Cree usted que los militares en los Estados Unidos pueden dar un golpe de estado algún día?
6. ¿Quiénes son los tres miembros de la junta militar de Andivia? ¿A cuáles cuerpos de las fuerzas armadas representan estos militares?
7. ¿Cómo celebró Andivia el aniversario de la fecha de su independencia?
8. ¿Cómo se celebra en los Estados Unidos el aniversario de la independencia?
9. ¿En qué año se independizó Estados Unidos de Inglaterra?
10. ¿Sabe usted si en América Latina hay gobiernos militares ahora? ¿En cuáles países, sabe usted?
11. ¿En qué consiste una dictadura militar?
12. El día de la independencia de Andivia, ¿qué y quiénes participaron en la parada militar?
13. ¿Por dónde pasaron las tropas primero y hacia dónde continuaron después?
14. ¿Cuánta gente vio el desfile? ¿Cómo era la mayoría de esa gente?
15. ¿Cree usted que los Estados Unidos deben mandar armamentos a los países latinoamericanos? ¿Por qué?

LISTENING COMPREHENSION EXERCISE C

Bogotá, Colombia: Military parade passing Bogotá Cathedral

Vocabulary

a sus órdenes at your service
a veces sometimes
absolutamente absolutely
alguno, -a some
el **almirante** admiral
atraer to attract
el **aumento** increase
la **barbaridad** terrible thing
caer to fall
el **capitán** captain
cierto, -a true
comentar to comment
el **comunismo** Communism
constitucional constitutional
contar (ue) to tell
el **coronel** colonel
el **curso** course
la **defensa** defense
la **democracia** democracy
democrático, -a democratic
derrocar to overthrow
la **dictadura** dictatorship
la **dificultad** difficulty
divertido, -a funny, amusing
el **edificio** building
el **ejército** army
la **embajada** embassy
el **embajador** ambassador
el **escándalo** scandal
escuchar to listen (to)
el **exilio** exile
frecuente frequent
las **fuerzas aéreas** air force
ganar to earn
el **general** general
el **gobierno** government
el **golpe** blow
el **golpe de estado** coup d'état
hace un rato a while ago
hacer silencio to be quiet
hacer un examen bueno to do well
  on a test
la **iglesia** church

imaginario, -a imaginary
el **impuesto** tax
la **infantería de la marina** marines
inmediatamente immediately
el **jefe** the chief
la **junta** junta
licenciado, -a title
  conferred on a graduate of a law
  school
lo de siempre the same old thing
loco, -a crazy, mad
la **marina** navy
matar to kill
el **mayor** major
militar military
el **ministro** government minister
el **motivo** reason, motive
muchísimo a great deal of; a great
  many
naturalmente naturally
necesario, -a necessary
la **noticia** (item of) news
la **orden** order
la **patria** (native) country
perder to lose
la **persona** person
el **poder** power
ponerse furioso become furious
el **presidente** president
el **presupuesto** budget
proponer to propose
¡qué barbaridad! how awful!
¡qué divertido! how amusing!
el, la **radio** radio
raro, -a strange
el **rato** while
la **rebaja** decrease
recientemente recently
refugiarse to take refuge
la **república** republic
el **rumor** rumor
salvar to save
el **sargento** sergeant

el **silencio** silence
simplemente simply
suicidarse to commit suicide
el **teniente** lieutenant
terrible terrible

todos everyone
el **trabajo** work
la **tragedia** tragedy
verdadero, -a true, real
volverse loco to go mad

Cultural Listening Passage
for Chapter 10

News from Home

(1) When we are far from home, there's nothing nicer (more pleasant) than getting letters from the family—very long letters full of news. It doesn't matter if the news is just a repetition of the last letter, of a routine nature (character) and about the same things that happen in every home; we still haven't painted the living room; the cat's still (has continued) sick; the maid has left us and has run (gone) away with the milkman; Uncle Antonio has finally decided to start looking for a job, but he hasn't found anything yet and seems very happy about it; we still haven't expressed (given) our condolences to the Mena family for don Chico's death—may he rest in peace; we've hurt Aunt Casilda's feelings (Aunt Casilda is offended) again, as usual, and she hasn't come back to visit us, etc., etc.

(2) The important thing is knowing that everybody is well and that nothing bad has happened. Then we are interested in the sensational news, good or bad, about the things that are happening in the country: that there have been many parties lately; that "Fulano" has won a hundred thousand pesos in the lottery; that "Zutano" has challenged "Mengano"* to a duel; that the cost of living has gone sky high (to the clouds); that the university students are on strike and there have been many demonstrations and riots on the streets; that there was a great bullfight last Sunday; that the Minister of Education has resigned; that it's been raining, that it hasn't been raining . . . In short, the longer the letters, the more we like them; and if they are interesting and full of news, after having read them once, we read them two or three times more.

(3) Sometimes, however, we get letters in which the one who is writing only talks about

*Fulano, Zutano, and Mengano are fictitious names used much like "John Doe" or "Tom, Dick, and Harry" in English.

198

the things *he* has done or complains about what others have done to him, about how sick he has been or how much he has suffered, but he hardly mentions the person to whom the letter is addressed (goes directed).

(4) Such is the case of Aunt Casilda—as we can see in the dialog that follows—who has written to her nephews, Aurelio and Vicente, who are studying in Germany. Being in a strange land and so far away from home (their fatherland), these fellows, like thousands of others, are always anxiously waiting for the mail. This time, however, there was (has been) only a letter from Aunt Casilda. It's nothing to be very happy about because they already know Aunt Casilda's letters, but . . . it's something (something is something).

(5) Aunt Casilda is Aurelio's godmother, and she's complaining that her godson hasn't written to her, not even to congratulate her on (for) her saint's day. This seems to be a new complaint because Aunt Casilda has never celebrated her saint's day, only her birthday. Aurelio didn't even know there was a saint named Casilda and, consequently, a Saint Casilda's day in the calendar.

(6) At any rate, she's very hurt and mad at her nephew, she says in her letter. She's one of those people who are very touchy and who for the slightest reason are always getting mad at everybody. In her letter Aunt Casilda also mentions that she's angry with her brother, the boys' father, because she's been very sick in bed, and everybody has come (gone) to see her and asked about her except her own brother.

(7) Oh, Aunt Casilda! She's like a little girl. But deep down in her heart (at the bottom) she's very good, better than all the other aunts. Vicente tells Aurelio that he ought to write to her congratulating her on her saint's day, but Aurelio thinks it's too late for that. Perhaps, but better late than never, says his brother.

Grammar Points

First, the present perfect; second, irregular past participles; third, impersonal forms of the verb **haber** (there to be); fourth, the future tense; fifth, comparisons; and sixth, some suffixes.

Chapter **10**

Basic Dialog

Noticias de la casa

A. *Aurelio*   V. *Vicente*

I

A. ¿No ha venido el correo?

V. Sí, hubo sólo una carta, de tía Casilda. Está resentidísima[1] contigo.

A. ¿Por qué? ¿Qué he hecho yo?

V. Dice que no le has escrito, ni para el día de su santo.

A. No le *hemos* escrito, mejor dicho.

V. ¿Yo por qué? ¡Tú! Tú eres el ahijado.

---

[1] *Resentidísima* is derived from *resentido*, an adjective used to describe a touchy person who is hurt and angry at someone. The suffix *-ísimo* is discussed in grammar section 57.

II

A. Ni siquiera sabía que había una Santa Casilda. ¿Qué más cuenta?

V. Dice que ha estado en cama y que sólo papá no ha ido a verla. Que está muy resentida con él.

A. ¡Oh tía Casilda! Parece una chiquita: por todo se resiente.

V. Pero en el fondo ella es muy buena, la mejor de la familia. Debieras escribirle felicitándola.

A. Ya es tarde para eso.

V. Más vale tarde que nunca. Se sentirá muy contenta.

News from home

A. *Aurelio*   V. *Vicente*

I

A. Hasn't the mail come?

V. Yes, there was only one letter, from Aunt Casilda. She's very mad at you.

A. Why? What have I done?

V. She says you haven't written her, not even for her saint's day.

A. *We* haven't written her, you mean.[2]

V. Why me? You! You're her godson.

II

A. I didn't even know there was a Saint Casilda. What else does she say?

V. She says she's been in bed and that Dad's the only person who hasn't come[3] to see her. She's very mad at him.

A. Oh, Aunt Casilda! She's like a little girl: she gets mad about everything.

V. But deep down in her heart[4] she's very good, the best in the family. You ought to write to her and congratulate her.

A. It's too late for that.

V. Better late than never. She'll feel very happy.

Cultural Notes

A. Many Spanish speaking people are named for a Catholic saint and every year celebrate their saint's day in the Catholic calendar, rather than, or in addition to, their birthday. The two days do not necessarily coincide.

B. *Madrina* and *padrino* are "godmother" and "godfather," the sponsors of a child at baptism. The relationship of a *madrina* or *padrino* to the godchild (*ahijado* or *ahijada*) is taken more seriously in Spanish speaking countries than in the United States.

[2]Better said.
[3]Gone.
[4]At the bottom.

Dialog Supplement

I

¿No ha venido el correo?
 cartero *mailman*
 lechero *milkman*

Noticias de la madrina
 del padrino *godfather*

Ni para el día de su santo
     cumpleaños *birthday*

II

Parece una chiquita.
 viejita *little old lady*

La mejor de la familia
 peor   *worst*

LISTENING COMPREHENSION EXERCISE A

Dialog and Supplement Check

Sentence Recall

Say the dialog phrase or sentence in which each of the following words or phrases occurs.

Santa Casilda	madrina	se resiente
resentidísima	en el fondo	ni siquiera
muy resentida	chiquita	hubo
mejor dicho	debieras	noticias
sólo papá	más vale	para eso

Questions

1. ¿Cómo se llaman los dos hermanos que están estudiando en Alemania?
2. ¿Recibieron ellos noticias de la casa hoy?
3. ¿Cuántas cartas hubo?
4. ¿De quién era la carta?
5. ¿Está la tía Casilda muy contenta con su ahijado?
6. ¿Por qué está resentidísima con Aurelio?
7. ¿Por qué está resentida con el papá de Aurelio?
8. ¿Por qué parece la tía Casilda una chiquita?
9. ¿Cómo es ella en el fondo, sin embargo?
10. ¿Cómo es ella en comparación con los otros parientes?
11. ¿Está usted resentido con alguien en esta clase?
12. ¿Se resiente usted por cualquier cosa?
13. ¿Recibió usted alguna carta ayer? ¿De quién?
14. ¿Hubo buenas o malas noticias?
15. ¿Cuántos tíos y tías tiene usted? ¿Le escriben con frecuencia?

Grammar

52. The present perfect

haber	+	*past participle*
he ⎫		
has ⎪		
ha ⎬		-ado, -ido
hemos ⎪		
han ⎭		

vosotros habéis	-ado, -ido

A. Although both *tener* and *haber* correspond to "have," only *haber* is used with a past participle in perfect tense constructions in Spanish. The corresponding English constructions contain a form of the verb "to have" followed by a past participle.

> Mucho gusto de **haber**la **conocido.**　*Glad to have met you.*
> No **hemos trabajado** mucho hoy.　*We haven't worked hard today.*

B. The past participle is formed by adding *-ado* to the stem of *-ar* verbs, and *-ido* to the stem of *-er* and *-ir* verbs.

> hablar　**hablado**　comer　**comido**
> estar　**estado**　ser　**sido**
> dar　**dado**　ir　**ido**

C. Past participles used as such are never inflected for number or gender.

> El chico no ha **comido.**　*The boy hasn't eaten.*
> Las chicas no han **comido.**　*The girls haven't eaten.*

However, past participles are often used as adjectives, just as in English, and as such are inflected for number and gender.

> Ellas han **estado** (*past participle*) muy　*They have been very worried.*
> **preocupadas** (*past participle used as adjective*).

D. *Haber* and the past participle are not normally separated by adverbs, as is frequently the case in English.

> Yo nunca he estado allí.　*I have never been there.*

E. Spanish has a "progressive" form of the present perfect, which is entirely analogous to the English "progressive" present perfect.

> He trabajado.　*I have worked.*
> **He estado trabajando.**　*I have been working.*

F. The position of object pronouns in perfect and progressive perfect constructions is the same as in the verb constructions you have already learned.

Se lo he compuesto.	*I have fixed it for him.*
Después de habér**selo** compuesto	*After having fixed it for him*
Se lo he estado componiendo. ⎫ He estado componiéndo**selo**. ⎭	*I have been fixing it for him.*

Paradigm Practice

Practice the present perfect tense with the following verbs.

dar	quejarse	tener	ser	sentirse
estar	enojarse	aprender	ir	vestirse
enseñar	sentarse	entender	irse	resentirse

Person–Number Substitution

1. La tía ha estado en cama.
    (yo, los niños, nosotros, todo el mundo, tú)
2. Sólo papá no ha ido a verla.
    (ustedes, su ahijado, usted y yo, sus sobrinos)
3. Es que no hemos podido.
    (I, they, she, you and I, you *fam*, he)
4. ¿Por qué no se ha vestido usted todavía?
    (ustedes, yo, la chiquita, tú, los chicos)
5. ¿Qué han estado haciendo ustedes todo el día?
    (tú, la criada, nosotros, Vicente, yo, ellos)
6. Nada; no me he sentido muy bien hoy.
    (you, they, she, we, I)

Construction Substitution

Change each sentence first to the present perfect and then to the present perfect progressive.

EXAMPLE: ¿Quién habla inglés aquí?
            ¿Quién ha hablado inglés aquí?
            ¿Quién ha estado hablando inglés aquí?

1. ¿La chica que estudia en la Facultad de Derecho?
2. Debemos dinero en todas partes.
3. El inglés me mata.
4. Te presto el diccionario.
5. Este año vivimos en Venezuela.
6. Yo no me quejo de nada.
7. ¿Aprenden ustedes mucho en esta clase?

Questions

Answer with a present perfect or present perfect progressive construction.

EXAMPLES: Hola, ¿ya comiste?
No, no he comido todavía.
¿Qué estás haciendo?
Estudiando; he estado estudiando toda la tarde.

1. ¿Has tenido noticias de tu familia?
2. ¿Cuánto tiempo ha estado estudiando usted en esta escuela?
3. Usted ha estado progresando mucho en español, ¿no?
4. ¿Alguno de ustedes ha estado en Latinoamérica?
5. ¿Han ido ustedes al cine esta semana?
6. ¿Cuánto tiempo me han conocido ustedes a mí?

53. Irregular past participles

hacer	**hecho**	volver	**vuelto**
decir	**dicho**	devolver	**devuelto**
morir	**muerto**	resolver	**resuelto**
abrir	**abierto**	ver	**visto**
poner	**puesto**	escribir	**escrito**

The chart lists most of the verbs that have irregular past participles. Notice that the past participles of *volver* and *devolver* have the same irregularity. In general, verb stems have the same irregularities, with or without a prefix.

revolver	**revuelto**	componer	**compuesto**	prever	**previsto**
envolver	**envuelto**	descomponer	**descompuesto**	prescribir	**prescrito**

The only exceptions among the verbs listed in the chart are *bendecir,* "to bless," and *maldecir,* "to curse," whose past participles are *bendecido* and *maldecido.*

Construction Substitution

EXAMPLE: ¿Qué hace usted?
¿Qué ha hecho usted?

1. Escribo una novela.
2. ¿Tú no pones el dinero en el banco?
3. Nosotros no vemos a nadie.
4. Mi novia me devuelve las cartas que yo le escribo.
5. Ni siquiera las abre.

Todavía no

EXAMPLE: ¿Le devolvió Emilio el diccionario a Luz María?
            No, todavía no se lo ha devuelto.

1. ¿Es verdad que ya murió Pirimpimpín?
2. ¿Vieron ustedes la película *Gone with the Wind?*
3. ¿Le escribió usted a su tía?
4. ¿Resolvieron los expertos el problema?
5. ¿Compuso el mecánico el motor del coche?
6. ¿Pusieron ustedes el dinero en el banco?
7. ¿Ya abrieron las tiendas?
8. ¿Ya le escribió Aurelio a su madrina, la tía Casilda?

54. The impersonal forms of *haber*

hay	*there is (are)*
había ⎫ hubo ⎬	*there was (were)*
ha habido	*there has (have) been*
va a haber	*there is (are) going to be*

A. Spanish uses the infinitive or third person singular forms of **haber** in the same way English uses "there is," "there were," etc.

Va a **haber** una fiesta.	*There's going to be a party.*
Había mucha gente.	*There were many people.*
No **ha habido** muchos problemas.	*There haven't been many problems.*

B. The present tense impersonal form is *hay* rather than *ha*.

Oral Translation

1. There's a party at her house.
2. There can't be a party at her house!
3. But there seems to be one now.
4. There has never been a party at her house!
5. Oh yes. There was one there last night.
6. And there's one there now.
7. And there's going to be another one tomorrow.
8. And we all are going to be there!

You Ask the Questions

Include in each of your questions the form of *haber* suggested by the following statements.

EXAMPLE: Hay pocos turistas en las playas porque no hace mucho calor todavía.
    ¿Por qué hay pocos turistas en las playas?

1. En Andivia hubo dos golpes de estado el año pasado.
2. Sí, creo que puede haber más revoluciones en América.
3. En la historia de Bolivia ha habido más de ciento cincuenta revoluciones y golpes de estado.
4. Va a haber una fiesta en mi casa para celebrar mi cumpleaños.
5. No va a haber cerveza en la fiesta porque no le gusta a nadie la cerveza.
6. ¡Tiene que haber cerveza porque a mí sí me gusta!
7. Usted tiene mucha razón, joven. Mañana no hay clases.

55. The future

trabajar comer vivir	-é -ás -á -emos -án

trabajar comer vivir	-éis

A. The future tense has only one set of endings for all verbs, regular and irregular. Future tense endings are attached to the infinitive rather than to the stem alone. It may be helpful to notice that, except for the *vosotros* forms, the future endings sound the same as the present indicative forms of *haber: he, has, ha, hemos, han,* (*habéis*).

B. In Spanish the future forms are quite often replaced by the simple present or the *ir a + infinitive* construction. Thus the three ways of referring to the future in Spanish are the following.

Trabajo mañana.   *I'm working tomorrow.*
Voy a trabajar mañana.   *I'm going to work tomorrow.*
Trabajaré mañana.   *I shall (will) work tomorrow.*

poner	**pondré**	saber	**sabré**
valer	**valdré**	poder	**podré**
tener	**tendré**	haber	**habré**
salir	**saldré**	querer	**querré**
venir	**vendré**	hacer	**haré**
		decir	**diré**

C. The verbs listed in the chart have irregular *stems* in the future, but take the same future *endings* as verbs with regular stems.

Paradigm Practice

Practice the three model regular verbs as illustrated. Then practice some of the irregular verbs.

EXAMPLE: **¿Trabajaré, comeré y viviré yo aquí?**
           ¿Trabajarás, comerás y vivirás tú aquí?
           Etc.

Future Form Substitution

Repeat each segment of the following paragraphs, substituting future forms for the verbs in the present tense or in *ir a* + *infinitive* constructions. Then repeat the whole paragraph.

EXAMPLE: Tenemos examen mañana y,...
   Tendremos examen mañana y,...

1. Como probablemente yo no voy a saber mucho,... lo mejor es no ir a la clase de español.
2. Pero tal vez puedo estudiar esta noche... ¡Claro! Esta noche estudio como loco... Leo el libro entero,... lo aprendo de memoria,... me acuesto a las tres de la mañana y... no, mejor no voy.
3. Le digo al maestro que estaba enfermo y... le voy a preguntar... cuándo puedo hacer el examen.
4. Probablemente él va a comprender mis razones y... me va a decir... que puedo hacerlo cualquier otro día... y que él me va a llamar a mi casa y... que me va a hacer un examen muy fácil.

Quién sabe

Follow the examples. The whole class answers.

EXAMPLE: ¿Van a venir ustedes mañana?
   Quién sabe si vendremos mañana.

1. ¿Cuándo es el examen?
2. ¿Van a ir ustedes al paseo?
3. ¿Cuánta gente va a haber allí?
4. ¿Qué van a comer ustedes?
5. ¿Quién trae las Coca-Colas?
6. ¿Cuándo llegan los estudiantes americanos?
7. ¿A qué hora van a acostarse ustedes esta noche?
8. ¿Van a volver ustedes a la escuela?
9. ¿Qué voy a hacer yo sin ustedes?
10. ¿Me invitan ustedes al paseo?
11. ¿Cuándo voy a tener otra oportunidad?

56. Comparisons

1. Yo soy **más inteligente que** él.	*I am more intelligent than he is.*
El es **menos grande que** yo.	*He is smaller (less big) than I am.*
2. Yo tengo **más de** 100 pesos.	*I have more than 100 pesos.*
El tiene **menos de** 50.	*He has less (fewer) than 50.*
3. Necesito un vestido **más pequeño.**	*I need a smaller dress.*

A. The most common type of comparison corresponds to the "-er than" or "more/less (fewer) . . . than" constructions in English. *De* is usually used for "than" before numbers (examples 2).

4. Es **el** hombre **más rico** del mundo.	*He's the richest man in the world.*
5. Esa es **la** parte **menos divertida** del libro.	*That's the least amusing part of the book.*

B. To express the notions "-est" or "most/least," Spanish uses the definite article with the noun before *más* or *menos*.

C. *De*, rather than *en*, is normally used to indicate the group of persons or things with respect to which the comparison is made (example 4).

mejor más bueno	*better*	**mayor** más viejo	*older*
peor más malo	*worse*	**menor** más joven	*younger*

D. These irregular comparatives are very common and in most cases are freely inter- changeable with their corresponding *más* forms. However, *mayor* is used for comparison only among people, either young or old, whereas *más viejo* is used to compare things or old people with one another.

    With a definite article, *mejor* means "best," *peor* means "worst," etc., as in the case of regular comparatives.

Comparison Drill

EXAMPLE: Luis es un buen alumno.
        First student: **Yo soy mejor que él.**
        Second student: **Pero yo soy el (*or* la) mejor de la clase.**

1. Pedro es muy alto.
2. María es inteligente.
3. Jorge es muy malo.
4. Luz María es muy gorda.
5. Alfredo tiene 18 años.
6. Beatriz es muy delgada.

Now repeat the drill, reversing the comparisons as shown in the example.

EXAMPLE: Luis es tonto.
        First student: **Yo soy menos tonto que él.**
        Second student: **Pero yo soy el (*or* la) menos tonto (-a) de la clase.**

Problemas

I

La primera montaña tiene 900 metros de altura, la segunda tiene 1,400, y la tercera 2,500.

1. ¿Cuál es más alta que la segunda?
2. ¿Cuáles son más bajas que la tercera?
3. ¿Cuál es la más alta de las tres?
4. ¿Cuántos metros más alta es la tercera que la primera?
5. ¿Solamente cuál tiene menos de 1,000 metros de altura?
6. ¿Solamente cuál tiene más de 2,000?

II

Tres hijos tiene doña Patricia: Alberto, que tiene 11 años de edad; Jorge, que tiene 13; y Violeta, que tiene 17. Alberto es un chico bastante bueno en la casa y en la escuela. Jorge es un diablo que no hace nada en la casa ni le gusta estudiar; no hay nadie más malo en toda la clase. Pero Violeta es una hija buenísima y siempre la primera de su clase.

1. ¿Es Alberto mayor o menor que Jorge?
2. ¿Cuál es el menor de los tres hijos? ¿Y el mayor?
3. ¿Es Violeta la mejor de su clase? ¿Y Jorge?
4. ¿Cuántos años menor que Jorge es Alberto?
5. ¿Cuántos años tienen los tres hermanos?

57. Suffixes

Diminutive *-ito, -cito*

silla	**sillita**
libro	**librito**
papel	**papelito**
hombres	**hombrecitos**
mujer	**mujercita**

A. The suffixes *-ito* and *-cito* add a connotation of "cute," "little," or both, to the meaning of the noun to which they are attached.

¡Qué **perrito** tan inteligente!   *What a smart puppy!*

B. The suffix *-ito, -ita* is added to the stem of nouns ending in *-o* and *-a*, and to nouns ending in *l*. All other nouns normally take the ending *-cito*. A few nouns can take either ending: *mamá,* **mamita, mamacita;** *papá,* **papito, papacito;** Juan, **Juanito, Juancito.**

Superlative *-ísimo*

bueno	**buenísimo**
mala	**malísima**
grande	**grandísimo**
fáciles	**facilísimos**

C. The suffix *-ísimo* is added to adjective stems and means "extremely." Thus, *grandísimo* is equivalent to *muy muy grande,* and *facilísimo* is equivalent to *extremadamente fácil.*

Adverbial *-mente*

aburrido	**aburridamente**
triste	**tristemente**
fácil	**fácilmente**

San José, Costa Rica:
In the post office

D. The suffix *-mente* corresponds to the adverbial ending *-ly* in English. This suffix is attached to the feminine form of adjectives with *-o*, *-a* endings, and directly at the end of other adjectives. When *-mente* is added to an adjective, the adjective keeps its original stress, and the first syllable of the suffix is also stressed: *fácilmente*.

E. The two suffixes *-ísimo* and *-mente* can be used together: *-ísimamente*.

> Este libro es malo, es malísimo, **malísimamente** escrito.
>
> *This book is bad, (it's) extremely bad, terribly badly written.*

F. It is customary—especially in writing—to omit *-mente* from all but the last of two or more consecutive adverbs.

> extraña y tristemente   *strangely and sadly*

Noun Substitution

In each of the following sentences, substitute the *-ito* or *-cito* form of each of the nouns listed, making whatever other changes may be necessary.

1. Es una cosita interesante.
   (libro, cartas, lápiz, ojos, mujer, señoras)
2. ¡Qué linda está la chiquita!
   (árbol, mañana, noche, paseo, abuelo, niño, madre)

Adjective Substitution

In each of the following sentences, substitute the *-ísimo* form of each of the adjectives listed.

1. La madrina de Vicente está resentidísima.
   (contenta, triste, preocupada, enferma, alegre)
2. Es un lugar lindísimo.
   (verde, feo, aburrido, alto, bueno, interesante)

Adverb Substitution

EXAMPLE: Es una carta perfectamente escrita.
           (horrible)
           Es una carta horriblemente escrita.

1. Es una montaña fácilmente visible.
   (perfecto, verdadero, clarísimo, facilísimo, difícil)
2. Verdaderamente, no entendemos nada.
   (franco, simple, desafortunado, obvio)

LISTENING COMPREHENSION EXERCISE B

Reading

Tres cartas[5]

I

27 de noviembre, 19—[6]

Queridos papá y mamá,

Me alegro mucho de saber que todos han estado bien y que la situación económica del país ha mejorado bastante. Papá, todavía no ha llegado el último

---

[5]There are many ways letters to friends can be started and closed. Some of the most common—which can be used with either the *usted* or the *tú* form of address—are:

Openings			Closings	
Querido, -a		*Muchos cariños*	Much love (affection)	
Estimado, -a	Dear	*Muchos abrazos*	Many hugs	
Recordado, -a		*Muchos besos*	Many kisses	
Queridísimo, -a	Dearest	*Muchos recuerdos*	(Many) regards	from your friend,
Adorado, -a		*Besos y abrazos*	Kisses and hugs	
		Saludos	Greetings	
		de tu amigo, -a		

[6]The English form for dates—month, day, year—is also acceptable in Spanish.

cheque y estoy casi sin un céntimo; he tenido que empeñar[7] el reloj. No quiero preocuparlos mucho pero he tenido un poco de mala suerte en los exámenes, especialmente en el de inglés y en el de historia. Yo he estudiado mucho y no comprendo qué ha pasado. Mala suerte, eso es todo. Por lo demás[8] estoy muy bien, un poco enfermo nada más, con el "flu", como llaman aquí a los resfríos largos y cuando uno tiene un poco de temperatura. Pero ya estoy mejor. Termino porque tengo que ir a clase.

Besos y abrazos de su hijo,

Juan

II

3 de diciembre, 19—

Adorada Julita,

¿Qué ha pasado, mi vida? ¿Por qué no me has escrito? Me siento desesperado porque tú no me has contestado mis últimas tres cartas. Tú sabes que te quiero muchísimo y no quiero nada más que estar contigo todo el tiempo. No quiero seguir estudiando; no me gusta la medicina; yo no nací para ser médico. Además, los estudios son eternos y dificilísimos. Yo solamente quiero regresar a mi patria y casarme contigo. Yo podré trabajar en cualquier cosa. Todavía no les he dicho nada de esto a mis padres. Es un secreto entre tú y yo y nadie más. Si ellos lo saben se mueren y no sé cómo empezar a decirles. Termino porque voy a llegar tarde a clase. Por favor, escríbeme pronto, muy pronto.

Mil besos de tu novio que te adora te adorará toda la vida.

Juan

III

18 de diciembre, 19—

Querido Juan,

Recibí tu última carta, es decir, tus últimas cuatro cartas. No te he contestado hasta ahora porque he tenido que pensar mucho antes de decirte lo que te voy a decir. Por fin he resuelto no dejar[9] pasar ni un día más y hacerlo hoy mismo porque comprendo que soy muy cruel si te hago esperar más. No sé cómo empezar.

Tú eres un hombre maravilloso que podrás hacer feliz a cualquier mujer. Sin embargo, las circunstancias nos han separado por mucho tiempo y el amor que antes sentía por ti debo confesarte, y perdón, mil veces perdón, ya no lo

---

[7]To pawn.
[8]*Por lo demás:* otherwise.
[9]Let.

siento. Estoy enamorada de otro y no lo puedo remediar. Estoy segura de que tú comprenderás. No puedo escribirte más. Te deseo lo mejor de lo mejor en todos tus trabajos y estudios. Adiós.

> Un abrazo y muchos recuerdos de tu sincera amiga,
>
> *Julita*

Conversation Stimulus

Summarize the contents of each of the three letters.

Written Composition

You are a North American spending a school year abroad as a guest student in the National University of Andivia, located in the capital city of Salsipuedes. There has just been a coup d'état and you are writing a hurried letter to your parents or a close friend, assuring them that you are safe and well, and describing the events surrounding the coup as far as you know them at this moment. If you need a guide, base your letter on the questions accompanying the Dialog "Golpe de estado en Andivia," pages 183–84.

LISTENING COMPREHENSION EXERCISE C

Remite:
Julia María Fernández de los Pinos
Avenida Simón Bolívar No. 359
Medellín, Colombia

Vocabulary

abrir to open
la **ahijada** goddaughter
el **ahijado** godson; godchild
la **altura** height
el **banco** bank
buenísima very good
la **cama** bed
el **cartero** mailman
celebrar to celebrate
componer to fix
con frecuencia frequently
el **correo** mail
el **cumpleaños** birthday
la **chiquita** little girl
de memoria by heart
debieras you ought to
desafortunado, -a unfortunate
el **diablo** devil
en comparación con in comparison with
el **experto** expert
felicitar to congratulate
el **fondo** bottom
franco, -a frank
el **lechero** milkman

la **madrina** godmother
mayor older
el **mecánico** mechanic
mejor dicho rather
la **memoria** memory
menor younger
el **metro** meter
el **motor** motor
ni siquiera not even
obvio, -a obvious
la **oportunidad** opportunity
el **padrino** godfather
prescribir to prescribe
prever to foresee
progresar to progress
resentido, -a hurt, angry
resentirse (ie) to become hurt and angry
resolver (ue) to resolve
la **revolución** revolution
el **santo** saint; saint's day
sentirse (ie) to feel
simple simple
la **viejita** little old lady
visible visible

Cultural Listening Passage
for Chapter 11

Problems of a Housewife

(1) Latin American housewives generally lead an easier (more rested) life than that of the American housewife, despite the fact that there one doesn't find the household conveniences that exist in the United States. There housewives don't have to get up early to dress their children, give them breakfast, and send them off to school. They don't have to cook; they don't have to wash or iron clothes; they don't have to sweep floors or clean the house. That's what the servants are for; they take care of all these jobs. (2) Housewives, naturally, direct and control the services of their employees, but in not having to do the manual labor themselves, even women of limited financial resources can live as easily as rich women. They can also lead a more active social life than an American housewife on the same economic level.

(3) Except for (excepting) the extremely poor people of the cities—those who live in what in Argentina are called "villas miseria," that is, the slums (extremely poor neighborhoods) that are so common (abound) in every Latin American city—it is rare to find a family with modest resources that doesn't have at least a cook and a maid. Families that are better off also have a laundress and a nursemaid, and rich people also enjoy (count with) the services of a gardener, a chauffeur, and even a seamstress.

(4) Obviously, the existence of this luxury or privilege as a normal aspect of life in Latin American homes derives from the bad socioeconomic conditions prevailing in our countries, which make it possible to obtain these services at very low prices. Thus sixty dollars is more than enough to cover the monthly salaries of a cook, a maid, and a nursemaid in most (the majority of the) countries of Latin America. We Latin Americans are so used to having servants that we can't live without them. At least that's what we think until we come to live in the United States.

(5) The dialog that follows presents a typical scene in the life of an ordinary family. It's early in the morning and all the children are getting ready to go off to school or to their respective jobs. They all need something and they all call (direct themselves to) poor Valentina to come help them. Lili calls her first, but Lola tells Valentina not to go because she wants her to come and help her first. At the same time Toño hands her his pants and tells her to tell the laundress to press them for him. (6) In the meantime their mother is still in bed and wants to have (take) her breakfast there. So Flora shouts to Valentina to bring it to her. Finally we hear Juan asking where Valentina is. He is in the bathroom and wants Valentina to bring him a towel. He doesn't ask anybody else, only Valentina. Poor Valentina! But, as we'll see, she won't stand for it any longer; she's fed up (up to the crown of her head).

(7) One thing that the housewife does customarily (has the custom of doing) is go in person to the market to buy groceries. Usually the cook or the maid accompanies her, carrying the shopping basket. She goes to the market for two reasons: first, in order to haggle over the prices, because in Latin America one has to haggle over everything, and anybody who doesn't haggle is a fool. Second, because she fears that her servant will steal from her if she sends her alone. Nobody trusts (has confidence in) the poor servants.

(8) Two days after the scene we have just described, we find the lady of the house haggling with don Vito over the price of some grapes. She says (that at) nine pesos a kilo is impossible, and that he should let her have them (that he leave them for her) for five. Don Vito says he won't make any profit (won't earn anything), that he'll give them to her for seven; she says no, they're too expensive. Finally she offers him six, and without waiting for don Vito's reply she tells him to give her two kilos and to put them in her basket. It is then that don Vito notices that the lady has come without Valentina, who always accompanies her to the market. The lady tells him not to even mention that name to her, that that dumbbell is an ungrateful so-and-so who quit her job (left the house) without giving notice (informing), and that all servants are alike.

Grammar Points

First, command forms; second, position of object pronouns in command verb forms; third, the forms of the present subjunctive; fourth, uses of the subjunctive in noun clauses.

Chapter 11

Basic Dialog

Problemas de una ama de casa

I

LI. *Lili*   LO. *Lola*   TO. *Toño*   FL. *Flora*   J. *Juan*

LI.   ¡Valentina! ¡Venga a ayudarme!
LO.   No vaya, Valentina. Yo quiero que venga aquí primero.
TO.   Valentina, dígale a la lavandera que me planche estos pantalones.
FL.   ¡Valentina! ¡Dice mamá que le lleve el desayuno a la cama!
J.   ¿Dónde está Valentina? ¡VALENTINA! ¡UNA TOALLA!

II *Dos días después.*

SRA. *Señora*   DON V. *Don Vito*

SRA.   ¡Qué caras están las uvas, don Vito! ¿Están dulces?

DON V.   Deliciosas, señora, pruébelas[1].

SRA.   Ah, pero a nueve pesos el kilo, imposible. Ojalá[2] que me las deje a cinco.

DON V.   No gano nada, señora. A siete, por ser usted.

SRA.   A seis, ni un centavo más.

DON V.   Está bien, no discutamos. A propósito, ¿dónde está la chica que le lleva siempre la canasta?

SRA.   ¿Valentina? ¡Ni me mencione a esa ingrata! Se fue sin avisar. ¡Todas son iguales!

Problems of a housewife

I

LI. *Lili*   LO. *Lola*   TO. *Toño*   FL. *Flora*   J. *Juan*

LI.   Valentina! Come help me!

LO.   Don't go, Valentina. I want you to come here first.

TO.   Valentina, tell the laundress to press these pants for me.

FL.   Valentina! Mother says for you to bring[3] her her breakfast in bed!

J.   Where's Valentina? VALENTINA! A TOWEL!

II *Two days later.*

LA. *Lady*   DON V. *Don Vito*

LA.   The grapes are so expensive, don Vito! Are they sweet?

DON V.   Delicious, ma'am, try them.

LA.   Oh, but nine pesos a kilo, impossible. I hope you'll let me have them[4] for five.

DON V.   I wouldn't make any profit,[5] ma'am. Seven, since it's you.

LA.   Six, not a penny more.

DON V.   All right, let's not argue. By the way, where's the girl that always carries the basket for you?

LA.   Valentina? Don't even mention that ungrateful woman to me. She left and didn't let me know.[6] They're all alike!

---

[1] From *probar.*

[2] *Ojalá* comes from an Arabic expression meaning "may Allah grant." It belongs to none of the parts of speech of Spanish.

[3] Carry, take.

[4] Leave them to me.

[5] I don't earn anything.

[6] She went away without informing.

Dialog Supplement

I

¡Valentina! ¡Venga a ayudarme!

barrer	*sweep*
sacudir	*dust*
limpiar	*clean*
jugar[7]	*play*

¡Valentina! ¡Una toalla!

un jabón	*a (piece of) soap*

II

¡Qué caras están las uvas!

naranjas	*oranges*
manzanas	*apples*
peras	*pears*
frutas	*fruit*
verduras	*green vegetables*
papas	*potatoes*
lechugas	*heads of lettuce*

¿Están dulces?

amargas	*bitter*
maduras	*ripe*
verdes	*green (unripe)*
saladas	*salty*
suaves	*soft*
duras	*hard*

A nueve pesos el kilo, imposible.

la libra	*the pound*

La chica que le lleva la canasta

bolsa	*bag*

Ojalá que me las deje a cinco.

Espero	*I hope*

Se fue sin avisar.

pagar	*paying*
regatear	*haggling*

LISTENING COMPREHENSION EXERCISE A

Dialog and Supplement Check

Sentence Recall

Say the dialog phrase or sentence in which each of the following words or phrases occurs.

kilo	ingrata	pantalones	uvas
canasta	ayudarme	a propósito	dígale
deje	lleve	lavandera	dulces
gano	problemas	discutamos	iguales
cama	planche	desayuno	avisar

---

[7]*Jugar: juego, juegas, juega, jugamos, juegan, (jugáis).*

Item Substitution

Repeat each of the following sentences, substituting a related word or phrase for the part in italics. If books are closed, your instructor will repeat the item at the end of each sentence.

1. ¡Qué *baratas* están las uvas!
2. Pero a nueve pesos *el kilo*, imposible.
3. ¿Dónde está la chica que le lleva siempre *la bolsa*?
4. Venga a *barrer*.
5. No *venga*.
6. ¡Qué caras están *las naranjas!*
7. ¡Valentina, *una toalla!*
8. ¡Qué baratos están *los tomates!*
9. Se fue *sin regatear*.
10. ¿Están *suaves*?

Questions

1. ¿Cómo se llamaba la sirvienta de esa casa?
2. ¿Se fue Valentina de esa casa o todavía está allí?
3. ¿Le avisó a la señora que ella quería irse?
4. ¿Adónde fue la señora unos días después?
5. ¿En ese momento estaba comprando frutas o verduras?
6. ¿Qué clase de frutas estaba comprando?
7. ¿Estaban baratas las uvas?
8. ¿A qué precio estaban?
9. ¿Qué precio acabó pagando[8] la señora?
10. ¿Qué tuvo que hacer ella para conseguir ese precio?
11. Cuando usted va a las tiendas o al mercado, ¿le gusta regatear?
12. ¿Se acostumbra[9] regatear en los Estados Unidos?
13. ¿Cómo son las naranjas, dulces o amargas?
14. ¿Cómo son mejores las frutas, maduras o verdes?
15. ¿Cuál es la fruta que más le gusta a usted?
16. ¿Es la vida de una ama de casa norteamericana muy suave o muy dura?
17. ¿Qué tienen que hacer ellas en la casa?
18. ¿Les ayudan los hijos?
19. ¿En qué ayuda usted en su casa?
20. ¿Sabe usted cocinar? ¿Sabe barrer? ¿Lavar ropa? ¿Planchar? ¿Jugar tenis?

Grammar

58. Commands

The verb forms of Spanish (and of many other languages) are inflected to show *mood*. The verb forms you have learned so far are the present, imperfect, preterit, present perfect,

[8] *Acabar* + present participle: to end up + present participle.
[9] Is it customary.

and future forms of the *indicative mood*. We are now going to take up the *usted, ustedes,* and *nosotros* forms of the *imperative mood*, often called "command forms." Later in this chapter the *subjunctive mood* will be introduced.

In general, the indicative mood is used for assertions or denials of *fact*. The imperative mood, on the other hand, is used in *commands* and *requests*, that is, to express the will of the speaker to influence the behavior of another.

> Henry, please *empty* the ashtrays.
> *Leave* immediately, all of you.

When the speaker includes himself in the group whose behavior he wishes to influence, the form "let's" is used in English.

> *Let's* not *do* anything rash.

Command Forms[10]

-ar *verbs*	-er *and* ir *verbs*
cante (usted)	aprenda, ponga escriba, salga } (usted)
canten (ustedes)	aprendan, pongan escriban, salgan } (ustedes)
cantemos (nosotros)	aprendamos, pongamos escribamos, salgamos } (nosotros)

A. The endings of the command forms are like those of the present indicative, except that the "opposite" vowel is used: the endings of *-ar* verbs have *e*, and those of *-er* and *-ir* verbs have *a*. There are no exceptions.

B. The stems of the command forms are the same as the stem of the first person singular of the present indicative. Whatever irregularity occurs in this form occurs in all command forms (*yo pongo: ponga, pongan, pongamos*). Three qualifications are necessary:

1. Those *-ar* and *-er* verbs that have the vowel-diphthong alternations *e → ie* and *o → ue* do not have diphthongs when the stress falls on the ending: *piense, piensen, pensemos; cuente, cuenten, contemos; vuelva, vuelvan, volvamos.*

2. In the few *-ir* verbs that have the alternation *e → ie* in the present indicative (*e.g., sentir*), the stem vowel changes to *i* in the "let's" form: *sienta, sientan, sintamos.* In those *-ir* verbs that have the alternation *o → ue* in the present indicative (*dormir, morir*), the stem vowel becomes *u* in the "let's" form: *duerma, duerman, durmamos; muera, mueran, muramos.*

3. The five verbs whose first person singular present indicative forms do not end in *-o* have the following command forms.

---

[10]The *tú* and *vosotros* command forms will be discussed in Chapter 14.

Peru: Slum area

saber (sé): **sepa, sepan, sepamos**
ser (soy): **sea, sean, seamos**
estar (estoy): **esté, estén, estemos**
dar (doy): **dé, den, demos**

ir (voy): **vaya, vayan,** $\begin{cases} \textbf{vamos} \textit{ (affirmative)} \\ \textbf{no vayamos} \textit{ (negative)} \end{cases}$

C. As is the case with other verb forms, subject pronouns are used with command forms only for emphasis or politeness. The pronouns, when used, normally follow the command forms.

Infinitive → Command

Give the specified command forms of the following verbs.

1. Usted

   EXAMPLE: venir, **venga**

hablar	suponer	mirar	decir
tomar	tener	dar	ir
comer	escribir	vivir	entender

2. Ustedes

   EXAMPLE: aprender, **aprendan**

salir	trabajar	discutir	estar
saber	ganar	vender	ver
ser	insultar	comprar	venir

3. Nosotros

    EXAMPLE: hacer, **hagamos**

ir	barrer	recordar	prestar
entrar	planchar	jugar	vivir
leer	dar	limpiar	decir

Completion

Read each of the following sentences aloud, then add an affirmative or negative command as in the examples.

EXAMPLES: ¿Por qué nunca llega temprano usted?
            ¿Por qué nunca llega temprano usted? Llegue temprano, por favor.
            ¡Ay, cómo fuma María!
            ¡Ay, cómo fuma María! No fume, María, por favor.

1. Usted no pregunta nada.
2. Y usted, Pedro, ¿no toma más café?
3. María y José, ustedes conversan tanto.
4. ¿Por qué no imitan a Margarita?
5. Ustedes no creen en mí, ¿verdad?
6. ¿Entramos y tomamos un café?
7. ¿Pero por qué no promete usted algo bueno?
8. Manuel, usted no estudia mucho.
9. Y usted, Felipe, nunca lee el periódico.
10. Señorita, ¿bailamos?
11. Señores, ¿comemos o no comemos?
12. ¿Cantamos?
13. ¿Vendemos esta casa y compramos otra?
14. En esta clase nunca leemos ni escribimos.
15. ¿Discutimos más?

Questions

Answer with a command form; do not use object pronouns.

EXAMPLES: ¿Voy al mercado ahora o después?
            Vaya ahora.
            ¿Voy yo solamente o vamos usted y yo?
            Vamos los dos.

1. ¿Llevamos la canasta o la bolsa?
2. ¿Dónde pongo esto?
3. ¿Ponemos la canasta en el coche?
4. ¿Qué traigo del mercado?

5. ¿Hago yo o hace usted la lista de las compras?
6. ¿Por qué no hacemos las dos la lista, mejor?[11]
7. Carne, verduras, leche... ¿qué más ponemos?
8. ¿Qué hago para la comida, señora, arroz con pollo o paella?

59. Position of object pronouns in commands

Affirmative	Negative
Díga**le**. *Tell him (her)*	No **le** diga. *Don't tell him (her).*
Déje**melas**. *Let me have them.*	No **me las** deje. *Don't let me have them.*
Discutámos**lo**. *Let's argue about it.*	No **lo** discutamos. *Let's not argue about it.*
Siénten**se**, señores. *Sit down, gentlemen.*	No **se** sienten, señores. *Don't sit down, gentlemen.*
Vámo**nos**. *Let's go.*	No **nos** vayamos. *Let's not go.*

A. Object pronouns always follow the verb in affirmative commands and precede it in negative commands. When they follow, they are attached to the verb.
B. In writing, when one or more object pronouns are attached to an affirmative command form, an accent mark must be placed over the stressed syllable of the verb in order to show that the stress remains on that syllable.
C. The -*mos* ending in affirmative commands drops the *s* when the pronoun *nos* is attached to it (last example in the chart).

Rejoinders

Your instructor will ask whether to do this or that. Half the class, answering together, will say to do it; the other half will say not to.

EXAMPLE: *Instructor:* ¿Le doy este libro a él?
            First half: **Sí, déle el libro.**
        Second half: **No, no le dé el libro.**
            Instructor: ¿Se lo doy?
            First half: **Sí, déselo.**
        Second half: **No, no se lo dé.**

[11]Rather, instead.

1. ¿Abro la ventana?
2. ¿Cierro la puerta?
3. ¿Empezamos?
4. ¿Hacemos el examen?
5. ¿Se lo doy mañana, mejor?
6. ¿Me voy a mi casa?

7. ¿Me quedo, mejor?
8. ¿Nos vamos todos?
9. ¿Se lo digo al jefe?
10. ¿Me levanto?
11. ¿Me siento?
12. ¿Me acuesto?

13. ¿Me pongo el sombrero?
14. ¿Llamo a la policía?
15. ¿Nos despedimos?
16. ¿Vengo mañana?
17. ¿No vuelvo?
18. ¿Les escribo una carta?

Written Translation

Make sure to place written accents and to drop the *s* of *-mos* wherever necessary.

PANCHO. Let's stay home today, let's not go to school.

JORGE. Great idea! But what shall we tell Mom? Perhaps if we tell her there's no school today . . . . Yes, let's tell her that.

PANCHO. No, better not. Come on (let's go). Let's get up. What excuse (*excusa*) are we going to give the teacher tomorrow?

JORGE. Let's not give him any, or let's tell him that Aunt Casilda was very sick.

MADRE. Come on, get up! You're going to be late! And don't tell me that there's no school today!

PANCHO. Valentina! Bring me a towel and a piece of soap!

JORGE. Valentina! Shine (clean) these shoes for me,[12] please.

60. Subjunctive forms

Present Subjunctive: *saber*

(que yo) **sepa**	(que nosotros) **sepamos**
(que tú) **sepas**	
(que él, *etc.*) **sepa**	(que ellos, *etc.*) **sepan**

(que vosotros) **sepáis**

The subjunctive is the third mood for which Spanish verbs are inflected (in addition to the indicative and the imperative). You already know the forms of the present subjunctive. They are the same as the command forms (*e.g., sepa usted, sepamos nosotros, sepan ustedes*), plus forms for *yo* and *tú*. The *yo* form is the same as the *usted* command form; the *tú* form adds *-s*, as in the present indicative. (The *vosotros* form has the same stem as the *nosotros* command form, and the ending *-éis* for *-ar* verbs and *-áis* for *-er* and *-ir* verbs.)

---

[12] See grammar section 35, part A.

Paradigm Practice

Before taking up the uses of the subjunctive, you should be absolutely certain of the forms. Since subjunctive verb forms are nearly always preceded by *que*, it is a good idea to practice them with this lead word, as in the chart.

Do paradigm practice with the verbs listed below, following the examples. Include object pronouns whenever they are attached to an infinitive.

EXAMPLES: hablar: **que yo hable, que tú hables, que él hable,** etc.
            comer: **que yo coma, que tú comas,** etc.
            pedir: **que yo pida, que tú pidas,** etc.
            irse: **que yo me vaya, que tú te vayas, que él se vaya,** etc.

venir	levantarse	quedarse	dar	barrer
decir	sentarse	quejarse	ser	sacudir
hacer	sentirse	vestirse	ir[13]	jugar
ponerse	traérselo	ponérmelo	saber	limpiar
estar	discutir	recordar	ver	haber[14]

61. Uses of the subjunctive

A. Perhaps the most common use of the subjunctive is one that is quite similar to that of the imperative: to express the intention to influence the behavior of another person.
  1. An imperative form alone expresses the speaker's intention to influence behavior.

      Cierre la puerta.   *Close the door.*

  2. A subjunctive form is used when *another* verb—such as *querer* (want), *pedir* (request), *decir* (tell), or *sugerir* (suggest)—expresses the intention of one person to influence the behavior of another.

      Juan *quiere* que yo **cierre** la puerta.   *Juan wants me to close the door.*
      *Díga*le que me **traiga** una toalla.   *Tell her to bring me a towel.*

  3. Object pronouns always precede subjunctive forms, although they follow affirmative imperatives.

      Imperative: Ciérre**la**.   *Close it.*
      Subjunctive: Quiere que **la** cierre.   *He wants you to close it.*

Subjunctive Formation

Using the verbs listed in the INFINITIVE → COMMAND exercise on pp. 224–25, form subjunctive phrases that begin with the fragment: *Quiero que...*

---

[13]The *nosotros* form of *ir* in the subjunctive is *vayamos* for both the affirmative and the negative forms.
[14]The subjunctive of *haber* is *haya*.

EXAMPLES: venir, **venga**

        Quiero que venga   I want you to come
        aprender, **aprendan**
        Quiero que aprendan I want you *pl* to learn
        hacer, **hagamos**
        Quiero que hagamos I want us to do

B. In addition, the subjunctive is used after verbs that indicate such emotions as sorrow, gladness, surprise, fear, hope, expectation, and doubt. Compare the use of the indicative and the subjunctive in the following examples.

Ind.:	*Creo* que **está** enfermo.	*I think he's sick.*
Subj.:	*Siento* que **esté** enfermo.	*I'm sorry he's sick.*
Ind.:	Yo *sé* que ella **viene.**	*I know she's coming.*
Subj.:	No, yo *dudo* que **venga.**	*No, I doubt that she'll come.*
Ind.:	*Dice* el médico que mamá **sigue** mejor.	*The doctor says Mom is doing better.*
Subj.:	*Me alegro* que mamá **siga** mejor.	*I'm glad Mom is doing better.*
Ind.:	¿*Piensa* usted que yo **soy** rico?	*Do you think I'm rich?*
Subj.:	¿Le *sorprende* a usted que yo **sea** rico?	*Does it surprise you that I'm rich?*
Ind.:	Ella *sabe* que Jorge **dice** la verdad.	*She knows Jorge is telling the truth.*
Subj.:	Ella *espera* que Jorge **diga** la verdad.	*She hopes Jorge will tell the truth* or *She expects Jorge to tell the truth.*

C. When *decir* and other verbs of communication such as *contestar* and *escribir* are used merely to convey information, they are followed by the indicative. When the same verbs express intention to influence behavior, they are followed by the subjunctive.

    Dice que Jorge **viene.**   *He says that Jorge is coming.*
    Le *dice* a Jorge que **venga.** *He tells Jorge to come.*

D. Either the subjunctive or the indicative may be used after *creer, pensar,* and *suponer* in negative and interrogative sentences.

    No *creo* que hoy **es** (*or* **sea**) lunes.   *I don't think today is Monday.*
    ¿*Cree* usted que hoy **es** (*or* **sea**) lunes? *Do you think today is Monday?*

E. In affirmative sentences, however, the indicative is always used.

    Creo que hoy **es** lunes.   *I think today is Monday.*

F. Except for *verdad, obvio, evidente, seguro,* and a few other expressions of truth or certainty, nouns and adjectives used with *ser* and *parecer* always call for the subjunctive.

$$\text{Es} \atop \text{Me parece} \left\{ \begin{array}{l} \text{necesario} \\ \text{una tragedia} \\ \text{fácil, difícil} \\ \text{bueno, malo} \\ \text{interesante} \\ \text{una lástima} \\ \text{posible, imposible} \\ \text{triste} \\ \text{mejor, peor} \end{array} \right\} \text{que Juan \textbf{vaya.}}$$

Indicative–Subjunctive Substitution

Make the second verb indicative or subjunctive, as required by the expression substituted at the beginning of the sentence.

EXAMPLE: Yo creo que somos amigos.
        (es imposible)
    Es imposible que seamos amigos.

1. Ojalá que[15] Valentina no se vaya de la casa.
    (estoy seguro, es mejor, pienso, espero, es bueno)
2. Nosotros sabemos que allí hace mucho calor.
    (es probable, dudamos, nos sorprende, creemos, es verdad)
3. Dicen que yo estoy loco.
    (dudan, sienten, saben, es posible, se alegran, quieren, es verdad)
4. Usted piensa que nosotros vamos al paseo, ¿verdad?
    (usted duda, a usted le parece, usted se alegra, es importante, es absolutamente seguro, usted piensa)
5. Tú sientes que yo no tenga dinero, ¿no, María?
    (sabes, te alegras, supones, esperas, dices, a ti te sorprende, quieres, piensas, prefieres)

Transformation

Use a sentence beginning with *El profesor quiere que* or *dice que,* followed by a subjunctive verb form, to repeat your instructor's commands. Use either the *usted* or the *tú* form in your answer. *Todos* is a signal for the whole class; include yourself when repeating the message.

EXAMPLES: Luis, abra la ventana.
    Luis, el profesor dice que abra(s) la ventana.
    Juan y María, siéntense.
    Juan y María, el profesor dice que se sienten.
    ¡Hagan silencio, todos!
    El profesor quiere que todos hagamos silencio.

[15] *Ojalá* may or may not be followed by *que.*

San José, Costa Rica:
Canasta game

1. Emilio y Luz María, no conversen tanto.
2. Usted, ¡ponga atención!
3. Vaya a abrir la puerta, Juan.
4. Quédese usted aquí, Cecilia.
5. Tráigame un vaso de agua, Pedro.
6. Présteme su libro, Alicia.
7. Jorge, dígame qué hora es.
8. Váyanse todos a la casa.
9. Vengan todos preparados para un examen mañana.

Questions

1. ¿Qué quiere Lili que Valentina haga?
2. ¿Qué quiere Toño que Valentina le diga a la lavandera?
3. ¿Qué quiere la mamá que Valentina le lleve a la cama?
4. ¿Y qué quiere Juan que Valentina le traiga al baño?
5. ¿Cree usted que la historia de Valentina es cierta, o duda que sea verdad?
6. ¿Con quién está regateando la señora después, en el mercado?
7. ¿Quiere don Vito que la señora pruebe las uvas o no quiere que las pruebe?
8. ¿A qué precio quiere ella que don Vito le deje las uvas?
9. ¿Por qué no quiere ella que don Vito le mencione el nombre de Valentina?

10. ¿Cree usted que yo sé, o duda que yo sepa jugar tenis?
11. ¿Quiere usted que yo le traiga una manzana mañana?
12. ¿Esperan las madres norteamericanas que sus hijas ayuden con el trabajo de la casa?
13. ¿Es importante que las mujeres sepan cocinar, lavar y planchar ropa?
14. ¿Es necesario que los hombres ayuden en el trabajo de la casa?
15. ¿Creen ustedes que hay mujeres que no saben hacer nada?
16. ¿Es bueno o es malo que las mujeres tengan muchos hijos?
17. ¿Creen ustedes que hay un exceso de población en el mundo?
18. ¿Es necesario, según usted, que haya un control de la población del mundo en este respecto?
19. ¿Qué recomienda usted que hagamos?
20. ¿Quiere usted que nos vayamos a la casa o que nos quedemos aquí?

62. Uses of the subjunctive: structural differences

1. El quiere **ir.**	*He wants to go.*
Juan espera **ir.**	*Juan expects to go.*
2. El quiere que Juan **vaya.**	*He wants Juan to go.*
Juan espera que él **vaya.**	*Juan expects him to go.*
3. El dice que Juan **va.**	*He says (that) Juan is going.*
El dice que Juan **vaya.**	*He says for (tells) Juan to go.*

A. Besides understanding how the subjunctive works in Spanish, you must learn to avoid the influence of English in certain types of constructions where Spanish uses the subjunctive. In the first pair of sentences in the chart, there is only *one* subject, and the subjunctive is not used in Spanish. In sentences like this, Spanish and English have similar constructions.

B. In the second pair of sentences, in which there are two different subjects—"Juan" and "he"—Spanish and English are structurally different. English places a noun ("Juan") or a pronoun ("him") before an infinitive, but Spanish uses the subjunctive, introduced by *que*.

C. In the first sentence of the third pair, the subjunctive is not called for because *dice* merely makes the announcement that Juan is going. Here Spanish and English are alike. The only difference is that in English the word "that" may or may not be used, whereas in Spanish *que* is always used.

In sentences like the last one, where *dice* expresses an intention to influence Juan's behavior and thus calls for the use of the subjunctive of the verb *ir*, English quite frequently uses the preposition "for" followed by a noun or a pronoun and an infinitive form.

D. It is important for you to be aware of the danger of saying totally unacceptable non-sentences like * *Yo quiero usted ir allí* (for *Yo quiero que usted vaya allí*) or * *Mamá dice por* (or *para*) *Valentina traer su café* (for *Mamá dice que Valentina le traiga el café*).[16]

Written Translation

Use the *usted* form throughout.

Monday, June 18

Dear Mom,

I'm glad you have a new cook and I hope you are well; I am not (well). I want you to know that I love[17] you and Dad very much, and I hope that you love me, too. I have to give you some bad news,[18] however. Do you remember when I told you that English and history were very difficult, and that I didn't know if I was going to pass or not? Well, I didn't pass. But that's not all. I didn't pass in any other subject[19] either. In other words, I flunked (stayed in) everything. I'm very sorry. I hope you won't tell anybody, except Dad. If you want me to tell him, I'll tell him, but I think it's better that you tell him. I believe it's also necessary for Julita to know. I want you to do me one favor, Mom. Tell Dad to send me a little money, if he can.

Your loving son (son who loves you),
Juan

LISTENING COMPREHENSION EXERCISE B

Reading

Se necesita sirvienta

La señora Dávila estaba desesperada porque Clotilde, la criada que le había durado casi tres años —tan buena, tan servicial, tan honrada y tan limpia— se había ido a trabajar a la casa de una familia americana.

—Ingrata, después de todo lo que hice por ella —le contaba por teléfono a una amiga—. La queríamos como a una de la familia, como hija. ¡Y ni siquiera nos avisó que se iba!

—Todas son iguales —le respondió su amiga—. Y tan difícil que es hoy día conseguir una sirvienta; hay que pagarles sueldos de presidente. ¿Y sabes quién tiene la culpa? Los americanos. ¿Sabes cuánto pagan ellos a una sirvienta?

---

[16]Utterances preceded by an asterisk are incorrect.
[17]*Querer.*
[18]One item of news is *una noticia.*
[19]*Materia.*

¡Veinte y hasta treinta al mes! ¡Dólares! Siento mucho que no puedas jugar canasta esta tarde. Ojalá que consigas a alguien pronto.

La señora Dávila estaba pasando una verdadera crisis. No podía tomar el café en la cama; tenía que levantarse temprano para vestir a los niños y mandarlos a la escuela; tenía que hacer las camas y arreglar la casa. Era una situación horrible. Puso varios anuncios en los periódicos pero sin resultado. Dos o tres muchachas fueron a ver el empleo pero ninguna quería trabajar por menos de cien pesos; y cuando se supo que en esa casa no ofrecían más de sesenta, no volvió nadie.

Sin saber qué otra cosa hacer, la señora Dávila puso en la ventana de la sala un rótulo que decía:

> *Se necesita sirvienta*

Divinidad Contreras era una humilde campesina[20] quien nunca había salido del remoto pueblo donde vivía. Había llegado hasta el tercer grado en la escuela pero tuvo que salir para empezar a trabajar y de esta manera ayudar en la casa con unos pocos centavos más cada semana. Un día, después de muchos años de estar sembrando[21] papas, cuidando vacas y cogiendo café, Divinidad resolvió irse a la capital a probar su suerte. Según le habían contado, era fácil conseguir un empleo de sirvienta en alguna casa y ganar así más dinero que el que ganaba en su pueblo. De esa manera podía ayudar mejor a sus padres que ya estaban viejos y a su hermana que recientemente había quedado viuda y con siete hijos, el mayor de siete años de edad.

[20] From the country (*campo*).
[21] *Sembrar:* to plant.

Con diez pesos en su cartera y sin más ropa que la que llevaba en un pequeño bulto[22] de mano, se despidió llorando de sus padres, hermana y sobrinos, y subió a un viejísimo autobús repleto de indios, con sus gallinas y sus cerdos[23], el cual dos veces por semana pasaba por ese pueblo con dirección a la capital.

Llegó allá y sin perder un minuto de tiempo empezó a caminar sin rumbo por las calles. Mirando de arriba a abajo los altos y modernos edificios de la ciudad, saltando a cada momento de un lado al otro para esquivar[24] los coches, taxis, bicicletas y camiones[25], llegó por fin a una casa donde había un rótulo que decía:

> *Se necesita sirvienta*

Golpeó tímidamente la puerta. Nadie abrió. Golpeó más fuerte. Tampoco. Golpeó mucho más fuerte y esta vez se abrió la puerta y apareció una señora furiosa:

—¡Va a tumbar[26] la casa! ¿Para qué cree que es el timbre[27]? ¿Qué quiere? No tenemos limosna.

—Es que en ese rótulo dice que aquí necesitan una sirvienta.

—Ah. ¿Ha estado empleada alguna vez?

—No, señora. Acabo de venir del campo. Yo vivo en Ojo del Diablo, allá muy lejos, en la montaña.

—Sí, ya sé. Entonces ni para qué[28] preguntarle si tiene referencias o certificado de salud.

—No, señora, ni pa[29] qué, no tengo na[29] más que mi persona. Pero estoy sanita, señora.

—¿Qué edad tiene?

—No sé, señora; como veintiocho años.

—No parece tener más de dieciocho.

—Debe ser menos, entonces.

—¿Qué sabe hacer?

—Pues pa decirle la verdá[30], no sé hacer mucho. Pero si me enseña, yo soy buena p'aprender[31].

—Bueno, vamos a ver. Entre. Yo pago cincuenta al mes.

—¡Cincuenta! ¡Claro!

Y así empezó Divinidad su nueva vida y la señora Dávila su nueva crisis. Divinidad no mentía cuando dijo que venía de la montaña, y la señora no podía dejarla sola ni un instante.

—¡Divinidad, no ponga las servilletas debajo de los platos! ¡Divinidad, no ponga los dedos adentro cuando trae los vasos a la mesa! ¡Divinidad, puso una cortina en la cama!

[22] Bundle.
[23] *Gallinas y cerdos:* hens and pigs.
[24] Dodge.
[25] Trucks.
[26] Knock down.
[27] Bell.
[28] *Ni para que:* there's no point in.
[29] *Pa* and *na,* from *para* and *nada,* are very common contractions in unguarded or substandard speech.
[30] Shortened form of *verdad.*
[31] *P'* represents Divinidad's contraction of *para.*

—A mí me pareció que era una sobrecama[32], señora.

—¡Divinidad esto, Divinidad aquí, Divinidad allá! —Era algo de volver loca a cualquiera.

Pero Divinidad poco a poco fue aprendiendo y después de un mes ya estaba más o menos domesticada. Un día la llamó la señora para darle su primer sueldo.

—Aquí tiene, Divinidad, su cheque. Nosotros tenemos la costumbre de pagar todo con cheque. —Pero viendo que la chica miraba el pedazo de papel con cierta desconfianza, la señora le explicó lo que debía hacer:

—Lleve este cheque al banco y allí le dan el dinero. Sí, el banco es el lugar donde guardan el dinero. Este cheque es del Banco Central, el edificio grande que está frente al mercado. Vaya ahora, si quiere.

Divinidad presentó el "pedazo de papel" en una de las ventanillas, según las instrucciones de la señora. El empleado examinó por un momento el cheque y luego se lo devolvió.

—Tiene que endosarlo.

—¿Qué es eso?

—Tiene que ponerle la firma.

—¿Qué es eso?

—Escribir su nombre aquí, ¿entiende? Igual como cuando termina una carta —le explicó el cajero[33].

Recordando las cartas que había escrito a su casa, Divinidad tomó entonces la pluma y con todo cuidado escribió: "Besos y abrazos de su hija, Divinidad Contreras."

For Oral or Written Composition

Retell the parts of the story suggested by the following key words and phrases.

Clotilde	rótulo en la ventana	viejo autobús
la culpa	humilde campesina	nueva crisis
pasando una verdadera crisis	tercer grado	después de un mes
anuncios en el periódico	a la capital a probar su suerte	con el cheque en el banco

LISTENING COMPREHENSION EXERCISE C

---

[32] Bedspread.
[33] Cashier.

Vocabulary

alegrarse (de)   to be happy
el **ama de casa** *f*   housewife
amargo, -a   bitter
avisar   to inform, give notice
ayudar   to help
bailar   to dance
barrer   to sweep
la **bolsa**   bag
la **cama**   bed
la **canasta**   basket
el **centavo**   penny
el **control**   control
dejar   to let, allow, leave (alone)
discutir   to argue, discuss
dudar   to doubt
dulce   sweet
duro, -a   hard
esperar   to hope, expect
evidente   obvious
el **exceso**   excess
la **fruta**   fruit
igual   same; alike
ingrato, -a   ungrateful
el **jabón**   (piece of) soap
jugar (ue)   to play
el **kilo**   kilogram (approximately 2.2 pounds)
la **lavandera**   laundress
la **lechuga**   lettuce
la **libra**   pound
limpiar   to clean

llevar   to carry
maduro, -a   ripe
la **manzana**   apple
la **materia**   subject, course
mencionar   to mention
la **naranja**   orange
ojalá   I wish; if only
pagar   to pay
la **papa**   potato
la **pera**   pear
el **peso**   Spanish American monetary unit
planchar   to iron
la **población**   population
el **pollo**   chicken
preparado, -a   prepared
probar (ue)   to taste, try
recomendar (ie)   to recommend
regatear   to haggle
sacudir   to dust
salado, -a   salty
sentir (ie)   to be sorry
sorprender   to surprise
suave   soft
suponer   to suppose
el **tenis**   tennis
la **toalla**   towel
el **tomate**   tomato
la **uva**   grape
verde   green, unripe
las **verduras**   green vegetables

Cultural Listening Passage
for Chapter 12

Individualism

(1) The belligerent attitude of the Spaniard toward the demands of the government and the community, which generally require the subordination of the individual to society, is almost legendary. But to what factors is this due? In Spain many artists, writers, and political figures, whose concept of freedom originated (was born) from a romantic impulse, are continually rebelling against the laws, many of which have been imposed by dictatorial regimes.

(2) The Latin American follows this Iberian tradition of individualism. For this reason he does not feel he is the same as others, but rather seeks to differentiate himself from them. He leads (lives) an intensely personal life. He doesn't enjoy being organized and he isn't interested in community projects. If he crosses a dangerous bridge, he doesn't think about what's going to happen to those who cross it behind him. He knows that many laws exist, but

he doesn't consider that they apply to (are for) him. Because of his attitude he doesn't understand impersonal relationships very well and rejects them whenever he can. He feels a strong loyalty toward his family and his friends. He thinks about his personal dignity more than about the usefulness of his actions. He loves ideals (ideals enchant him) and hates the empirical method.

(3) Many examples of this individualistic attitude can be cited (named). A clerk or a worker seldom (few times) identifies with the interests of his firm. In the government offices people are waited on sullenly or are told to come back the next day. College and even high school students are almost always willing and ready to declare themselves on strike. Professors and deans resign from their positions for minor reasons (easily) and frequently, and high government officials do the same for any personal reason.

(4) As Don Quixote demonstrated, individ-

ualism naturally comes into conflict with the law, which is made for everybody and is based on impersonal reasons. Therefore an automobile driver will take (give himself) the privilege of obeying his own impulses rather than the traffic laws. And when his actions have created a conflict with the law, he will find a way out (to save himself) on the basis of something very personal. If he is poor, he will avail himself of this same condition; if he is rich, he would be foolish not to take advantage of this privileged situation, since that's what one is rich for in a Latin American society.

A Case of Individualism

(5) It was approximately midnight when the taxi came to a corner where the traffic signal was red (with the red light). The taxi driver, who was in a hurry, stopped for a moment, looked both ways, and since nobody was coming, crossed the corner.

(6) Unfortunately, there was a traffic officer hidden behind a tree on the other side of the street. While the officer examined the taxi driver's license, both started to argue. The taxi driver insisted that he hadn't committed any crime since, to his way of thinking, it is illogical and absurd that a human being like him, who thinks with his head, should have to obey a stupid mechanical signal at that hour of the night and at a moment when there wasn't a soul coming down the other street. (7) Naturally the representative of the law told him that laws are made to be respected and became very angry with the taxi driver because of his nonsensical explanations. Then the taxi driver, in his efforts to avoid punishment for his crime, appealed to the fact that he was a poor man and the father of ten children. The traffic officer wasn't moved.

Grammar Points

First, additional verb constructions; second, a group of verbs that undergo a small irregularity in the preterit and the present participle; third, the infinitive as a verb complement; and fourth, review of verb constructions.

Lima, Peru: Avenida
Arequipa

Chapter **12**

Basic Dialog

Un caso de individualismo

o. *Oficial de tránsito*   t. *Taxista*

I

o. Su licencia de manejar, por favor. Continúe, ¿qué estaba usted diciendo?

t. Que yo no sabía que habían puesto una señal en esa esquina. Pero le juro que yo paré primero. Si me pasé la luz, como dice usted, es porque no venía nadie del otro lado. No iba a quedarme allí toda la noche esperando el cambio de luz.

II

o. Señor, las leyes se hacen para ser respetadas.

t. Yo comprendo, señor oficial, pero yo soy una persona civilizada y sé pensar con la cabeza.

o. ¡No me venga con cuentos! ¡Aquí todos manejan como salvajes! ¡Vamos, sígame!

t. ¡Tenga compasión, señor! ¡Yo soy un hombre pobre, padre de diez hijos!

o. Yo también soy un hombre pobre, pero debo cumplir con mi deber. ¡Vamos!

A Case of individualism

o. *Traffic Officer*   t. *Taxi Driver*

I

o. Your driver's license, please. Go on, what were you saying?

t. That I didn't know they had put a light[1] on that corner. But I swear (to you) I stopped first. If I went through the light, as you say, it's because there was nobody coming from the other side. I wasn't going to stay there all night waiting for the light to change.[2]

II

o. Sir, laws are made to be respected.

t. I understand, officer, but I'm a civilized person and I know how to use my head.

o. Don't give me that![3] Everybody here drives like savages! Come on, follow me!

t. Have a heart, officer! I'm a poor man, the father of ten children!

o. I'm a poor man too, but I must do[4] my duty. Let's go!

Dialog Supplement

I

Yo no sabía
    no me había fijado   *hadn't noticed*

Si me pasé la luz...
    el alto   *the stop sign (halt)*

Una señal en esa esquina
    esa carretera   *highway*
    ese camino   *road*

Es porque no venía nadie.
    ni un alma[5]   *not a soul*

---

[1] Signal.
[2] The change of light.
[3] Don't come to me with stories.
[4] Fulfill, comply.

[5] *Alma* is feminine. However, the form of the definite article used immediately before all singular nouns beginning with stressed *a* (or *ha*) is *el* rather than *la*. The form of the indefinite article immediately preceding such nouns is either *un* or *una*. The plural forms are the expected ones: *las almas, unas almas.*

II

¡No me venga con cuentos!

| tonterías | *nonsense* |
| excusas | *excuses* |

Yo soy un hombre pobre.

| honrado | *honest* |
| humilde | *humble* |

LISTENING COMPREHENSION EXERCISE A

Dialog and Supplement Check

Sentence Recall

Say the dialog phrase or sentence in which each of the following words and phrases occurs.

diciendo	leyes	diez hijos	deber
juro	cuentos	salvajes	del otro lado
civilizada	el cambio de luz	señal	compasión

Questions

1. ¿Se había fijado el taxista en que habían puesto una señal en esa esquina?
2. ¿Estaba la luz en verde o en rojo?
3. ¿Paró el taxista cuando llegó a la esquina?
4. ¿Se acercaba alguien del otro lado?
5. ¿Ni un alma?
6. ¿Se quedó el taxista toda la noche esperando el cambio de luz?
7. ¿El oficial de tránsito le pidió dinero al taxista o le pidió su licencia de manejar?
8. ¿Sabe usted manejar coche?
9. ¿Qué debe hacer usted cuando llega a una señal de tránsito que dice "alto"?
10. Y si una luz está en rojo, ¿cuándo puede pasar?
11. ¿Por qué no puede pasar cuando la luz está en rojo?
12. ¿Las leyes se hacen para ser respetadas o para ser violadas?
13. ¿Manejan los jóvenes americanos como personas civilizadas o como salvajes?
14. ¿A cuántas millas por hora maneja usted generalmente en las carreteras?
15. Según las leyes de tránsito, ¿a qué velocidad más o menos debe uno manejar en las calles de una ciudad?
16. ¿Tiene usted licencia de manejar?
17. ¿Qué debe uno hacer para conseguir una licencia?
18. En la conversación entre el oficial de tránsito y el taxista, ¿le pide el taxista al oficial que tenga compasión de él o que cumpla con su deber?
19. ¿Por qué dice que tenga compasión?
20. ¿Piensan ustedes con la cabeza cuando manejan o piensan con los pies?

Written Composition

Using the above questions as your guide, write a short dialog describing a dispute between a taxi driver and a policeman concerning an alleged traffic violation.

Grammar

63. Additional verb constructions

	Present	**Past**
PROGRESSIVE	Está diciendo *He is saying*	Estaba diciendo *He was saying*
PERFECT	Han puesto *They have put*	Habían puesto *They had put*
PERFECT PROGRESSIVE	Hemos estado pensando *We have been thinking*	Habíamos estado pensando *We had been thinking*
"IR A"	Voy a quedarme *I'm going to stay*	Iba a quedarme *I was going to stay*

A. The past progressive with an imperfect form of *estar* is equivalent to the simple imperfect with the meaning "was . . .ing." The progressive construction emphasizes the notion of action in progress.

Construction Substitution

Read the following dialog aloud; then read it once more, this time changing the imperfect verb forms to the corresponding progressive constructions.

EXAMPLE: Hablaba por teléfono.
  Estaba hablando por teléfono.

DIEGO.   ¿Qué hacías anoche, Pedro? Te llamé varias veces.
PEDRO.   Estudiaba en casa de Juan. Estudiamos hasta casi la una. Y tú, ¿qué hiciste anoche? ¿Viste televisión?
DIEGO.   No, hombre. Escribí unas cartas nada más. ¡Qué frío hacía! ¿no?
PEDRO.   No solamente hacía frío; nevaba y llovía en cantidades, como nunca.

Ayer a esta hora

Following the cues, tell what the people listed below were doing yesterday at this time.

EXAMPLE: Emilio / preguntarle / Carlos María / quién ser / maestra
            Ayer a esta hora Emilio le estaba preguntando a Carlos María quién era la maestra.

1. Vickie y Linda / hablar / Manuel y Enrique
2. Nosotros / quejarnos / clase de español
3. Juan José / tomar café y mirar / hija del dueño
4. Lucrecia / aprender a / poner / mesa
5. Estudiantes latinos / conversar / dormitorio
6. Luz María / preguntarle / empleado / precio / gramática
7. Tú / no hacer nada / como siempre
8. Anita / llamar / Cecilia / teléfono
9. General Méndez / dar golpe de estado y poner / presidente / avión
10. Tía Casilda / quejarse / ahijado
11. Señora / regatear / don Vito / precio / uvas
12. Taxista / explicarle / oficial de tránsito / ser hombre pobre / padre / diez hijos

B. The past perfect, **había comido** (I had eaten), is formed with the imperfect of *haber*. The past perfect progressive is formed in the obvious way; see the chart on page 244.

Tense Substitution

EXAMPLE: ¿Qué he hecho yo?
            ¿Qué había hecho yo?

1. No le has escrito a la tía Casilda.
2. Ella ha estado muy enferma.
3. No le hemos escrito, mejor dicho.
4. Todos han estado muy preocupados.
5. Sólo papá no ha ido a verla.
6. Yo no he podido escribirle.
7. Mis amigos se han quejado de mi conducta.

Tense Substitution

EXAMPLE: ¿Qué han estado haciendo todos?
            ¿Qué habían estado haciendo todos?

1. Jorge ha estado afeitándose y peinándose.
2. Nosotros hemos estado quejándonos del español.
3. Mis padres han estado pensando ir a Europa.
4. Tú no has estado haciendo absolutamente nada.
5. Yo he estado pensando comprar una casa más grande.

Rejoinders

EXAMPLES: Ahora no puedo; estoy comiendo.
Yo creí que ya habías comido.

1. Amadeo y su mujer se van a divorciar.
2. Tú y yo no hemos estudiado para el examen.
3. ¡Qué barbaridad! No ha venido el doctor.
4. El tico no ha recibido el cheque de su casa todavía.
5. Están poniendo una señal de tránsito en esa esquina.
6. Las chicas se van para Nicaragua mañana.
7. Dicen que el hijo del peón se casa con Valentina.
8. Usted no le ha escrito a su madrina todavía.
9. Con permiso, tengo que bañarme.

C. The **ir a** + *infinitive* construction with the imperfect of *ir* means "was going to."

Iba a comer.   *I was going to eat.*

Tense Substitution

EXAMPLE: Voy a decirles una cosa.
Iba a decirles una cosa.

1. ¿Ah sí? ¿Qué vas a contarnos?
2. ¿No va a venir nadie a la fiesta?
3. Nosotros no vamos a quedarnos aquí toda la noche.
4. Sí, pero todos van a llegar tarde.
5. ¿Y tú vas a esperarlos?

Questions

Include in your answers the same type of verb construction that appears in the questions.

EXAMPLES: Perdón, ¿qué iba a decir usted?
Iba a decir que usted habla muy rápido.
¿Qué estaba haciendo usted?
Yo no estaba haciendo nada.

1. ¿Dónde había estudiado usted español antes?
2. ¿Cuál de ustedes dijo que iba a ir al centro esta tarde, usted?
3. ¿Qué estaban haciendo ustedes dos, hablando?
4. Y usted, ¿qué estaba haciendo ayer a esta misma hora, bañándose o leyendo el periódico?
5. ¿No habíamos estado pensando hacer un examen hoy, eh?
6. Usted nunca me había dicho que usted era hijo del ex-presidente de Andivia, ¿verdad?

7. ¿Iban ustedes a preguntarme algo?
8. ¿En quién estaba pensando usted en este momento, en su novia?
9. ¿No dije yo que hoy íbamos a tener un examen?
10. ¿Dije yo entonces que hoy no íbamos a tener clase?

64. Additional stem changes in *-ir* verbs

	pedir
pedí	pedimos
pediste	(pedisteis)
pidió	**pidieron**
pidiendo	

	morir
morí	morimos
moriste	(moristeis)
murió	**murieron**
muriendo	

A. All *-ir* verbs that have vowel alternations in the present tense—like *pedir* (*yo pido*) and *morir* (*yo muero*)—have additional alternations in the preterit and in the present participle, as shown in the charts.
B. Other verbs like *pedir* that you know are *despedir, preferir, seguir, conseguir, sentir, resentirse,* and *vestir.*
C. Other verbs like *morir* are *dormir* (to sleep) and *dormirse* (to fall asleep).
D. The present participles of *decir* and *venir* are *diciendo* and *viniendo.*

Paradigm Practice

Do paradigm practice with all the verbs listed in B and C above.

Person–Number Substitution

Change only the clause in italics.

EXAMPLE: Yo no conseguí el dinero; *lo conseguiste tú.*
          (ellos)
          Yo no conseguí el dinero; lo consiguieron ellos.

1. Tú preferiste irte; *ellos prefirieron quedarse.*
   (nosotros, el taxista, usted, las chicas, yo, él)
2. ¿Se resintió usted? *Más me resentí yo.*
   (la tía Casilda, nosotros, mi novia, tus padres, yo)
3. El no pidió nada; *yo pedí un café negro.*
   (ella, tú, este señor, mis amigos, nosotros, nadie)

4. Si ella durmió mal anoche, *peor dormí yo.*
   (el marido, los hijos, tú, nosotros, usted, ellos)
5. ¿Te dormiste en la clase? *Yo también me dormí.*
   (la maestra, los alumnos, nosotros, todo el mundo, él)

Verb Substitution

EXAMPLE: ¿Qué estaba haciendo usted, trabajando?
        (decir tonterías)
     ¿Qué estaba haciendo usted, diciendo tonterías?

1. A mí no me pasa nada, pero Jorge está muriéndose.
   (sentir el calor, dormirse, manejar como un salvaje, discutir, decir barbaridades)
2. ¿Había estado usted tomando cerveza esa noche?
   (dormir en el parque, vestirse en la calle, maldecir, llamarme a mí, pedir dinero, morirse)

Quito, Ecuador:
Avenida Guayaquil

65. The infinitive as a verb complement

I		**II**	
Quiero		Voy	
Puedo		Vengo	
Necesito		Entro	
Debo	estudiar.	Aprendo	a estudiar.
Sé		Empiezo	
Prefiero		Te invito	
Juro		Te llamo	
Me gusta		Te ayudo	

A. In English most verbs require the particle "to" before an infinitive.

$$
\text{I} \left\{ \begin{array}{l} \text{want} \\ \text{need} \\ \text{prefer} \\ \text{promise} \\ \text{hope} \\ \text{swear} \end{array} \right\} \textit{to} \text{ study.}
$$

Only a handful of verbs omit "to."

$$
\text{I} \left\{ \begin{array}{l} \text{will} \\ \text{must} \\ \text{shall} \\ \text{can} \end{array} \right\} \text{study.}
$$

B. Spanish is quite different: Many verbs may be followed directly by an infinitive (group I); many others require the preposition *a* (group II).

C. Whether a verb belongs to one group or another is largely unpredictable and in most cases must simply be memorized. The important thing to remember is that English usually provides the *wrong* model for Spanish, since most English verbs require "to." You must try to avoid the habit of automatically inserting *a* before every infinitive in Spanish.

D. There are three special cases. *Tener* and *haber* are followed by *que: Tengo que estudiar* (I have to study); *Hay que estudiar* (One has to study). *Acabar* is followed by *de: Acabo de estudiar* (I just studied).

Verb Substitution

EXAMPLE: No iba a quedarme allí toda la noche.
(no pude)
No pude quedarme allí toda la noche.

1. ¿De veras vas a vender esta casa, papá?
(debes, tienes, acabas, vas, prefieres)
2. Te prometen cuidar a los niños.
(habían jurado, habían estado pensando, salieron, van a venir, sabían, les gustaba, van a empezar)
3. ¿Vas a preguntarle al panameño?
(juras, no has podido, acabas, debes, tienes, hay)
4. Julita estaba pensando jugar tenis.
(está empezando, tuvo, había, no sabe, acababa, le gustaba, había aprendido)

66. Review of verb constructions

Substitution

EXAMPLE: Anita habla conmigo.
(is talking)
Anita está hablando conmigo.
(talked)
Anita habló conmigo.
(used to talk)
Anita hablaba conmigo.
(was talking)
Anita estaba hablando conmigo.
(is going to talk)
Anita va a hablar conmigo.
(was going to talk)
Anita iba a hablar conmigo.

(has talked)
Anita ha hablado conmigo.
(has been talking)
Anita ha estado hablando conmigo.
(had talked)
Anita había hablado conmigo.
(had been talking)
Anita había estado hablando conmigo.
(has to talk)
Anita tiene que hablar conmigo.
(has just talked)
Anita acaba de hablar conmigo.

1. Yo digo que no.
(said, was going to say, have said, have just said, used to say)
2. Estos niños comen mucho.
(have eaten, ate, had been eating, are eating, have to eat)
3. Estudiamos español.
(have been studying, used to study, were going to study, are going to study)
4. ¿Le escribe usted a su tía?
(did you write, are you going to write, did you use to write, do you have to write, are you writing, have you just written)

5. Ellos no hacen nada.
   (are not doing, haven't done, haven't been doing, don't have to do, hadn't done, weren't doing)
6. Tú trabajas mucho.
   (have to work, have just worked, have been working, used to work, are working, were going to work, have worked)

Written Translation

Spanish differs from English in the punctuation of dialog within prose. In particular, dashes are used instead of quotation marks. The following selection is punctuated as though it were Spanish. Observe this punctuation and imitate it in your translation.

I

—I hadn't noticed it was so late —said Consuelo to her husband—. ¿Do you know what time it is? ¡It's five after four! If you don't hurry up (give yourself haste), we're going to be (arrive) late.

—¿(At) what time is the wedding? —asked Ramón.

—The wedding *was* at four o'clock.

—There's plenty of (much) time, then. I'm sure the bride hasn't left the house yet. ¿Where are my black socks? Tell the maid, what's her name, to bring me a pair and to shine (clean) these shoes for me, ¿will you (do you want), Consuelo? ¡For Pete's sake! ¡I can't wear (put on) this suit, I've gotten (am) too fat!

II

—Here we are at last —said Ramón—. ¿But why isn't anybody here?

—Because this is not the church.

—¿Why didn't you tell me that before?

—Because I thought you knew —replied his wife—. Besides, you were driving so fast and going through all the stop signs and everything that I was afraid (of) to open my mouth.

—Oh, don't give me that (don't come to me with stories). I only went through two red lights, and I did it because nobody was coming the other way.

—But you have to respect the laws.

—¿Laws? ¿What laws? I know what I'm doing. Besides, I am Ramón Fuentes de la Torre y Gómez, the Minister of Education's cousin (cousin of. . .).

—Okay, dear, let's not argue —said his wife impatiently—. You have to turn left at (on) this corner.

LISTENING COMPREHENSION EXERCISE B

Reading

La esquina

La esquina de mi casa es mi teatro. Es una esquina muy amplia y transitada[6] donde se cruzan calle y avenida, ricos y pobres, viejos y jóvenes, mujeres y niños, camiones y bicicletas, Cádilacs de último modelo y coches tan viejos y enfermos como yo. Sentado al lado de mi ventana paso las horas observando las muchas escenas que se desarrollan ante mis ojos, algunas interesantes, otras aburridas. La que voy a describir aquí es sobre un choque. Ocurrió ayer por la tarde, cuando ya comenzaba a oscurecer.

Acercándose hacia mi esquina por la avenida, venía una elegante dama manejando un reluciente Mercedes Benz de último modelo. Por la calle opuesta venía un viejísimo taxi recién pintado en brillante combinación de amarillo con verde.

La señal de tránsito que en grandes letras decía ALTO no produjo ningún efecto en la señora, y su Mercedes Benz entró tranquilamente a la intersección. El taxista también tenía una señal de su lado, pero como él creyó que no venía nadie por la otra dirección, le pareció absurdo parar. Ocurrió entonces lo inevitable: un fuerte y ruidoso[7] impacto entre los dos vehículos, que segundos después se vieron rodeados de una numerosa y variada multitud. Todos o casi todos gritaban exaltadamente.

Había entre ellos niños, mujeres, señores de respetable presencia, mendigos, limpiabotas y todo tipo de vendedores ambulantes quienes, aprovechando[8] la oportuna ocasión, anunciaban con mayor entusiasmo sus productos: ¡Helados![9] ¡Tamales calientes! ¡Lotería para el domingo! ¡LOTERÍAAA! Y cada uno de los presentes en aquella multitud, incluso los vendedores, limpiabotas y mendigos, parecía tener un interés personal en las causas y efectos del choque. Todos discutían y opinaban al mismo tiempo, unos a favor de la dama, otros a favor del taxista.

Yo, imitando al público de la ópera, miré con mis binóculos para observar más de cerca los detalles. ¡Ajá! ¡Allí también estaban ellos! Sí, eran ellos, los había visto en otras ocasiones y los reconocí inmediatamente, "La Pulga"[10] y "El Santo", dos de los muchos carteristas[11] que siempre abundan en los estadios, en las procesiones religiosas, en las corridas de toros[12] y en toda clase de conglomeraciones públicas.

Un guardia civil, única autoridad que en ese momento circulaba por ese lugar, se acercó sin entusiasmo. Después de varios intentos pudo por fin abrirse paso

---

[6] Busy.
[7] Noisy.
[8] *Aprovechar:* to take advantage of.
[9] Ice cream.

[10] The Flea.
[11] Pickpockets.
[12] *Corridas de toros:* bullfights.

entre la multitud. La dama y el taxista estaban ya en acalorada discusión:

—¡Usted tuvo la culpa, señora! —insistía el taxista—. ¡Usted se pasó el alto! ¡Hay testigos![13] ¡Yo soy un hombre pobre que tengo que trabajar mucho para llevarles el pan a mis hijos! ¡Mire mi pobre carro!

—¡Insolente! ¡La culpa la tuvo usted! —gritaba ella.

—¡La señora pasó primero, ella no tuvo la culpa! —exclamó vehementemente uno de los "testigos"—. ¡Yo lo vi con mis propios ojos!

—¡La vieja rica es la culpable! —gritó otro—. ¡Esa gente se cree ser los dueños de todo, hasta de las calles!

—¡Comunista! —le respondieron otros.

Intervino entonces el guardia civil exigiendo calma y menos intromisión[14] de parte del público.

—Sus credenciales de manejar, señora —y al taxista también le pidió su licencia.

—¡Pero este hombre insolente tuvo la culpa! —exclamó ella—. ¡Hay testigos!

—Su licencia, señora, por favor —dijo el guardia con voz seca.

—No la traje. La puse en otra cartera. —Y luego, en un tono pretencioso y mirando de pies a cabeza a la autoridad, dijo: —No sé si usted sabe quién soy yo. Usted está hablando con una tía del ingeniero Rafael Antonio Robles. Supongo que usted sabe quién es él. Puede arreglar este asunto[15] con él. Yo me voy.

El guardia sintió el efecto y se puso un poco nervioso, pero no queriendo dejarse intimidar ni humillar enfrente de todos, exclamó:

—Yo soy un hombre humilde, señora, y al ingeniero Robles le tengo mucha consideración y respeto. Sin embargo, usted debe comprender que yo soy la autoridad y debo proceder de acuerdo con la ley. Señora, no puedo permitirle manejar este vehículo si usted no tiene su licencia.

Pero ella no le hizo el menor caso y subió a su coche cerrando furiosamente la puerta.

—¡No la deje irse, señor guardia, tiene que pagarme! —exclamó el taxista.

Voces de protesta y de contra-protesta, brazos que se agitaban ante su cara, dedos que apuntaban directamente a su nariz; esa era la situación del infeliz representante de la ley.

—¡¡SILENCIO TODO EL MUNDO, YO SOY LA AUTORIDAD!! —exclamó con desesperación. Nadie le hizo caso y continuó el tumulto de la gente, el ruido espantoso que la elegante dama hacía con el motor de su coche, y las voces de los que vendían helados, tamales y lotería. El pobre guardia estaba perdido y sin saber qué hacer. Pero de pronto ocurrió algo que vino a sacarlo de tan precaria situación.

—¡LADRONES! ¡MI CARTERA! —gritó súbitamente un hombre de presencia

[13] Witnesses.
[14] Intrusion.
[15] Affair.

distinguida y uno de los más exaltados testigos del accidente de tránsito—. ¡Me han dejado sin cartera y sin bolsillo[16]! ¡POLICÍA! —gritaba levantando su saco para mostrar a los muchos curiosos un espacio vacío en la parte trasera[17] de su pantalón, donde momentos antes había estado su bolsillo izquierdo... y su cartera.

—¡Allá van! —exclamó alguien, apuntando hacia "La Pulga" y "El Santo", que en ese instante pasaban como un rayo bajo mi ventana. Probablemente —yo no los vi— pero probablemente habían colaborado para dar el golpe; uno discutiendo con la víctima sobre el choque mientras el otro con gran habilidad y rapidez cortaba el bolsillo de su pantalón con una gillette.

—¡Allá van! ¡Deténganlos! ¡Policía! —gritaron otros, y todo el mundo empezó a correr tras los carteristas, incluso el guardia civil, quien alegremente obedeció al llamado, encontrando así una excusa perfecta para salir de aquel lío.[18]

En la semi-oscuridad que ahora cubría el escenario del teatro sólo quedaron dos figuras que seguían discutiendo acaloradamente.

Questions for Oral or Written Composition

Summarize the preceding narrative within the framework of the following questions.

1. ¿Por qué compara el narrador la esquina de su casa con un teatro?
2. ¿Qué tipos de personajes y de vehículos se cruzan en esa esquina?
3. ¿Qué ocurrió ayer por la tarde?
4. ¿Quién se acercaba a la esquina por la avenida?
5. ¿Puede usted describir el otro vehículo?
6. ¿Qué efecto produjo en la señora la señal de tránsito que había al final de la avenida?
7. ¿Y el taxista, por qué no paró tampoco?
8. ¿Qué ocurrió, entonces?
9. ¿De qué se vieron rodeados los dos vehículos segundos después del choque?
10. Describa usted a esa multitud y diga qué hacían todos.
11. ¿Quiénes eran "La Pulga" y "El Santo", y dónde abunda ese tipo de individuos?
12. ¿Quién era la única autoridad que circulaba por allí en esos momentos?
13. ¿Qué estaban haciendo la dama y el taxista cuando el policía pudo por fin abrirse paso?
14. ¿Qué le decía el taxista a la señora y qué le decía ella a él?
15. ¿Qué les pidió el guardia civil a la dama y al taxista?
16. ¿Qué excusa dio ella para explicar por qué no tenía su licencia?
17. ¿Qué le dijo la dama al guardia para intimidarlo?

[16]Pocket.
[17]Back.
[18]Mess.

18. ¿Qué empezó de pronto a gritar el señor de distinguida presencia?
19. ¿Qué le habían robado?
20. ¿Cómo salió el guardia civil de tan precaria situación?

LISTENING COMPREHENSION EXERCISE C

Vocabulary

acercarse to approach
el **alma** *f* soul
el **alto** stop sign
el **cambio** change
el **camino** road
la **cantidad** quantity
la **carretera** highway

civilizado, -a civilized
la **compasión** compassion
comprender to understand
la **conducta** conduct
continuar to continue
el **cuento** story
cumplir con mi deber to do my duty

Mérida, Mexico: Street scene

deber must
el **deber** duty
dormir (ue) to sleep
dormirse to fall asleep
estar en rojo (verde) to be red (green)
la **excusa** excuse
fijarse (en) to notice
honrado, -a honest
humilde humble
jurar to swear
el **lado** side
la **ley** law
la **licencia** license
la **luz** light
maldecir (i) to curse
manejar to drive
máximo, -a maximum
la **milla** mile
no me venga con cuentos don't give
   me that (story)
el **oficial** officer
parar to stop
pasarse la luz to go through the light
por hora per hour
respetado, -a respected
responder to answer
el **salvaje** savage
la **señal** traffic sign, signal
el **taxista** taxi driver
la **tontería** nonsense
el **tránsito** traffic
la **velocidad** speed
violado, -a violated

Cultural Listening Passage for Chapter 13

The Single Woman

(1) As life changes in Latin America, women also adapt to modern times—perhaps more than men, because in the past they had much less freedom than did the men. But it isn't easy to speak of *one* attitude concerning single women in Latin America, because that depends in great part on their class and social environment. Nowadays high society women live (carry on) a fast and modern life. They don't need to work and they have time, freedom, and money to spare to flirt and travel. Generally they marry well, which means that they select a husband of their same class. The newspapers with their society (social) pages full of women in wedding gowns and with very long (last) names that become longer as they add that of the man they marry are constant evidence of this practice.

(2) But the upper class is small, whereas the lower class always constitutes the majority of the population in many Latin American countries. Among the poor people things are quite different. Young women work, frequently from the age of twelve, whether it be as a servant, a laborer, or a peasant in the rural zones. They are considered lucky if they find a hard-working and responsible man who will treat them well. (3) A high percentage of these women live with a man without being officially married. It is estimated that half the children born among the lower classes are illegitimate. One must read studies such as *Five Families* or *The Children of Sánchez* by the sociologist Oscar Lewis in order to understand the difficult life of these young women.

(4) There remains the middle class, which little by little is extending itself upward and downward. This class is quite synonymous with what is called the bourgeoisie, which looks after their children's morals and meddles in other people's as well. Curiously enough, their

daughters are divided into two groups. The younger ones follow modern trends and are quite independent. They go out with their friends at any time, try to make (create) a professional career for themselves, and demand, in order to marry, a companion who shares their dreams. The older women who are still unmarried are the victims of a period of transition; that is, they don't know whether to follow the norms of filial obedience and let themselves be dominated by the old traditions of their parents, or to become independent also. Most of them will choose the former. They will marry only with the family's approval, and afterward they will accept the role of the housewife who depends completely on her husband.

(5) But at any rate, to marry is not so easy. Although there may be a great number of bachelors, many of them at the age of thirty have not finished their studies or attained an economic level that permits them to think about marriage. And then there's the old problem with its proverb, "a married man wants a house"; and cheap housing is lacking everywhere.

(6) In one of these upper middle class families where the traditional norms still prevail, the matrimonial possibilities and probabilities of Dolores, the still unmarried daughter, are being discussed. Gathered in the living room at this moment are, besides her parents, her older sister, fortunately already married; her younger brother, of more liberal ideas; and a maiden aunt. Dolores is not present, but that doesn't matter.

(7) The aunt is worried because her niece still hasn't found a fiancé in spite of the fact that she has already passed the age of twenty, and she says that something has to be done in order for her to find a suitor. Her smart-aleck brother suggests that they light a candle to Saint Anthony, the patron saint of single girls. The aunt didn't know, however, that Dolores already has a suitor, a man by the name of Cabeza who, according to her sister, is crazy about her. The bad part is that Dolores doesn't like him because, besides being about twenty years older than she is, he is very fat. As her brother says, he must weigh about a thousand pounds. But according to her mother, Mr. Cabeza is a great catch, a very rich, decent, and honest man, from a very good family.

(8) Dolores' father agrees (is in agreement) that his daughter should accept this suitor, because the important thing in marriage is that the man have the qualities his wife has just mentioned. The aunt also agrees. According to her, women cannot afford (give themselves) the luxury of choosing too much because men are always scarce. Love is a secondary thing, she says; it grows in time. One must take advantage of the opportunities, not waste them. In short, the whole family, except the younger brother, agrees that Dolores should marry Mr. Cabeza. Now it's only a matter of convincing Dolores. But that will be easy.

Grammar Points

First, indicative and subjunctive forms in adverb and adjective clauses; second, the generic use of the definite article; third, contrast of the verb **gustar** with the verb "to like"; and fourth, the neuter article **lo**.

Chapter 13

Basic Dialog

¿Sra. Dolores de Cabeza?

TÍA. *Tía*   HNO.[1] *Hermano*   HNA. *Hermana*   MA. *Madre*   PA. *Padre*

TÍA.   ¿Qué hacemos para que Dolores consiga novio?

HNO.   Yo sugiero que le encendamos una vela a San Antonio.

HNA.   No te hagas el chistoso. Dolores ya tiene un pretendiente, tía Marta. ¿No sabía? Se llama Armando Cabeza. Está loco por ella, pero a ella no le gusta.

MA.   Es muy tonta porque él es un gran partido. Sólo que es un poquito gordo.

HNO.   ¡Un poquito! Debe pesar mil libras. Además, es como veinte años mayor.

PA.   Con tal que sea un hombre decente y honrado, eso es lo importante.

HNO.   ¡Qué risa: Sra. Dolores de Cabeza! Además, Dolores no está enamorada. ¿Por qué no busca a alguien que sea más joven, menos gordo y que tenga otro apellido?

TÍA.   ¿Con la escasez de hombres que hay aquí? Hay que aprovechar las oportunidades. El amor crece con el tiempo.

---

[1] Abbreviation of *hermano*.

259

Mrs. Dolores de Cabeza?

A. *Aunt*   B. *Brother*   S. *Sister*   M. *Mother*   F. *Father*

A.   What can we do so that Dolores can catch a man?

B.   I suggest that we light a candle to Saint Anthony.[2]

S.   Don't be funny.[3] Dolores already has a suitor, Aunt Marta. Didn't you know? His name is Armando Cabeza. He's crazy about her, but she doesn't like him.

M.   She's very silly because he's a great catch. Only he's a little heavy.

B.   A little! He must weigh a thousand pounds. Besides, he's about twenty years older.

F.   As long as he's a decent and honest man, that's the important thing.

B.   What a laugh[4]: Mrs. Headache! Besides, Dolores isn't in love. Why doesn't she look for someone younger, less fat, and with a different last name?

A.   With the shortage of men we have here? You've got to take advantage of the opportunities. Love grows with time.

Cultural Note

A married woman's legal name includes *de* (meaning "the wife of") before her husband's last name. Thus, if Marta Campos marries Pedro Molina, she signs her name Marta Campos de Molina, or simply Marta de Molina. She doesn't need to include the title *Sra.* in her signature, or to call herself Sra. Marta de Molina, except for reasons of emphasis: *¿Sabe usted quién soy yo? ¡Soy la Sra. Marta de Molina!*

Dialog Supplement

Con tal que sea un hombre decente
                              sin vicios   *without vices*

Eso es lo importante.
         lo que importa ⎱
         lo que cuenta ⎰   *what counts, matters*

El amor crece con el tiempo.
         odio   *hate*
         La amistad   *friendship*

¡Qué risa!
         chiste   *joke*
         broma   *joke*[5]

---

[2] Saint Anthony is the patron saint of women who wish to marry. (See the reading at the end of this chapter.)

[3] Don't make yourself the funny one.

[4] What laughter.

[5] *Un chiste* is a funny story; *una broma* is a practical joke.

¿Por qué no busca a alguien que tenga otro apellido?

mejor porvenir   *better future*

¿Con la escasez de hombres que hay aquí?

abundancia   *abundance*

Hay que aprovechar las oportunidades.

olvidar   *forget*
desperdiciar   *throw away, waste*

LISTENING COMPREHENSION EXERCISE A

Dialog and Supplement Check

Sentence Recall

Say the dialog phrase or sentence in which each of the following words or phrases occurs.

enamorada	menos gordo	mil libras	loco por ella
pretendiente	escasez	San Antonio	tonta
consiga	gran partido	aprovechar	chistoso
decente y honrado	crece	poquito	qué risa

Item Substitution

Substitute each of the following words and phrases from the Dialog Supplement for a related word or phrase in one of the sentences in the Basic Dialog of this chapter. Repeat the whole new sentence.

EXAMPLE: *Instructor:* qué chiste

Student: **¡Qué chiste: Sra. Dolores de Cabeza!**

desperdiciar	el odio	que tenga porvenir
sin vicios	abundancia	lo que cuenta

Questions

1. ¿Hay abundancia de hombres solteros aquí, o escasez?
2. Y de chicas solteras, ¿hay abundancia?
3. ¿Cómo se llama el pretendiente de Dolores?
4. Si Dolores se casa con él, ¿cómo se va a llamar ella?
5. ¿Qué quiere decir "dolores de cabeza" en inglés?
6. ¿Cómo es él físicamente? ¿Es importante eso?
7. ¿Cuántas libras pesa él, según el hermano de Dolores?
8. ¿Quiere él a Dolores? ¿Cuánto la quiere?

Peru: Sewing class

9. Y Dolores, ¿está ella loca por él?
10. ¿Por qué cree la madre de Dolores que su hija debe casarse con el Sr. Cabeza?
11. ¿Es él mayor o menor que Dolores? ¿Cuántos años?
12. ¿Cree usted que una diferencia de edad de veinte años entre la mujer y el hombre tiene importancia?
13. ¿Cuántos años, máximo, debe ser el hombre mayor que la mujer, según usted?
14. ¿Qué es para una mujer "un gran partido"?
15. ¿Cuáles de ustedes están enamorados? ¿Cuándo piensan casarse?
16. ¿Es una persona chistosa alguien que cuenta cosas tristes?
17. ¿Quién es el más chistoso de esta clase?
18. ¿Le gusta a usted dar bromas? ¿Contar chistes?
19. ¿Olvida usted fácilmente las cosas o tiene buena memoria?
20. ¿Aprovecha usted su tiempo o lo desperdicia?

Grammar

67. Indicative and subjunctive in adverb clauses

A. In Chapter 11 you studied the use of the subjunctive in *noun clauses*. These clauses are called noun clauses because they function in sentences just like nouns and noun phrases. In the following example the noun clause "that John pay me" functions as the object of the verb "demand," just as the single noun "payment" does.

I demand $\begin{cases} \text{payment.} \\ \text{that John pay me.} \end{cases}$

Adverb clauses function in sentences just like simple adverbs and adverb phrases.

I always get up $\begin{cases} \text{early.} \\ \text{before the sun comes up.} \end{cases}$

I. Adverbial expressions always followed by indicative

porque	es tarde	*because it is late*
ya que **como** }	es tarde	*since, inasmuch as it is late*

II. Adverbial expressions always followed by subjunctive

a menos que		*unless it is late*
antes (de) que		*before it is late*
con tal que	sea tarde	*provided it is late*
para que		*so that it is (may, will be) late*
sin que		*without (its) being late*

B. 1. Charts I and II list some of the most common expressions that introduce adverb clauses.
2. Clauses introduced by *porque, ya que,* and *como* (chart I) always contain information that agrees with the facts in the real world. For example, one doesn't say "because it is raining" unless it is in fact raining. These clauses always contain indicative verb forms.
3. Clauses introduced by *a menos que, antes que,* and the other expressions in chart II contain information that may or may not agree with the facts in the real world. For example, if you say "I won't go *unless* Mary goes," you don't know whether Mary will go or not. These clauses always contain subjunctive verb forms.

Clause Substitution

The following exercises contain adverb clauses introduced by expressions from charts I and II, where the choice of indicative or subjunctive is automatically determined by the expression that introduces the clause. These exercises will prepare you for the explanation of the choice of indicative or subjunctive in adverb clauses introduced by a third group of expressions.

EXAMPLE: Ojalá, porque Dolores *no está muy joven.*
(ser buena)
Ojalá, porque Dolores es buena.

1. Ya que Armando *es un hombre honrado,* eso es lo que cuenta.
(pesar apenas mil libras, ser un gran partido, querer a Dolores)
2. ¿Qué hacemos para que *Dolores consiga novio?*
(Dolores casarse, Dolores tener pretendiente, Dolores querer a Armando, Armando venir a verla, Armando proponerle matrimonio, Dolores estar enamorada de Armando, Dolores decir que sí)
3. Con tal que *Armando tenga porvenir,* eso es lo importante.
(Armando ser honrado y decente, Dolores no quedarse soltera, Armando no irse con otra, Armando y Dolores tener muchos hijos)
4. No pueden casarse a menos que *ella tenga veintiún años.*
(ella terminar sus estudios, ella decidirse definitivamente, los padres tener más dinero para la fiesta)
5. No deben hacerlo sin que *nadie lo sepa.*
(nosotros investigar quién es su familia, Dolores conocer a su suegra, Armando hablar con nosotros, nosotros saber cuándo)

Substitution–Translation Exercise

EXAMPLE: Yo no digo nada porque Armando viene.
(provided)
Yo no digo nada con tal que Armando venga.

1. Ya que usted y yo somos amigos, eso no importa.
(unless, so that, provided, since)
2. Yo no voy a ir sin que ustedes vayan.
(because, unless, since, so that, without, before)

III. Adverbial expressions followed by indicative or subjunctive

aunque es	*even though it is, although it is*
aunque sea	*even if it is, although it may be*
donde está	*where it (usually) is*
donde esté	*wherever it may be*
cuando es	*when it (usually) is*
cuando sea	*whenever it may be*
hasta que es	*until it is (as it always is)*
hasta que sea	*until (this time) it is*
tan pronto es	*as soon as it is (as it always is)*
tan pronto sea	*as soon as it is (this time)*
después (de) que es	*after it (usually) is*
después (de) que sea	*after it is (this time)*

C. Charts I and II illustrate the basis for the choice of indicative or subjunctive in adverb clauses introduced by the third group of expressions. Study the following pairs of sentences.

INDICATIVE: **Cuando sale** el sol, estoy contento.   *When the sun comes out I'm happy.* (The sun does in fact come out regularly, and it makes me happy.)

SUBJUNCTIVE: **Cuando salga** el sol, avíseme.   *When the sun comes out, let me know.* (The sun is *not* out now, but I want to know when it subsequently does come out.)

INDICATIVE: Nos vamos, **aunque está** nevando.   *We're leaving, although (even though) it's snowing.* (It *is* snowing right now, but we're leaving anyway.)

SUBJUNCTIVE: Nos vamos, **aunque esté** nevando.   *We're leaving, even if it's snowing.* (I don't know whether it's snowing now or not, but we're leaving in any event.)

Written Translation

1. *Aunque*
He wants to marry (with) her, even though she's dumb and ugly.
He wants to marry (with) her, even if she's dumb and ugly.
2. *Donde*
She wants to be wherever he may be.
She's always where he is.
3. *Cuando*
Come (to) see us when you have money.
You never come to see us when you have money.
4. *Hasta que*
The man always waits until his daughter arrives.
Today, however, he's not going to wait until she arrives.
5. *Tan pronto*
I'll call you as soon as I have some news.
I always call you as soon as I have some news, don't I?
6. *Después (de) que*
I always eat after he does (eat).
I'm going to eat after he eats.

Questions

Provide an answer that includes the phrases in parentheses. If books are closed, your instructor will give the cue. Follow the example.

EXAMPLE: ¿Tiene usted hambre si no come? (sí, cuando)
Sí, cuando no como, tengo hambre.

1. ¿Va a comer tan pronto tenga hambre? (sí, cuando)
2. Su novia probablemente no sabe cocinar. ¿Va a casarse con ella de todos modos? (sí, aunque)
3. Usted no pone atención; por eso no aprende nada, ¿verdad? (sí, como)
4. Si usted sabe alguna noticia, ¿me avisa? (sí, tan pronto)
5. Como hoy es domingo, ¿podemos ir al cine? (sí, ya que)
6. ¿Cree que un joven y una chica deben casarse si están enamorados pero no tienen dinero? (sí, aunque)
7. Si Armando es un hombre decente y honrado, ¿le recomienda usted a Dolores que se case con él? (sí, con tal)

68. Indicative and subjunctive in adjective clauses

> 1. a. Busco un libro **que tiene muchas fotos.**
>   b. Busco un libro **que tenga muchas fotos.**
>
> 2. a. Espero a una chica **que habla inglés.**
>   b. Espero a una chica **que hable inglés.**
>
> 3. a. Hay mucha gente **que sabe hacer paella.**
>   b. No hay nadie **que sepa hacer paella.**

A. *Adjective clauses* modify nouns and pronouns, just like simple adjectives and adjective phrases.

I want to study something { easier. / that won't take so much time.

B. The decision to use the indicative or subjunctive in adjective clauses is made in essentially the same way as in adverb clauses: If the description given in the clause applies to a specific, known noun, then the indicative is used; if the description does not so apply, the subjunctive is used.

For instance, in the (a) examples in the chart, the speaker is (1) looking for a particular book that he knows about that has a lot of pictures; (2) waiting for a particular girl who in fact speaks English; and (3) referring to many people who exist and who know how to make paella. In the (b) examples, on the other hand, the speaker is (1) looking for *any* book (he has no particular one in mind) with a lot of pictures; (2) waiting for some girl (not yet identified and perhaps nonexistent) who speaks English; and (3) denying that people who know how to make paella exist.

In short, the indicative is used in adjective clauses that describe nouns that exist and that have been identified or "picked out." The subjunctive is used when the described noun is unidentified, not "picked out," or nonexistent.

Opinions

Listen to each of the following statements. One student agrees with it, the other disagrees. Begin your responses with *Sí, yo conozco a unos (algunos)* or *No, yo no conozco a ningún(a)* or *a nadie.*

EXAMPLE: Hay muchos americanos que son millonarios.
First student: **Sí, yo conozco a unos americanos que son millonarios.**
Second student: **No, yo no conozco a ningún americano que sea millonario.**

1. Los maestros saben mucho.
2. Las mujeres saben cocinar muy bien.
3. Hay algunos hombres que pesan más de mil libras.
4. Todas las mujeres hablan muchísimo.
5. Hay algunas personas que saben contar buenos chistes.
6. Hay hombres que son un gran partido y tienen un gran porvenir.
7. La gente inteligente pone su dinero en el banco.
8. Los latinoamericanos llegan a tiempo.

Written Composition

Follow the cues given below and write a composition about the ideal type of a woman a man wants for a wife, or man a woman wants for a husband. You may make changes or add some details if you wish to express a different opinion. Make sure you use the subjunctive in the proper places, make the necessary noun-adjective agreements, etc.

Mi tipo ideal

Yo buscar / mujer / no ser / muy viejo / y / (ella) querer tener / mucho / hijo. Yo querer / ella ser / bonito / y estar bonito / día / noche / noche / día. No ser importante / ella no tener / mucho dinero / con tal / ella quereme. Ojalá / futuro / suegra / ser simpático / y creer / yo ser / gran partido / su hija. Cuando casarnos / yo pensar invitar / mis amigos / para que / ellos venir / casa / tomar cerveza. Ojalá / ella no oponerse.

Hasta que / yo encontrar / ese tipo / mujer / yo no casarme.

69. **Generic use of the definite article**

Las mujeres son mejores como maestras.	*Women are better as teachers.*
El amor crece con **el** tiempo.	*Love grows in time.*

In Spanish the definite article normally precedes the subject noun in sentences that mention a property or characteristic of a whole group or class. In English the article is used only with singular subjects in sentences like "The dog is man's best friend," "The three-toed thrig is extinct."

Generalizations

EXAMPLE: ¿Cuáles hombres son malos, nosotros?
No, los hombres en general son malos.

1. ¿Estas chicas nada más son bonitas?
2. ¿Sólo este idioma extranjero es difícil?
3. ¿Sólo esas mujeres rubias y de ojos azules son simpáticas?
4. ¿Cuál vida es amarga, la suya?
5. ¿Dice usted que solamente su casa cuesta mucho?

Oral Translation

1. Money is what counts.
2. Love is good; hate is bad.
3. All vices are bad.
4. Students must help other students.
5. Americans have no problems.
6. Latin Americans need money.
7. Children have to eat.
8. Clothes (*ropa*) are expensive.
9. Meat, vegetables, apples, pears, rice, eggs, butter, tomatoes . . . all food (*comida*) is very expensive.
10. Americans must help.

70. The verb *gustar*

A Juan le gustan las uvas.	*John likes grapes.*
A mí me gusta María.	*I like María.*
Pero a María no le gusto yo.	*But María doesn't like me.*

A. The literal meaning of **gustar** is "to please, to be pleasing." Thus Spanish says "Grapes are pleasing to Juan," whereas English says "Juan like grapes." In other words the Spanish subject and object are the reverse of the English.

   In order to correct any tendency to say non-sentences like *Juan gusta las uvas*, it may help to remember that an indirect object pronoun (*me, te, le, nos, les*) must always be used with *gustar*, and that the preposition *a* must precede the object noun in Spanish (the subject in English): *A Armando **le** gusta Dolores.*

B. The third person singular and plural are the most frequently used forms of *gustar*. The first person singular is normally used only in a situation of contrast, as in the third sentence in the chart, which is in contrast with the second. The more usual equivalent of "María doesn't like me" is *María no me quiere* or *Yo no le caigo bien a María.*[6]

[6]Literally, "I do not fall well to María."

Written Translation

1. Pedro likes María.
   María likes Pedro.
2. Pedro and Carlos like Carmen.
   Carmen doesn't like them.
3. Dolores is going to like her mother-in-law.
   But her mother-in-law is not going to like her.
4. The children liked (*imperfect*) the maid.
   And the maid liked the children.
5. The maid didn't like (*preterit*) the lady.
   The lady didn't like the maid.
6. I hope Dolores likes her new suitor.
   Let's hope that her new suitor likes her.

Translation

Don't forget that the definite article precedes any noun subject that refers to a class as a whole.

1. I like coffee.
2. You like tea.
3. I like girls.
4. And girls like me.
5. One person likes to go to the movies.
6. Another likes to play tennis.
7. Many don't like to do anything.
8. But we like everything.

Questions

1. ¿Le gustó el desayuno esta mañana?
2. ¿Qué clase de frutas le gustan a usted más?
3. ¿Le gusta Dolores al Sr. Cabeza o el Sr. Cabeza le gusta a Dolores?

La Paz, Bolivia: Indian wedding

4. ¿Les gusta a todos ustedes el español?
5. ¿Me gustan a mí mis alumnos?
6. ¿Cuál es la película que más le ha gustado a usted en su vida?

71. The neuter article *lo*

Eso es **lo** importante.	*That's the important thing.*
Eso es **lo** que cuenta.	*That's what counts.*

A. The article **lo** never precedes a noun and consequently has nothing with which it can agree in gender. Like the demonstratives *esto* and *eso* (grammar section E, p. 63), *lo* is thus neuter, rather than masculine or feminine.

B. *Lo* can precede an adjective, an adjective phrase introduced by *de,* or an adjective clause:

ADJECTIVE: lo importante   *the important thing (part, aspect)*
PHRASE: lo de la casa   *the thing (matter, bit, part) about the house*
CLAUSE: lo que cuenta   *what counts, matters, the part (aspect, thing) that counts*

English has no exact counterpart to *lo;* the English equivalents of Spanish expressions with *lo* usually have a cover word such as *thing, part, side, aspect, bit,* and so on.

C. Of the three constructions with *lo,* the most common are *lo* before a simple adjective (*lo bueno*) and *lo* before an adjective clause (*lo que cuenta, lo que me gusta*). Only these two are included in the following exercises.

Transformation

EXAMPLE: La parte mejor de la casa es la sala.
            Lo mejor de la casa es la sala.

1. La cosa importante es que sea un hombre honrado.
2. El aspecto malo de esta situación es el dinero.
3. La parte más buena de este libro es el color.
4. La parte triste en la vida de una mujer es que no puede casarse cuando quiere.
5. El aspecto más feo de la casa es que la cocina es muy vieja.

Transformation

EXAMPLE: Todas las cosas que me gustan son caras.
            Todo lo que me gusta es caro.

1. Nadie tiene las cosas que yo tengo.
2. La parte que no me gusta de mi suegra es que habla mucho.
3. La cosa que ellos no entienden es que Dolores no está enamorada.
4. Nunca encontramos las cosas que buscamos.
5. El problema que ella menciona en su carta es terrible.

Oral Translation

1. The important (thing) is the truth.
   What is important is the truth.
2. The best (thing) is to be honest.
   The (thing) that counts is to be honest.
3. Good (things) are expensive.
   What is good is expensive.
4. The bad (part) about this book is that it is not cheap.
   The (thing) that I don't like about this book is that it is not cheap.

LISTENING COMPREHENSION EXERCISE B

Reading

Catalina y San Antonio
Una leyenda del Ecuador

En una casa grande cerca de la antigua iglesia de San Francisco en Quito vivía, hace muchos años, una viuda con su hija Catalina. Desde la edad de quince años, cuando la linda señorita fue presentada a la alta sociedad en un baile elegante y costoso, muchos pretendientes le habían pedido la mano. Pero Catalina, algo consentida[7] y un poco orgullosa por tantas atenciones, no encontraba ningún pretendiente a su gusto. Los rehusó[8] a todos, uno después de otro.

—Es lástima que tú, una señorita tan bella como un amanecer[9], no te cases —le decían a Catalina sus amigos.

—Cuidado, chica, o vas a quedarte soltera —le avisaban las amigas recién casadas.

De buen humor, Catalina escuchaba estos consejos[10] sin seguirlos, y el resultado fue que a la edad avanzada de dieciocho años todavía no había encontrado esposo.

[7] Spoiled.
[8] *Rehusar:* to turn down.
[9] Dawn.
[10] (Pieces of) advice.

Quito, Ecuador:
Church of San
Francisco

—Esto no puede continuar así —le dijo la buena madre a Catalina—. ¿No quieres casarte con Carlos que anoche te dio la serenata?

—¿Con ese gordo? No, mamacita. ¡Qué barril!

—Pues, no entiendo por qué no quieres a Luis que tiene una familia tan distinguida.

—No, no, es tan pálido como un muerto.

—¿Y Eduardo que es el más guapo[11] de todos los jóvenes de la capital?

—No, no, es tan alto como un palo[12].

—Pues, dime, hijita, ¿quieres quedarte para vestir santos[13]?

—¡Oh, no, no! —contestó Catalina llorando—; pero, ¿qué voy a hacer cuando no encuentro a ningún pretendiente a mi gusto?

Por algunos momentos, la madre se quedó pensando. Entonces habló como si fuera[14] inspirada:

—He oído decir que San Antonio de Padua sabe dar buenos maridos a las jóvenes que le piden devotamente este favor. Creo que debemos pedir ayuda al buen santo.

[11] Handsome.
[12] Pole, stick.
[13] The expression *quedarse para vestir santos* refers to the stereotype of the unmarried woman in Spanish-speaking countries who spends her time in Catholic churches doing various tasks, among them changing the robes of the statues of saints.
[14] (She) were.

—Bueno, mamacita —contestó Catalina, secando sus lágrimas—. Vamos a rezar[15] en seguida[16] en la iglesia de San Francisco.

Así, día tras día, las dos, madre e hija, fueron a la iglesia a rezar al buen santo. Sin embargo, ningún pretendiente agradable se presentó. Por supuesto, la señorita se puso triste.

—Debes tener fe y paciencia, hija —avisó la madre—. Ahora tengo otra idea. En tu cuarto vamos a arreglar un altarcito con una estatua de San Antonio. Entonces, por nueve noches le rezaremos al santo, pidiéndole que te consiga un esposo a tu gusto. Sé que te dará lo que pides.

—Voy a hacerlo por obediencia —respondió Catalina, tristemente—. Pero si al fin de nueve días no me ha ayudado San Antonio, haré algo terrible, absolutamente terrible.

Así, el altarcito de San Antonio fue arreglado con flores frescas y dos velas grandes que quemaron constantemente. Aunque las dos mujeres rezaron por nueve noches, el novio del milagro[17] no apareció.

Pacientemente, Catalina esperó unos días más. Entonces una tarde la señorita, llorando a lágrima viva, corrió al altarcito. Tomando la estatua del santo en las manos, le dijo:

—Perdóname, santo mío, pero como no me has dado un esposo, no quiero verte más.

Dicho esto, la señorita arrojó la estatua por una ventana abierta a la calle. En ese mismo momento pasaba un caballero elegantemente vestido. Y el santo cayó exactamente en la copa[18] alta de su fino sombrero.

El caballero reaccionó violentamente con el golpe recibido en la cabeza. Se puso furioso. Recogiendo la estatua, fue a la puerta de la casa de donde había sido arrojada. Con su bastón[19] llamó ruidosamente. Pronto apareció la madre.

—Arrojar una estatua a la calle es una cosa terrible, señora. Y mire cómo está arruinado mi fino sombrero que compré en París.

—Lo siento mucho, señor.

—Pues, explíqueme, señora, ¿por qué arrojó la estatua? ¿No sabe que ha cometido un gran pecado?

—Tenga paciencia, buen caballero, y se lo contaré todo.

Al final de la explicación la madre añadió:

—Pero mi hija es amable y bella, señor.

Ahora el caballero, más curioso que enojado, contestó:

—Le ruego que me disculpe, señora, que tal vez estuve un poco violento. Y ahora espero que me haga el favor de presentarme a su preciosa hija que ha sufrido tanto.

[15] To pray.
[16] At once.
[17] Miracle.
[18] Crown.
[19] Cane.

—El gusto es mío, caballero. Pase y siéntese. Esta es su casa —dijo la madre, abriendo la puerta de la sala.

El señor aceptó la invitación y la madre salió en busca de Catalina. Sin entusiasmo, la señorita acompañó a su madre a la sala donde extendió la mano al caballero cuyo apellido indicaba que pertenecía a una de las familias más ricas y distinguidas del Ecuador.

El caballero quedó asombrado de la belleza de Catalina y le dijo:

—Le ruego, doña Catalina, que me considere su sincero admirador. Y permítame ser el primer servidor de su casa.

—Mi madre y yo estamos honradas con su presencia. Tendremos mucho gusto en recibirle, caballero —contestó la hija con modestia.

Después de esos discursos sinceros y entusiásticos, los tres platicaron[20], hora tras hora, como si hubieran sido[21] viejos amigos. Catalina estaba encantada del buen joven amable e inteligente que acababa de volver de Europa donde había estudiado por muchos años. Y el caballero estaba encantado de la modestia y hermosura de Catalina.

Al fin del año se casaron los jóvenes en la antigua iglesia de San Francisco, celebrando las bodas con pompa y esplendor.

Si hoy día visita la iglesia, puede ver en una de las capillas una preciosa estatua de San Antonio de Padua. Se dice que es el regalo de dos personas muy agradecidas —Catalina y su esposo.

For Oral or Written Composition

una viuda
ningún pretendiente
edad avanzada
para vestir santos
piden devotamente
arreglar un altarcito
arrojó la estatua
se puso furioso
apellido
platicaron
la modestia
agradecidas

LISTENING COMPREHENSION EXERCISE C

---

[20] *Platicar:* to chat.
[21] As if they had been.

Vocabulary

a menos que unless
la **abundancia** abundance
la **amistad** friendship
antes (de) que before
aprovechar to take advantage of
el **aspecto** aspect
aunque although
la **broma** (practical) joke
como since, inasmuch as
con tal que provided that
contar (ue) to matter, be important
contrario, -a opposite
crecer (zc) to grow
cuando whenever
el **chiste** joke
chistoso, -a funny
dar bromas to play jokes
decente decent
definitivamente definitively, decisively
desperdiciar to waste, throw away
después (de) que *conj* after
la **diferencia** difference
encender to light
la **escasez** shortage
el **estudio** study
físicamente physically
gustar to be pleasing (to)

hasta que until
la **importancia** importance
importar to matter
investigar to investigate
el **matrimonio** marriage
millonario, -a millionaire
el **odio** hate
olvidar to forget
oponerse to object
para que so that, in order that
el **partido** match (for marriage)
pesar to weigh
el **porvenir** future
el **pretendiente** suitor
probablemente probably
querer (ie) to love
querer decir to mean
la **risa** laugh, laughter
sin que *conj* without
la **situación** situation
soltero, -a unmarried
sugerir (ie) to suggest
tan pronto (como) as soon as
terminar to finish
la **vela** candle
el **vicio** vice
ya que since, inasmuch as

Cultural Listening Passage
for Chapter 14

Lack of Punctuality:
Defect or Virtue?

(1) The North American visitor who has a date with his Latin American friend in a café at seven o'clock and has to wait for him till eight twenty no (without) doubt will get angry. Perhaps the uproar (shouting) of the people in the café, the typical effusiveness of the Latins, and the almost interminable conversation in social gatherings will also bother him. And possibly it will displease him that without connections (the intervention of friendships) it is difficult to open a checking (running) account in a bank or to obtain the cooperation of the municipal authorities.

(2) This reaction is understandable, because the visitor judges such conduct from the point of view of his own culture. In the same way there are thousands of Latin American students who have come to the United States and have gone back (away) after one semester because they couldn't adapt to local life.

(3) The North American must try to understand that the social structure in Latin America is different and that, as a result, what motivates the conduct of the Latin American is different also. This doesn't mean that he must imitate that conduct. The anthropologist who studies the customs of a civilization does not necessarily utilize them for himself, but examines them, knowing that they are the result of national cultural values. If in the Latin culture sentimentalism and emotion occupy a prominent place, the gestures and phrases that seem exaggerated have their reason for being so. While in the Anglo-Saxon culture the control of emotions is a virtue, in the Latin culture such a disposition is considered (as) cold and undesirable.

(4) Returning to the question of punctuality

and the lack of it, time is a subjective thing (to the) south of the Rio Grande,* because the Latin American, like Don Quixote, not only creates his own reality, but also lives comfortably within it. To arrive late is not a social crime, because time is quite elastic. The same concept prevails during a social gathering: one doesn't look at his watch, but rather lives it up (lives the hour).

(5) Where he can (it is possible for him), the Latin American considers work as an extension of his own reality, and therefore he will seek to modify it by chatting, drinking coffee, and above everything else, watching out for his social standing—in sum, by imposing an intensely personal rhythm on it. Here too time is subordinated to personal reality and, as a result, in some public offices that are open to the public only from fourteen to eighteen hours from Monday to Friday, the bosses will arrive a little late and perhaps leave early too, if they feel like it (have desires). This is a privilege that only the fortunate can enjoy, but it is also an ideal that those less fortunate dream of turning into a reality (achieving) some day. Each culture has its priorities.

(6) In the dialog of this chapter we see poor Slim Hernández sad and disappointed because his friend Andrés, who had agreed to pick him up (come by for him) to take him to a party, stood him up (left him planted). This wouldn't have bothered Slim so much if the occasion had been different (another). After all, to be stood up (that they stand him up) is not unheard of (something of the other world). But this time it was different: Slim—everyone knows him by that nickname because he is tall and thin like bamboo—Slim was dying (crazy) to go to that party, because it was the opportunity of his life to meet Luz María Terán Marín and declare his love for her.

(7) His friend Andrés had told him to wait for him on the corner by the shoe store. Right there was where Slim waited until almost eleven, but finally he got tired and had no other recourse but to go to (put himself in) a movie. He couldn't take a taxi to go to the party because he couldn't even find out where it was. What happened to Andrés was that he was delayed a little, that was all. When he passed by the corner it was already going on (to be) twelve.

(8) Another friend of Slim's, called (whom they call) Chino, began to tease (annoy) him and make his mouth water telling him about the party. He told him that the party had been ter-rif-ic, that they had gone all out (thrown the house out the window). He said that Luz María had looked out of this world (simply divine), and that he had danced with her all night and she had asked (told) Chino to say hello to Slim. And poor Slim was almost crying listening to his friend. Finally Andrés intervened and told Chino to shut up.

Grammar Points

First, forms of the past subjunctive; second, uses of the past subjunctive; third, the construction **ojalá + subjunctive;** fourth, additional uses of **ser;** and fifth, the command forms for **tú.**

*In Latin America the Rio Grande is known as the *Río Bravo.*

Viña del Mar, Chile:
Discothèque

Chapter 14

Basic Dialog

Falta de puntualidad

FL. *El Flaco*   AN. *Andrés*   CH. *El Chino*

I

FL.   Ni me digas nada. Me dejaste plantado.

AN.   Un momento. ¿No te dije que me esperaras en la esquina de la zapatería?

FL.   ¿Ah sí? ¿Y dónde crees que estuve hasta casi las once? Por fin me cansé y me fui a un cine.

AN.   Lo siento, no fue culpa mía.

FL.   ¡Tantas ganas que tenía de ir a esa fiesta! Pero ni siquiera pude averiguar dónde era.

II

CH. ¡La fiesta estuvo fe-no-me-nal! Tiraron la casa por la ventana, no te miento. ¡Ah, y Luz María estaba divina!

AN. ¿Por qué no te callas, Chino?

FL. ¿Bailaste con ella?

CH. Ajá, y me dijo que te saludara.

FL. Ojalá fuera cierto. No te creo.

CH. Palabra. Lástima que no fuiste.

AN. ¡Ah, caramba! ¡Qué lata eres, Chino!

Lack of punctuality

SL. *Slim*   AN. *Andrés*   CH. *Chino*

I

SL. Don't say anything to me. You stood me up.[1]

AN. Just a moment. Didn't I tell you to wait for me on the corner by the shoe store?

SL. Oh yeah? And where do you think I was until almost eleven? I finally got tired and went to a movie.

AN. I'm sorry, it wasn't my fault.

SL. I really wanted[2] to go to that party! But I couldn't even find out where it was.

II

CH. The party was ter-rif-ic! They went all out;[3] I'm not lying. Oh, and Luz María looked out of this world.

AN. Why don't you shut up, Chino?

SL. Did you dance with her?

CH. Uh-huh, and she told me to say hello to you.

SL. I wish it were true. I don't believe you.

CH. I swear. Too bad you didn't go.

AN. Oh, good grief! What a nuisance you are, Chino!

Cultural Notes

The use of nicknames involving adjectives like *flaco,* "skinny," *chino,* "with slanted eyes" (literally, "Chinese"), *negro,* "dark complexioned," and *indio,* "Indian," is not offensive, and persists well beyond school age in Latin America.

---

[1] Left me planted.
[2] So many desires I had.
[3] Threw the house out the window.

Dialog Supplement

I

¿No te dije que me esperaras...
                  pasaras por mí   *come by for me*

...en la esquina de la zapatería?
                  peluquería   *barber shop, beauty salon*
                  panadería   *bakery*
                  cafetería   *coffee shop*
                  carnicería   *butcher shop*
                  sastrería   *tailor shop*
                  tintorería   *cleaner's*

Por fin me cansé.
             me aburrí   *got bored*

II

La fiesta estuvo fe-no-me-nal.
El baile   *the dance*
El concierto   *the concert*
La conferencia   *the lecture*

LISTENING COMPREHENSION EXERCISE A

Dialog and Supplement Check

Sentence Recall

Say the dialog phrase or sentence in which each of the following words and phrases occurs.

ganas	hasta casi	esperaras	averiguar
ni siquiera	nada	zapatería	por la ventana
lástima	por fin	divina	plantado
te callas	ojalá	bailaste	culpa

Questions

1. ¿Por qué no fue el Flaco a la fiesta?
2. ¿Quién dejó plantado al Flaco?
3. ¿Lo han dejado a usted plantado alguna vez?
4. Y usted, ¿ha dejado plantado a alguien?
5. ¿Dónde estuvo esperando el Flaco a Andrés?
6. ¿Hasta qué hora estuvo esperándolo allí?
7. ¿Por qué no pasó Andrés por su amigo?

8. ¿Qué hizo el Flaco entonces?
9. ¿Por qué se fue a un cine?
10. ¿Por qué no tomó un taxi para ir a la fiesta?
11. ¿Por qué no preguntó dónde era la fiesta?
12. ¿Por qué tenía el Flaco tantas ganas de ir a la fiesta?
13. ¿Y cómo estuvo la fiesta, según el Chino?
14. ¿Qué tiraron por la ventana?
15. ¿Quiere Andrés que el Chino se calle o que continúe hablando de la fiesta?
16. ¿Bailó el Chino con Luz María?
17. ¿Cómo estaba ella, según él?
18. ¿Qué le dijo ella al Chino que le dijera al Flaco?
19. ¿Qué le respondió su amigo?
20. ¿Qué le dice Andrés al Chino?

Grammar

72. Forms of the past subjunctive

Third person plural preterit		Past subjunctive
Regular verbs	habla comie vivie	
Verbs with vowel alternations	pidie murie	**supiera** **supieras** **supiera** **supiéramos** **supieran**
Irregular verbs	estuvie pusie supie dije fue	
	-ron	**supierais**

A. For *all* verbs, regular or irregular, the stem of the past subjunctive is based on the third person plural form of the preterit. There are absolutely no exceptions.
B. The *nosotros* form is stressed on the third syllable from the end: *habláramos, comiéramos,* etc. All other forms are stressed on the next-to-last syllable.
C. There is an alternate set of endings for the past subjunctive in which -*se*- replaces -*ra*- in all forms; for example, *hablase, hablases,* etc., *supiese, supieses,* etc. However, for active use you need learn only the set shown in the chart, since these are far more commonly used in the spoken language in Spanish America.

Infinitive → Preterit → Past Subjunctive

Give the third person plural forms of the preterit and the past subjunctive for each of the following infinitives.

EXAMPLE: tomar: **tomaron, tomaran**

ser	estar	traer	crecer	prometer	preguntar
pedir	deber	poner	sentir	enseñar	levantarse
decir	tener	morir	costar	robar	refugiarse
leer	saber	pesar	cuidar	enojarse	afeitarse
ir	beber	entrar	servir	vestirse	quejarse
creer	hacer	cortar	llegar	quedarse	suicidarse

Paradigm Practice

Do the complete past subjunctive paradigm of as many of the verbs in the previous exercise as you can. Start each phrase with the lead word *que*.

EXAMPLE: **que yo me levantara, que tú te levantaras, que usted se levantara, que él se levantara, que nosotros nos levantáramos, que ustedes se levantaran, que ellos se levantaran**

73. Uses of the past subjunctive

I. Noun Clauses

> PRESENT: Le estoy diciendo a usted **que espere.**
> *I'm telling you to wait.*
>
> PAST: Le dije a usted **que esperara.**
> *I told you to wait.*

II. Adjective Clauses

> PRESENT: Busco a alguien **que sepa** cocinar.
> *I'm looking for someone who knows how to cook.*
>
> PAST: Buscaba a alguien **que supiera** cocinar.
> *I was looking for someone who knew how to cook.*

III. Adverb Clauses

> PRESENT: Nunca voy al cine **a menos que tenga** tiempo.
> *I never go to the movies unless I have time.*
>
> PAST: Nunca iba al cine **a menos que tuviera** tiempo.
> *I never went to the movies unless I had time.*

As illustrated in the charts, the use of the past subjunctive in noun, adjective, and adverb clauses follows the same general principles that apply to the use of the present subjunctive. The difference is that the present subjunctive refers to the *present* or the *future*, while in general the past subjunctive refers to the *past*.

Before you do the following exercises, you should review grammar sections 61 and 62 in Chapter 11, and 67 and 68 in Chapter 13, and their accompanying exercises, which deal with the present subjunctive.

Tense Substitution

Change the present subjunctive forms to the past subjunctive. Remember that for all verbs, regular or irregular, the stem of the past subjunctive is based on the third person plural form of the preterit.

EXAMPLE: que estudien
que estudiaran

Madrid, Spain: (above) Cuatro Caminos, subway station and busy intersection (right) Fuente de la Cibeles

1. *Clauses with* -ar *verbs*

con tal que te calles

para que ellos no nos dejen plantados

hasta que Catalina se canse

que Dolores se case con Armando

para que nos levantemos temprano

aunque no baile bien

que no me acueste tarde

a menos que usted cante

sin que te calles

que me esperes

tan pronto averigüemos

que no hable y no fume mucho

que me dejes plantado

que te salude

con tal que tiren la casa por
   la ventana

2. *Clauses with* -er *and* -ir *verbs,* dar, andar, *and* estar

aunque él no tenga dinero

antes que mi suegra se aburra

con tal que sea honrado

para que no digamos nada

que sepa hablar inglés

que los chicos no coman mucho

aunque haga mucho frío

que le escriban a su madre

hasta que ella se vaya

cuando venga el cartero

que vivamos muchos años

después que vaya a la fiesta

que le digan a la señora

antes que ustedes lean ese libro

que estén todos muy bien

para que me den el dinero

cuando andemos de compras

que ustedes aprendan

sin que ellos vendan la casa

hasta que salgan de la otra

tan pronto puedan

y que vayamos allá pronto

aunque él no quiera

que no me digas nada

Clause Substitution

Remember that the present subjunctive refers to the *present* or the *future,* while the past subjunctive refers to the *past.*

EXAMPLE: No quiso que su amigo fuera a la fiesta.
        (es necesario)
     Es necesario que su amigo vaya a la fiesta.

Noun clauses
   1. Andrés le dijo que esperara en la esquina.
      (es mejor, yo no creí, fue bueno, él quería)
   2. Siento mucho que tengas tantos problemas.
      (es malo, ellos no creyeron, me alegro, fue una lástima)

Adjective clauses
   1. Queremos una mujer[4] que sepa cocinar.
      (busco, no había, no encontrábamos, no conocen)

---

[4]The personal *a* is omitted when the speaker thinks primarily of the services rendered by the person referred to, rather than his human qualities, as in this sentence and the next. Compare, for example, the following sentences: *María quiere un médico,* "María wants a doctor," and *María quiere a un médico,* "María loves a doctor."

2. ¿Buscabas un hombre que tuviera experiencia?
(quieres, encontraste, hay, necesitabas, buscas)
3. No necesito a nadie que hable francés.
(no teníamos, no quieren, no encontré, no conozco)

Adverb clauses

1. Quiero esperar hasta que Andrés venga por mí.
(iba a, estoy, era necesario, es imposible, estaba)
2. Nunca voy allí a menos que tenga dinero.
(iba, estudiaba, me quedo, vuelvo, vivía)
3. Se fueron para que estudiáramos más.
(vienen, estuvieron aquí, trajeron el libro, están aquí)

Tense Substitution

Shift the following sentences to the past. Say each segment first, then the entire paragraph. Use the past tense indicated in parentheses for the indicative verb forms, as in the example.

EXAMPLE: La madre de Dolores quiere (*imperf.*)... que su hija vaya a la fiesta,... aunque no tenga muchas ganas,... para que conozca a muchos chicos... y consiga novio... para que se case pronto.
    La madre de Dolores quería... que su hija fuera a la fiesta,... aunque no tuviera muchas ganas,... para que conociera a muchos chicos... y consiguiera novio... para que se casara pronto.

1. Andrés le dice (*pret.*) al Chino... que él es (*imperf.*) una lata... y que a menos que se calle... se va (*imperf.*) a enojar.
2. No me importa (*imperf.*)... que el novio de mi hija sea viejo y feo... y que no sepa bailar,... con tal que sea un hombre honrado... y tenga porvenir.
3. Le pido (*pret.*) a mi amigo... que me espere en la esquina... hasta que yo llegue,... Pero como él es (*imperf.*) muy tonto,... no me espera (*pret.*)... y se va (*pret.*).
4. Dice (*pret.*) el maestro... que es (*imperf.*) necesario... que pongamos atención... y estudiemos más... para que sepamos bien esto... cuando tengamos el examen final.

Rejoinders

The instructor repeats the same questions each time, and the whole class answers.

EXAMPLE: *Instructor:*   ¡Hablen! ¿Qué quiero yo?
    Class: **Usted quiere que hablemos.**
    Instructor: ¿Qué les dije yo?
    Class: **Usted nos dijo que habláramos.**

1. ¡Digan algo!
2. ¡Pongan atención!
3. ¡Abran la ventana!
4. ¡Cierren la puerta!
5. ¡Siéntense!
6. ¡Levántense!
7. ¡Hagan silencio!
8. ¡Váyanse a la casa!
9. ¡No vengan aquí más!
10. ¡Vuelvan! ¡Vuelvan!
11. ¡No me dejen solo!
12. ¡Quédense conmigo!

Questions

1. ¿Le dijo Andrés a su amigo que lo esperara en la esquina de una carnicería, de una peluquería, o de una zapatería?
2. ¿Qué venden en una carnicería?
3. ¿Qué hacen en una sastrería?
4. ¿Qué hacen en una tintorería?
5. ¿En qué clase de tienda venden pan?
6. ¿Adónde van para comprar libros?
7. ¿Qué venden en una cafetería?
8. ¿Dónde se corta usted el pelo?
9. ¿Dónde compra zapatos?
10. ¿Dónde compran ustedes sus libros?

74. *ojalá* + subjunctive

Ojalá (que) estén aquí.	*I hope they're here (and perhaps they are).*
Ojalá (que) estuvieran aquí.	*I wish they were here (but they aren't).*

Ojalá followed by the present subjunctive means "I hope . . . ." Followed by the past subjunctive, it means "I wish . . . ." *Que* is often omitted.

Oral Translation

1. I hope you have time.
   I wish you had time.
2. I hope you'll be my friend.
   I wish you were my friend.
3. I hope my dad will say (that) yes.
   I wish my dad would say (that) yes.
4. I hope the girl speaks Spanish.
   I wish the girl would speak Spanish.
5. I hope you'll shut up.
   I wish you'd shut up.
6. I hope you won't eat with your (the) mouth open (*abierta*).
   I wish you wouldn't eat with your mouth open.
7. I hope we don't have problems.
   I wish we didn't have problems.
8. I hope you don't have to work tomorrow.
   I wish you didn't have to work tomorrow.

75. Additional uses of *ser*

> María **estaba** allí.   *María was there.*
> La fiesta **era** allí.   *The party was (being held) there.*

In Chapter 2 you learned that only *estar* can be used when the verb complement expresses location, for example *donde, allí, en mi casa* (first example). However, when the subject refers to an activity (*una fiesta, un baile, una conferencia*) rather than an object or a person (*la mesa, María*), only *ser* is used, and has the meaning "to take place," "to be held" (second example).

Translation

1. Where is Andrés?
   Where is the dance?

2. The dinner was (*imperf.*) on the table.
   The dinner was being held at (in) the Grand Hotel.[5]

3. The president was (*pret.*) here.
   The coup d'état was (*pret.*) here.

4. The guest (*invitado*) is going to be here at eight.
   The lecture is going to be here at eight.

5. The bride (*novia*) was going to be at (in) her aunt's house.
   The wedding was going to be at (in) Saint Joseph's Church.

6. Where will the groom (*novio*) be?
   Where will the ceremony (*ceremonia*) be?

7. He won't be in the back yard (*patio*).
   The wedding won't be in the back yard.

8. I don't want anybody to be here.
   I don't want the party to be here.

9. Luz María wanted Flaco to be at (in) her party.
   Luz María wanted the party to be held at the country club.[6]

10. I hope (*ojalá*) Dolores is there.
    I hope the lecture is there.

11. I wish you were here.
    I wish the picnic were here.

[5] *El hotel.*
[6] *El country club.*

Replacement

1. ¿Dónde va a estar la gente?

   ¿_____ el baile?

   ¿_____ fue _____?

   ¿_____ la conferencia?

   ¿_____ era _____?

   ¿_____ ustedes?

2. El profesor está en la casa.

   La fiesta _____.

   _____ iba a ser _____.

   Yo _____.

   _____ aquí.

   El examen _____.

3. Ojalá que el examen sea en este cuarto.

   _____ mi libro _____.

   _____ en la escuela.

   _____ estuviera _____.

   _____ la fiesta _____.

76. *tú* command forms[7]

	Affirmative		**Negative**	
-ar	Habla (tú).	*Talk.*	No hables (tú).	*Don't talk.*
-er	Bebe (tú).	*Drink.*	No bebas (tú).	*Don't drink.*
-ir	Escribe (tú).	*Write.*	No escribas (tú).	*Don't write.*

-ar	Hablad (vosotros).	No habléis (vosotros).
-er	Bebed (vosotros).	No bebáis (vosotros).
-ir	Escribid (vosotros).	No escribáis (vosotros).

A. The *affirmative tú* command forms are the same as those of the third person singular present indicative.

   El habla inglés; habla tú inglés también.

   El bebe mucho; bebe tú mucho también.

   El escribe bien; escribe tú bien también.

B. The *negative tú* command forms are the same as the *tú* forms of the present subjunctive.

   No quiero que hables. ¡No hables!

   Es malo que bebas. ¡No bebas!

   No es necesario que escribas. ¡No escribas!

[7]For the reasons given in Chapter 1 (page 17), *tú* verb forms have not, in general, been emphasized in this book. Correspondingly, the purpose of the following explanations and exercises is not to enable you to use the *tú* command forms actively yourself, but only to enable you to recognize them when you encounter them in speech or writing.

C. A few common verbs have irregular *affirmative tú* command forms.

hacer:	**Haz** algo.	*Do something.*
tener:	**Ten** paciencia.	*Be patient.*
poner:	**Pon** atención.	*Pay attention.*
decir:	**Di** algo.	*Say something.*
venir:	**Ven** acá.	*Come here.*
salir:	**Sal** de aquí.	*Get out of here.*
ser:	**Sé** bueno.	*Be good.*
ir:	**Ve** a tu casa.	*Go home.*

The *negative tú* commands of these verbs are formed as described in the previous paragraph: *No hagas nada, No tengas paciencia,* etc.

D. The *affirmative vosotros* commands are formed by replacing the final *r* of the infinitive with a *d*. There are no exceptions.

ir:	**Id.**	*Go.*
ser:	**Sed** buenos.	*Be good.*

The *negative vosotros* command forms are the same as the *vosotros* forms of the present subjunctive.

No quiero que vayáis. ¡No vayáis!
No quiero que seáis malos. ¡No seáis malos!

E. The position of object pronouns with respect to *tú* command forms is the same as for the *usted, ustedes,* and *nosotros* command forms. That is, object pronouns follow affirmative command forms (and are attached to them in writing), but precede negative command forms.

Mánda**melo.**	*Sent it to me.*
No **me lo** mandes.	*Don't send it to me.*
Dí**selo.**	*Tell it to him.*
No **se lo** digas.	*Don't tell it to him.*

Written Translation

Use a *tú* command in the second clause of each sentence.

1. If he calls, you call too.
2. If he learns, you learn too.
3. If Luz María gets married, you get married too.
4. If Mr. Gómez sells his house, you sell your house too.
5. If he bathes, you bathe too.
6. If your godmother writes to you, you write to her too.

Completion

Write completions containing negative *tú* commands, using the same verb and addressing the commands to Juanito, as in the model.

EXAMPLE: Hable usted, señor, pero...
   no hables tú, Juanito.

1. Cásese usted, tía Marta, pero...
2. Lea usted, don Pedro, pero...
3. Quédese usted, señora, pero...
4. Acuéstese usted, doña María, pero...
5. Escríbale usted a ella, señor, pero...

Written Translation

Use *tú* commands only.

1. Don't come now, come tomorrow.
2. Do me a favor, will you (*¿quieres?*) Don't do anything.
3. Don't put that on the table, put it here.
4. Be good, don't be foolish.
5. Leave in the morning, don't leave now.
6. Come here. Don't come to me with stories.
7. Don't be afraid (don't have fear); have patience.
8. Don't tell me lies, tell me the truth.

Substitution

Change the following sentences to *usted* command forms.

EXAMPLE: Ponte los zapatos, Juan.
   Póngase los zapatos, Juan.

1. Ven acá, Pedro, y siéntate.
2. Cállate, hazme el favor, ¿quieres?
3. No seas malo, sé un hombre bueno toda la vida.
4. Dile a María que te devuelva el libro.
5. ¡No quiero verte más! ¡Sal de aquí!
6. Ve a cualquier parte, pero vete. ¡Vete, por el amor de Dios!
7. Ponte algo en la cabeza si vas a entrar a la iglesia.
8. ¡Diez años más, María, eso es todo! ¡Ten paciencia, y dime que me esperarás! ¡Dímelo!

LISTENING COMPREHENSION EXERCISE B

Reading

El tiempo y el espacio*
por Julio Camba

Tengo un asunto urgente a ventilar[8] con un amigo. Desde luego el amigo se opone a que lo ventilemos hoy.

—¿Le parece a usted que nos veamos mañana?

—Muy bien. ¿A qué hora?

—A cualquier hora. Después de almorzar, por ejemplo...

Yo le hago observar a mi amigo que eso no constituye una hora. Después de almorzar es algo demasiado vago, demasiado elástico.

—¿A qué hora almuerza usted?—le pregunto.

—¿Que a qué hora almuerzo? Pues a la hora en que almuerza todo el mundo: a la hora de almorzar...

—Pero ¿qué hora es la hora de almorzar para usted? ¿El mediodía? ¿La una de la tarde? ¿Las dos...?

—Por ahí, por ahí... —dice mi amigo—. Yo almuerzo de una a dos. A veces me siento a la mesa cerca de las tres... De todos modos a las cuatro siempre estoy libre.

—Perfectamente. Entonces podríamos citarnos[9] para las cuatro.

Mi amigo asiente.

—Claro que, si me retraso unos minutos—añade—, usted me esperará. Quien dice a las cuatro, dice a las cuatro y cuarto o cuatro y media. En fin, de cuatro a cinco yo estaré sin falta en el café. ¿Le parece a usted?

Yo quiero puntualizar:

—Digamos a las cinco.

—¿A las cinco? Muy bien. A las cinco... Es decir, de cinco a cinco y media... Uno no es un tren, ¡qué diablo! Supóngase usted que me rompo una pierna...

—Pues citémonos para las cinco y media—propongo yo.

Entonces a mi amigo se le ocurre una idea genial.[10]

—¿Por qué no citarnos a la hora del aperitivo?—sugiere.

Hay una nueva discusión para fijar en términos de reloj la hora del aperitivo. Por último, quedamos en reunirnos de siete a ocho. Al día siguiente dan las ocho, y claro está, mi amigo no comparece.[11] Llega a las ocho y media echando el bofe,[12] y el camarero[13] le dice que yo me he marchado.[14]

---

*"El tiempo y el espacio," from Volume I of Julio Camba, *Obras completas*. Reprinted by permission of Editorial Plus-Ultra, Madrid.
[8]Clear up.
[9]Get together.
[10]Terrific.
[11]Doesn't show up.
[12]Out of breath.
[13]Waiter.
[14]Gone.

—No hay derecho—exclama días después al encontrarme en la calle—. Me hace usted fijar una hora, me hace usted correr, y resulta que no me aguarda[15] usted ni diez minutos. A las ocho y media en punto yo estaba en el café.

Y lo más curioso es que la indignación de mi amigo es auténtica. Eso de que dos hombres que se citan a las ocho tengan que reunirse a las ocho, le parece algo completamente absurdo.

Lo lógico, para él, es que se vean media hora, tres cuartos de hora o una hora después.

—Pero fíjese usted bien—le digo—. Una cita es una cosa que tiene que estar tan limitada en el tiempo como en el espacio. ¿Qué diría usted si habiéndose citado conmigo en la Puerta del Sol, se enterase de que yo había acudido[16] a la cita en Cuatro Caminos? Pues eso digo yo de usted cuando, habiéndonos citado a las ocho, veo que usted comparece a las ocho y media. De despreciar[17] el tiempo, desprecie usted también el espacio. Y de respetar el espacio, ¿por qué no guardarle también al tiempo un poco de consideración?

—Pero con esa precisión, con esa exactitud, la vida sería imposible—opina mi amigo.

¿Cómo explicarle que esa exactitud y esa precisión sirven, al contrario, para simplificar la vida? ¿Cómo convencerle de que, acudiendo puntualmente a las citas, se ahorra[18] mucho tiempo para invertirlo en lo que se quiera?

Imposible. El español no acude puntualmente a las citas, no porque considere que el tiempo es una cosa preciosa, sino,[19] al contrario, porque el tiempo no tiene importancia para nadie en España. No somos superiores, somos inferiores al tiempo. No estamos por encima, sino por debajo, de la puntualidad.

[15]Wait.
[16]I had come.
[17]Ignore.

[18]Save.
[19]But rather.

For Oral or Written Composition

ventilar
a cualquier hora
me siento a la mesa
de cuatro a cinco
podríamos citarnos
sin falta
idea genial
me hace usted correr
la indignación
limitada en el tiempo
Puerta del Sol
la vida sería imposible
acudiendo puntualmente

LISTENING COMPREHENSION EXERCISE C

Vocabulary

aburrirse   to be bored, become bored
acá   here
averiguar   to find out, ascertain
el **baile**   dance
la **cafetería**   coffee shop
callarse   to be quiet, become quiet, shut up
cansarse   to get tired
la **carnicería**   butcher shop
el **concierto**   concert
la **conferencia**   lecture
la **culpa**   fault
dejar plantado, -a   to stand up
divino, -a   out of this world, divine
la **experiencia**   experience
la **gana**   desire, interest

mentir (ie)   to lie
palabra   I swear; word of honor
la **panadería**   bakery
pasar por   to come by for, go by for
la **peluquería**   barber shop, beauty salon
perdonar   to pardon
plantado, -a   stood up
la **puntualidad**   punctuality
saludar   to greet, say hello
la **sastrería**   tailor shop
tener ganas   to feel like
la **tintorería**   (dry) cleaner's
tirar   to throw, toss
tirar la casa por la ventana   to go all out, to throw a lavish party
la **zapatería**   shoe store

Cultural Listening Passage
for Chapter 15

Immigration and Migration

(1) The great urban centers such as Buenos Aires, Mexico City, and Sao Paulo each have a minimum population of nine to ten million inhabitants, and every year hundreds of thousands of people coming from the interior of the country increase this figure. Something similar occurs in almost every important Latin American city, although, unfortunately, these cities do not have the facilities to assimilate such migratory waves.

(2) At this point we should take a look at (do a little) history. Domingo Faustino Sarmiento, the famous writer, educator, and president of Argentina in the last century, said that the basic social conflict in Latin America was the struggle between civilization and the forces of unrefinement (barbarism). According to Sarmiento's thesis, no one was interested in establishing schools, housing, or trade in the interior of the country; and consequently the prairies, jungles, and mountains remained desolate. The cities, founded almost always along the coast, grew; millions of immigrants came from Europe, particularly to the ports of the Atlantic, and settled down where there was culture and industry.

(3) Meanwhile, in the provinces of the interior, the peasants, mostly Indians and mestizos, went on cultivating their own small parcels of land or working for the owners of great haciendas or plantations. Schools and roads were not being built, and the way of life of the peasants changed little. However, despite the high infant mortality, their number continued to increase and, when it was no longer possible to subdivide the land or the work among so many, they would start moving to the cities, where they hoped to find a job and a school for their children.

(4) Unfortunately these peasant families that get off the bus or the train, carrying their chil-

dren in their arms and their cardboard boxes on their backs, come poorly prepared to face the struggle for modern life. Without money, without any technical knowledge, and in the majority of cases without even knowing how to read or write, these people have to manage any way they can. In the capital of Mexico many peasant families settle down (install themselves) in some corner of the humble room where some generous but equally poor relatives live. In the morning, after eating a tortilla and beans, they will all go around the city offering their services—the mother and older daughters no doubt as servants. (5) On the outskirts of Buenos Aires, for instance, there are a number of the so-called *villas miseria,* a very appropriate (adequate) name for the dense clusters (conglomerations) of shacks, made of boards, sheets of tin, and canvas, where there is no electricity or running water, and where each rainfall causes a flood. There live thousands and thousands of mestizos from the north of Argentina, and Bolivian and Paraguayan Indians, all of them in search of a life that may some day offer them a little dignity, comfort, and a better future for their children.

(6) In the conversation that follows we find a peasant and his wife discussing the possibility of moving away from the place where they live. He is furious and desperate because of the drought in that region, because he is without a job, and because someone (they) has been stealing even the few chickens he has left.

(7) His wife suggests that they move to some other place, but he says that everywhere the situation is as bad as it is there, and that the only place worth (the trouble) going to would be the capital. She agrees.

(8) Now the question is where or how to get the money for the trip. The only way, he suggests, would be to sell their old cow; if they sold that cow, he says, then he could go alone first, and later send for her and the children. His wife thinks it's a good idea.

(9) And thus, like many other families before them, these poor peasants begin with great enthusiasm to make their plans, in the hope of finding a better life in the capital. They don't know what awaits them.

Grammar Points

First, the conditional; second, indicative and subjunctive in clauses introduced by the conjunction **si**; third, more on comparisons; and fourth, the use of **hace** in expressions of time.

Montevideo, Uruguay

Chapter 15

Basic Dialog

¡Todos se van para la capital!

CA. *Campesino*   MU. *Su mujer*

I

CA.   ¡Qué ladrones! ¡Nos robaron dos gallinas más anoche!

MU.   ¡NO!

CA.   ¡SÍ! ¡Si pudiera coger al ladrón, con este machete le daría! ¡Con esta sequía, sin empleo, y ahora hasta las gallinas me roban! ¡Qué vida!

MU.   ¿Por qué no nos vamos a vivir lejos de aquí?

CA.   Como si fuera tan fácil. Además, en todas partes la situación está tan mala como aquí. El único lugar adonde valdría[1] la pena irse sería a la capital.

[1]The infinitive is *valer* (like *salir*).

II

MU.   Tu primo, el carnicero, hace un año que está allá. Yo creo que él nos haría un campito en su casa.

CA.   Tal vez, si vendiéramos la vaca vieja, podría irme yo primero, y los traería a ustedes después. ¿Qué dice, viejita²?

MU.   Los chiquitos se pondrían felices. ¡Ay, pero me da lástima la vaca!

CA.   Esa vaca ya no sirve. No da ni una botella al día.

Everybody is leaving for the capital!

P. *Peasant*   W. *His wife*

I

P.   What thieves! They stole two more chickens from us last night!

W.   NO!

P.   YES! If I could catch the thief, I would let him have it with this machete! With this drought, no job, and now even the chickens they steal from me! What a life!

W.   Why don't we go live far away from here?

P.   As if it were that easy. Besides, everywhere conditions are as bad as they are here. The only place where it would be worth the trouble to go would be the capital.

II

W.   Your cousin, the butcher, has been there for a year. I think he'd make room for us in his house.

P.   Maybe, if we sold the old cow, I could go first, and I would bring you all later. What do you say, Ma?

W.   The children would be³ so happy. Oh, but I feel bad about the cow!⁴

P.   That cow is no good⁵ anymore.⁶ She doesn't even give a bottle a day.

Dialog Supplement

I

¡Con este machete le daría!	
palo	*stick*
esta piedra	*rock*

¡Y ahora hasta las gallinas me roban!	
¡Y ahora hasta los gallos me roban!	*the roosters*
cerdos	*pigs*
caballos	*horses*
bueyes	*oxen*
perros	*dogs*
gatos	*cats*
pájaros	*birds*
burros	*donkeys*
las mulas	*mules*

---

² *Viejita* is one of the many pet names a husband may use to address his wife.
³ Become.
⁴ The cow gives me pity.
⁵ Doesn't serve (the purpose).
⁶ No longer.

¡Con esta sequía!

lluvia	*rain*	
humedad	*humidity*	
suerte	*luck*	
este polvo	*dust*	

¡Qué ladrones:

bandidos	*robbers, bandits*
canallas	*rascals, rats*
sinvergüenzas	*scoundrels,*[7] *cads*

El único lugar adonde valdría la pena irse . . .

mudarse *move*

. . . irse sería a la capital.

selva	*jungle*
finca	*farm*

II

Tu primo, el carnicero

panadero	*baker*
zapatero	*shoemaker*
carpintero	*carpenter*
electricista	*electrician*
peluquero	*barber*
sastre	*tailor*
tintorero	*dry cleaner*

No da ni una botella al día.

un litro *a liter*[8]

LISTENING COMPREHENSION EXERCISE A

Dialog and Supplement Check

Sentence Recall

Say the dialog phrase or sentence in which each of the following words or phrases occurs.

dos gallinas más	como si fuera	carnicero	vaca vieja
hasta las gallinas	viejita	machete	lástima
lejos	felices	situación	botella
en todas partes	ya no	valdría la pena	campito

Item Substitution

Make as many contextually related substitutions as you can for the word in italics. If books are closed, your instructor will repeat the item to be replaced.

[7]Without shame.
[8]Approximately one quart.

1. El único lugar adonde valdría la pena *mudarse* sería a la capital.
2. ¡Si pudiera coger al *sinvergüenza*, con este machete le daría!
3. No da ni una *taza* al día.
4. Tu primo, el *zapatero*.
5. Hasta los *gatos* me roban.
6. ¡Con este *zapato* le daría!
7. ¡Con esta *lluvia*, sin trabajo... qué vida!

Questions

1. ¿Qué se robaron anoche de la casa del campesino?
2. ¿Le daría él con un zapato al ladrón, si pudiera cogerlo?
3. ¿Están estos campesinos en buena o en mala situación económica?
4. ¿Cuáles son las causas de esa situación?
5. ¿Qué sugiere la mujer que hagan, que se queden allí o que se vayan a vivir lejos de allí?
6. ¿Y cómo está la situación en todas partes, según el campesino?
7. Según él, ¿cuál es el único lugar adonde valdría la pena mudarse?
8. ¿Por qué creen ustedes que en América Latina casi todo el mundo se va a vivir a la capital del país?
9. ¿Qué es un carnicero, un hombre que compra carne?
10. ¿Y un zapatero? ¿Y un panadero? ¿Y un peluquero? ¿Y un ladrón?

Peru: Foothills of the Andes

11. ¿Ganan más dinero los electricistas que los carpinteros en este país, o ganan más o menos lo mismo?
12. ¿Cuál animal quiere vender el campesino?
13. ¿Por qué no sirve esa vaca? ¿Cuánta leche da al día, diez litros?
14. ¿Tiene usted animales en su casa? ¿Qué prefiere usted, los gatos o los perros?
15. ¿Le gustan a usted los caballos? ¿Sabe montar a caballo?
16. ¿Son los tigres y los leones animales salvajes o animales domésticos? ¿Dónde viven esos animales?
17. ¿Y en cuál continente hay muchísimos canguros? ¿Y elefantes?
18. ¿Prefiere usted vivir en el campo o en la ciudad?
19. ¿En qué parte del año caen las lluvias en esta región de los EE. UU.? ¿Hay grandes sequías algunas veces?
20. Si ustedes tienen que escoger entre la humedad y el polvo, ¿cuál prefieren?

Grammar

77. The conditional

trabajar comer vivir	-ía -ías -ía -íamos -ían

trabajar comer vivir	-íais

A. The conditional in Spanish is equivalent to "would + *verb*" in English.

   ¿Comería usted allí?   *Would you eat there?*

If, however, "would + *verb*" in English refers to a customary action in the past (meaning "used to"), the *imperfect*, not the *conditional*, is used in Spanish.

   Cuando teníamos dinero **íbamos** al cine.   *When we had money we would (used to) go to the movies.*

B. There is only one set of conditional endings for all verbs. These are the same as those of the imperfect of *-er* and *-ir* verbs, but they are attached to the infinitive rather than to the stem.

   IMPERFECT: Yo **comía** mucho.   *I used to eat a lot.*
   CONDITIONAL: Yo **comería** mucho.   *I would eat a lot.*

poner	**pondría**	saber	**sabría**
valer	**valdría**	poder	**podría**
tener	**tendría**	haber	**habría**
salir	**saldría**	querer	**querría**
venir	**vendría**	hacer	**haría**
	decir	**diría**	

C. The verbs listed in the chart, which have irregular future stems, have the same irregular stems in the conditional.

Subject–Verb Substitution

EXAMPLE: Yo no trabajaría allí, ni por mil pesos.
     (nosotros/vivir)
  Nosotros no viviríamos allí, ni por mil pesos.

1. ¿Comprarían ustedes una vaca vieja? ¡Nunca!
   (matar/el carnicero, vender/tú, pensar/usted en, regalar/tus amigos, cuidar/yo, conversar/el panadero con, robarse/los ladrones)
2. Dolores se casaría a las dos de la mañana, tal vez.
   (nosotros/divorciarnos, nadie/afeitarse, yo/bañarme, los panaderos/levantarse, los peluqueros/acostarse)
3. Un zapatero no haría eso.
   (nosotros/saber, tú/decir, la casa/valer, el electricista/tener, un peluquero/querer)
4. ¿A qué hora vendrías tú?
   (poder/ellos, salir/yo, querer/usted, decir/ustedes, levantarnos/nosotros, irse/ella)

Oral Translation

1. If we sold the old cow . . .
2. I could go to the capital first.
3. My wife would stay with the children.
4. But the children would get (put themselves) very sad.
5. And they wouldn't have any milk.
6. The butcher would kill the poor cow.
7. I would feel very bad about the cow (the cow would give me much pity).
8. Besides, I couldn't sell it for more than (*de*) ten pesos.
9. We would have to buy another one, anyway.
10. No, I don't think we would sell the old cow.

78. Indicative and subjunctive in "if" clauses

"If" Clause	*"Then" Clause*
1. Si **vendemos** la vaca, *If we sell the cow,*	**llevaremos** a los niños a la capital. *we will take the children to the capital.*
2. Si **vendiéramos** la vaca, *If we sold (were to sell, should sell) the* *cow,*	**llevaríamos** a los niños a la capital. *we would take the children to the capital.*

A. "If/then" sentences are almost identical in English and Spanish. Sentences like the first example are entirely analogous in the two languages. Note the *indicative* in both clauses. Sentences like the second example are slightly different: English uses "were to," "should," or a past tense form in the "if" clause and "would" in the "then" clause; Spanish uses the *past subjunctive* in the "if" clause and the *conditional* in the "then" clause.

B. The expression **como si,** "as if, as though," is always followed by the past subjunctive.

Como si fuera tan fácil.	*As if it were so easy.*
Hablas **como si** no **tuviéramos** que vender la vaca.	*You're talking as though we didn't have to sell the cow.*

Written Translation

1. If he comes, are you going to call me?
   If he came, would you call me?
2. If they sell the oxen, they're going to buy a horse.
   If they sold the oxen, they would buy a horse.
3. If they catch the thief, they won't tell me anything.
   If they caught the thief, they wouldn't tell me anything.
4. If you tell Mr. Coco, he's not going to mention it to anyone.
   If you told Mr. Coco, he wouldn't mention it to anyone.
5. If we go to the movies, she's not going to stay home.
   If we went to the movies, she wouldn't stay home.
6. Why don't you eat, if you are hungry?
   Why wouldn't you eat, if you were hungry?

Clause Substitution

EXAMPLE: Si vendiéramos la vaca vieja, seríamos muy felices.
          (tener dinero)
          Si tuviéramos dinero, seríamos muy felices.

1. Si tú no fueras tan sinvergüenza, viviríamos mejor.
     (levantarte temprano, buscar empleo, no quejarte tanto, no robar gallinas, no jugar[9] mi dinero, hacer algo)
2. Si yo te contara un cuento, no te quejarías tanto.
     (decirte una cosa, darte dinero, comprarte un caballo, traerte una criada, ser un canalla)
3. Si los chiquitos tuvieran un gato, se pondrían felices.
     (ir a la escuela, saber leer y escribir, hablar inglés, vivir en una finca, conocer la capital)
4. Si no hubiera tanta sequía, valdría la pena vivir aquí.
     (no hacer tanto calor, no haber tanto polvo, no llover tanto, no caer tanta lluvia, hacer buen tiempo)

Oral Translation

You talk . . .

1. as if you knew everything.
2. as if I didn't know you.
3. as if he were a scoundrel.
4. as if we were dumb.
5. as if your teacher didn't like (*querer*) you.
6. as if life were that (so) easy.
7. as if there weren't enough problems in the world.
8. as if you were in love.
9. as if we didn't study enough.
10. as if they lived in the jungle.
11. as if man were a wild (savage) animal.
12. as if you lived very far from here.

Questions

Answer each of the following questions with a sentence containing several "if" clauses.
EXAMPLE: ¿Bajo qué condiciones se casaría usted?
    Me casaría si tuviera novia, si estuviera enamorado, si yo tuviera porvenir, si ella fuera rica...

¿Bajo qué condiciones...

1. viviría usted en el campo?
2. sería usted feliz?
3. me prestaría usted dinero a mí?
4. estudiaría usted el idioma ruso?
5. iría usted a vivir a un país de Latinoamérica?

[9]Gamble.

79. More on comparisons

No soy **tan** alto **como** él.	*I am not as tall as he (is).*
Sé **tanto como** él.	*I know as much as he (does).*
Tengo **tantos** libros **como** él.	*I have as many books as he (does).*

The only differences between English and Spanish in this type of construction are (1) the gender-number agreement in Spanish between *tanto* and the noun it refers to; and (2) the lack of a Spanish equivalent for the English tags "is," "does," "would," etc.

Comparison Drill

Make a comparison based on the information given.

EXAMPLES: Pedro tiene cinco bueyes; Juan tiene dos.
Pedro tiene más bueyes que Juan.
El campesino tiene muchos problemas; yo también.
El campesino tiene tantos problemas como yo.

1. Los electricistas ganan mucho dinero; los carpinteros también.
2. El panadero tiene diez hijos; el carnicero tiene catorce.
3. El peluquero pesa sesenta kilos; su mujer pesa casi cien.
4. Aquí cae mucha lluvia; allá también.

Bolivia: "Villas miseria"

5. Yo trabajo mucho; un caballo también trabaja mucho.
6. La vaca negra no da ni un litro de leche; la blanca da cinco.
7. Los pájaros son muy bonitos; las flores también.
8. Aquí roban mucho; en la capital también.
9. Yo tengo mucho calor; ustedes tienen menos.
10. Nosotros no pesamos mucho; el novio de Dolores pesa casi mil libras.
11. El lago está muy lejos de aquí; la montaña está más cerca.
12. El maestro llegó muy tarde a la clase hoy; los alumnos también llegaron muy tarde.
13. Los gallos cuestan cien pesos; las gallinas, veinte.

Rejoinders with Comparative Constructions

Compare yourself to your instructor as illustrated.

EXAMPLES: Yo estoy muy bien.
    Yo estoy tan bien como usted.
    Yo me siento mal.
    Yo me siento peor (mejor) que usted.

1. Yo sé mucho.
2. Yo tengo diez hermanos.
3. Yo no sé casi nada.
4. Yo trabajo muchísimo.
5. Yo tengo cien años.
6. Yo compré muchas cosas ayer.
7. Yo he visto muchas cosas en la vida.
8. Yo soy muy tímido.

80. *Hace* in expressions of time

Hace un año se fue Chepín para la capital.	*A year ago Chepín left for the capital.*
Hace un año que vive allá.	*He's been living there for a year.*
¿Cuánto tiempo hace que usted estudia español?	*How long have you been studying Spanish?*

A. In a sentence where the main verb is in the past tense, *hace* means "ago" (first example). In English the main verb is also in the past tense.

B. English uses the present perfect ("has lived," "has been living") to express the duration of an event that is still going on or a condition that still exists. This is expressed in Spanish by the use of *hace* in a sentence with the main verb in the present tense preceded by *que*. A Spanish construction parallel to the English with the present perfect is also grammatically correct: *Ha vivido allá por un año.* However, its use is much less frequent than *Hace un año que vive allá.*

¿Cuándo?

Using *hace* in a full sentence, give an approximation of the time passed.

EXAMPLE: ¿Cuándo se fue Chepín para la capital?
Chepín se fue para la capital hace más de un año.

1. ¿Cuándo mataron al presidente Kennedy?
2. ¿Cuándo descubrió Colón el continente de América?
3. ¿Cuándo nació usted?
4. ¿Cuándo empezó esta clase?
5. ¿Cuándo murió Jesucristo?
6. ¿Cuándo llegó el barco *Mayflower* a la costa de Massachusetts?
7. ¿Cuándo descendió a la luna el primer astronauta?
8. ¿Cuándo nació Jorge Washington?
9. ¿Cuándo empezó la Guerra Civil de los Estados Unidos?
10. ¿Cuándo empezó usted a estudiar español?
11. ¿Cuándo se casó usted?

Transformation

EXAMPLE: Chepín ha vivido en la capital más de un año.
Hace más de un año que Chepín vive en la capital.

1. Yo he estudiado español casi seis meses.
2. Nosotros no hemos comido por tres días.
3. Chepín no ha escrito por mucho tiempo.
4. Mi suegra ha vivido en mi casa casi catorce años.
5. Ella no me ha hablado a mí por trece años y medio.
6. Yo he sido maestro de idiomas más de cincuenta años.
7. He estado aquí casi diez años.
8. Tú y yo hemos sido amigos apenas un mes.
9. El campesino ha trabajado como un buey por dos años.
10. ¡Hola, amigo! No lo he visto por mucho tiempo.
11. ¡Por tres semanas no hemos ido al cine!

Written Translation

Use *hace* each time.

1. How long have you been studying Spanish?
2. I started a year ago.
3. I've been studying this language for over five years.
4. I haven't written to my family in two months.
5. They called me a little while ago and asked me what was wrong (*pasar*) with me.
6. How long have they been working in this place?
7. How long have you known Dr. Campos?
8. How long have you been sick?

Reading

Un campesino ingenioso

Un campesino tenía una hermosa vaca que daba mucha leche, y un perro. La vaca daba leche para sus hijos y también para venderla y comprar comida para la familia. Así vivían muy bien.

Pero un día se enfermó la mujer. Vino el doctor a verla, pero ella no se mejoró. Cada día parecía estar más enferma. El marido estaba triste y preocupado porque no sabía qué hacer para curar a su esposa.

Decidió entonces ir a la iglesia para hacerle una promesa a la Virgen. Arrodillado ante la estatua de la Santa Patrona, dijo devotamente:

—Prometo, Madre Santísima, vender mi vaca y dar todo el dinero a la iglesia para los pobres si le devuelve la salud a mi vieja. —Luego rezó varios Padrenuestros y Avemarías.

Al salir de la iglesia, el campesino contó al sacerdote[10] lo que había prometido a la Virgen.

—Muy bien, hijo mío —dijo el padre—, pero no te olvides de tu promesa. La Virgen castiga[11] a los que no cumplen sus promesas.

La mujer empezó a sentirse mejor y en unos pocos días ya estaba completamente sana. Su marido estaba muy contento, pero también muy preocupado por la promesa a la Virgen.

—Si vendo la vaca —pensaba—, no tendré leche para mis hijos ni dinero para comprar la comida. Pero al mismo tiempo me remuerde[12] la conciencia y tengo miedo de que si no cumplo mi promesa, la Virgen me va a castigar. —Por fin pensó en un ingenioso plan. Llevó la vaca y el perro a una feria que había en el pueblo, para vender la vaca. Pronto se acercó un señor y le preguntó:

—¿Cuánto quiere por la vaca?

—Diez pesos, señor —contestó el campesino.

—No le haga caso[13], señor —dijo otro señor que había llegado—. Ese hombre está loco. No sabe lo que dice. Una vaca buena como ésa vale mucho más de quinientos pesos.

—Pues es todo lo que pido por ella —agregó el campesino—, porque quiero venderla pronto.

—Bueno, la compro —dijo el primer señor, después de examinar la vaca con cuidado—. Aquí tiene el dinero.

---

[10]Priest.
[11]Punishes.

[12]Bothers.
[13]Don't pay any attention to him.

El Salvador:
Country town

Ya iba el señor a llevarse la vaca cuando el campesino le advirtió[14]:

—Un momentito, señor. Quiero explicarle una cosa. La vaca está acostumbrada a estar con este perro. Si el perro no está con ella, la vaca no da leche.

—¡Qué raro! —exclamó el señor—. ¿Y cuánto quiere por el perro?

—Ah, señor, éste es un magnífico perro. Es muy inteligente. Lo vendo en quinientos pesos.

—¡Qué barbaridad, hombre! Un perro no vale tanto —dijo el señor.

—Pues éste sí —dijo el campesino—, porque si no compra el perro, la vaca no le va a dar leche.

El señor no quería comprar el perro, pero le gustaba mucho la vaca y pensó que el precio de los dos animales no estaba mal.

—Bueno, aquí tiene los quinientos pesos por el perro —dijo el señor, y se fue contento con la vaca y el perro.

El campesino se fue directamente a la iglesia y le dio al sacerdote los diez pesos que había recibido por la vaca. Así cumplió su promesa a la Virgen. Y con los quinientos pesos que había recibido por el perro se compró otra vaca.

[14] Warned him.

Conversation Stimulus

Give a brief oral summary of the preceding story using the following key words and phrases:

hermosa vaca
curar
rezar
sacerdote
promesa
castigar
feria
diez pesos
¡Qué raro!
quinientos pesos

LISTENING COMPREHENSION EXERCISE C

Vocabulary

apenas barely
el **astronauta** astronaut
bajo under
el **bandido** robber, bandit
la **botella** bottle
el **buey** ox
el **burro** donkey
el **campesino** peasant
el **campito** room, space
el **canalla** rascal, rat
el **canguro** kangaroo
el **carnicero** butcher
el **carpintero** carpenter
el **cerdo** pig
la **ceremonia** ceremony
coger catch
el **continente** continent
dar lástima to make (someone) feel
 pity
doméstico, -a domestic
económico, -a economic
el **electricista** electrician
el **elefante** elephant

el **empleo** job
escoger to choose
la **finca** farm
la **flor** flower
la **gallina** hen
el **gallo** rooster
el **gato**, la **gata** cat
la **humedad** humidity
el **invitado**, la **invitada** guest
Jesucristo Jesus Christ
el **ladrón** thief
el **león** lion
el **litro** liter
la **luna** moon
la **lluvia** rain
el **machete** machete, field knife
mudarse to move (to a new house)
la **mula** mule
la **paciencia** patience
el **pájaro** bird
el **palo** stick
el **panadero** baker
el **peluquero** barber

el **perro**   dog
la **piedra**   stone
el **polvo**   dust
la **región**   region
   robar(se)   to steal
   salvaje   wild
el **sastre**   tailor
la **selva**   jungle
la **sequía**   drought
el **sinvergüenza**   scoundrel, cad
el **tigre**   tiger
el **tintorero**   dry cleaner
   único, -a   only (one)
la **vaca**   cow
   valer   to be worth
   valer la pena   to be worthwhile
   ya no   no longer, not any more
el **zapatero**   shoemaker

Appendix

Regular Verbs

1. cantar *to sing*

PRESENT PARTICIPLE	cantando
PAST PARTICIPLE	cantado
PRESENT INDICATIVE	canto, cantas, canta, cantamos, cantan, (cantáis)
PRESENT SUBJUNCTIVE and COMMAND (usted)	cante, cantes, cante, cantemos, canten, (cantéis)
IMPERFECT	cantaba, cantabas, cantaba, cantábamos, cantaban, (cantabais)
PRETERIT	canté, cantaste, cantó, cantamos, cantaron, (cantasteis)
PAST SUBJUNCTIVE	cantara, cantaras, cantara, cantáramos, cantaran, (cantarais)
FUTURE	cantaré, cantarás, cantará, cantaremos, cantarán, (cantaréis)
CONDITIONAL	cantaría, cantarías, cantaría, cantaríamos, cantarían, (cantaríais)
COMMAND (tú; vosotros)	canta, no cantes; cantad, no cantéis

2. beber *to drink*

PRESENT PARTICIPLE	bebiendo
PAST PARTICIPLE	bebido
PRESENT INDICATIVE	bebo, bebes, bebe, bebemos, beben, (bebéis)
PRESENT SUBJUNCTIVE and COMMAND (usted)	beba, bebas, beba, bebamos, beban, (bebáis)
IMPERFECT	bebía, bebías, bebía, bebíamos, bebían, (bebíais)
PRETERIT	bebí, bebiste, bebió, bebimos, bebieron, (bebisteis)
PAST SUBJUNCTIVE	bebiera, bebieras, bebiera, bebiéramos, bebieran, (bebierais)
FUTURE	beberé, beberás, beberá, beberemos, beberán, (beberéis)
CONDITIONAL	bebería, beberías, bebería, beberíamos, beberían, (beberíais)
COMMAND (tú; vosotros)	bebe, no bebas; bebed, no bebáis

3. vivir *to live*

PRESENT PARTICIPLE	viviendo
PAST PARTICIPLE	vivido
PRESENT INDICATIVE	vivo, vives, vive, vivimos, viven, (vivís)
PRESENT SUBJUNCTIVE and COMMAND (usted)	viva, vivas, viva, vivamos, vivan, (viváis)
IMPERFECT	vivía, vivías, vivía, vivíamos, vivían, (vivíais)
PRETERIT	viví, viviste, vivió, vivimos, vivieron, (vivisteis)
PAST SUBJUNCTIVE	viviera, vivieras, viviera, viviéramos, vivieran, (vivierais)
FUTURE	viviré, vivirás, vivirá, viviremos, vivirán, (viviréis)
CONDITIONAL	viviría, vivirías, viviría, viviríamos, vivirían, (viviríais)
COMMAND (tú; vosotros)	vive, no vivas; vivid, no viváis

Stem-changing Verbs

Forms with vowel changes are shown in **boldface.** Tenses in which no vowel alternation occurs are omitted.

e → ie

4. pensar (ie) *to think; to intend*

PRESENT INDICATIVE	**pienso, piensas, piensa,** pensamos, **piensan,** (pensáis)
PRESENT SUBJUNCTIVE and COMMAND (usted)	**piense, pienses, piense,** pensemos, **piensen,** (penséis)
COMMAND (tú)	**piensa, no pienses**

5. perder (ie) *to lose*

PRESENT INDICATIVE	**pierdo, pierdes, pierde,** perdemos, **pierden,** (perdéis)
PRESENT SUBJUNCTIVE and COMMAND (usted)	**pierda, pierdas, pierda,** perdamos, **pierdan,** (perdáis)
COMMAND (tú)	**pierde, no pierdas**

6. sentir (ie, i)   *to feel; to regret, be sorry*

PRESENT PARTICIPLE	sintiendo
PRESENT INDICATIVE	siento, sientes, siente, sentimos, sienten, (sentís)
PRESENT SUBJUNCTIVE and COMMAND (usted)	sienta, sientas, sienta, sintamos, sientan, (sintáis)
PRETERIT	sentí, sentiste, sintió, sentimos, sintieron, (sentisteis)
PAST SUBJUNCTIVE	sintiera, sintieras, sintiera, sintiéramos, sintieran, (sintierais)
COMMAND (tú)	siente, no sientas

e ⟶ i

7. pedir (i)   *to ask*

PRESENT PARTICIPLE	pidiendo
PRESENT INDICATIVE	pido, pides, pide, pedimos, piden, (pedís)
PRESENT SUBJUNCTIVE and COMMAND (usted)	pida, pidas, pida, pidamos, pidan, (pidáis)
PRETERIT	pedí, pediste, pidió, pedimos, pidieron, (pedisteis)
PAST SUBJUNCTIVE	pidiera, pidieras, pidiera, pidiéramos, pidieran, (pidierais)
COMMAND (tú)	pide, no pidas

o ⟶ ue

8. contar (ue)   *to count; to tell*

PRESENT INDICATIVE	cuento, cuentas, cuenta, contamos, cuentan, (contáis)
PRESENT SUBJUNCTIVE and COMMAND (usted)	cuente, cuentes, cuente, contemos, cuenten, (contéis)
COMMAND (tú)	cuenta, no cuentes

9. volver (ue)   *to return*

PRESENT INDICATIVE	vuelvo, vuelves, vuelve, volvemos, vuelven, (volvéis)
PRESENT SUBJUNCTIVE and COMMAND (usted)	vuelva, vuelvas, vuelva, volvamos, vuelvan, (volváis)
COMMAND (tú)	vuelve, no vuelvas

10.   dormir (ue, u)   *to sleep*

PRESENT PARTICIPLE	**durmiendo**
PRESENT INDICATIVE	**duermo, duermes, duerme,** dormimos, **duermen,** (dormís)
PRESENT SUBJUNCTIVE and COMMAND (usted)	**duerma, duermas, duerma, durmamos, duerman,** (**durmáis**)
PRETERIT	dormí, dormiste, **durmió,** dormimos, **durmieron,** (dormisteis)
PAST SUBJUNCTIVE	**durmiera, durmieras, durmiera, durmiéramos, durmieran,** (**durmierais**)
COMMAND (tú)	**duerme, no duermas**

u ⟶ ue

11.   jugar (ue)   *to play, gamble*

PRESENT INDICATIVE	**juego, juegas, juega,** jugamos, **juegan,** (jugáis)
PRESENT SUBJUNCTIVE and COMMAND (usted)	**juegue, juegues, juegue,** juguemos, **jueguen,** (juguéis)
COMMAND (tú)	**juega, no juegues**

Irregular Verbs

Only those tenses having irregular forms are shown, and these forms are printed in **boldface.** Past subjunctive forms are not listed, since they have the same stem—regular or irregular—as the preterit forms. Stem vowel alternation, if any, is indicated parenthetically after the infinitive. Irregular verbs that are not treated in the grammar sections of the textbook are not included in these verb charts. Also not shown are regularly formed negative *vosotros* commands.

12.   andar   *to walk, go*

PRETERIT	**anduve, anduviste, anduvo, anduvimos, anduvieron,** (**anduvisteis**)

13.   caer   *to fall*

PRESENT INDICATIVE	**caigo,** caes, cae, caemos, caen, (caéis)
PRESENT SUBJUNCTIVE and COMMAND (usted)	**caiga, caigas, caiga, caigamos, caigan,** (**caigáis**)

14. conocer   *to know, be acquainted with; to meet*

PRESENT INDICATIVE   **conozco,** conoces, conoce, conocemos, conocen, (conocéis)
PRESENT SUBJUNCTIVE and
   COMMAND (usted)   **conozca, conozcas, conozca, conozcamos, conozcan, (conozcáis)**

15. dar   *to give*

PRESENT INDICATIVE   **doy,** das, da, damos, dan, (dais)
PRESENT SUBJUNCTIVE and
   COMMAND (usted)   **dé, des, dé, demos, den, (deis)**
PRETERIT   **di, diste, dio, dimos, dieron, (disteis)**

16. decir (i)   *to say, tell*

PAST PARTICIPLE   **dicho**
PRESENT INDICATIVE   **digo,** dices, dice, decimos, dicen, (decís)
PRESENT SUBJUNCTIVE and
   COMMAND (usted)   **diga, digas, diga, digamos, digan, (digáis)**
PRETERIT   **dije, dijiste, dijo, dijimos, dijeron, (dijisteis)**
FUTURE   **diré, dirás, dirá, diremos, dirán, (diréis)**
CONDITIONAL   **diría, dirías, diría, diríamos, dirían, (diríais)**
COMMAND (tú)   **di**

17. estar   *to be*

PRESENT INDICATIVE   **estoy, estás, está,** estamos, **están,** (estáis)
PRESENT SUBJUNCTIVE and
   COMMAND (usted)   **esté, estés, esté,** estemos, **estén,** (estéis)
PRETERIT   **estuve, estuviste, estuvo, estuvimos, estuvieron, (estuvisteis)**

18. haber   *to have*

PRESENT INDICATIVE   **he, has, ha, hemos, han,** (habéis)
PRESENT SUBJUNCTIVE   **haya, hayas, haya, hayamos, hayan, (hayáis)**
PRETERIT   **hube, hubiste, hubo, hubimos, hubieron, (hubisteis)**
FUTURE   **habré, habrás, habrá, habremos, habrán, (habréis)**
CONDITIONAL   **habría, habrías, habría, habríamos, habrían, (habríais)**

19. hacer *to do; to make*

PAST PARTICIPLE	**hecho**
PRESENT INDICATIVE	**hago,** haces, hace, hacemos, hacen, (hacéis)
PRESENT SUBJUNCTIVE and COMMAND (usted)	**haga, hagas, haga, hagamos, hagan,** (hagáis)
PRETERIT	**hice, hiciste, hizo, hicimos, hicieron,** (hicisteis)
FUTURE	**haré, harás, hará, haremos, harán,** (haréis)
CONDITIONAL	**haría, harías, haría, haríamos, harían,** (haríais)
COMMAND (tú)	**haz**

20. ir *to go*

PRESENT PARTICIPLE	**yendo**°
PRESENT INDICATIVE	**voy, vas, va, vamos, van,** (vais)
PRESENT SUBJUNCTIVE and COMMAND (usted)	**vaya, vayas, vaya, vayamos, vayan,** (vayáis)
IMPERFECT	**iba, ibas, iba, íbamos, iban,** (ibais)
PRETERIT	**fui, fuiste, fue, fuimos, fueron,** (fuisteis)
COMMAND (tú)	**ve**

21. oír *to hear*

PRESENT INDICATIVE	**oigo, oyes, oye,** oímos, **oyen,** (oís)
PRESENT SUBJUNCTIVE and COMMAND (usted)	**oiga, oigas, oiga, oigamos, oigan,** (oigáis)

22. poder (ue) *to be able*

PRESENT PARTICIPLE	**pudiendo**
PRETERIT	**pude, pudiste, pudo, pudimos, pudieron,** (pudisteis)
FUTURE	**podré, podrás, podrá, podremos, podrán,** (podréis)
CONDITIONAL	**podría, podrías, podría, podríamos, podrían,** (podríais)

23. poner *to put*

PAST PARTICIPLE	**puesto**
PRESENT INDICATIVE	**pongo,** pones, pone, ponemos, ponen, (ponéis)

° *Yendo* is listed only to show its spelling. It is actually regular.

PRESENT SUBJUNCTIVE and	
COMMAND (usted)	ponga, pongas, ponga, pongamos, pongan, (pongáis)
PRETERIT	puse, pusiste, puso, pusimos, pusieron, (pusisteis)
FUTURE	pondré, pondrás, pondrá, pondremos, pondrán, (pondréis)
CONDITIONAL	pondría, pondrías, pondría, pondríamos, pondrían, (pondríais)
COMMAND (tú)	pon

24. querer (ie)   *to want; to love*

PRETERIT	quise, quisiste, quiso, quisimos, quisieron, (quisisteis)
FUTURE	querré, querrás, querrá, querremos, querrán, (querréis)
CONDITIONAL	querría, querrías, querría, querríamos, querrían, (querríais)

25. saber   *to know*

PRESENT INDICATIVE	sé, sabes, sabe, sabemos, saben, (sabéis)
PRESENT SUBJUNCTIVE and	
COMMAND (usted)	sepa, sepas, sepa, sepamos, sepan, (sepáis)
FUTURE	sabré, sabrás, sabrá, sabremos, sabrán, (sabréis)
CONDITIONAL	sabría, sabrías, sabría, sabríamos, sabrían, (sabríais)

26. salir   *to go out*

PRESENT INDICATIVE	salgo, sales, sale, salimos, salen, (salís)
PRESENT SUBJUNCTIVE and	
COMMAND (usted)	salga, salgas, salga, salgamos, salgan, (salgáis)
FUTURE	saldré, saldrás, saldrá, saldremos, saldrán, (saldréis)
CONDITIONAL	saldría, saldrías, saldría, saldríamos, saldrían, (saldríais)
COMMAND (tú)	sal

27. ser   *to be*

PRESENT INDICATIVE	soy, eres, es, somos, son, (sois)
PRESENT SUBJUNCTIVE and	
COMMAND (usted)	sea, seas, sea, seamos, sean, (seáis)
IMPERFECT	era, eras, era, éramos, eran, (erais)
PRETERIT	fui, fuiste, fue, fuimos, fueron, (fuisteis)
COMMAND (tú)	sé

28. tener (ie) *to have*

PRESENT INDICATIVE	**tengo,** tienes, tiene, tenemos, tienen, (tenéis)
PRESENT SUBJUNCTIVE and COMMAND (usted)	**tenga, tengas, tenga, tengamos, tengan, (tengáis)**
PRETERIT	**tuve, tuviste, tuvo, tuvimos, tuvieron, (tuvisteis)**
FUTURE	**tendré, tendrás, tendrá, tendremos, tendrán, (tendréis)**
CONDITIONAL	**tendría, tendrías, tendría, tendríamos, tendrían, (tendríais)**
COMMAND (tú)	**ten**

29. traer *to bring*

PRESENT INDICATIVE	**traigo,** traes, trae, traemos, traen, (traéis)
PRESENT SUBJUNCTIVE and COMMAND (usted)	**traiga, traigas, traiga, traigamos, traigan, (traigáis)**
PRETERIT	**traje, trajiste, trajo, trajimos, trajeron, (trajisteis)**

30. valer *to be worth*

PRESENT INDICATIVE	**valgo,** vales, vale, valemos, valen, (valéis)
PRESENT SUBJUNCTIVE and COMMAND (usted)	**valga, valgas, valga, valgamos, valgan, (valgáis)**
FUTURE	**valdré, valdrás, valdrá, valdremos, valdrán, (valdréis)**
CONDITIONAL	**valdría, valdrías, valdría, valdríamos, valdrían, (valdríais)**
COMMAND (tú)	**val**

31. venir (ie, i) *to come*

PRESENT INDICATIVE	**vengo,** vienes, viene, venimos, vienen, (venís)
PRESENT SUBJUNCTIVE and COMMAND (usted)	**venga, vengas, venga, vengamos, vengan, (vengáis)**
PRETERIT	**vine, viniste, vino, vinimos, vinieron, (vinisteis)**
FUTURE	**vendré, vendrás, vendrá, vendremos, vendrán, (vendréis)**
CONDITIONAL	**vendría, vendrías, vendría, vendríamos, vendrían, (vendríais)**
COMMAND (tú)	**ven**

32. ver *to see*

PAST PARTICIPLE	**visto**
PRESENT INDICATIVE	**veo,** ves, ve, vemos, ven, (veis)
PRESENT SUBJUNCTIVE and	
COMMAND (usted)	**vea, veas, vea, veamos, vean, (veáis)**
IMPERFECT	**veía, veías, veía, veíamos, veían, (veíais)**

Summary of the Forms of a Sample Verb: *aprender,* to learn

1. Ana aprende inglés. *Ana learns, is learning, will learn English.*
2. Ana está aprendiendo inglés. *Ana is learning English.*
3. Ana va a aprender inglés. *Ana is going to learn English.*
4. Ana ha aprendido inglés. *Ana has learned English.*
5. Ana ha estado aprendiendo inglés. *Ana has been learning English.*
6. Ana aprendió inglés. *Ana learned English.*
7. Ana aprendía inglés. *Ana used to learn, was learning English.*
8. Ana estaba (estuvo) aprendiendo inglés. *Ana was learning English.*
9. Ana había aprendido inglés. *Ana had learned English.*
10. Ana había estado aprendiendo inglés. *Ana had been learning English.*
11. Ana iba a aprender inglés. *Ana was going to learn English.*
12. Aprenda usted inglés, Ana. *Learn English, Ana.*
13. Aprende tú inglés, Ana. *Learn English, Ana.*
14. (Ojalá que) Ana aprenda inglés. *(I hope) Ana learns English.*
15. (Ojalá que) Ana aprendiera inglés. *(I wish) Ana would learn English.*
16. (Ojalá que) Ana haya aprendido inglés. *(I hope) Ana has learned English.*
17. (Ojalá que) Ana hubiera aprendido inglés. *(I wish) Ana had learned English.*
18. Ana aprenderá inglés. *Ana will learn English.*
19. Ana aprendería inglés. *Ana would learn English.*
20. Ana habría aprendido inglés. *Ana would have learned English.*
21. Si Ana aprendiera inglés *If Ana should learn English*
22. Si Ana hubiera aprendido inglés *If Ana had learned English*

Vocabularies

The Spanish-English Vocabulary includes all Spanish words and expressions used in the text and the Student Manual except personal proper nouns; the names of most places; regular past participles used as adjectives, when the corresponding infinitive is listed and English equivalents are exact derivations of the English forms given for the verb; and regular adverbs ending in -*mente*, when the corresponding adjective form is listed. The English-Spanish Vocabulary includes all words and expressions used in the text except those found exclusively in the Readings.

The vowel alternation of stem-changing verbs is given in parentheses after the infinitive. A number in parentheses following the infinitive of an irregular verb refers to the paradigm in the Appendix (page 315) for the conjugation of that verb or a verb with the same irregularity.

Abbreviations

adj	*adjective*	*f*	*feminine noun*	*pl*	*plural*
adv	*adverb*	*m*	*masculine noun*	*pp*	*past participle*
dim	*diminutive*	*n*	*noun*	*s*	*singular*

Spanish-English Vocabulary

A

a to; at

abajo below; **de arriba a —** up and down; **venirse —** to fall down, collapse

abierto, -a open; *pp of* **abrir**

el abogado lawyer

el abrazo embrace, hug

el abrigo overcoat

abril April

abrir to open; **—se paso** to make one's way

absolutamente absolutely

absurdo, -a absurd

la abuela grandmother

la abuelita granny

el abuelo grandfather

la abundancia abundance

abundar to abound

aburrido, -a bored; boring

aburrirse to get bored

abusar to abuse

acá, here; **hacia—** this way

acabar to finish, end; **—** **(pagando)** to end up (paying); **— de (salir)** to have just (left)

la **academia** academy

académico, -a academic

acaecido, -a taken place, occurred

acalorado, -a heated (discussion or argument)

accesible accessible

accidentado, -a uneven, rough

el **accidente** accident

el **aceite** oil; olive oil

el **acento** accent

aceptar to accept

acercarse to approach

aclamado, -a acclaimed

acomodar to accommodate

acompañar to accompany

acostarse (ue) to go to bed

acostumbrar to accustom; to be accustomed to, be used to

la **actividad** activity

activo, -a active

el **acto** act

actual present-day

acudir to respond

el **acuerdo** accordance, agreement; **de — con** in accordance with

además (de) besides

adentro within, inside

la **adhesión** adhesion; loyalty

adinerado, -a wealthy

adiós good-bye

administrativo, -a administrative

la **admiración** admiration

el **admirador** admirer

admirar to admire

admitir to concede

el **adobe** sun-dried clay brick

adónde where (to)

adoptar to adopt

adorable adorable

adorado, -a dearest, adored

adorar to adore

aducir to adduce

advertir (ie, i) to warn; to advise

afanosamente eagerly

afeitarse to shave

el **aficionado** fan, enthusiast

afirmativo, -a affirmative

aflojar to weaken

afuera outside

las **afueras** outskirts

ágil agile, quick

agitar to agitate

agosto August

agradable pleasant

agradecer (14) to be grateful, thank

agrario, -a agrarian

agregar to add

la **agricultura** agriculture

agrupar to group

el **agua** (*f*) water

aguantar to endure, stand

aguardar to wait for

ahí there; **por —** over there

la **ahijada** goddaughter

el **ahijado** godson

ahora now; **— mismo** right now

ahorrar to economize, save

ajá uh-huh

ajeno, -a another's; foreign

el **ají** pepper (green)

el **ajo** garlic

al to the; at the

alarmante alarming

la **albóndiga** meatball

alcanzar to reach, attain

aleccionar to instruct

alegrarse (de) to be glad (about)

alegre happy, gay

la **alegría** happiness

alemán, -ana German

Alemania Germany

el **alfabeto** alphabet

algo something

alguien someone, anyone, anybody

alguno (algún), -a some, any; someone

aliado, -a allied

el **alimento** food

aliviar to relieve

el **alma** (*f*) soul

el **almirante** admiral

el **almuerzo** lunch

aló hello

alrededor (de) around

el **altarcito** tiny altar

alto, -a tall; **el alto** stop sign

la **altura** height

el **alumno, la alumna** student

allá there, over there; **hacia —** that way (in that direction)

allí there

el **ama** (*f*) **de casa** housewife

amable kind

el **amanecer** dawn

amargo, -a bitter

amarillo, -a yellow

el **Amazonas** Amazon (river)

la **ambición** ambition

ambicioso, -a ambitious

el **ambiente** atmosphere, environment

ambos, -as both

ambulante traveling; **el vendedor —** street vender

la **amenaza** threat

americano, -a American

la **amiga** friend, girlfriend

el **amigo** friend, boyfriend

el **amor** love

amplio, -a large, wide

amueblado, -a furnished

el **análisis** analysis

anaranjado, -a orange

andaluz, -za Andalusian
andar (12) to walk, go;
— **de compras** to go
shopping
andino, -a Andean
Andivia fictional Spanish
American country
andiviano, -a Andivian
el **angloparlante** English
speaker
anglosajón, -ona Anglo-
Saxon
angosto, -a narrow
animar to enliven; to encourage
aniquilar to annihilate
el **aniversario** anniversary
anoche last night
anónimo, -a anonymous
ansioso, -a anxious
ante before (in the presence of)
anteanoche night before
last
anteayer day before yesterday
el **antepasado** ancestor
antes (de) (que) before
antidemocrático, -a anti-
democratic
antiguo, -a old, ancient;
former (before noun)
antipático, -a unpleasant,
disagreeable
antiquísimo,-a *superlative
of* **antiguo**
anunciar to announce
el **anuncio** announcement
añadir to add
el **año** year; **(el) Año Nuevo**
New Year
apagado, -a extinguished,
out (fire or light); dull
aparecer (14) to appear
aparentemente apparently
la **aparición** appearance
la **apariencia** appearance
apartado, -a distant, remote
el **apartamento** apartment

apelar to appeal
el **apellido** surname
apenas barely
el **aperitivo** appetizer
el **aplauso** applause
aplicar to apply
el **apogeo** peak, high point
apostar (ue) to bet
apoyado, -a supported
aprender to learn
el **aprendizaje** apprentice-
ship
apresurado, -a hasty,
hurrying
apropiado,-a appropriate,
suitable
aprovechar(se) de to take
advantage of
aproximadamente ap-
proximately
aproximarse (a) to approach
apuntar to point; to jot
down
el **apunte** note
aquel, aquella that
aquél, aquélla that one
aquello that
aquí here
la **araña** spider
arbitrario, -a arbitrary
el **árbol** tree
el **archivo** archives
la **aritmética** arithmetic
el **arma** (*f*) weapon
el **armamento** armament
el **aroma** aroma, scent
arquitectónico, -a archi-
tectural
la **arquitectura** architecture
el **arraigo** deep-rootedness,
embedment
arreglar to arrange,
straighten up
arriba up, upward, up
high; **de — a abajo** up
and down
arriesgar to risk
arrodillado, -a kneeling
arrogante arrogant

arrojar to throw
el **arroz** rice
arruinar to ruin
el **arte** art
las **artes** arts, skills, crafts
artístico, -a artistic
el **ascenso** promotion
asentir (ie, i) to assent,
agree to
el **asesino** murderer
así thus, so, like that, this
way
asiático, -a Asian, Asiatic
el **asiento** seat
asimilar(se) to assimilate
la **asistencia** aid, assistance
asociar(se) (a) to associ-
ate (with)
asombrar to astonish
asombroso,-a astonishing
el **aspecto** aspect
la **aspiración** aspiration
la **aspirina** aspirin
el **astronauta** astronaut
astronómico,-a astronom-
ical
la **astucia** cleverness, cun-
ning
el **asunto** matter, subject
asustadísimo,-a extremely
frightened
atacar attack
el **ataque** attack
la **atención** attention
atractivo, -a attractive
atraer (29) to attract
atreverse (a) to dare (to)
atrevido, -a bold; fresh,
insolent
aumentar to increase
el **aumento** increase
aun even
aunque although, even
though
ausente absent
auténtico, -a authentic
el **autobús** bus
automáticamente auto-
matically
el **autor** author

la autoridad authority
la autosuficiencia self-sufficiency
el avance advance; progress
avanzar to advance
la avenida avenue
averiguar to find out, as-certain
el avión airplane
avisar to warn; to inform; to give notice
¡ay! oh!
ayer yesterday
la ayuda help, aid
ayudar to help
el azúcar sugar
azul blue

B

el bachiller secondary-school graduate
el bachillerato secondary-school diploma
bailar to dance
el baile dance
Baja California Lower California (part of Mexico)
bajo, -a low, short; **bajo** under; **— (qué) condiciones** under (what) conditions
el balcón balcony, window
el banco bank; bench
el bandido robber, bandit
bañar to bathe; **—se** to take a bath
el baño bathroom
barato, -a cheap, inexpensive
la barbaridad terrible thing; **¡qué —!** how terrible!
el barco boat, ship
el barítono baritone
barrer to sweep
el barril barrel
la base base
básico, -a basic
bastante enough; quite, fairly

el bastón cane
el bateador batter (baseball)
la batería battery
beber to drink
el béisbol baseball
la belleza beauty
bello, -a beautiful
bendecir (i) (16) to bless
beneficiarse to benefit
el beso kiss
la biblioteca library
la bicicleta bicycle
bien well; okay; **el —** good (welfare)
el billete ticket
los binóculos binoculars
la biología biology
blanco, -a white
el bloque block
la blusa blouse
la boca mouth
la bocina (automobile) horn
la boda wedding
el bofe: echando el — out of breath, panting
bogotano, -a from Bogotá, Colombia
la bolsa bag
el bolsillo pocket
la bomba bomb
bonito, -a pretty
borrar to wipe out, eliminate, erase
la bota boot
la botella bottle
el boxeo boxing
el brazo arm
brillante brilliant, shiny
el brillo shine
la brisa breeze
la broma joke, practical joke
el bronce bronze
brusco, -a brusque
bueno (buen), -a good, nice; **bueno** well (now); **buenos (buenas)** common response to **buenos días, buenas tardes, buenas noches**

el buey ox
la bufanda scarf
el bulto bundle
burgués, -esa bourgeois
la burguesía bourgeoisie, middle class
el burro burro, donkey
buscar to look for

C

el caballerito young gentleman
el caballero gentleman; sir (as a form of address)
el caballo horse
la cabecera headboard
la cabeza head
el cácher catcher
cada each
el cadete cadet
caer (13) to fall; **— de inocente** to be made a fool of (as a practical joke)
el café coffee; cafe; *adj* brown
la cafetería coffee shop
el cajero cashier
el calamar squid
el calcetín sock
calcular to calculate, figure, estimate
el cálculo calculation
el caldo broth
calentar (ie) to heat
la calidad quality
caliente hot
el califa caliph
la calma calm
el calor heat; **hacer —** to be warm (weather); **tener — ** to be (feel) warm
callarse to be quiet, shut up
la calle street
el callo callous
la cama bed
el camarero waiter
el camarón shrimp

cambiar to change, exchange; **— de mano** to change hands

el cambio change

el camino road

el camión truck

la camisa shirt

la campana bell

el campeón champion

el campesino, la campesina peasant, farm worker

campestre rural

el campito: hacer(me) — to make room for (me)

el campo country; field

el canalla scoundrel

la canasta canasta; market basket

el canguro kangaroo

cansado, -a tired

cansarse to get tired

cantar to sing

la cantidad quantity

la cantina bar, tavern

el cañón cannon

la capacidad capacity

capaz capable

la capilla chapel

la capital capital city

el capitán captain

la cara face

el carácter character, nature

la característica characteristic

caramba for Pete's sake; damn

carecer (14) de to lack

el cariño affection

carismático, -a charismatic

la carne meat

la carnicería butcher shop

el carnicero butcher

caro, -a expensive

el carpintero carpenter

la carrera career; run (baseball); **meter —s** to score runs

la carretera highway

el carro car

la carta letter

la cartera purse; wallet

el carterista pickpocket

el cartero mailman

la casa house, home; **en —** at home; **(ir) a —** (to go) home

casar to marry, marry off; **—se (con)** to marry, get married (to)

casi almost, nearly

el caso case; **hacer —** to pay attention

la casta caste

castigar to punish

el castillo castle

la catástrofe catastrophe

la catedral cathedral

catorce fourteen

el caudillismo rule by political bosses

el caudillo political boss

la causa cause; **a — de** because of

causado, -a caused

el cayo islet, key

la caza hunt

el cazador hunter

la cebolla onion

celebrar to celebrate

celoso, -a jealous

el cementerio cemetery

la cena supper

el centavo cent

el céntimo cent

central central

el centro center; downtown

centroamericano, -a Central American

cerca (de) near, nearby

cercano, -a near

el cerdo pig

la ceremonia ceremony

el cero zero

cerrao regional variant of **cerrado**

cerrar (ie) to close

el cerro hill

el certificado certificate

la cerveza beer

el cielo sky

la ciencia science

científico, -a scientific

ciento (cien) one hundred; **por —** percent

cierto, -a certain, true

el cigarrillo cigarette

el cigarro cigar; cigarette

cimentar to establish; to consolidate

cinco five

cincuenta fifty

el cine movies

circular to circulate

el círculo circle

la circunstancia circumstance

citarse to make a date (appointment)

la ciudad city

el ciudadano citizen

civil civil

civilizado, -a civilized

claro, -a clear; **¡—!** of course!

la clase class

clasificar to classify

la clientela clientele

el clima climate

el club club

el cobrador collector

cobrar to collect; to acquire

la coca-cola Coke

la cocina kitchen; stove

cocinar to cook

la cocinera cook

el coctel cocktail

el coche car

coger to seize; to catch; to pick up; to pick, harvest

coherente coherent

la cola tail

la colaboración collaboration

colaborar to collaborate

la colección collection

colectivo, -a collective

colgar (ue) to hang
colombiano,-a Colombian
Colón Columbus
la **colonia** colony
el **combate** combat
el **combatiente** combatant
la **combinación** combination
el **comedor** dining room
comentar to comment
el **comentario** comment
comenzar (ie) to begin
comer to eat, dine
comercial commercial
el **comestible** food
cometer to commit; **— un error** to make an error
la **comida** meal; food; dinner
como like, as; since; about, around
cómo how; ¿**— es (ella)?** what is (she) like?; **— no** of course; ¿**— se dice?** how do you say?
cómodo, -a comfortable, convenient
el **compañero,** la **compañera** companion, pal
la **compañía** company; **Compañía de Jesús** Society of Jesus, Order of Jesuits
comparecer (14) to appear
la **compasión** compassion
el **compatriota** countryman
completo, -a complete
complicado, -a complicated
el **componente** component
componer (23) to compose; to fix
la **compra** purchase; **andar de —s** to go shopping
comprar to buy
comprender to understand; to include
la **comprensión** comprehension, understanding
el **comprobante** proof
común common

la **comunicación** communication
el **comunismo** communism
el **comunista** Communist (*n* and *adj*)
con with; **— tal que** provided that
la **conciencia** conscience
el **concierto** concert
la **condición** condition
la **conducta** conduct
la **conferencia** lecture
confesar (ie) to confess
confiado, -a confident
la **confusión** confusion
la **conglomeración** conglomeration
el **congreso** congress
conmigo with me
la **conmoción** commotion
conocer (14) to know, be acquainted with; to meet
la **Conquista** the conquest of America by the Spaniards
conquistar to conquer
consciente conscious
la **consecuencia** consequence
consecuentemente consequently
conseguir (i) to get, obtain
el **consejo** (piece of) advice
consentido, -a pampered, spoiled
conservador, -ra conservative
conservar to preserve
la **consideración** consideration; **guardar(le) —** to show (him or her) respect
considerar to consider
consiguiente: por — therefore
consistir en to consist of, be made up of
la **consonante** consonant

constante constant
la **constitución** constitution
constitucional constitutional
constituir to constitute, make up
la **construcción** construction
construir to build
consultar to consult
el **contacto** contact
contar (ue) to tell; to count
contemporáneo, -a contemporary
contener (ie) (28) to contain
contento, -a content, happy, satisfied
contestar to answer
contigo with you
continental continental
el **continente** continent
continuar to continue
la **contorsión** contortion; grimace
contra against; **en — de** against
contradecir (i) (16) to contradict
contraer (29) to contract; **—se** to shrink
la **contra-protesta** counterprotest
el **contrario** opponent; **al —** on the contrary; **al — de** unlike
la **contribución** contribution
el **control** control
controlar to control
controversial controversial
convencer convince
la **conveniencia** convenience; advantage; agreement
convenir (ie, i) (31) to suit, be suitable
conversar to converse, chat
convertir (ie, i) to change,

convert; **—se en** to become, turn into

la cooperación cooperation

cooperar to cooperate

la copa crown (of a hat)

la corbata necktie

la cordillera mountain range

el coro choir

el coronel colonel

correctamente correctly

el correo mail

la corrida (de toros) bullfight

corrompido, -a corrupted

cortar to cut

la corteza bark; surface

la cortina curtain

corto, -a short

la cosa thing

el coscorrón knock on the head

la costa coast

costar (ue) to cost

costoso, -a expensive

la costumbre custom

creador, -ra creative

creativamente creatively

crecer (14) to grow

el credencial credential

la creencia belief

creer to believe

la crema cream

la criada maid

el criado servant

el crimen crime

el crisantemo chrysanthemum

la crisis crisis

Cristo Christ

el criterio criterion, judgment

la crónica chronicle

cruel cruel

el cuaderno notebook

cuadro: el — interior infield

cuál which, what

la cualidad quality

cualquier(a) any, whatever; *pl* **cualesquiera**

cuando when; whenever

cuándo when

cuanto: en — a as to, in regard to

cuánto, -a how; how much; *pl* how many; **— lo siento** I'm very sorry; **¿— tiempo?** how long?

cuarenta forty

cuarto, -a fourth; **el cuarto** room; bedroom; quarter (of an hour)

cuatro four

Cuatro Caminos well-known sector of Madrid

cuatrocientos, -as four hundred

cubano, -a Cuban

los cubiertos silverware

cubrir to cover

la cuchara tablespoon

la cucharada tablespoonful

la cucharita teaspoon

el cuchillo knife

la cuenta bill; **a fin de —s** after all; **darse — (de)** to realize

el cuento story

cuerdo, -a sane

el cuero leather

el cuerpo body; corps

la cuestión question, matter

el cuidado care; caution; **¡—!** be careful! **tener —** to be careful

cuidar to take care of

la culpa guilt, blame; **tener la —** to be to blame

el cultivo cultivation

cultural cultural

el cumpleaños birthday

cumplir to fulfill; **— con (mi) deber** to do (my) duty

la cuñada sister-in-law

el cuñado brother-in-law

la cuota dues; quota, share

curar to cure

curioso, -a curious, strange

la curva curve

cuyo, -a whose

CH

el cha-cha-cha cha-cha

el chal shawl

chao so long (from Italian *ciao*)

el chapín nickname for Guatemalan

el cheque check

chicano, -a Chicano, Mexican American

chico, -a small; **el chico** boy, child; **la chica** girl, child

chileno, -a Chilean

el chilito hot pepper

chino, -a Chinese

la chiquita little girl

el chisme rumor

el chiste joke

chistoso, -a funny; **el chistoso** smart-aleck

el chofer driver

el choque collision; shock

la chuleta pork chop

D

la dama lady

dar (15) to give; **— bromas** to play jokes; **— el golpe** to strike; **— lástima** to make (a person) feel sorry; **— resultado** to produce results; **— un suspiro** to sigh; **—se cuenta (de)** to realize; **—se vuelta** to turn around

datar to date

de from; of; about

debajo de under

deber must; to owe; **el —** duty

la **decadencia** decline
decente decent, nice
decidir to decide
décimo, -a tenth
decir (i) (16) to say; to tell
decisivo, -a decisive
declarar to declare
decorativo, -a decorative
dedicar(se) to devote (one-self)
el **dedo** finger; **— del pie** toe
defender (ie) to defend
la **defensa** defense
definitivamente decisively, definitively
dejar to let; to leave, let (go); **—(lo)** to stop (it); **—(me) plantado** to stand (me) up
del from the; of the, about the
delante de in front of
delatar to reveal
delgado, -a slender
delicioso, -a delicious, delightful
demandar to ask, to request
demás rest (remaining)
demasiado, -a too much; *pl* too many
democrático, -a democratic
demostrar (ue) to show, demonstrate
denominar to name; to refer to
dentro (de) inside, within
el **departamento** apartment
depender (de) to depend (on)
el **deporte** sport
la **derecha** right
derecho, -a right; **el derecho** right (privilege); law; **la facultad de —** law school; *adv* straight; **seguir todo —** to go straight ahead

la **derivación** derivation
derivar to derive
derramado, -a spread out; spilled
derrocar to overthrow
desafortunado, -a unfortunate, unlucky
desagradable unpleasant
desaparecer (14) to disappear
desarrollar to develop
el **desarrollo** development
el **desastre** disaster; mess
el **desayuno** breakfast
el **descamisado** shirtless man (follower of Juan Perón)
descansar to rest
descender (ie) to descend
el **descendiente** descendant
descifrar to decipher
descomponer (23) to decompose; to break down
la **desconfianza** mistrust
desconocido, -a unknown
describir to describe
descubrir to discover
el **descuido** carelessness
desde from; since; **— hoy en adelante** from today on
deseoso, -a eager
la **desesperación** desperation
desesperado, -a desperate
desfilar to parade
el **desfile** parade
desgraciadamente unfortunately
deshacer (19) to tear down
la **desigualdad** inequality
desinteresado, -a disinterested
desmayarse to faint
desnutrido, -a undernourished
desocupado, -a unoccupied, free

la **despedida: de —** farewell (*adj*)
despedir (i) to fire; **—se (de)** to say good-bye (to)
desperdiciar to waste, throw away
despintado, -a faded
despreciar to despise; disdain
después afterwards; **— de** after
destinado, -a destined; intended
el **destino** destiny, fate
destruir to destroy
el **detalle** detail
detener (ie) (28) to detain, stop; **—se** to stop, come to a stop
determinado, -a determined
detrás (de) behind
devolver (ue) to return (an object)
devoto, -a devout
el **día** day; **al —** a day, per day; **buenos —s** good morning; **Día de los Inocentes** Fools' Day (December 28)
el **diablo** devil
el **dialecto** dialect
diario, -a daily
dibujar to draw
el **diccionario** dictionary
diciembre December
el **dictador** dictator
la **dictadura** dictatorship
dicho *pp of* **decir; mejor —** rather
dichoso, -a lucky
diecinueve nineteen
dieciocho eighteen
dieciséis sixteen
diecisiete seventeen
el **diente** tooth
la **diferencia** difference
diferente different
difícil difficult; **es —** it is unlikely

la **dificultad** difficulty

¡**diga!** hello! (to answer the telephone in Spain)

la **dignidad** dignity

dinámico, -a dynamic

el **dinero** money

Dios God; **como — manda** as it should be (done), the right way, the proper way

el **diploma** diploma; title

diplomático, -a diplomatic; **el diplomático** diplomat

el **diputado** delegate

la **dirección: con — a** in the direction of

directamente directly

dirigirse (a) to go toward; to address

el **disco** record

la **disculpa** excuse

disculpar to forgive

el **discurso** talk, speech

la **discusión** discussion, argument

discutir to argue; discuss

disminuir to decrease

disolver (ue) to dissolve

dispensar to excuse

la **disposición** disposal; **a su entera —** completely at your disposal

la **disputa** argument

distinguido, -a distinguished

distinto, -a different

la **distribución** distribution

diverso, -a different

divertido, -a amusing, funny

dividido, -a divided

divino, -a divine, out of this world

divorciarse to get a divorce

doblar to turn; to fold

doble double; **el —** twice as much

doce twelve

el **doctor** doctor

el **dolor** pain, ache

domesticado, -a domesticated

doméstico, -a domestic

dominador, -ra dominating

dominar to master, dominate

(el) **domingo** Sunday

dominicano, -a Dominican, from the Dominican Republic

don a title used with masculine first name

donar to donate

donde where

dónde where

doña a title used with feminine first names

dormir (ue, u) to sleep

dos two; **en un — por tres** in a jiffy; **los —** both

doscientos, -as two hundred

dotado, -a gifted; provided

dramático, -a dramatic

dramatizar to dramatize

drástico, -a drastic

dudar to doubt

dudoso, -a doubtful

el **dueño, la dueña** owner, boss

dulce sweet

la **duración** duration, length

durante during

durar to last

duro, -a hard

E

e and; regional variant of **de**

económico, -a economic

la **ecuación** equation

ecuatoriano, -a Ecuadorian

echando el bofe out of breath, panting

la **edad** age

la **edición** edition

el **edificio** building

la **educación** education, training

los **EE.UU.** U.S.A.

el **efecto** effect; **a ese—** in that respect; **en—** as a matter of fact, really

efectuar to achieve; to carry out

eficiente efficient

el **ejemplo** example

el **ejercicio** exercise

el **ejército** army

el the; the one; *pl* them, you

él he; him; it

elástico, -a elastic

la **elección** election

electo, -a elected

el **electricista** electrician

el **elefante** elephant

elegante elegant

el **elemento** element

elevado, -a noble

ella she; her; it

ellos they; them

la **embajada** embassy

el **embajador** ambassador

embargo: sin — however

eminente eminent

empeñar to pawn

empezar (ie) to begin

el **empleado, la empleada** employee

el **empleo** job

emprendedor, -ra enterprising

la **empresa** undertaking, enterprise

en in; on; at

enamorado, -a (de) in love (with)

encaminarse (hacia) to make one's way (toward)

encantado, -a charmed, delighted; delighted to meet you

encantador, -ra charming, delightful

encantar to charm
encender (ie) to light
la **enciclopedia** encyclopedia
encima (de) on top (of), above
encontrar (ue) to find; **—se** to be
el **encuentro** meeting
la **enchilada** Mexican dish, tortilla stuffed with meat or other filling and baked in chile-seasoned sauce
endosar to endorse
enemigo, -a enemy
enero January
enfermarse to get sick
la **enfermedad** illness
enfermo, -a sick
enfrente (de) in front (of)
engañar to deceive
enojarse to get angry
enorme enormous
enriquecer (14) to make wealthy; **—se** to become wealthy, get rich
la **ensalada** salad
enseñar to teach; to show
entender (ie) to understand
entero, -a whole, entire
entonces then
la **entrada** entrance
entrar to enter
entre between; among
entreabierto, -a partially open
entregar to hand over, deliver
entretener (ie) (28) to entertain
entusiasmado, -a enthusiastic
el **entusiasmo** enthusiasm
entusiástico, -a enthusiastic
la **envidia** envy
envolver (ue) to wrap

la **época** epoch, period
el **equivalente** equivalent
errático, -a erratic
la **escala** scale, degree
el **escándalo** scandal
escandinavo, -a Scandinavian
la **escasez** shortage
escaso, -a scarce
la **escena** scene; stage
el **escenario** scene
la **esclavitud** slavery
el **esclavo** slave
escoger to choose
escondido, -a hidden
escribir to write
el **escrúpulo** scruple
escuchar to listen
la **escuela** school
la **ese** the letter *s*
ese, -a that; **esos, -as** those
ése, ésa that one; **ésos, ésas** those
esencial essential
el **esfuerzo** effort
eso that; **por —** therefore, that's why
el **espacio** space
espantoso, -a frightening
español, -la Spanish; *n* Spaniard; **el español** Spanish (language); **a la española** Spanish style
especial special
la **especie** sort, kind
específico, -a specific
el **espectáculo** spectacle
el **espectador** spectator
la **espera** wait, waiting
la **esperanza** hope
esperar to hope; to wait
espiritual spiritual
el **esplendor** splendor
esporádico, -a sporadic
la **esposa** wife
el **esposo** husband
la **esquina** corner
esquivar to dodge

la **estabilidad** stability
establecer (14) to establish; **—se** to settle
el **establecimiento** establishment; settlement
la **estación** station; season
estacionado, -a positioned, placed
el **estadio** stadium
el **estado** state
los **Estados Unidos** United States
el **estadounidense** inhabitant of the United States
estante shelf
estar (17) to be; **— mal (de salud)** to be ill; **está bien** very well, OK
la **estatua** statue
este eh, uh
este, -a this; **estos, -as** these
éste, ésta this one; the latter; **éstos, éstas** these; the latter
el **estilo** style
estimado, -a dear, esteemed
esto this
el **estómago** stomach
estratégico, -a strategic
estrecho, -a narrow; **el estrecho** strait
la **estrella** star
estricto, -a strict
la **estructura** structure
estudiar to study
el **estudio** study
estúpido, -a stupid
eterno, -a eternal; interminable
étnico, -a ethnic
etnográfico, -a ethnographic
Europa Europe
europeo: a lo europeo the European way
evidente evident, obvious
Evita *dim* of **Eva**
exacerbado, -a aggravated

la **exactitud** precision, accuracy

exacto, -a exact

exaltado, -a excited, zealous

el **examen** test, exam

examinar to examine

la **excelencia** excellence

la **excepción** exception

excepto except

el **exceso** excess

exclamar to exclaim

la **excusa** excuse

el **ex-chofer** former driver (chauffeur)

la **ex-colonia** former colony

exigir to demand

el **exilio** exile

la **existencia** existence

existir to exist

la **expansión** expansion, increase

la **experiencia** experience

el **experimento** experiment

el **experto** expert

la **explicación** explanation

el **explorador** explorer

la **expresión** expression

expulsado, -a expelled

extender (ie) to extend, stretch

extendido, -a extended

extinto, -a extinct

extraer (29) to extract

extranjero, -a foreign

extraño, -a strange, odd; foreign

extraordinariamente extraordinarily

extravagante extravagant

extremadamente extremely

el **extremista** extremist

el **extremo** extreme

F

la **fábrica** factory

las **facciones** features

facial facial

fácil easy

factible feasible, workable

la **facultad** school (of a university); **— de derecho** law school

la **falda** skirt

la **falta** lack; **sin —** without fail

faltar to be missing, lacking

famoso, -a famous

fantástico, -a fantastic, wonderful

la **farmacia** pharmacy

fascinante fascinating

la **fe** faith

febrero February

febril feverish

la **fecha** date

felicitar to congratulate

feliz happy

femenino, -a feminine

fenomenal great, terrific

el **fenómeno** phenomenon

feo, -a ugly

la **feria** fair

el **ferrocarril** railroad

ferviente fervent, intense

fétido, -a stinking

feudal feudal

la **fiebre** fever

fiel faithful

la **fiesta** party

figurar appear

fijarse (en) to fix (upon), notice

fijo: término — fixed time, fixed length

la **filosofía** philosophy; **— y letras** liberal arts

fin: a — de cuentas in the end; **por —** at last

finalmente finally

la **finca** farm

finlandés, -esa Finnish; *n* Finn; **el finlandés** Finnish (language)

fino, -a fine, thin

la **firma** signature; firm

firme firm

físico, -a physical

flaco, -a slim

la **flor** flower

fomentar to encourage, promote

el **fondo** bottom; **en el —** at heart

forjado, -a forged, shaped, made

la **formación** formation; training

formar to form

el **foro** forum

la **fortuna** fortune, luck

forzado, -a forced

la **foto** photo

francamente frankly

francés, -esa French; *n* French man or woman; **el francés** French (language)

Francia France

franco, -a frank

la **frase** phrase; sentence

la **frecuencia** frequency; **con —** often

frecuente frequent, often

freír (i) to fry

frente: hacer — (a) to stand up (to, against)

fresco, -a cool; fresh

frío, -a cold; **el —** cold; **hacer —** to be cold (weather); **tener —** to be (feel) cold

frito, -a fried

la **fruta** fruit

la **fuente** source; fountain

fuera (de) outside

fuerte *adj* strong; *adv* hard

la **fuerza** force; **—s aéreas** air force; **—s armadas** armed forces

fumar to smoke

el **funcionamiento** functioning, working

el **funcionario** official

el fundamento basis, foundation
furioso, -a furious
la fusión fusion
el fútbol soccer

G

las gafas eyeglasses
la gallina hen
el gallo rooster
la gana desire; **de buena —** gladly; **tener —s** to want to
ganar to earn; to win
la garganta throat
gastado, -a worn-out
gastar to spend
el gato, la gata cat
el gemelo, la gemela twin
general general; **el— general; por lo —** generally
genial genial, brilliant
el genio genius
la gente people
genuinamente genuinely
geográficamente geographically
germánico, -a Germanic
la gillette razor blade
glorioso, -a glorious
gobernar (ie) to govern
el gobierno government
el golpe blow; **— de estado** coup d'état
golpear to knock; to hit
la góndola gondola
gordo, -a fat
el gorila gorilla
gozar (de) to enjoy
gracias thank you; **dar las —** to thank
el grado grade
el graduado, la graduada graduate
la gramática grammar; grammar book
gramatical grammatical
grande (gran) big, large; great

grandioso, -a grandiose
gratis free
grave grave; seriously ill
Grecia Greece
griego, -a Greek
gris gray
gritar to shout
el grito scream, shout
grueso, -a thick
el guante glove
guapo,-a handsome,good-looking
guardar to keep
el guardia guard; policeman; **— civil** policeman
el guardián guardian
la guayaba guava
la guerra war
la guerrilla band of guerrillas
el guerrillero guerrilla; partisan
la guitarra guitar
gustar to be pleasing
el gusto pleasure; taste; **con mucho —** gladly; **mucho —** glad to meet you

H

habano, -a brown
haber (18) to have
la habilidad ability, skill
el habitante inhabitant
habitar to reside in, dwell in
el hábito habit
el habla (*f*) speech
hablar to speak
hacer (19) to do; to make; **— caso** to pay attention; **— frente (a)** to stand up (to, against); **— silencio** to be quiet; **— un examen bueno** to do well on a test; **hace (buen) tiempo** the weather

is (good); **hace (dos años)** (two years) ago; **hace (sol)** it is (sunny)
hacia toward
halagador, -ra flattering
el hambre (*f*) hunger; **tener —** to be hungry
hasta until, up to; even; **— mañana** see you tomorrow
hay there is, there are; **— que** it is necessary; **¿qué —?** how are things? **¿qué — de nuevo?** what's new?
hemisférico, -a hemispheric
el hemisferio hemisphere
la herencia heritage; inheritance
la hermana sister
el hermano brother
hermoso, -a beautiful
la hermosura beauty
el héroe hero
hervir (ie, i) to boil
la hija daughter
el hijito *dim* of **hijo**
el hijo son; *pl* children; **cualquier — de vecino** anybody at all
hipnotizado, -a hypnotized
la hipótesis hypothesis
el hispanoparlante Spanish speaker
la historia history
el historiador historian
histórico, -a historical
la hoja leaf; page, sheet
hola hi
el hombre man
honesto, -a upright, honest
el honor honor
honrado, -a honest
honrar to honor
la hora hour; **¿qué — es?** what time is it?
el horario schedule

horizontal horizontal
el hotel hotel
hoy today; — **mismo** today for sure
el huevo egg
la humanidad humanity
humanitario, -a humanitarian
humano, -a human
la humedad humidity
humillar to humiliate
el humor humor; mood; **estar de (buen) —** to be in a (good) mood

I

ibérico, -a Iberian
la ida departure
la idea idea
ideal ideal
el idealista idealist
identificar to identify
el idioma language
el idiota idiot
la iglesia church
ignorante ignorant; stupid
igual alike; — **que** same as
ilegal illegal
ilimitado, -a unlimited
ilustre illustrious
imaginable imaginable
imaginario, -a imaginary
imaginar(se) to imagine
el impacto impact
impecable impeccable
impedir (i) to prevent
imperceptible imperceptible
el imperio empire
el impermeable raincoat
implacable inexorable, implacable
imponente impressive
imponer (23) (a) to impose
importante important
importar to import; to matter, be of importance
imposible impossible

la impresión impression
el impuesto tax
inacentuado, -a unaccented
inaugurar to inaugurate, open, initiate
el inca Inca
incluir to include
inclusive including
incómodo, -a uncomfortable
incondicional unconditional
increíble incredible
la indecisión indecision
indeciso, -a undecided
indefenso, -a defenseless
la independencia independence
independizarse to become independent
el index index
indicar to indicate
el indicio indication
indígena *adj m and f* native
la indignación indignation
el indio, la india Indian
la indirecta hint
individual individual
individualista individualistic
indoeuropeo, -a Indo-European
la índole nature
industrial industrial
la industrialización industrialization
inédito, -a unpublished
inesperado, -a unexpected
inevitable inevitable
la infantería infantry
infeliz unhappy, unfortunate
inferior inferior
infernal infernal, infuriating
infinitamente infinitely
el infinitivo infinitive (grammar)

la influencia influence
la información information
informar to inform
el ingeniero engineer
ingenioso, -a clever, ingenious
inglés, -esa English; *n* English man or woman; **el inglés** English (language)
ingrato, -a ungrateful; *n* ingrate
el ingrediente ingredient
la inicial initial
iniciar to start, begin
inmediato, -a immediate
inmenso, -a immense
la inmigración immigration
el inmigrante immigrant
inmigrar to immigrate
innegable undeniable
el inning inning
inolvidable unforgettable
insistir to insist
la insolación sunstroke
insolente insolent
inspirar to inspire
instalarse to settle down
el instante instant
el instinto instinct
la institución institution
la instrucción instruction
insultar to insult
el insulto insult
el insurgente rebel
integrante constituent
inteligente intelligent
el intercambio exchange
el interés interest
interesante interesting
interesarse to become interested
interior interior
interminable endless
internacional international
interno, -a internal
interrumpir to interrupt
la interrupción interruption
la intersección intersection

la **intervención**   intervention
intervenir (ie, i) (31)   to intervene
intimidar   to intimidate
intolerable   intolerable
la **intromisión**   intrusion, butting in
inútil   useless, futile
la **invasión**   invasion
invertir (ie, i)   to invest
la **investigación**   investigation
investigar   to investigate
el **invierno**   winter
la **invitación**   invitation
el **invitado, la invitada**   guest
invitar   to invite
ir (20)   to go; **—se** to leave, go out
la **irresponsabilidad**   irresponsibility
irresponsable   irresponsible
irrevocable   irrevocable
la **isla**   island
italiano, -a   Italian
itálico, -a   Italic
izquierdo, -a   left

J

el **jabón**   soap
el **jamón**   ham
japonés, -esa   Japanese (*n* and *adj*); **el japonés** Japanese (language)
el **jardín**   garden
el **jardinero**   gardener
el **jefe**   head, chief, leader; boss
Jesucristo   Jesus Christ
el **jonrón**   home run
joven   young; **el —** young man, youth; **la —** young woman, youth
el **juego**   game
(el) **jueves**   Thursday
el **jugador**   player
jugar (ue)   to play; to gamble

el **jugo**   juice
julio   July
junio   June
la **junta**   junta, ruling council
junto   together
jurar   to swear
justo, -a   just, right
juvenil   youthful

K

el **kilo**   kilogram (approximately 2.2 pounds)
el **kilómetro**   kilometer (approximately 0.6 mile)

L

la   the; the one; it, her, you; *pl* them, you
el **labio**   lip
el **lado**   side; **al —** (de) beside, alongside; **por otro —** on the other hand
el **ladrón**   thief
el **lago**   lake
la **lágrima**   tear; **llorar a — viva** to cry one's eyes out
lamentable   lamentable, deplorable
la **laguna**   lagoon
el **lápiz**   pencil
largo, -a   long
la **lástima**   pity
la **lata**   nuisance
la **lavandera**   laundress
lavar   to wash; **—se** to get washed
le   you; (to, for) him, her, you, it; *pl* (to, for) them, you
la **lección**   lesson
la **leche**   milk
el **lechero**   milkman
la **lechuga**   lettuce
leer   to read

legítimo, -a   legitimate, authentic
lejos (de)   far (from)
la **lengua**   tongue; language
el **lenguaje**   language
lentamente   slowly
el **león**   lion
la **letra**   letter (of the alphabet); **las —s** humanities
levantar   to lift, raise; **—se** to get up
la **ley**   law
la **leyenda**   legend
la **libra**   pound
librarse   to (get) rid
libre   free
la **librería**   bookstore
el **libro**   book
la **licencia**   license; **— de manejar**   driver's license
el **licenciado**   title conferred upon a graduate of a law school
el **líder**   leader
limitado, -a   limited
el **limón**   lemon
la **limosna**   alms
la **limosnita**   *dim* of **limosna**
el **limpiabotas**   shoeshine boy
la **limpiadita**   cleaning, shine
limpiar   to clean
limpio, -a   clean
lindo, -a   pretty, nice
la **línea**   line
lingüístico, -a   linguistic
el **lío**   mess
Lisboa   Lisbon
la **literatura**   literature
el **litro**   liter (approximately 0.95 quart)
lo   him, it, you; *pl* them, you; the; **— que** that, which, what
local   local
loco, -a   crazy
el **locutor**   radio announcer
la **lógica**   logic

lógico, -a logical
lograr to achieve, attain
la lotería lottery
luego presently, immediately, next; later; then;
hasta— see you later
el lugar place
el lujo luxury
la luna moon
(el) lunes Monday
Lupe *dim* of **Guadalupe** (woman's name)
la luz light

LL

llamar to call; **—se** to be called, named
la llegada arrival
llegar to arrive
llenar to fill
lleno, -a full
llevar to carry; to wear
llorar to weep, cry; **— a lágrima viva** to cry one's eyes out
llover (ue) to rain
la lluvia rain

M

el machete machete, field knife
la madera wood
la madre mother; **—superiora** mother superior
la madrecita *dim* of **madre**
la madrina godmother
maduro, -a ripe; mature
el maestro, la maestra teacher
el magnetismo magnetism, appeal
magnífico, -a magnificent
el maíz corn
el mal illness; evil; *adv* badly, poorly
maldecir (i) (16) to curse
la maleta suitcase
malo (mal), -a bad; ill
la mamá mama, mom

la mamacita *dim* of **mamá**
mandar to send; to command
manejar to drive; to manage
la manera way, fashion
el manifiesto manifesto, public declaration; **poner de —** to reveal
el maní peanuts
la maniobra maneuver
la mano hand; **cambiar de —** to change hands
el mantel tablecloth
mantener (ie) (28) to maintain
la mantequilla butter
el manual handbook
la manzana apple
la mañana morning; **el mañana** tomorrow; **— mismo** tomorrow for sure; **mañana por la —** tomorrow morning
el mar sea
maravilloso, -a marvelous
marcado, -a marked
marcar to dial (a telephone number)
marcha: ponerse en — to set out
marchar to march; to go away, leave
el marido husband
la marina navy
el mariscal marshal
marrón, -ona brown
(el) martes Tuesday
marzo March
más more; **— o menos** more or less
la masa mass
masivo, -a massive
el matador matador; *adj* murderous
matar to kill
las matemáticas Mathematics
la materia subject matter

material material
materno, -a maternal
máximo, -a maximum; **el máximo** maximum
maya Maya, Mayan
mayo May
el mayor major; *adj* older, bigger
la mayoría majority
mayoritario, -a (of the) majority
me me; (to, for) me; myself
mecánico, -a mechanical
la media stocking
mediados: a — de about the middle of (a period of time)
la medicina medicine
el médico doctor; **médico, -a** medical
la medida measure
medio, -a half, half a; middle; **el medio** means, way
el mediodía noon
medir (i) to measure
mejor better; best
mejorar to improve
melódico, -a melodic
la memoria memory; **de —** by heart
mencionar to mention
el mendigo beggar
el menor younger one; *adj* younger; smaller
menos less; minus; **al —** at least
mental mental
la mentalidad mentality; attitude; viewpoint
mentir (ie, i) to lie
la mentira lie; **¡—!** that's not true!
el mentor mentor, teacher
el mercado market
el mes month
la mesa table
la mesera waitress
el mesero waiter

mestizo, -a mestizo, born of Indian and white parents

meter to put in; **—se en** to get inside; **— un jonrón** to make a homerun

el metro meter (approximately 1.1 yards)

mexicano, -a Mexican

México Mexico

la mezcla mixture

mezclar to mix

mezquino, -a nasty, mean

mi my

mí me

el miedo fear; **¡qué—!** what a scare!; **tener—** to be afraid

el miembro member

mientras while; **— más (menos)** . . . the more (less) . . . ; **— tanto** meanwhile

(el) miércoles Wednesday

migratorio, -a migratory

el mil thousand

el milagro miracle

el militar military man; *adj* military

la milla mile

el millón million

el millonario millionaire

la mina mine

el ministro minister

minoritario, -a (of the) minority

el minuto minute

la mirada look, glance

mirar to look, look at

miserable miserable, wretched

la miseria misery, poverty, wretchedness

la misión mission

mismo, -a same

misterioso, -a mysterious

la moda fashion

el modelo model

la moderación moderation

moderado, -a moderate

la modestia modesty

modificar to modify

el modo way, manner; **de — que** so (that); **de todos —s** anyway

molestar to bother, annoy

molesto, -a annoying, bothersome

molido, -a ground

momentáneo, -a momentary

el momentito *dim* of **momento**

el momento moment

la moneda coin

el mono monkey

el monopolio monopoly

la montaña mountain

montañoso, -a mountainous

montar to mount; **— a caballo** to ride horseback

el montón pile, stack, heap; **a montones** in crowds

morado, -a purple

morir(se) (ue, u) to die

moro, -a Moorish

mostrar (ue) to show

el motivo reason, motive

el motor motor

mover(se) (ue) to move

el movimiento movement

la muchacha girl

el muchacho boy

mucho plenty, much, a lot; *pl* many

mudarse to move (to another house)

la muela tooth (molar)

muerto, -a dead; *pp* of **morir**; *n* dead person

la mujer woman; wife; "dear"

la mula mule

mulato, -a mulatto

multiplicado, -a multiplied, increased

mundial world(wide)

el mundo world; **todo el —** everybody

el murmullo murmur

la música music

mutuo, -a mutual

muy very

N

na regional variant of **nada**

nacer (14) to be born

naciente growing; incipient

nacional national

la nacionalidad nationality

nacionalista nationalist

nacionalizar to nationalize

nada nothing; anything (after negative); **de —** you're welcome; **— más** only, nothing more

nadie no one, nobody; anyone (after negative)

napoleónico, -a Napoleonic

la naranja orange

la nariz nose

natural natural

la naturaleza nature; **por —** by nature

la naturalización naturalization

la náusea nausea

naval naval

la Navidad Christmas

necesario, -a necessary

la necesidad necessity

necesitar to need

negar (ie) to deny

los negocios business

negro, -a black

el nene, la nena baby

nervioso, -a nervous

nevar (ie) to snow

ni neither, nor; not even

nicaragüense Nicaraguan

el **nido** nest
la **nieta** granddaughter
el **nieto** grandson
ninguno (ningún), -a no, none, no one; any, anyone (after negative)
el **nivel** level
no no, not
la **noción** notion, idea
la **noche** night
el **nómada, la nómada** nomad; *adj* nomadic, wandering
el **nombre** name
normal normal
el **normando** Norman
el **norte** north
nos us; (to, for) us; ourselves
nosotros, -as we, us
la **noticia** (item of) news
novecientos, -as nine hundred
la **novela** novel
noveno, -a ninth
noventa ninety
la **novia** sweetheart, fiancée, girlfriend; bride
noviembre November
el **novio** sweetheart, fiancé, boyfriend; bridegroom
el **núcleo** nucleus
la **nuera** daughter-in-law
nuestro, -a our, ours
nueve nine
nuevo, -a new; **de —** again
el **número** number
numeroso, -a numerous
nunca never; ever (after negative)

O

o or
obedecer (14) to obey
la **obediencia** obedience
obligado, -a obligated, forced; **verse — a** to be forced to
el **obrero** worker, laborer
observar to observe
el **observatorio** observatory
obstinado, -a obstinate
obtener (ie) (28) to obtain
obvio, -a obvious
la **ocasión** occasion
occidental western
octavo, -a eighth
octubre October
ocultar to hide
ocupar to occupy; to fill
ocurrir to occur
ochenta eighty
ocho eight
ochocientos, -as eight hundred
odiado, -a hated
el **oficial** officer
la **oficina** office
ofrecer (14) to offer
el **oído** (inner) ear
oír (21) to hear
ojalá I wish; I hope
el **ojo** eye
la **oligarquía** oligarchy
olvidar to forget
once eleven
la **ópera** opera
la **operación** operation
opinar to express an opinion
oponer(se) (23) to oppose
la **oportunidad** opportunity
oportuno, -a opportune, timely, convenient
la **opresión** oppression
el **opresor** oppressor
el **optimista** optimist
opuesto, -a opposite
el **orden** order (orderly arrangement); **la orden: a sus órdenes** how do you do
la **oreja** (outer) ear
el **organismo** organism
la **organización** organization
organizar to organize

orgulloso, -a proud
el **oriente** east
el **origen** origin
originado, -a originating
original original
originarse to originate
la **orquídea** orchid
os you; (to, from) you; yourselves
oscurecer (14) to get dark
la **oscuridad** darkness
oscuro, -a dark
el **otoño** autumn
otro, -a other, another
oxidado, -a rusty, rusted

P

pa regional variant of **para**
la **paciencia** patience
paciente patient
pacífico, -a peaceful
padecer (14) to suffer
el **padre** father; **los —s** parents
el **Padre Nuestro** Lord's Prayer
el **padrino** godfather
la **paella** saffron-flavored rice cooked with seafood, chicken, and other ingredients
pagar to pay (for)
la **página** page
el **país** country
el **pájaro** bird
la **palabra** word; word of honor
el **palacio** palace
la **palangana** washbowl
pálido, -a pale; **ponerse —** to turn pale
la **palmera** palm tree
el **palo** pole, stick
la **palomita** fly ball
el **pan** bread
la **panadería** bakery
el **panadero** baker

panameño, -a Panamanian

panamericano, -a Pan-american

los pantalones pants

la papa potato; **—s fritas** fried potatoes

el papá dad, papa

la papaya papaya fruit

el papel paper

el par pair

para for; in order to; to; by (a certain time); **— que** so that

la parada parade

el paraguas umbrella

parar to stop

pardo, -a brown

parecer (14) to seem

parecido, -a alike, similar

la pared wall

el pariente relative

el parque park; **— zoológico** zoo

la parte part; **de — de** on behalf of; **en todas —s** everywhere; **la mayor —** most; **por — de (padre)** on (my father's) side

la participación participation

el participante participant

participar to participate

particular particular, special

el partido game, match; political party; **un gran —** a great catch (in marriage)

partir to depart

pasado, -a past, last; **el —** past

el pasaje passage

pasar to happen; to pass; to spend (time); **— hambre** to go hungry; **— por** to pick up, come by for; **—se una luz** to go through a traffic light

el paseo walk, drive, outing, picnic

el paso step; way

paterno, -a paternal

el patio patio

la patria fatherland

patrio, -a national

el patriota patriot

la patrona: Santa Patrona patron saint

la pausa pause

la paz peace

la pe the letter *p*

el pecado sin

el pedacito small piece

el pedazo piece

pedir (i) to ask for

peinarse to comb one's hair

pelear to fight

el pelele punk

la película film

el pelo hair; **tomar(me) el —** to tease (me)

la pelota ball

la peluquería barber shop

el peluquero barber

la pena trouble

la península peninsula

penoso, -a painful, difficult

pensar (ie) to think; to intend; **— de** to think of (have an opinion); **— en** to think of (bring to mind)

el peón manual laborer

peor worse; worst

pequeño, -a small, short

la pera pear

perder (ie) to lose; **— de vista** to lose sight of

el perdón pardon

perdonar to pardon

perezoso, -a lazy

perfecto, -a perfect

el periódico newspaper

el período period, era

permanecer (14) to remain, stay

permanentemente permanently

el permiso permission; **con —** excuse me

permitir to permit

pero but

el peronista follower of Juan Perón

el perro dog

el perso, la persa Persian

la perseverancia perseverance

la persona person

el personaje character

personalista personalist

pertenecer (14) to belong

peruano, -a Peruvian

pesar to weigh; **el —** sorrow; **a — de** in spite of

el pescador fisherman

pescar to fish

el peso Spanish American monetary unit

el piano piano

picado, -a chopped, minced

picante hot (spicy)

el pícher pitcher

el pie foot; **a —** on foot

la piedad pity; piety

la piedra stone, rock

la pierna leg

la pimienta pepper

pintado, -a painted

pintoresco, -a picturesque

la piña pineapple

la pipa pipe

la piscina swimming pool

el piso floor, story (of a building)

la placa license plate

el placer pleasure

el plan plan

planchar to iron, press

el planeta planet

la plantación plantation

plateresco, -a plateresque, fancifully ornamented

platicar to chat

el plato dish, plate

la playa beach

la plaza (city or town) square

pleno, -a full, complete; **en —** **(verano)** in the middle of (summer)

la pluma pen

la población population, people; town

pobre poor

poco, -a little, scanty; *pl* few; **el poco** little; **un —** a little bit; *adv* little, in or to a small degree; **— a —** little by little

poder (ue) (22) to be able, can; **el —** power

el poderío might

el poeta poet

el policía policeman

la policía police (force, department)

la política politics

el polvo dust

el pollo chicken

la pompa pomp, splendor

poner (23) to put; **— atención** to pay attention; **— la mesa** to set the table; **—se** to put on (clothing); to become; **—se pálido** to turn pale

popular popular

popularísimo, -a exceedingly popular

poquísimo, -a extremely few

poquito *dim* of **poco**

por by; for; through; along; per; as; on account of, because of; **— favor** please; **— (la mañana)** in (the morning); **— qué** why

el porcentaje percentage

la porción portion, bit

porque because

el portador bearer

el portón large, heavy door

el porvenir future

la posibilidad possibility

posiblemente possibly

la posición position

posponer (23) to postpone

postizo, -a false

el postre dessert

la postura posture, attitude

práctico, -a practical

precario, -a precarious

el precio price

precioso, -a precious

la precisión precision

preciso, -a precise, exact

predominar to predominate

preferir (ie, i) to prefer

la pregunta question

preguntar to ask

prehistórico, -a prehistoric

premiado, -a awarded, (prize) winning

el premio prize

prender to catch; to turn on (a light)

la preocupación worry, concern

preocuparse to worry

preparar to prepare

prescribir to prescribe

la presencia presence; appearance

presentar to present; to introduce

presidencial presidential

el presidente president

prestar to lend

el prestigio prestige

el presupuesto budget

pretencioso, -a haughty

el pretendiente suitor

prevalecer (14) to prevail

prevenir (ie, i) (31) to prevent; to warn

prever to anticipate, foresee

la primavera spring

primero, -a first

primitivo, -a primitive, rudimentary

el primo, la prima cousin; **—hermano** first cousin

principal principal

la prisa haste; **estar de —** to be in a hurry; **tener —** to be in a hurry

probable probable

probar (ue) to taste, try

el problema problem

procedente (de) coming (from)

proceder to proceed

el procedimiento procedure

la procesión procession

el proceso process

la proclamación proclamation

productivo, -a productive

el producto product

la profesión profession

el profesor professor

profundo, -a deep, profound

progresivo, -a progressive

el progreso progress

el proletariado proletariat

la promesa promise

prometer to promise

pronto soon; **tan — como** as soon as

la pronunciación pronunciation

pronunciar to pronounce

propicio, -a favorable

la propiedad property

proponer (23) to propose

el propósito purpose; **a —** by the way, incidentally

proscrito, -a banished, outlawed

la protesta protest

protestar to protest

provenir (de) (ie, i) (31) to originate (in)

provisional provisional

próximo, -a next

la publicidad publicity

público, -a public

pue regional variant of **pues**

el pueblo people; town
la puerta door; **la Puerta del Sol** historic intersection of old Madrid
el puerto port
puertorriqueño, -a Puerto Rican
la pulga flea
el punto point; **en —** on the dot
la puntualidad punctuality
puntualizar to describe (report) in detail
puntualmente punctually
el puño fist; fistful

Q

que that, which; who, whom; than; **lo —** that which, what
qué what, which; **¿— tal?** hi, how are you? **¿— tal es (ella)?** what is (she) like?
el quechua Quechua, Indian language of the Andes region
quedar to remain, be left over; to be (located); **—se** to stay, remain; **—se para vestir santos** to become an old maid
quejarse to complain
quemar to burn
querer (ie) (24) to want; to love
querido, -a dear
el queso cheese
el quiché Quiche, Indian language of Central America
quien who, whom
quién who, whom
la química chemistry
quince fifteen
quinientos, -as five hundred
quinto, -a fifth

quitar to remove, take away; **—se** to take off (clothing)
quiteño, -a from Quito, Ecuador

R

racial racial
la radio radio (broadcast); **el radio** radio (apparatus)
la ramificación ramification
ranchero, -a ranch-style
la rapidez rapidity
rápido, -a rapid, fast
raro, -a strange
rascar to scratch
el ratito *dim* of **rato**
el rato while
el rayo flash
la razón reason; **con —** no wonder, of course; **tener —** to be right
razonable reasonable
reaccionar to react
la realidad reality
realizar to carry out, accomplish
realmente really
la rebaja reduction
la receta recipe
recibir to receive
recién recently
reciente recent
el recipiente container, dish
recíproco, -a mutual
recitar to recite
reclamar to demand, insist (on)
recoger to pick up, gather, collect
recomendar (ie) recommend
reconocer (14) to recognize
el reconocimiento recognition; examination
recordado, -a dear (in greeting of a letter)

recordar (ue) to remember; to remind
el recuerdo memory; souvenir; *pl* regards
la redistribución redistribution
redondo, -a round
reducido, -a reduced
la referencia reference
referente a with, in reference to, relating to
el referí umpire
referirse (ie, i) to refer
la reforma reform
la refrigeradora refrigerator
refugiarse to take refuge
regalar to give
el regalo gift
regatear to haggle
el régimen regime
la región region, part, section
regir (i) to rule
la regla rule
regresar to return
el regreso return
regular regular; so-so, fair
rehusar to refuse
reír(se) (de) to laugh (at)
la reja wrought iron grillwork
la relación relation
relajado, -a relaxed
relativo, -a relative
religioso, -a religious
el reloj watch; clock
reluciente shiny
remediar to help, remedy
el remedio remedy
remorder (ue) to disturb
remoto, -a remote
renacer (14) to be reborn
repente: de — suddenly
repetir (i) to repeat
repleto, -a full
replicar to answer, reply
reponer (23) to replace
el representante representative

representar to represent; to perform

la república republic

republicano,-a republican

requerir (ie, i) to require

resentirse (ie,i) to become angry or hurt

el resfrío cold (illness)

residencial residential

resignado, -a resigned

la resistencia resistance

resolver (ue) to resolve

respectivamente respectively

el respecto respect

respetable honored; respectable

respetar to respect

el respeto respect (deference)

responder to respond; **¡o no respondo de mis actos!** or I don't know what will happen!

responsable responsible

restablecer (14) reestablish

el restaurante restaurant; also **restorán**

el resto rest (remainder)

la restricción restriction

resuelto, -a resolved

el resultado result

resultar to result, turn out

retener (ie) (28) to retain

retórico, -a rhetorical

retrasarse to fall behind

la reunión meeting

la revelación revelation

revelar to reveal

la revista magazine

la revolución revolution

revolver (ue) to stir

el rey king

rezar to pray

rico, -a rich, wealthy

el río river

la riqueza wealth

riquísimo, -a extremely delicious

la risa laughter, laugh; **¡qué —!** what a joke!

robar to steal

la roca rock

el rock rock music

rodeado, -a (de) surrounded (by)

rodear to surround

la rodilla knee

rogar (ue) to beg

rojo, -a red

romance romance

romano, -a Roman

romántico, -a romantic

romper(se) to break

el ron rum

la ropa clothing, clothes

el rótulo sign

rubio, -a blond

rubio-gris grayish blond

el ruido noise

ruidoso, -a noisy

la ruina ruin

rumano, -a Rumanian

la rumba rumba

el rumbo direction; **sin —** aimlessly

el rumor rumor, gossip; murmur

rural rural

Rusia Russia

ruso, -a Russian

S

(el) sábado Saturday

saber (25) to know; to know how

sacar to take out

el sacerdote priest

el saco suit jacket

el sacrificio sacrifice

sacudir to shake

sagrado, -a sacred, holy

la sal salt

la sala living room

salado, -a salty

salir (26) to go out; to leave

la salsa sauce

saltar to jump

el salteador hijacker, attacker, mugger

el salto jump

saludar to greet, say hello

el saludo greeting

salvadoreño, -a Salvadoran, from El Salvador

el salvaje savage; *adj* wild

salvar to save

salvo, -a safe

el sandwich sandwich

sanguíneo, -a blood

sanito, -a *dim of* **sano**

sano, -a healthy

el sánscrito Sanskrit

el santo (san) saint; saint's day; **quedarse para vestir —s** to become an old maid

el sargento sergeant

la sartén frying pan

el sastre tailor

la sastrería tailor shop

satisfactorio, -a satisfactory

satisfecho, -a satisfied

se himself, herself, yourself, oneself, itself, yourselves, themselves

sea whether it be

secar to dry

seco, -a dry; unemotional

el secretario, la secretaria secretary

el secreto secret

el sector sector, section

el secuestrador kidnapper

secundario, -a secondary

la sed thirst; **tener —** to be thirsty

seguida: en — at once

el seguidor follower

seguir (i) to follow; to continue; **— (hablando)** keep on (talking); **¿cómo sigue (Juan)?** how is (John) coming along?

según according to

segundo, -a second; **el segundo** second

seguro, -a sure, certain

seis six

seiscientos, -as six hundred

la selva jungle

la semana week

el semáforo traffic light

sembrar (ie) to sow, plant

la semioscuridad twilight, dim light

semioscuro, -a dim

semiparalizado, -a half-paralyzed

semipodrido, -a half-decayed, half-rotten

sencillo, -a simple

sentarse (ie) to sit down

sentir (ie, i) to feel; to regret

la señal signal

señor Mr.; sir; **el —** gentleman

señora Mrs.; madame; **la —** lady

señorita Miss; **la —** girl, young lady

separar to separate

septiembre September

séptimo, -a seventh

la sequía drought

ser (27) to be

la serenata serenade

la serie series

serio, -a serious

servicial helpful

el servicio service

el servidor servant

el seviche South American variety of shrimp cocktail

la servilleta napkin

servir (i) to serve

sesenta sixty

setecientos, -as seven hundred

setenta seventy

sexto, -a sixth

si if

sí yes

siempre always

la sierra sierra, jagged mountain range

siete seven

el siglo century

significativo, -a significant

siguiente following

el silencio silence

la silla chair

similar similar

simpático, -a nice, pleasant, charming

simple simple

simplificar to simplify

sin without; **— que** without

sino but, except

el sinvergüenza bum, cad

siquiera at least; even **ni —** not even

el sirviente, la sirvienta servant

el sistema system

el sitio place

la situación situation

situado, -a located

sobre on, upon; about; **el —** envelope

la sobrecama bedspread

la sobrina niece

el sobrino nephew

social social

la sociedad society

la soga rope, cord

el sol sun; **hace —** it is sunny

solamente only

el soldado soldier

solemnemente solemnly

solitario, -a solitary, lone

solo, -a alone

sólo only

soltero, -a unmarried

la solución solution, answer

solucionar to resolve, solve

la sombra shade

el sombrero hat

sonar (ue) to sound; to blow

el sonido sound

la sonrisa smile

soñar (ue) (con) to dream (about)

la sopa soup

la soprano soprano

sorprender to surprise

la sorpresa surprise

el sorteo drawing (of lottery)

la sospecha suspicion

su your, his, her, its; their

suave soft

la subdivisión subdivision

el subgrupo subgroup

súbitamente suddenly

subterráneo, -a underground

subversivo, -a subversive

la sucesión succession

sucio, -a dirty

suculento, -a tasty, succulent

sudar to sweat

el sudor sweat

la suegra mother-in-law

el suegro father-in-law

el sueldo salary, pay

suelto, -a loose

el sueño dream; sleep; **tener —** to be sleepy

la suerte luck

suficiente enough, sufficient

sufriente suffering

el sufrimiento suffering

sufrir to suffer; undergo

sugerir (ie, i) to suggest

suicidarse to commit suicide

el sujeto person; subject (grammar)

sumamente extremely

sumiso, -a meek, docile

superior superior

suponer (23) to suppose

supuesto: por — of course

el sur south

Suramérica South America

surgir to arise, appear

suspirar to sigh

el suspiro sigh; **dar un —** breathe a sigh

T

el taco Mexican dish, fried tortilla stuffed with cheese, chicken, roast pork, etc.

la táctica strategy, tactic

tal such, such a; **con — que** provided that; **¿qué —?** how are things?; **¿qué — es (ella)?** what is (she) like?; **— vez** perhaps

el talento talent

el tamal Mexican dish, chile-seasoned meat or other filling steamed in soft cornmeal casing

también too, also

tampoco neither; either (after negative)

tan so, as

el tango tango

el tanque tank

tanto, -a so much, as much; *pl* so many, as many; *adv* so much, to such an extent; **tanto como** as well as

la tardanza delay

tardar to delay; to be late or take (time)

la tarde afternoon; **buenas —s** good afternoon, good evening; *adv* late: **— o temprano** sooner or later; **llegar —** to be late

tartamudear to stutter, stammer

el taxi taxi

el taxista taxi driver

la taza cup

te you; (to, from) you; yourself

el té tea

el teatro theater

la técnica technique

técnico, -a technical

la tecnología technology

el techo ceiling; roof

el teléfono telephone

la televisión television

temblar (ie) to tremble, shake

temer to fear

el temperamento temperament

la temperatura temperature

el templo temple

temporal time

temprano early; **tarde o —** sooner or later

la tendencia tendency

tender (ie) to tend

el tenedor fork

tener (ie) (28) to have; **— calor** to be (feel) warm; **— ganas (de)** to feel like; **— hambre** to be hungry; **— la culpa** to be to blame; **— miedo** to be afraid; **— prisa** to be in a hurry; **— que (trabajar)** to have to (work); **— razón** to be right; **— sed** to be thirsty; **— sueño** to be sleepy

el teniente lieutenant

el tenis tennis

la tensión tension

el tequila tequila, liquor made from distilled juices of the Mexican century plant

tercero (tercer), -a third

el tercio third

terminar to finish, end; to close

el término term; **— fijo** fixed time, fixed length

el terreno field, terrain

terrible terrible, awful

el tesoro treasure

el testigo witness

ti you

la tía aunt

el tico, la tica nickname for Costa Rican

el tiempo time; weather; **a —** on time

la tienda store

la tierra land

el tigre tiger

el timbre bell

tímido, -a timid

la tintorería dry cleaner's shop

el tío uncle

típico, -a typical

el tipo type; guy

el tirano tyrant

tirar to throw; to draw, pull; **— la casa por la ventana** to go all out

la toalla towel

tocar to touch; to play (music); **— la puerta** to knock at the door, ring the bell

todavía still, yet

todo, -a all; every; **el todo** all; whole; everything; *pl* everybody, all

tolerar to tolerate

tolteca-azteca Toltec-Aztec

la toma seizure, takeover

tomar to take; to drink; to eat; **—(me) el pelo** to tease (me)

el tomate tomato

el tomo volume

el tono tone

la tontería nonsense

tonto, -a dumb, silly

el toro bull

la tortilla thin cornmeal pancake (Mexican)

tostar (ue) to toast, roast; **—se** to get a tan

total total

la totalidad whole, totality

trabajar to work

el trabajo work

el trabalenguas tongue twister

tradicional traditional

tradicionalista traditionalistic

traer (29) to bring

la tragedia tragedy

el traje suit; gown

tranquilamente calmly

transformar to transform

transitado, -a busy (as a street)

el tránsito traffic

el transporte transport

tras after

trasero, -a back

la trasmisión transmission

el tratamiento treatment

tratar (de) to try (to)

través: a — de in the course of; across; through

trazar to draw

trece thirteen

treinta thirty

tremendo, -a tremendous, awful

el tren train

tres three

trescientos, -as three hundred

la tribu tribe

triste sad

triunfalmente triumphantly

triunfar to triumph

la tropa troops

tropical tropical

el trópico tropics

tu your

tú you

tumbar to knock down

el tumulto tumult

el turista tourist

tuyo, -a your, yours, of yours

U

último,-a last; **por último** at last, finally

unánimemente unanimously

único, -a unique, only

la unidad unit; unity

unido, -a united

el uniforme uniform

la universidad university

uno (un), -a one; a; *pl* some

urgente urgent

el uso use

usté regional variant of **usted**

usted you

la usurpación usurpation

usurpado, -a usurped

útil useful

utilitario, -a utilitarian

la uva grape

V

la vaca cow

las vacaciones vacation

vacilar to hesitate

vacío, -a empty

vago, -a vague

valenciano, -a Valencian, of the city of Valencia, Spain

valer (30) to be worth; **— la pena** to be worthwhile; **—se de** to make use of

válido, -a valid

el valor value

el vals waltz

vano: en — in vain

la variante variation, variant

variar to vary

la variedad variety

varios, -as various

el vaso glass

vegetal vegetable

el vehículo vehicle

veinte twenty

la vela candle

la velocidad speed

vencer to defeat

el vendedor, la vendedora vender

vender to sell; **— en** to sell for

venidero, -a future, coming

venir (ie, i) (31) to come; **—se abajo** to fall down

la ventana window

la ventanilla window

ventilar to air, discuss

ver (32) to see; **—se obligado a** to be forced to

el verano summer

veras: de — really

el verbo verb

verdá regional variant of **verdad**

la verdad truth; **¿—?** isn't that so? right?

verdadero, -a real, true

verde green; unripe

las verduras green vegetables, greens

la versión version

los versos poetry, poems

vespertino, -a evening, vesper

el vestido dress

vestir (i) to dress; **—se** to get dressed; **quedarse para — santos** to become an old maid

la vez time; **algunas (unas) veces** sometimes; **a veces** sometimes; **de — en cuando** from time to time; **en — de** instead of; **muchas veces** often; **tal —** perhaps, maybe

el viaje trip

el vice-presidente, la vice-presidenta vice president

viceversa vice versa
el vicio vice
la víctima victim
la victoria victory
victorioso, -a victorious, winning
la vida life
el vidrio glass
viejísimo, -a extremely old
la viejita little old lady
viejo, -a old
el viento wind; **hace —** it is windy
(el) viernes Friday
la villa town; **— miseria** conglomeration of hovels and shacks that house the poor
el vino wine
violar to violate
violento, -a violent

el virrey viceroy
la visita visit; visitor
la visa de residencia resident visa
la vista view, sight; **la — fija al frente** looking straight ahead
la viuda widow
la vivienda housing
vivir to live
vivo, -a live, lively, alive
el vocabulario vocabulary
volar (ue) to fly
la voluntad will
volver (ue) to return; **—se loco** to go crazy
vosotros, -as you
el voto vote
la voz voice; **en — baja** under one's breath
vuestro, -a your

Y

y and; plus
ya now; yet; already; still; **— no** no longer, not any more; **— que** since
el yanqui Yankee; *adj* Yankee
el yerno son-in-law
yo I

Z

zambo, -a born of black and Indian parents
la zapatería shoestore; shoemaker's shop
el zapatero shoemaker
el zapato shoe
la zona zone, region

English-Spanish Vocabulary

A

a un, una
able: be — poder (ue, u) (22)
abound abundar
about de, acerca de, sobre; como (approximately)
above sobre, encima (de)
abroad en el extranjero
absolutely absolutamente
absurd absurdo
abundance la abundancia; **be in** — abundar
accent el acento
accept aceptar
accompany acompañar
according to según
account la cuenta; **on** — **of** por, a causa de
accumulate acumular
accustom acostumbrar
accustomed: be — acostumbrar; **become** — acostumbrarse
ache el dolor
achieve realizar
acquisition la adquisición
action la acción
active activo
activity la actividad
adapt adaptar
add agregar
addition: in — **to** además de

adequate adecuado
adjective el adjetivo
administrative administrativo
admiral el almirante
advance avanzar
advantage la ventaja; **take** — **of** aprovechar
affection el cariño
affirmative afirmativo
afford (give, provide) dar (15)
afraid: be — tener (ie) (28) miedo
after después (de)
afternoon la tarde; **good** — buenas tardes
afterwards después
again otra vez; — **and** — una y otra vez
against contra
age la edad
agency la agencia, el servicio
ago: (ten years) — hace (diez años)
agree estar (17) de acuerdo; — **to** quedar en
agreement el acuerdo; la concordancia (grammar)
agricultural agrícola
ahead: get — adelantarse
aid ayudar; la ayuda
air el aire
alarm alarmar; la alarma
alike parecidos, iguales

all todo(s)
almost casi
alms la limosna
alone solo
alongside al lado de
alphabet el alfabeto
alphabetical alfabético
already ya
also también
although aunque
always siempre
America América; **Central** — Centroamérica; **North** — Norteamérica; **Spanish** — Hispanoamérica; **South** — Suramérica
American americano
among entre
amusing divertido
an un, una
and y, e
Anglo-Saxon anglosajón, -ona
angry enojado; resentido; furioso; **get** — enojarse; resentirse (ie, i)
annihilate aniquilar
annoy molestar
another otro
answer contestar
anthropologist el antropólogo
anticipate prever (32)
any cualquier; alguno; ninguno (after negative)

anybody alguien; nadie (after negative)
anyone alguien; nadie (after negative)
anything cualquier cosa; nada (after negative)
anyway de todos modos
apartment el apartamento
appeal apelar
appear aparecer (14)
appearance la apariencia
apple la manzana
apply aplicar
approach acercarse (a)
approval la aprobación
approximately aproximadamente
April abril
Argentinean argentino
argue discutir
arise surgir
arm el brazo
armed armado
army el ejército
around alrededor de; por
arrive llegar
art el arte; **liberal —s** (los) artes
article el artículo
artist el artista
as como; a medida que; **— for (me)** en cuanto a (mí); **— soon —** tan pronto como; **— well —** tanto como
ask preguntar; **— for** pedir (i)
aspect el aspecto
assimilate asimilar
astronaut el astronauta
at en; a
Atlantic el Atlántico; atlántico
attain obtener (ie) (28)
attend asistir; atender (ie) (wait on, look after)
attention: pay — poner (23) atención; hacer (19) caso
attitude la actitud
attract atraer (29)
August agosto
aunt la tía

authority la autoridad
autumn el otoño
avoid evitar
away: right — inmediatamente; **go —** irse (20); **throw —** desperdiciar
awful terrible; **— thing** la barbaridad

B

baby el bebé, la bebé
bachelor el soltero
back la espalda
bad malo
bag la bolsa
baker el panadero
bakery la panadería
bamboo el bambú
banana la banana (fruit); el banano (tree)
band la banda
bank el banco; la orilla (shore)
barbarianism la barbarie
barber el peluquero; **—shop** la peluquería
barely apenas
barrier la barrera
base la base
basic básico
basket la canasta; **shopping —** la canasta de compras
bath el baño; **take a —** bañarse
bathe bañarse
bathroom el baño
be estar (17); ser (27)
beach la playa
bean el frijol
beautiful lindo; bello
because porque; **— of** a causa de, por
become ponerse (23); hacerse (19); convertirse (ie, i) en
bed la cama; **go to —** acostarse (ue)
bedroom el cuarto
beer la cerveza
before antes (de)
beforehand de antemano
beggar el mendigo

begin comenzar (ie); empezar (ie)
behalf: on — of a favor de
behind atrás; detrás (de)
being el ser
believe creer
belligerent beligerante
belong pertenecer (14)
below abajo
bench el banco
beside al lado de
besides además (de)
best mejor
bet apostar (ue)
better mejor
better-off acomodado
between entre
beyond más allá
big grande
bill la cuenta
biology la biología
bird el pájaro
birthday el cumpleaños
bit: a little — un poco; un poquito
bitter amargo
black negro
bless bendecir (16, *pp* bendecido)
block el bloque
blond rubio
blouse la blusa
blow el golpe
blue azul
board la tabla
boat el barco
Bogotá: person from — bogotano
boiling hirviendo
Bolivian boliviano
book el libro
bookstore la librería
bored aburrido; **get —** aburrirse
boring aburrido
born: be — nacer (14)
boss el dueño; el jefe
both ambos; los dos
bother molestar
bottle la botella

bottom el fondo
bourgeoisie la burguesía
boy el muchacho; el chico;
    little — el niño
Brazil Brasil
bread el pan
break down descomponer (23)
breakfast el desayuno
bring traer (29); **— about**
    causar; **— closer** estrechar
broth el caldo
brother el hermano
brother-in-law el cuñado
brown café; de color café;
    marrón; pardo; castaño;
    habano
brunette de pelo negro; el
    moreno, trigueño, la mo-
    rena, trigueña
budget el presupuesto
build construir
building el edificio
bull el toro
bullfight la corrida (de toros)
bum el sinvergüenza
bus el autobús
busy ocupado
but pero; sino (que)
butcher el carnicero; **—shop**
    la carnicería
butter la mantequilla
buy comprar
by por; para

C

cabinet el gabinete
cad el sinvergüenza
café el café
calendar el calendario
caliph el califa
call llamar
calm la calma
can poder (ue, u) (22)
canal el canal
candle la vela
canvas la lona
capable capaz
capital la capital (city)
captain el capitán

car el carro; el coche
caravel la carabela
cardboard el cartón
cardinal cardinal
care (el) cuidado; **to take — of**
    cuidar
career la carrera
carefully con cuidado
Carribbean el Caribe
carpenter el carpintero
carry llevar
case el caso
cat el gato, la gata
catch coger; **a great —** un gran
    partido
cause causar; la causa
caution (el) cuidado
cease cesar
celebrate celebrar
cemetery el cementerio
center el centro
central central; **Central Amer-**
    ica Centroamérica; **Cen-**
    tral American centroame-
    ricano
century el siglo
ceremony la ceremonia
certain cierto
chair la silla
chance la oportunidad
change cambiar; el cambio
chapter el capítulo
character el carácter; el
    personaje
charge: take — encargarse;
    in — encargado
charming simpático
chat conversar
chauffeur el chofer
cheap barato
check el cheque
cheerful alegre
cheese el queso
chemical químico
chemistry la química
chicken el pollo; la gallina
    (hen)
chief el jefe; principal
child el niño, la niña; el hijo, la
    hija

Chilean chileno
choose escoger; elegir (i);
    optar (por)
chop picar
Christmas la Navidad
church la iglesia
cigarette el cigarro, el ciga-
    rrillo
circulate circular
circumstance la circunstancia
citizen el ciudadano
city la ciudad
civic cívico
civil civil
civilization la civilización
civilize civilizar
class la clase
clause la cláusula
clean limpiar; limpio
cleaner: dry —'s shop la tin-
    torería
clear claro
clock el reloj
close cerrar (ie)
close (to) cerca (de); **pay —**
    attention poner (23) mu-
    cha atención
closer: bring — estrechar
clothes la ropa
cloud la nube
club el club
coast la costa
coat el abrigo
coffee el café; **— shop** la ca-
    fetería
Coke la coca-cola
cold el frío; **to be —** (weather)
    hacer (19) frío; **to be**
    (feel) — tener (ie) (28) frío;
    el resfrío (illness)
collect cobrar
collector el cobrador
college la universidad; univer-
    sitario
Colombian colombiano
colonel el coronel
colony la colonia
color el color
colossus el coloso
Columbus Colón

comb peinar; — **one's hair** peinarse
come venir (ie, i) (31); — **about** ocurrir; — **back** regresar, volver (ue); — **by for** pasar por; — **in** entrar; **how is (he) coming along?** ¿cómo sigue (él)?
comfort el confort
comfortably cómodamente
command el mando; el imperativo (grammar)
comment comentar; el comentario
commit cometer; — **suicide** suicidarse
commonly comúnmente
communism el comunismo
community la comunidad; comunal
companion el compañero
comparison la comparación
compassion la compasión
complain quejarse
complaint la queja
complement el complemento
complete completo
compose componer (23)
conceive concebir (i)
concentrate concentrar
concentration la concentración
concept el concepto
concert el concierto
condition la condición
conditional condicional
condolence el pésame
conduct la conducta
confess confesar (ie)
conflict el conflicto
confuse confundir
conglomeration la conglomeración
congratulate felicitar
congress el congreso
consequently por consiguiente; consecuentemente; por consecuencia
consider considerar
consolation el consuelo
consonant la consonante

constant constante
constitute constituir
construction la construcción
contain contener (ie) (28)
content contento
continent el continente
continually continuamente
continue continuar; seguir (i)
continuously continuamente
contract contraer (29)
contraction la contracción
contradict contradecir (16)
contrast el contraste; **in —** en cambio
contribute contribuir
control controlar; el control
controversy la controversia
convenience la comodidad
conversation la conversación
converse conversar; charlar
convert convertir (ie, i); **be —ed to** convertirse en
convertible convertible
convince convencer
cook cocinar; el cocinero, la cocinera
cooperation la cooperación
corner el rincón (of room); la esquina (of street)
correct correcto
corresponding correspondiente
cost costar (ue); el costo
Costa Rican costarricense; tico (nickname)
count contar (ue)
country el país; el campo
countryside el campo
coup d'état el golpe de estado
course (class) el curso; — **(of an evening, etc.)** transcurso; **of —** cómo no, claro
cousin el primo, la prima; **first —** el primo hermano
cover tapar, cubrir
cow la vaca
crazy loco; **go —** volverse (ue) loco
create crear
creditor el acreedor
crew la tripulación

crime el delito
cross cruzar
cry llorar
Cuban cubano
cultivate cultivar
cultural cultural
culture la cultura
cup la taza
curiosity la curiosidad
curious curioso
curse maldecir (16, *pp* maldecido)
custom la costumbre
customary: be — acostumbrarse
customer el cliente
cut cortar
cute simpático

D

dad el papá
daily diario
damn! ¡caramba!
dance bailar; el baile
dangerous peligroso
date la fecha; la cita (appointment); **make a —** citarse
daughter la hija
daughter-in-law la nuera
day el día; — **before yesterday** anteayer
deal: a great — mucho
dean el decano
dear querido, estimado, recordado
dearest adorado, queridísimo
death la muerte
debt la deuda
decade la década
deceive engañar
December diciembre
decent decente
decide decidir
decisively definitivamente
declare declarar
decompose descomponer (23)
decrease la rebaja
defect el defecto
defense la defensa
definite definido

definitely definitivamente
delayed: be — atrasarse
delicious delicioso, rico
delighted encantado
delightful delicioso
deliver entregar
demand exigir; la exigencia
democratic democrático
demonstration la demostra-
ción; la manifestación
demonstrative demostrativo
depart partir
department el departamento
depend (on) depender (de)
derive provenir (ie, i) (31)
describe describir
descriptive descriptivo
desire desear; las ganas
desolate desolado
despair la desesperación
desperate desesperado
despite a pesar de
dessert el postre
detail el detalle
detain detener (ie) (28)
develop desarrollar
dialog el diálogo
dictate dictar
dictator el dictador
dictatorial dictatorial
dictatorship la dictadura
dictionary el diccionario
die morir (ue, u)
difference la diferencia
different distinto, diferente
differentiate diferenciar
difficult difícil
difficulty la dificultad
dignity la dignidad
dine comer
dining room el comedor
dinner la comida
diplomatic diplomático
direct dirigir; directo
dirty sucio
disappear desaparecer (14)
disappointed decepcionado
disaster el desastre
discover descubrir
discoverer el descubridor
discovery el descubrimiento

discuss discutir
dish el plato
displease disgustar
distance la distancia
divide dividir
divine divino
divorce el divorcio; **get a —**
divorciarse
do hacer (19)
doctor el médico, el doctor
dog el perro
dollar el dólar
domestic doméstico
dominate dominar
donkey el burro
door la puerta
dormitory el dormitorio
dot: on the — en punto
doubt dudar; la duda; **without**
a —, no — sin duda
down: tear — deshacer (19)
downtown el centro
draw (out) extender (ie)
dream soñar (ue); el sueño
dress vestir (i); el vestido;
get —ed vestirse
drink beber, tomar; **soft —** el
refresco
drive manejar
driver el automovilista; el
chofer; **taxi —** el taxista
drought la sequía
dry-cleaning shop la tintorería
duel el duelo
dull apagado
dumb tonto
dumbbell el tonto
during durante
dust el polvo
duty el deber; **do (my) —** cumplir con (mi) deber

E

each cada; **— other** el uno al
otro
ear el oído (inner); la oreja
(outer)
earache el dolor de oídos
early temprano
earn ganar

easily con facilidad; cómodamente
Easter (las) Pascuas; **— Week**
la Semana Santa
easy fácil
eat comer
educational educativo
educator el educador
effectively eficazmente
efficient eficiente
effort el esfuerzo
effusiveness la efusión
egg el huevo
eight ocho
eighteen dieciocho
eighth octavo
eight hundred ochocientos
eighty ochenta
either o; ni; tampoco (after
negative)
elastic elástico
elect elegir (i)
electrician el electricista
electricity la electricidad
elegant elegante
elephant el elefante
eleven once
else más
elude eludir
embassy la embajada
emerge surgir
emotion la emoción
empirical empírico
employee el empleado, la empleada
empty vacío; **— table** la mesa
desocupada
enchant encantar
end terminar; acabar
English inglés, -esa
English speaker el inglés-ha-
blante
enjoy disfrutar, gozar (de)
enormous enorme
enough bastante
enter entrar
enterprising emprendedor, -ra
entertain entretener (ie) (28)
enthusiasm el entusiasmo
entire entero
environment el ambiente

envy envidiar; la envidia
epoch la época
equal igual
equality la igualdad
era la era
erroneous erróneo
error el error
especially especialmente
essentially esencialmente
establish establecer (14)
Europe (la) Europa
European europeo
even parejo; hasta; — **though** aunque; **not —** ni (siquiera)
evening la tarde; la noche; **good —** buenas noches
event el acontecimiento
ever siempre; jamás (after negative); nunca (after negative)
every todos; cada (each)
everybody todo el mundo; todos
everyone todo el mundo; todos
everything todo
everywhere por todas partes; en todas partes
exact exacto
exaggerate exagerar
exam el examen; **do well on an —** hacer (19) un examen bueno
examine examinar
example el ejemplo
excellent excelente
except exceptuar; excepto
exception la excepción
excess el exceso
exclaim exclamar
excuse la excusa; **— me** perdón; con permiso
exercise el ejercicio
exhibit la exposición
exile el exilio
exist existir
existence la existencia
expense el gasto
expensive caro
experience la experiencia
expert el experto
explain explicar

explanation la explicación
explorer el explorador
export la exportación
express expresar
expression la expresión
extension la extensión
extreme el extremo; extremado
eye el ojo
eyeglasses las gafas

F

fabric la tela
face enfrentarse; la cara; **in the — of** ante
facility la facilidad
facing enfrente (de)
fact el hecho, el dato
factor el factor
faint desmayarse
fair regular; así, así
fairly bastante
fall caer (13); la caída, el otoño (season)
fame la fama
family la familia
famous famoso
fantastic fantástico
far lejos; **— from** lejos de
farewell adiós; **say —** despedirse (i)
farm la finca
farmer el agricultor
fast rápido, veloz; rápidamente
fat gordo
father el padre
father-in-law el suegro
fatherland la patria
fault la culpa
favor el favor
fear el temor, el miedo
feat la hazaña
feature el aspecto
February febrero
fed: be — up estar hasta la coronilla
feel sentir (ie, i); **— like** tener (ie) (28) ganas (de); **make (someone) — sorry** dar(le) (15) lástima

feeling el sentimiento; el sentido
fellow el chico
few pocos, pocas
fiancé el novio
fiancée la novia
ficticious ficticio
field el campo
fifteen quince
fifth quinto
fifty cincuenta
figure la figura; la cifra
filial filial
film la película
finally finalmente; por fin
financial económico
find encontrar (ue); **— out** averiguar
fine bien; **— arts** (los) artes; las letras
finger el dedo
finish acabar; terminar
fire despedir (i)
firm la firma
first primero; **— cousin** el primo hermano
five cinco
five hundred quinientos
flat plano
flirt flirtear
flood la inundación
floor el piso
flower la flor
follow seguir (i)
following siguiente
food la comida
fool el tonto
foot el pie
footstep el paso
for por; para
force la fuerza; **air —** las fuerzas aéreas
foreign extranjero
forget olvidar, olvidarse de
fork el tenedor
form formar; componer (23); la forma
formal formal
formality la formalidad
formation la formación
former aquél; antiguo

formidable formidable
formula la fórmula
forth: and so — etcétera
fortunate afortunado
forty cuarenta
found fundar
four cuatro
four hundred cuatrocientos
fourteen catorce
fourth cuarto
France (la) Francia
frank franco
frankly francamente
fraternity la fraternidad
free gratis; libre
freedom la libertad
French francés, -esa
Frenchman el francés
frequency la frecuencia
frequent frecuente
frequently frecuentemente; a menudo
fresh fresco; atrevido (bold)
Friday (el) viernes
friend el amigo, la amiga
friendship la amistad
from de; desde; **— (table) to (table)** de (mesa) en (mesa)
front: in — of delante de, enfrente de; frente a
fruit la fruta
fry freír
frying pan la sartén
fulfill cumplir
full lleno; pleno (complete)
fun la alegría
funny chistoso
furious furioso
further: — (down) más (abajo)
future el porvenir, el futuro

G

gamble jugar (ue)
gap el abismo
garden el jardín
gardener el jardinero
garlic el ajo

gather reunir(se); recoger (pick up)
gathering la reunión
gay alegre
gender el género
general el general; general
generally por lo general
generic genérico
generous generoso
genius el genio
Genoa Génova
gentleman el señor, el caballero
geographical geográfico
geography la geografía
German el alemán; alemán, -ana
Germanic germánico
Germany Alemania
gesture el gesto
get conseguir (i); obtener (ie) (28); recibir; **— inside** meterse (en); **— off** (a bus) bajar; **— ready** alistarse; prepararse; **— somewhere** llegar; **— up** levantarse
gift el regalo
girl la muchacha, la chica; **little —** la niña
girlfriend la amiga; la novia
give dar (15); regalar; **don't — me that** no me venga con cuentos
glad: be — alegrarse
gladly con mucho gusto
glass el vaso
glove el guante
go ir (20); andar (12); **— all out** echar la casa por la ventana; **— around** andar (12); **— away** irse; **— in** entrar; **— on** seguir (i); **— out** salir (26); **— through the light** pasarse la luz
God Dios
goddaughter la ahijada
godfather el padrino
godmother la madrina
godson el ahijado
golden dorado

good bueno
good-bye adiós; **say —** despedirse (i)
government el gobierno
gown el traje; **wedding —** el traje de boda
grammar la gramática; gramatical; **— book** la gramática
granddaughter la nieta
grandfather el abuelo
grandmother la abuela
grandson el nieto
granny la abuelita
grape la uva
gravely: very — ill gravísimo
gray gris
great grande; **—!** ¡fantástico!
greater mayor
green verde; **the light is —** la luz (el semáforo) está en verde
greens las verduras
greet saludar
greeting el saludo
grief: good —! ¡por Dios!
ground molido
group el grupo
grow crecer (14)
Guatemalan guatemalteco; el chapín (nickname)
guest el invitado
guitar la guitarra
guy el tipo

H

habit el hábito; la costumbre
hacienda la hacienda
haggle regatear
hair el pelo
half la mitad; medio
ham el jamón
hand la mano; **— over** entregar; **on the other —** en cambio, por otra parte
happen ocurrir, pasar
happy alegre, contento, feliz; **be —** alegrarse (de)
hard duro
hardly apenas

hard-working trabajador, -ra
haste la prisa
hat el sombrero
hate odiar, detestar; el odio
have tener (ie) (28); haber (18); **— just (gone out)** acabar de (salir); **— (something to eat)** tomar; **— to (leave)** tener que (salir); **one has to (study)** hay que (estudiar)
he él
head la cabeza; el jefe (leader)
hear oír
heart el corazón; **by —** de memoria
heat calentar (ie); el calor
height la altura
hello aló (on phone)
help ayudar; la ayuda
hemisphere el hemisferio
hen la gallina
hence de ahí
her la; le; ella; su; suyo
here aquí; **over —** por aquí
hers suyo
herself se
hesitation la cavilación
hi! ¡hola!
hide esconder
high alto; **— up** arriba
high school el colegio, la (escuela) secundaria; **— student** estudiante secundario
highway el camino; la carretera
him lo; le; él
himself se
hint la indirecta
his su; suyo
historical histórico
history la historia
Holy Mary! ¡Santa María!
home la casa; **be —** estar (17) en casa; **go —** ir (20) a casa
homeland la patria
homely feo
Honduran hondureño
honest honrado; honesto

honor: word of — palabra (de honor)
hope esperar; la esperanza
horse el caballo; **ride a —** montar a caballo
hot caliente; picante (spicy); **be — (weather)** hacer (19) calor; **be (feel) —** tener (ie) (28) calor
hotel el hotel
hour la hora
house la casa
household el hogar
housewife el ama (f) de casa
housing la vivienda
how cómo; **— are you?** ¿qué tal? ¿cómo estás? **— do you do?** a sus órdenes; **— many** cuántos; **— much** cuánto; **— (nice)!** ¡qué (bueno)!
however sin embargo
hug el abrazo
human humano
humanities filosofía y letras
humble humilde
humidity la humedad
humor el humor
hundred cien, ciento
hunger (f) el hambre
hungry: be — tener (ie) (28) hambre
hurry: be in a — tener (ie) (28) prisa; estar (17) de prisa
hurt resentido; **become —** resentirse (ie) (i)
husband el marido, el esposo

I

I yo
Iberian ibérico
idea la idea
ideal ideal
identify identificar
if si; **even —** aunque
ill grave; enfermo; malo
illegitimate ilegítimo
illness el mal
illogical ilógico

imaginary imaginario
imagine imaginarse
imitate imitar
immediate inmediato
immediately en seguida
immigrant el inmigrante
immigration la inmigración
impenetrable impenetrable
imperfect imperfecto
impersonal impersonal
importance la importancia
important importante; **to be —** importar
impose imponer (23)
impossible imposible
impression la impresión
impressive impresionante
impulse el impulso
in en, de (after superlative)
inasmuch as como
incidentally a propósito
increase aumentar
independence la independencia
independent independiente
Indian el indio; indio
indication la indicación
indicative indicativo
indirect indirecto
individual el individuo
individualism el individualismo
individualistic individualista
industry la industria
inevitable inevitable
inexact inexacto
inexpensive barato
infinite infinito
infinitive el infinitivo (grammar)
inform avisar
information la información
ingrate ingrato
ingredient el ingrediente
inhabitant el habitante
initial la inicial; inicial
initiate iniciar
inside dentro (de); **get —** meterse en
insist insistir

insolent insolente
install instalar
instance la ocasión; **for —** por ejemplo
instead of en vez de
institution la institución
intelligent inteligente
intend pensar (ie)
intense intenso
interest el interés
interested: become — (in) interesarse (en)
interesting interesante
interior interior
interminable interminable
interrogative interrogativo
interrupt interrumpir
interruption la interrupción
intervene intervenir (ie, i) (31)
intervention la intervención
introduce presentar
investigate investigar
investigation la investigación
invitation la invitación
invite invitar
iron planchar; el hierro
irregular irregular
irresponsible irresponsable
island la isla
it lo, la; él, ella
Italian italiano
Italy Italia
its su

J

jail la cárcel
January (el) enero
Japan (el) Japón
jealous celoso
Jesus Christ Jesucristo
job el oficio; el empleo
join unirse (a)
jointly conjuntamente
joke bromear; el chiste; la broma
judge juzgar; el juez
judgment el juicio
juice el jugo
July julio

jump saltar
June junio
jungle la selva
junta la junta
just justo; nada más; **have — (gone out)** acabar de (salir)

K

kangaroo el canguro
keep mantener (ie) (28); **— quiet** callarse, hacer silencio
kill matar
kilogram el kilo
kilometer el kilómetro
kind amable; la especie, la clase
king el rey
kiss besar; el beso
kitchen la cocina
knife el cuchillo
know conocer (14); saber; **— how** saber (25)
knowledge el conocimiento

L

labor el trabajo
laborer: day — el peón
lack faltar; la falta
lady la señora; **young —** la señorita
lake el lago
land la tierra
language la lengua, el idioma, el lenguaje
large grande
largely en gran parte
last durar
last último; **at —** por fin; **— name** apellido; **— night** anoche; **— week** la semana pasada
late tarde
later más tarde
Latin el latín; latino
Latin America América Lati-na, Latinoamérica

Latin American latinoamericano
laugh reír; la risa
laughter la risa
laundress la lavandera
law la ley; **— school** la facultad de derecho
lawyer el abogado
lead dirigir; **— a life** llevar una vida
learn aprender
leave salir (26); irse (20); marchar
leave salir (26); irse (20); marchar
lecture la conferencia
left la izquierda; izquierdo
leg la pierna
legal legal
legendary legendario
lend prestar
length la longitud
lesson la lección
let dejar; **— go** dejar
letter la carta; la letra, el carácter (of the alphabet)
lettuce la lechuga
level el nivel
liberator el libertador
library la biblioteca
license la licencia; **driver's —** licencia de manejar
lie mentir (ie, i); la mentira
lieutenant el teniente
life la vida
light encender (ie); la luz; **traffic —** el semáforo, la luz
like: (I) — these (me) gustan éstos
like como; **— that** así
limit limitar
linguistic lingüístico
lion el león
Lisbon Lisboa
listen (to) escuchar
liter el litro
literature la literatura
little poco; **— by —** poco a poco; pequeño
live vivir; vivo

living residente; — **room** la sala

local local

located situado

long largo; **how —** cuánto tiempo; **so —** hasta luego

look parecer (14); — **after** atender (ie), guardar; — **at** mirar; — **for** buscar; **they — alike** son parecidos

lose perder (ie)

lot: a — mucho

lottery la lotería

love querer (ie) (24); el amor; **in — (with)** enamorado (de)

low bajo

Lower California Baja California

loyalty la lealtad

luck la suerte

lucky dichoso, afortunado; con suerte

lunch el almuerzo

luxury el lujo

M

machete el machete

mad: get — enojarse; resentirse (ie, i); **go —** volverse (ue) loco

magazine la revista

maid la criada

maiden: — aunt la tía soltera

mail el correo

mailman el cartero

main principal

maintain mantener (ie) (28)

maintenance la manutención

major el mayor

majority la mayoría

make hacer (19)

man el hombre; **military —** el militar

mango el mango

mankind la humanidad

manner la manera; el trato; **in (this) —** de (esta) manera

manual manual

many muchos; **a great —** muchísimos

March marzo

marines la infantería de la marina

market el mercado

marriage el casamiento

marry casarse (con); **get married** casarse

marvelous maravilloso

mass la masa

master el señor

match el partido (sport); **a good —** un buen partido

material material

mathematics las matemáticas

matter importar; el asunto; la cuestión; **what's the —?** ¿qué pasa?

maximum máximo

May mayo

maybe tal vez

me me; mí

meal la comida

mean significar; malo

meaning el significado

means el medio

meantime: in the — mientras tanto

measure medir (i)

meat la carne

mechanic el mecánico

mechanical mecánico

meddle meterse

medicine la medicina

Mediterranean el Mediterráneo; mediterráneo

meet conocer (14); recibir

memory la memoria

mention mencionar; la mención

mess el desastre; el lío

meter el metro

method el método

Mexican mexicano

México Mexico

middle el medio

midnight la medianoche

migratory migratorio

military militar

milk la leche

milkman el lechero

million el millón

millionaire el millonario

mine mío

miniature la miniatura

minimum el mínimo

minister el ministro

minute el minuto

miss (la) señorita

missionary el misionero

mister (el) señor

mix mezclar; la mezcla

mobility la movilidad

modern moderno

modest modesto

modify modificar

mom la mamá

moment el momento

monarch el monarca

Monday (el) lunes

money el dinero

month el mes

monthly mensual

moon la luna

morals la moral

more más

morning la mañana; **good —** buenos días; **tomorrow —** mañana por la mañana

mortality la mortalidad

most la mayor parte

mother la madre

mother-in-law la suegra

motive el motivo

motor el motor

mountain la montaña

mouth la boca; **make (his) — water** hacer(le) (19) la boca agua

move mover(se) (ue); mudarse (de casa) (to another house)

moved: be — conmoverse (ue)

movie la película

movies el cine

Mrs. (la) señora

much mucho; **as —** tanto; **how —?** ¿cuánto? **so —** tanto

mule la mula

municipal municipal
must deber
my mi; mío
myself me

N

nail clavar
name nombrar; el nombre;
  last — el apellido; **(my) —**
  is (me) llam(o)
napkin la servilleta
nation la nación
nationalism el nacionalismo
nationalistic nacionalista
nationality la nacionalidad
native nativo
naturalization la naturalización
naturally naturalmente
nature la naturaleza
navigation la navegación
navy la marina
near cerca (de)
nearby cerca
nearly casi
necessary necesario; **it is —**
  hay que (followed by infinitive)
need necesitar
negative negativo
neighborhood el barrio
neither tampoco; **— . . . nor**
  ni... ni
nephew el sobrino
never nunca
new nuevo
news las noticias; la noticia
  (item)
newspaper el periódico
New York Nueva York
next próximo; **— to (him)** a
  (su) lado
nice simpático; **how —!** ¡qué
  bien!
nickname el apodo
niece la sobrina
night la noche; **last —** anoche;
  — before last anteanoche
nine nueve

nine hundred novecientos
nineteen diecinueve
ninety noventa
ninth noveno
no no; ninguno
nobody nadie, ninguno
nominalization la substan-
  tivación
none ninguno
nonsense la tontería
no one nadie, ninguno
norm la norma
normal normal
north el norte
North American norteamericano
nose la nariz
not no; **— even** ni siquiera
note el apunte
note notar
notebook el cuaderno
nothing nada
notice notar; fijarse (en);
  give — avisar
notion la noción; la idea
noun el substantivo; **— clause**
  la cláusula substantiva
novel la novela
November noviembre
now ahora; ya
nowadays hoy en día
nuisance la molestia
number el número
numerous numeroso
nursemaid la niñera

O

obedience la obediencia
obey obedecer (14)
obligate obligar
obscure obscuro
observe observar
obtain obtener (ie) (28)
obvious obvio, evidente
occident el occidente
occupy ocupar
occur ocurrir
o'clock: it is (two) — son las
  (dos); **it is one —** es la una

October octubre
of de
offer ofrecer (14)
office la oficina
officer el oficial
official el funcionario; oficial
oil el aceite
okay bien; **if it's — (with you)**
  si (te) parece bien
old viejo
oligarchy la oligarquía
on en, sobre
once una vez
one uno
onion la cebolla
only solamente, sólo, nada
  más; único; **not — . . . but**
  also no sólo ... sino también
open abrir; abierto
opinion la opinión; **to venture**
  an — opinar
opponent el oponente
opportunity la oportunidad
oppose oponer (23)
opposite enfrente de; lo contrario; contrario
optimism el optimismo
or o
orange la naranja (fruit); anaranjado (color)
order pedir (i); el orden (arrangement); la orden
  (command); **in — that** para
  que; **in — to** para
ordinal ordinal
organize organizar
orient el oriente
originate (in) provenir (de) (ie,
  i) (31)
orquid la orquídea
ostentation la ostentación
other otro
our nuestro
ours nuestro
outdoors al aire libre
outing el paseo
outside fuera (de)
outskirts las afueras
over sobre; más (more);

— **here** (por) acá; — **there** (por) allá
overcoat el abrigo
overthrow destituir, derrocar
ow! ¡ay!
owe deber
own tener (ie) (28); propio
owner el dueño
ox el buey

P

page la página
pain el dolor
pair el par
pan: frying — la sartén
Panama Panamá; — **Canal** el Canal de Panamá
Panamanian panameño
pants los pantalones
paper el papel; el periódico (newspaper)
paragraph el párrafo
Paraguayan paraguayo
parallel el paralelo; paralelo
parcel la parcela
pardon perdonar; el perdón; — **me** perdón
parent la madre; el padre; **—s** los padres
park el parque
part la parte
participate participar
particle la partícula
particularly especialmente, particularmente
party la fiesta; el partido (political)
pass pasar
passage el pasaje
past pasado; **(five)** — **(twelve)** las (doce) y (cinco)
patience la paciencia
patio el patio
patron el patrón
pay pagar; — **attention** poner (23) atención, hacer (19) caso; — **a visit** hacer una visita
payment el pago

peace la paz
peanut el maní
pear la pera
peasant el campesino
pen la pluma; **ballpoint** — el bolígrafo
pencil el lápiz
penny el centavo
peon el peón
people la gente; el pueblo
pepper la pimienta; el chile; el ají
percentage el porcentaje
perfect perfecto
perhaps tal vez
period la época, el período
permission el permiso
perseverance la perseverancia
person la persona
personal personal
Peru Perú
phenomenon el fenómeno
philosophy la filosofía
phone el teléfono
photograph la foto
phrase la frase
physically físicamente
physics la física
piano el piano
pick up coger; recoger; pasar por
picnic el paseo, el picnic
picture el cuadro
picturesque pintoresco
piece el pedazo; **small** — el pedacito
pig el cerdo
pity la lástima
place el lugar
plan el plan
plane el avión
plantation la plantación
plate el plato
play jugar (ue) (game); tocar (music); — **jokes** hacer bromas
pleasant agradable; simpático
please gustar; **be** **—ing to** gustar; por favor
pleasing agradable

pleasure el placer
plenty mucho; bastante
plus más; y
point el punto; — **of view** punto de vista; — **out** señalar
police la policía
policeman el policía
political político
politics la política
pool: swimming — la piscina
poor pobre
poorly mal
population la población
port el puerto
Portuguese el portugués; portugués, -esa
position la posición
possessive posesivo
possibility la posibilidad
possible posible
postpone posponer (23)
potato la papa
pound la libra
power el poder
practically prácticamente
practice la práctica
prairie la llanura
precisely precisamente
predecessor el predecesor
prefer preferir (ie, i)
prepare preparar
preposition la preposición
prescribe prescribir
present presentar; presente, actual; la actualidad; — **(tense)** el presente; — **perfect (tense)** el antepresente
president el presidente
press planchar
prestige el prestigio
pretend aparentar
preterit el pretérito; pretérito
pretext el pretexto
pretty bonito, lindo
prevail prevalecer (14)
prevailing prevaleciente
prevent prevenir (ie, i) (31)
price el precio

principal   principal
privilege   el privilegio
privileged   privilegiado
probability   la probabilidad
probably   probablemente
problem   el problema
produce   producir (14)
product   el producto
professor   el profesor, la profesora
progress   el progreso
progressive   progresivo
project   el proyecto
prominent   prominente
promise   prometer; la promesa
pronoun   el pronombre
pronounce   pronunciar
pronunciation   la pronunciación
propose   proponer (23)
protection   la protección
protest   protestar; la protesta
proverb   el refrán
provide   proveer
provided that   con tal que
province   la provincia
provoke   provocar
psychology   la (p)sicología
punctuality   la puntualidad
punishment   el castigo
purchase   la compra
purple   morado
purpose   el fin; **for the — of** para
purse   la cartera
push   empujar
put   poner (23); **— in** meter; **—on(clothing)** ponerse(23)

Q

quality   la calidad; la cualidad
quantity   la cantidad
quarter   el cuarto
queen   la reina; **the king and —** los reyes
question   la pregunta; la cuestión; la frase interrogativa
quickly   pronto
quiet: be —   callarse; hacer (19)

silencio; **keep —** callarse, hacer (19) silencio
quite   bastante

R

radio   la radio (broadcast); el radio (apparatus)
rain   llover (ue); la lluvia
raincoat   el impermeable
rainfall   la lluvia
rapid   rápido
rare   raro
rate: at any —   de todos modos, de cualquier modo
rather 'mejor dicho; **— than** en vez de
reach   llegar
reaction   la reacción
read   leer
ready   listo; **get —** alistarse
real   real
reality   la realidad
realization   la realización; la comprensión
realize   darse (15) cuenta (de)
really   de veras; realmente
reason   la razón; el motivo
reasonable   razonable
reasoning   el razonamiento
rebel   rebelar
rebellion   la rebelión
receive   recibir
recipe   la receta
recognize   reconocer (14)
recommend   recomendar (ie)
recourse   el recurso, el remedio
red   rojo; **the light is —** la luz (el semáforo) está en rojo
reduction   la rebaja
reflexive   reflexivo
refrigerator   la refrigeradora
refuge   el refugio; **take —** refugiarse
regard   el recuerdo
regime   el régimen
region   la región
regret   sentir (ie, i)
regular   regular
reject   rechazar

relating (to)   relativo (a)
relation   la relación
relationship   la relación
relative   el pariente; relativo
relaxed   relajado
religion   la religión
remain   quedar (to be left); quedarse (to stay)
remember   recordar (ue)
remind   recordar (ue)
repeat   repetir (i)
repetition   la repetición
replace   reponer (23)
reply   responder; la respuesta
represent   representar
representative   el representante
republic   la república
require   requerir (ie, i); pedir (i)
resemblance   la semejanza
resign   renunciar
resolve   resolver (ue)
resource   el recurso
respect   respetar; el respeto (esteem or regard); **in this —** a este respecto; **with — to** respecto a
respectable   respetable
respective   respectivo
responsibility   la responsabilidad
responsible   responsable
rest   descansar; el resto; demás
result   resultar; el resultado
retain   retener (ie) (28)
return   regresar, volver (ue); devolver (ue) (give back an object)
review   repasar; el repaso
revolution   la revolución
rhythm   el ritmo
rice   el arroz
rich   rico
ride a horse   montar a caballo
right   la derecha, el derecho (privilege); derecho; **be —** tener (ie) (28) razón; **isn't that —?** ¿verdad? **— away** ahora mismo; **— now** ahora mismo; **turn —** doblar a la derecha

riot el disturbio
ripe maduro
river el río
road el camino
rob robar
robber el bandido
rock la piedra
role el papel
Roman romano
romance romance
romantic romántico
roof el techo
room el cuarto
rooster el gallo
round redondo
route la ruta
routine rutinario
rule la regla
ruling dominador, -ra
rumor el rumor
run correr
running corriente
rural rural
Russia Rusia
Russian ruso

S

sad triste
sail navegar
sailor el marinero
saint el santo, la santa; —'s
  day el día del santo, el
  santo
sake: for Pete's —! ¡caramba!
  for heaven's —! ¡por Dios!
salad la ensalada
salary el sueldo
salty salado
Salvadoran salvadoreño
same igual, mismo; in the —
  way de la misma manera;
  the — as igual a, igual que;
  the — old thing lo de
  siempre
sandwich el sandwich
sargeant el sargento
satisfied contento
Saturday (el) sábado
sauce la salsa

savage el salvaje
save salvar
say decir (i) (16); — goodbye
  despedirse (i); that is to —
  es decir
saying el dicho
scandal el escándalo
Scandinavian escandinavo
scanty escaso
scarce escaso
scarcely apenas
scarf la bufanda
scene la escena
scholarship la beca
school la escuela; high — el
  colegio, (escuela) secundaria; — of a university la
  facultad
scientifically científicamente
scoundrel el canalla
sea el mar
seaman el marinero
seamstress la costurera
seaport el puerto
search buscar; la busca
season la estación
seat sentar (ie); el asiento
second segundo
secondary secundario
see ver (32); I'll — you chao
seek buscar
seem parecer (14)
seize usurpar
select elegir (i)
-self mismo; (him)— (él)
  mismo
sell vender
semester el semestre
send mandar
sensational sensacional
sentence la frase
sentimentalism el sentimen-
sentimentalism el sentimen-
  talismo
separate separar
September septiembre
sergeant el sargento
serious serio
servant el sirviente, la sirvienta
serve servir (i)

service el servicio
set: — the table poner (23) la
  mesa
settle establecerse (14)
settler el colonizador
seven siete
seventeen diecisiete
seventh séptimo
seventy setenta
several varios
sex el sexo
shack la choza
shade la sombra; in the — a la
  sombra
shake sacudir
share compartir
shave afeitarse
shawl el chal
she ella
shine limpiar; la limpiada
ship el barco
shipwrecked: be — naufragar
shirt la camisa
shoe el zapato; — store la
  zapatería
shoemaker el zapatero
shoeshine boy el limpiabotas
shopping: go — ir (20) (andar)
  (12) de compras
short corto; bajo (stature);
  pequeño (small); in — en
  fin, en breve
shortage la escasez
shorten acortar; abreviar
shortening el acortamiento
shout gritar; el grito
shouting el griterío
show mostrar (ue); enseñar
shrimp el camarón
shut up callarse
sick enfermo, grave, mal
side el lado; at the — of al
  lado de
sight divisar; la vista
sign el rótulo; stop — el alto
signal la señal
silence el silencio
silly tonto
silverware los cubiertos
similar parecido

simple simple

since pues; ya que; como

sing cantar

single solo; soltero (unmarried)

sir (el) señor

sister la hermana; — **in-law** la cuñada

sit sentarse (ie); — **down** sentarse (ie)

sitting sentado

situated situado

situation la situación

six seis

six hundred seiscientos

sixteen dieciséis

sixth sexto

sixty sesenta

skill la pericia, la habilidad

sky el cielo

sleep dormir (ue, u); el sueño

sleepy: be — tener (ie) (28) sueño

slender delgado

slightest menor

slim flaco

small pequeño

smart-aleck el chistoso

smile sonreír; la sonrisa

smoke fumar; el humo

snow nevar (ie); la nieve

so así; — **and —** tal por cual; — **called** llamado; — **long** hasta luego; — **much** tanto; **so-so** regular, así así; — **that** para que; — **they say** según dicen

soap el jabón

social social

society la sociedad

socioeconomic socio-económico

sociologist el sociólogo

sock el calcetín

soft suave

some alguno

somebody alguien, alguno

someone alguien, alguno

something algo

sometimes algunas veces, a veces, unas veces

son el hijo

son-in-law el yerno

soon pronto

sorry: be — sentir (ie, i)

sort el estilo; **and of the —** y por el estilo

soul el alma (*f*)

sound el sonido

soup la sopa

south el sur

southern sur, al sur

space el espacio

Spain España

Spaniard el español, la española

Spanish el español; español, -la; — **America** (la) Hispanoamérica; — **American** hispanoamericano

spare: to — de sobra

speak hablar

speech el lenguaje; el discurso

speed la velocidad; la rapidez

spell escribir; **the word is —ed** la palabra se escribe

spelling la ortografía; ortográfico

spend pasar (time); gastar (money)

spinster la soltera

spite: in — of a pesar de

splendorous esplendoroso

sponsor patrocinar

spoon la cucharita (teaspoon); la cuchara (tablespoon)

spot el sitio (place)

spring la primavera

stability la estabilidad

stage la etapa

stand estar (17) de pie; aguantar (tolerate)

standing de pie; **social —** el status social

stand up levantarse; **stand (someone) up** dejar plantado (a alguien)

start empezar (ie), comenzar (ie); ponerse (23) a; el principio; **from the —** desde un principio

starve morirse (ue, u) de hambre

state el estado

statistic la estadística

stay quedarse

steal robar

step el paso

stick el palo

still todavía

stinking cochino

stir revolver (ue)

stocking la media

stomach el estómago

stone la piedra

stop detener(se) (ie) (28), parar(se); — **sign** el alto

store la tienda

story el cuento, la historia

straight derecho; — **ahead** derecho

strange extraño

street la calle

stressed acentuado

strict estricto

strike la huelga; **on —** en huelga

strong fuerte

struggle la lucha

student el estudiante, la estudiante; el alumno, la alumna

study estudiar; el estudio

stupid estúpido

style el estilo

subdivide subdividir

subject sujeto (grammar); **school —** la materia

subjective subjetivo

subjunctive el subjuntivo

subordinate subordinado

subordination la subordinación

success el éxito

such (a) tal

suddenly de repente

suffer sufrir
suffering el mal
sufficient suficiente, bastante
suffix el sufijo
sugar el azúcar
suggest sugerir (ie, i)
suicide: to commit — suicidarse
suit convenir (ie, i) (31); el traje
suitable: be — convenir (ie, i) (31)
suitor el pretendiente
sullenly de mala gana
summer el verano
sun el sol
Sunday (el) domingo
superior superior; **mother —** la madre superiora
supper la cena
support el apoyo
suppression la supresión
sure seguro; cómo no
surname el apellido
surprise sorprender; la sorpresa
swear jurar
sweep barrer
sweet dulce
sweetheart el novio, la novia
swim nadar
swimming: — pool la piscina
syllable la sílaba
synonym el sinónimo
synonymous sinónimo
system el sistema

T

table la mesa
tablecloth el mantel
tablespoon la cuchara
tact el tacto
tailor el sastre; **— shop** la sastrería
take tomar; **— advantage of** aprovechar; **— a bath** bañarse; **— care of** cuidar; **— refuge** refugiarse
talk hablar, conversar
tall alto

task la tarea
taste saber (25); probar (ue)
tax el impuesto
taxi el taxi; **— driver** el taxista
tea el té
teach enseñar
teacher el maestro, la maestra; el profesor, la profesora
tear down deshacer (19)
teaspoon la cucharita
technical técnico
telephone el teléfono; **by —** por teléfono; **on the —** por teléfono
television la televisión
tell decir (i) (16), contar (ue); **— time** decir la hora
temporarily temporalmente
ten diez
tend tender (ie)
tendency la tendencia
tennis el tenis
tense el tiempo; tenso
tenth décimo
term el término
terrible terrible; **— thing** la barbaridad
terrific fenomenal
territorial territorial
than que; de
thanks (las) gracias
that ese, esa; aquel, aquella; eso; aquello; que; **— one** ése, ésa; aquél, aquélla; **like —** así; **is to say** es decir; **—'s why** por eso
the el, la, los, las
theater el teatro; **movie —** el cine
their su
theirs suyo
them los, las; les; ellos, ellas
theme el tema
themselves se
then entonces, luego
there allí; **— is, — are** hay
therefore por consiguiente, por eso
these estos, estas; éstos, éstas

thesis la tesis
they ellos, ellas
thief el ladrón
thin delgado
thing la cosa; **how are —s?** ¿qué tal? **the same old —** lo de siempre
think pensar (ie)
third tercero
thirst la sed
thirsty: be — tener (ie) (28) sed
thirteen trece
thirty treinta; media (telling time): **two —** las dos y media
this este, esta, esto; **— one** éste, ésta; **— way** por aquí
those esos, esas; aquellos, aquellas; ésos, ésas; aquéllos, aquéllas
though: even — aunque
thousand mil
three tres
three hundred trescientos
throat la garganta; **sore —** el dolor de garganta
through a través de; por; **go — (the light)** pasarse (la luz)
throw echar; tirar; **— away** desperdiciar
Thursday (el) jueves
thus así, así pues
ticket: lottery — el pedacito de lotería
tie la corbata
tiger el tigre
till hasta
time el tiempo; la vez; **at a —** a la vez; **at —s** a veces; **in —** con el tiempo; **on —** a tiempo; **what — is it?** ¿qué hora es?
tin la lata
tiny diminuto
tire la llanta
tired cansado; **get —** cansarse
to a; para
today hoy, hoy día

together junto con; juntos
tomato el tomate
tomorrow mañana; — **(morning)** mañana por (la mañana)
too demasiado; también; — **much** demasiado; — **many** demasiados
tooth el diente; la muela (molar)
toothache el dolor de muelas
top: on — (of) encima (de)
toss tirar
touch tocar
touchy delicado
tourist el turista, la turista
toward hacia
towel la toalla
town el pueblo; **center of —** el centro
trade el comercio
tradition la tradición
traffic el tráfico, el tránsito; — **light** el semáforo, la luz; — **signal** la señal de tránsito
tragedy la tragedia
train el tren
tranquillity la tranquilidad
transition la transición
trap atrapar
treat tratar
tree el árbol
trend la tendencia
trip el viaje
trivial trivial
tropical tropical
tropics el trópico
trouble la pena; la dificultad; **the — is** lo malo es; **to be worth the —** valer (30) la pena
trousers los pantalones
true verdadero; **it is —** es verdad, es cierto
trumpet la trompeta
truth la verdad
try tratar (de); probar (ue)
Tuesday (el) martes
tune afinar

turn doblar; **to — out** resultar
twelve doce
twin el gemelo, la gemela
twist torcer (ue)
two dos
two hundred doscientos
type el tipo
typical típico

U

ugly feo
uh eh
uh-huh ajá
umbrella el paraguas
uncle el tío
under bajo; debajo de
undergo sufrir
underline subrayar
underneath bajo; debajo de
understand comprender; entender (ie)
understandable comprensible
undesirable indeseable
undoubtedly indiscutiblemente
uneven disparejo
unfortunate desafortunado
unfortunately desgraciadamente
ungrateful ingrato
unite unir
United States Estados Unidos (*s*), los Estados Unidos (*pl*)
university la universidad; universitario
unless a menos que
unlike al contrario de
unmarried soltero
unpleasant antipático
unripe verde
unspecified no especificado
unstressed inacentuado
until hasta; hasta que
up arriba; **get —** levantarse; — **to** hasta
upright honesto
urban urbano
USA EE.UU. (*s*), los EE.UU. (*pl*)
us nos; nosotros
use usar; el uso

used to acostumbrado (accustomed)
usefulness la utilidad
usual corriente; acostumbrado; **as —** de costumbre
utilize utilizar

V

vacation las vacaciones
vegetables: green — las verduras
vegetation la vegetación
velocity la velocidad
vender el vendedor
Venezuelan venezolano
verb el verbo; verbal
very muy
vice el vicio
victim la víctima
view la vista
violated violado
Virgin Islands las Islas Vírgenes
virtue la virtud
visa: resident — la visa de residencia
visit visitar; la visita; **pay a —** hacer (19) una visita
visiting: to be — estar (17) de visita
visitor la visita; el visitante
voice la voz
vote el voto
vowel la vocal
voyage el viaje

W

wait esperar; — **on** atender (ie)
waiter el camarero, la camarera
walk andar (12), caminar
wall la pared
wallet la cartera
want querer (ie) (24)
war la guerra
warn advertir (ie, i); prevenir (ie, i) (31)

warning la advertencia
wash lavar; **get —ed** lavarse
waste desperdiciar
watch mirar; el reloj
water el agua (*f*)
wave la ola
way la manera, el modo; **by the —** a propósito; **in this —** de esta manera; **that —** para allá; **this —** para acá; **— over there** allá lejos
we nosotros, -as; **— like (them)** nos gusta(n) ellos
weapon el arma (*f*); **—s** los armamentos
weather el tiempo; **it is (good) —** hace (buen) tiempo
weaver el tejedor
wedding la boda
Wednesday (el) miércoles
week la semana
weigh pesar
welcome: you're — de nada
well bien
what qué, cuál; lo que (that which); **— else?** ¿qué más? **— for?** ¿para qué?
whatever cualquier, cualquiera
when cuando; cuándo
whenever cuando
where donde; dónde
wherever donde
whether si
which cuál; qué; que
while el rato; **a little —** un ra-

tito, un poco; mientras, mientras que; **a — ago** hace un rato
white blanco
who quién; que
whom quién; quien; que
whose cuyo; de quién
why por qué
wide ancho
wife la esposa, la mujer
willing dispuesto
win ganar
wind el viento
window la ventana
windy: it is — hace viento
wine el vino
winter el invierno
wish desear; el deseo; **I —** ojalá
with con
within adentro; dentro (de)
without sin; sin que
woman la mujer; **young —** la señorita
wonder: and no — y con razón
wool la lana
word la palabra; **— of honor** palabra
work trabajar; el trabajo
worker el obrero
world el mundo; mundial; **out of this —** divino
worn-out gastado
worried preocupado
worry (about) preocuparse (de)
worse peor

worst peor
worth: be valer (30); **be — while** valer la pena
wrap envolver (ue)
write escribir
writer el escritor
writing la escritura

Y

year el año; **New Year** (el) Año Nuevo
yellow amarillo
yes sí
yesterday ayer; **day before —** anteayer
yet todavía
you tú; usted, ustedes; vosotros
young joven; **— man** el joven; **— woman** la joven
younger menor
your tu, vuestro, su
yours tuyo, vuestro, suyo
yourself te, se; os, se
youth la juventud

Z

zero el cero
zone la zona

Index

Picture Credits

F
G   2
H   3
I   4

ESTADOS UNIDOS

Tijuana

30°

BAJA CALIFORNIA

GOLFO DE CALIFORNIA

Ciudad Juarez

Río Conchos

Chihuahua

BOLSÓN DE MAPIMÍ

SIERRA MADRE OCCIDENTAL

SIERRA MADRE ORIENTAL

Río Bravo (Río Grande)

Nuevo Laredo

Monterrey

GOLFO DE M

M
É
X
I
C
O

20°

Puerto Vallarta

Río Grande de Santiago

Guadalajara

Río Pánuco

Tampico

GOLFO DE CAMPECHE

Mérida

México, D.F.

Veracruz

PENÍNSULA DE YUCATÁN

Cuernavaca

Taxco

Río Balsas

SIERRA MADRE DEL SUR

Oaxaca

Acapulco

Belmo

BELIC

GOLFO DE TEHUANTEPEC

Puerto Barrios

Pu
Co

GUATEMALA

HO

Guatemala

Teguci

San Salvador

Acajutla

EL SALVADOR

10°

OCÉANO PACÍFICO

0   500 Millas
0   500 Kilómetros

110°   100°   90°